Canada Among Nations
1992–93

A NEW WORLD ORDER?

Canada Among Nations 1992–93

A NEW WORLD ORDER?

Fen Osler Hampson
and
Christopher Maule
Editors

Carleton University Press
Ottawa — Canada
1992

CARLETON
UNIVERSITY
1942-1992

ISBN   0-88629-167-4 (paperback)
ISBN   0-88629-166-6 (casebound)

Printed and bound in Canada
Carleton Public Policy Series 8

Canadian Cataloguing in Publication Data
The National Library of Canada has catalogued this publication as follows:
　　Canada among nations
　　　　1984–
　　　　Annual.
　　　　1992–93 ed.: A new world order?
　　　　Each vol. also has a distinctive title.
　　　　Produced by the Norman Paterson School of International Affairs
　　　　of Carleton University.
　　　　Includes bibliographical references.
　　　　ISSN 0832-0683

1. Canada–Foreign relations–1945–　–periodicals.　2. Canada–Politics and
government–1984–　–periodicals.　3. Canada–Politics and government–
1980–1984–periodicals.　I. Norman Paterson School of International Affairs.
FC242.C345　　　　　　　　　　327.71　　　　　　　　　　C86-031285-2

Distributed by　Oxford University Press Canada,
　　　　　　　　70 Wynford Drive,
　　　　　　　　Don Mills, Ontario,
　　　　　　　　Canada. M3C 1J9
　　　　　　　　(416) 441-2941

Cover design:　Aerographics Ottawa
Cover photos:　Courtesy of the Novosti Press Agency

Acknowledgements

Carleton University Press gratefully acknowledges the support extended
to its publishing programme by the Canada Council and the Ontario Arts
Council.

Table of Contents

List of Figures and Tables

List of Contributors

Ivan Bernier is professor in the Centre Québécois de Relations Internationales, Université Laval.

Maxwell A. Cameron is assistant professor in The Norman Paterson School of International Affairs, Carleton University.

Andrew Clark is a researcher in the North-South Institute, Ottawa.

Lenard Cohen is professor in the Department of Political Science, Simon Fraser University.

Fanny Demers is associate professor in the Department of Economics, Carleton University.

Michel Demers is associate professor in the Department of Economics, Carleton University.

Lorraine Eden is associate professor in The Norman Paterson School of International Affairs, Carleton University.

Charlotte Gray is the Ottawa editor of *Saturday Night*.

Giles Gherson is the bureau chief of the *Financial Times of Canada*.

Fen Osler Hampson is associate professor in The Norman Paterson School of International Affairs, Carleton University.

Keith Krause is associate professor in the Department of Political Science, York University.

Christopher Maule is a professor in the Department of Economics and Director of The Norman Paterson School of International Affairs, Carleton University.

Maureen Appel Molot is a professor with a joint appointment in The Norman Paterson School of International Affairs and the Department of Political Science, Carleton University.

Raymond Moriyama is senior partner, Moriyama and Teshima Architects, Toronto.

Maureen O'Neil is President of the North-South Institute, Ottawa.

Gerry Schmitz is program director, Human Rights and Democratic Government, the North-South Institute, Ottawa.

Iain Wallace is a professor in the Department of Geography, Carleton University.

David Welch is assistant professor in the Department of Political Science, University of Toronto.

Greg Wirick is an associate of the Parliamentary Centre for Foreign Affairs, Ottawa.

Gil Winham is professor in the Department of Political Science, Dalhousie University.

Glossary

Acronyms for *Canada Among Nations 1992-93*

ASEAN	Association of South-East Asian Nations
BCNI	Business Council on National Issues
CAFE	U.S. corporate average fuel economy
CAP	Common Agricultural Policy
CCIC	Canadian Council for International Co-operation
CFE	Conventional Forces in Europe
CIDA	Canadian International Development Agency
CIIPS	Canadian Institute for International Peace and Security
CIS	Commonwealth of Independent States
COAT	Coalition to Oppose the Arms Trade
COCOM	Co-ordinating Committee
COPAZ	National Commission for the Consolidation of Peace
COS	central office switch
CPC	Conflict Prevention Centre
CSCE	Conference on Security and Co-operation in Europe
CSIS	Canadian Security and Information Service
CUSFTA	Canada United States Free Trade Agreement
DAC	Development Assistance Committee (OECD)
DARPA	Defence Advanced Research Projects Agency
DEAITC	Department of External Affairs and International Trade Canada
DFI	direct foreign investment
DIPP	Defence Industry Productivity Program
DND	Department of National Defence
EAI	Enterprise for the Americas Initiative
EC	European Community
EDC	Export Development Corporation
EEA	European Economic Area
EFTA	European Free Trade Area
EMDI	Environmental Management Development Project in Indonesia
EMU	European Monetary Union
ESPRIT	European Strategic Program for R & D in Information Technology

FDI	foreign direct investment
FTA	Free Trade Agreement
G-7	Group of Seven
GATT	General Agreement on Tariffs and Trade
GDP	gross domestic product
GNP	gross national product
IAEA	International Atomic Energy Agency
ICHRDD	International Centre for Human Rights and Democratic Development
IDA	International Development Assistance (Fund)
IDRC	International Development Research Council
IMF	International Monetary Fund
IPCC	Intergovernmental Panel on Climate Change
IRPP	Institute for Research on Public Policy
LAVs	light armoured vehicles
LDC	less developed country
MFN	most favoured nation
MINURSO	UN Mission for the Referendum in Western Sahara
MMPA	U.S. Marine Mammals Protection Act
MNE	multinational enterprises
MTCR	Missile Technology Control Regime
MTN	multilateral trade negotiations
NAFTA	North American Free Trade Agreement
NASA	National Aeronautics and Space Administration
NATO	North Atlantic Treaty Organization
NDP	New Democratic Party (Canada)
NGO	Non-government organizations
NPT	Nuclear Non Proliferation Treaty
NSG	Nuclear Suppliers' Group
OAS	Organization of American States
OAU	Organization of African Unity
ODA	official development assistance
OECD	Organization for Economic Co-operation and Development
ONUSAL	UN Observer Mission in El Salvador
PP-5	Permanent Five (UN Security Council)
PABX	private automatic branch exchange
PAMSCAD	Plan of Action to Mitigate the Social Costs of Adjustment

PICC	Paris International Conference on Cambodia
PMO	Prime Minister's Office
PRI	Institutional Revolutionary Party (Mexico)
R & D	Research and Development
SAP	Structural Adjustment Program (Guyana)
SCEAIT	Standing Committee on External Affairs and International Trade
STA	Semiconductor Trade Agreement
UN	United Nations
UNAVEM II	UN Angola Verification Mission
UNCED	UN Conference on the Environment and Development
UNCHE	UN Conference on the Human Environment
UNCHR	UN High Commission for Refugees
UNDP	UN Development Program
UNICEF	UN International Children's Emergency Fund
UNIKOM	UN Iraq-Kuwait Observer Mission
UNITA	Union for the Total Independence of Angola
UNPAAERD	UN Program of Action for African Economic Recovery and Development
UNTAC	UN Transitional Authority on Cambodia
USAID	US Agency for International Development
VOCs	volatile organic chemicals
WEU	Western European Union
WID	Women in Development Policy (CIDA)

Preface

This is the eighth volume on Canada in international affairs produced by The Norman Paterson School of International Affairs. The book is organized around the most recent calendar year and contains an analysis and assessment of aspects of Canadian foreign policy and the environment that shapes the policy. Our intention is to contribute to the debate about appropriate policy choices for Canada by calling upon the services of experts from across the country.

The theme of this edition is "A New World Order?" Perhaps "disorder" should be used in the title, because as the year unfolded there were examples of disorderly events — the dissolution of the Soviet Union and the fragmentation of Yugoslavia into separate states. In the same period, the Gulf War ended and further moves towards integration took place in Europe. Events therefore suggest a balance of order and disorder outside Canada which provided the context for the continuing debate within Canada on its constitutional arrangements. This volume attempts to assess the impact of external events on Canadian foreign policy, and to set out new agenda items.

Financial support for this volume has been provided by the Social Science and Humanities Research Council of Canada, the Canadian Institute for International Peace and Security, the Military and Strategic Studies program at the Department of National Defence, and The Norman Paterson School of International Affairs. The authors appreciate the willingness of the contributors to participate in an undertaking which posed the challenge of coping with the rapidity of change, and they are grateful for the guidance and assistance offered by the faculty and staff of The Norman Paterson School of International Affairs.

Once more we are indebted to Brenda Sutherland for her advice and efficiency in producing the manuscript. The experience she has gathered over the years assists the editors immeasurably in meeting tight deadlines. Our thanks also go to Janet Doherty for organizing the authors' workshop which is an integral part of the volume's preparation. This is the third volume of *Canada Among Nations* to be published by Carleton University Press and we are pleased to acknowledge the assistance provided by Anne Winship, Steven Uriarte and Noel Gates. We would also like to thank Pauline Adams and Evan Ross Gill for proofreading the final manuscript.

Fen Osler Hampson
Christopher J. Maule
Ottawa, March 1992

Introduction

1

A New World Order?

Fen Osler Hampson and Christopher J. Maule

"G-7 dumps Canada!", proclaims the headline in the morning newspaper. The date is July 20, 1993. The lead story discusses how the G-7, the world's most exclusive club and the economic executive committee of the industrialized countries, has dropped Canada from its membership following the break-up of the country after the Quebec referendum on sovereignty-association. The decision follows a stormy debate by the other six heads of state behind closed doors. After noting the important contribution made by Canada to the work of the G-7, the communiqué expresses the "deep regret" of the heads of government at their decision. Since Canada had been a junior partner and a minor economic player compared to the other G-7 countries, its case for membership was always somewhat tenuous. The article explains that Canada had the smallest population in the G-7 (one half the size of the next smallest country, France) and the smallest GNP (one tenth of the largest, that of the United States). As a result of the division into two parts, Quebec and the rest of Canada, Quebec now has 25 percent of the population and GNP of the rest of Canada, and has become a minor player in the world economy. The rest of Canada has dropped to 10th place in world GNP (behind Spain, Brazil, and India), no longer qualifying even for junior membership status in the G-7. It is expected that the decision will send further shock waves through the Canadian and Quebec economies, already weakened by rapidly rising inflation, declining investor confidence, a massive outflow of capital, and skyrocketing unemployment. Rumours are reported that Washington wants to renegotiate the North American free trade agreement with the new sovereign state of Quebec and the remaining nine Canadian provinces. Already Tokyo and London financial markets are reporting a massive run on the Canadian dollar.

Is this a far-fetched scenario? In 1992 Canada's economic performance was lacklustre. The recession, combined with Canada's continuing constitutional difficulties, contributed to the decline in industrial production and the creation of an uncertain political climate for investors. There can be little doubt that continuing political uncertainty, or an outcome which leads to Quebec's separation, does not augur well for the Canadian economy and the well-being of either Canadians or Quebeckers. But the dilemma does not end there. Canada has built its economic future on the far from foreseeable outcome of the Canada-United States Free Trade Agreement (CUFTA). Some argue that this arrangement may turn Canada into another "spoke" of the North American "hub," centred on the United States, but it is not clear that the alternative proposed by many critics of free trade, i.e., a return to protectionism, would halt the exodus of investment given cheaper labour costs, better infrastructure, and lower taxes south of the border. The context in which the original CUFTA agreement was negotiated has changed dramatically with the appearance of Mexico as a probable member of a continental free trade area, which may include other western hemispheric partners.

The lowering of trade barriers is occurring in the context of a more general restructuring of the world's economy, involving increased mobility of capital and globalization of factors of production. For countries like Canada, dependent on the export sector for their economic growth and development, this restructuring is creating new strains and pressures to which they are ill-equipped to adjust. The problems of Canadian competitiveness have been clearly diagnosed in a number of recent studies and reports. All of these point to a shortage of skilled labor, declining productivity, high capital costs, and excessive reliance on unprocessed raw material exports. The government's strategy, which is based on the opening up of the Canadian economy to the North American market, is also being called into question because the United States is losing its competitive edge to the dynamic economies of Asia and the Pacific. It is one thing to be hitched to a rising star; quite another to cling to a falling one. Finally, domestic policies have worked against the adjustment to freer trade. The high value of the Canadian dollar and high interest rates have discouraged exports. And while interest rates fell sharply in 1991, the differential with the U.S. still places Canada at a competitive disadvantage.

Canada's constitutional crisis is also diverting much-needed political attention away from the economy. In a world in which "competitiveness" is the codeword for giant global corporations, which often enjoy direct subsidies, tax shelters, and other forms of state support in their countries of origin, Canada has few corporate champions ready or able to compete on the world stage. Continuing political uncertainty, interprovincial trade barriers, and monetary and fiscal policies which have sapped investor confidence, are not helping Canada confront the mounting demands of global competitiveness.

This year's volume of *Canada Among Nations* explores the linkages between Canada's domestic troubles and the larger world scene. Although the end of the Cold War and the outbreak of the Gulf War heralded the beginnings of what American President George Bush called "a new world order," this new "order" is characterized more by disorder stemming from the breakup of the Soviet empire and the legacy of failed communism. The war in the Persian Gulf quickly dispelled any delusions that the end of the Cold War would mark the end of international conflict or what some have called "the end of history." At the same time, the break-up of the Soviet empire in Eurasia and Eastern Europe has left the field clear for longstanding ethnic conflicts and territorial disputes, which have been exacerbated by deteriorating economic conditions and the inability of market forces to take hold. As the civil wars in Yugoslavia, Georgia, and Armenia testify, these new wars of independence are proving to be just as bloody as many of those in the Third World. But they are not the only sources of danger. The alarming and very real possibility that the nuclear arsenals of the former Soviet Union will be divided up among the republics of the new Commonwealth, or, worse still, find their way into the wrong hands as military and command control structures disintegrate, makes nuclear proliferation the number one global security challenge.

For Canadians, accustomed to dealing with their own internal political troubles through dialogue and consensus, nationalistic unrest abroad has raised the spectre of civil unrest and armed confrontation at home, if Quebec nationalism cannot be accommodated through constitutional reform and peaceful change. As bits of the Soviet Union broke off — first the Baltic republics, then the Ukraine followed by the other republics — the Canadian government was also faced with a more immediate quandary: whether to opt for speedy recognition of these newly declared sovereign states and be at the front of the pack, or to be cautious and follow the lead of others. It opted for the former in the case of the Ukraine, though not without strong domestic criticism.

As Canada confronts the disorder of a changing world, its own foreign policies and international image are coming under increased scrutiny. Some Canadians are looking to their country's international role to salvage what remains of Canada's sense of identity and self-worth as the hourglass on the constitution runs out. However, as the essays in this volume clearly show, Canada's foreign policy is riddled with its own internal contradictions, appreciably worsened by bureaucratic infighting and the diminished importance of the Department of External Affairs. To be sure, the Mulroney government has given a new gloss to Canadian foreign policy in the past year, underscoring its commitment to the promotion of human rights and democracy, to strengthened relations with Canada's western hemisphere partners, and to "multilateralism" in all of its various forms and guises. In spite of the rhetoric, however, Canada's foreign policy has been driven far more by the dictates of free trade and the government's narrow political agenda than by a broader vision or a sense of purpose regarding Canada's rightful place in the new world order — a world which is at once more threatening and more riddled with uncertainty than it was in the bipolar era of the Cold War.

To address these and other themes, the book is organized around the following questions:

- Who are the key personalities and decision-makers in the making of Canadian foreign policy?
- What are the foreign policy implications of Canada's constitutional crisis?
- What are we to make of the "new multilateralism" which has characterized international politics since the Cold War?
- Is there a special role for Canada in the newly emerging system of multilateral institutions?
- What are the implications of the new regionalism and increasing global competitiveness for Canada's economic future?
- What are the key challenges which confront Canadian foreign policy at the end of the Cold War?

Politics, Personalities and Places

The first section addresses the politics, personalities, and places involved in the making of decisions on Canadian foreign policy. In the lead chapter, Charlotte Gray explores the making of Canadian foreign policy and the changes wrought by the transition from Joe Clark to Barbara McDougall as Secretary of State for External Affairs. She argues that foreign policy decision-making is increasingly concentrated in the Prime Minister's Office, and that most of the big decisions about Canadian foreign policy in the past year have been taken there. Although Barbara McDougall has recovered from her shaky start as Secretary of State for External Affairs and the damage to her reputation resulting from the Al-Mashat affair, she is very much junior to Michael Wilson, the former Minister of Finance who now serves in two portfolios as the Minister for International Trade and Industry and for Science and Technology respectively. This has weakened External Affairs and contributed to a further erosion of morale in the department.

Raymond Moriyama, the architect of the exciting and critically acclaimed new Canadian chancery building in Tokyo, discusses the political challenges, design, and rationale behind Canada's new "ambassador extraordinaire." His building stands as a monument to the growing importance of the Pacific in Canadian foreign policy and of Japan, in particular, as a factor in Canada's trade and investment relations with the region. At the same time, it represents the promise of Canada's future and its own dynamic potential as a Pacific partner.

The final chapter in the first section is by Ivan Bernier. Professor Bernier addresses the foreign policy implications of Canada's current constitutional quagmire, and outlines the implications for foreign and domestic policy of different outcomes or scenarios for the future. Although he concludes that Canada's key political and trading partners will be able to do business with an independent Quebec and the rest of Canada, a divided Canada will face greater difficulties in international negotiations with its key trading partners than one which remains united.

The New Multilateralism

Some argue that the end of the Cold War will see the emergence of a new multilateralism in international politics. The essays by David Welch, Greg Wirick, Gil Winham, and Iain Wallace together explore the possibilities and prospects for multilateral diplomacy in a variety of contexts: the economy, security, and the environment.

David Welch argues that the bipolar security system of the Cold War will be replaced by an embryonic concert system centred on the great powers which make up the G-7, plus a complex of institutional structures which include the CSCE (Conference on Security and Cooperation in Europe), NATO (North Atlantic Treaty Organization), and the European Community (EC) and WEU (Western European Union). He argues that NATO will continue to remain at the core of the Western security system where it is successfully articulating a new rationale of response to the security challenges brought about by the demise of the Soviet Union. These include the risks of ethnic violence and territorial conflicts in Eastern Europe and the danger of Soviet nuclear weapons falling into the wrong hands. However, he notes that NATO is performing an increasingly political and consultative role as its members reduce the size of their armed forces. Although there is public uncertainty about NATO's future, there is no desire among its leading members to weaken or dissolve the alliance.

Greg Wirick addresses the mounting commitments of the United Nations with respect to peacekeeping — an area of traditional Canadian involvement. He argues that the nature of peacekeeping has changed dramatically; it is no longer just a quasi-military operation, but has taken up a plethora of new challenges that include disaster relief, refugee assistance, civil administration, and even election monitoring. If Canada is to remain at the forefront of international peacekeeping activities, it will have to adapt to these new realities and prepare for them accordingly. This will require a reorientation of Canada's defence capabilities, particularly if the defence of Europe is no longer the central mission of our armed forces.

Gil Winham looks at the future of the world trading system and the implications for Canada's trade policies of the stalled Uruguay Round of negotiations. He observes that U.S. trade policies have increasingly departed from a "rule-oriented" to a "results-oriented" approach as the United States Congress moves towards protectionism. The failure of the Uruguay Round would reduce the legitimacy of the General Agreement on Tariffs and Trade (GATT) system. The result would be increasing instability in international trade that would severely harm Canadian economic interests. Winham also notes that a series of new issues will continue to occupy the GATT. These include the widening interface between trade and environmental regulations, competition rules, immigration and security. In particular, environmental issues are being forced on to the international trade agenda not only by the action of domestic groups who fear that trade agreements will encourage environmental abuse, but also by differing national environmental standards and regulations which are fast becoming a new source of opportunistic protectionism.

Iain Wallace picks up on this theme in his chapter. In discussing the origins of the forthcoming United Nations Conference on the Environment and Development (UNCED) in Rio de Janeiro, Wallace argues that there is growing international recognition that economic well-being and environmental health are linked. In spite of this recognition, perceptions and interests vary among the world's nations. For this reason, UNCED's achievement in devising an action plan to save the global commons is likely to be modest. Wallace highlights the dilemmas of international co-operation by noting that Canada's own non-renewable resource policies have yet to demonstrate any serious commitment to reshaping current development and consumption patterns in terms of sustainable growth.

The New Regionalism and Global Competitiveness

Since the recession began in 1990, Canada's economic performance has compared poorly with that of its G-7 partners. Its growth rate, measured in terms of real gross domestic product (GDP) ranked it 5th out of 7 with 2.4 percent for 1988 to 1991 and 0.9 percent in 1991. Canada has the third highest unemployment rate over the same period — a rate that is almost 50 percent higher than the United States. It also had the second highest debt burden from 1988–91, in 1991 and forecast for 1992, with its burden increasing in percentage terms to an expected 74 percent in 1992. In comparison to its neighbour, the United States, with which it must compete most directly for investment, Canada in 1991 had higher unemployment, higher inflation, a larger public debt burden and a lower rate of return on capital.

Much of what ails the Canadian economy has been attributed to poor productivity performance. Giles Gherson argues that mounting concern about Canada's "competitiveness gap" is prompting a fundamental reassessment of national economic policy and a reconsideration of the appropriateness of free trade with the United States, particularly if current negotiations lead to an expanded free trade area that includes low-wage Mexico. As a federal election approaches, the government is under increasing pressure to develop an industrial policy that will address Canada's competitiveness requirements. However, there is growing realization that competitiveness and free trade are not two sides of the same coin. Those countries which enjoy a competitive advantage have done so through interventionist policies which have nurtured and marshalled appropriate technologies and encouraged a commitment to product innovation and marketing. The key players in the global economy are giant multinational corporations which enjoy the active support of their home governments in developing new markets abroad. This new mercantilism in international economic relations, often involving subsidies to industries, does not sit easily alongside the free market and free trade philosophy of the current Conservative government.

Gherson's provocative assessment of the dilemmas of free trade and competitiveness is reinforced in the chapter on North American Free Trade co-authored by Maxwell Cameron, Lorraine Eden, and Maureen Appel Molot. Their chapter explores in detail the asymmetrical nature of economic linkages across the Canadian, American, and Mexican economies and shows how patterns of dependence have prompted Canada and Mexico to seek a special trading relationship with the United States. Although they conclude that Canada had little choice but to seek a seat at the table when Mexico entered into free trade negotiations with the United States, they emphasize that the stakes are enormously high. Moreover, the outcome is likely to be dictated by U.S. domestic interests and the U.S. political timetable.

Next to the United States, the EC is Canada's most important trading partner. The EC is also the most important foreign investor in Canada (after the United States) with a 34 percent share of foreign direct investment. Michel and Fanny Demers assess Canada's evolving economic relations with the EC and the likely course of relations after the Maastricht Summit. The core of Europe 1992 is the elimination of the physical, technical and fiscal barriers to the free movement of goods, services, capital and labor. Tax harmonization and company laws still need to be dealt with, although there has been much progress in these and other areas, including the removal of restrictions on money and capital movements, greater co-operation among central banks, and movement towards European monetary union (EMU).

As European integration deepens and widens, Canada may feel the effects of trade diversion in wood products and fisheries if Sweden and Norway enter into the European Economic Area (EEA) or even the EC. Europeans have also indicated that if Canadian financial institutions want access to the EC, EC financial institutions will want to receive the same treatment as the United States under the CUFTA. Canada is also having to deal with unforeseen consequences of European anti-trust policy for its own competition policies, as evidenced by the cancelled sale of De Havilland to European interests. Although the Demers's reject the notion of a new "fortress Europe," they argue that Canadian access to the EC will increasingly depend upon business-government co-operation at the federal and provincial levels and active promotion of joint research and marketing ventures between Canadian and European business interests.

New Agendas

The collapse of the Soviet Union, the increasing marginalization of the poorest developing countries, the growing tide of democratization coupled with rising concern about human rights, the mounting dangers of proliferation of weapons of mass destruction — these are just some of the issues that have been thrown on to the Canadian foreign policy agenda. The final section of this book examines how effective Canada has been in addressing the new and emerging challenges of the post-Cold War era. On the one hand, as Lenard Cohen argues in his chapter on the Soviet Union and Eastern Europe, Canada has successfully moved to the forefront of Western nations as they rush to recognize the newly emerging nations of Eastern Europe and the former territories of the Soviet Union. Canada has also been a leader in international efforts to provide economic assistance and investment funds to Eastern Europe, although the investment climate in the Soviet Union is clouded by political uncertainty and domestic turmoil.

On the other hand, Canada's record in development assistance, human rights, and the control of arms transfers is marked by a clear mismatch between deeds and rhetoric. Maureen O'Neil and Andrew Clark note that Canada has expressed strong support for Third World economic interests while cutting its aid budget, making only limited movement on debt forgiveness, and pursuing trade policies which are inimical to developing countries. In human rights, Canadian policy has been caught on the horns of two dilemmas: whether to continue to do business with authoritarian regimes while tying aid to performance in human rights, and to support "just wars" while calling for humanitarian and peacemaking interventions. Gerald Schmitz pinpoints these and other contradictions in Canadian foreign policy which have become more, not less, acute with the dizzying turn of events of the past year.

Finally, Keith Krause argues that Canadian foreign policy with respect to the international arms trade lies somewhere between "sniffing the wind" and "setting the agenda." Domestic concern about Canada's role in the Gulf War prompted the government to actively pursue controls on the conventional arms trade. According to Krause, however, Canada was not responsible for any concrete measures or proposals that would directly or indirectly control the arms trade, and Canada's own behaviour concerning foreign arms sales has left it open to charges of hypocrisy.

Conclusion

All of the essays in this volume reinforce the conclusion that Canada's ability to conduct a proactive foreign policy will critically depend on the country's own political and economic health. Aid to the Third World, Eastern Europe and the former Soviet Union, adjustment assistance to industries affected by trade negotiations, and influence in international organizations and other global fora, like the G-7, require sound economic performance and internal political stability that will boost rather than diminish, Canada's influence on the world scene. For much of the post-war period, Canada enjoyed one of the highest growth rates in the world, one of the highest standards of living, and domestic political stability. It is no accident that Canada's unrivalled status as a "middle power" in international politics was enhanced (indeed made possible) by its sound political and economic base. It is ironic that with the end of the Cold War, when new global opportunities and challenges confront the nation, its very future has been called into doubt. The dramatic restructuring of the world economy and the world map by the new engines of economic and political change, so ably documented by the contributors to this volume, underscore the growing realization that it would be suicidal for Canadians to face these challenges apart rather than together.

Politics,
Personalities
and Places

2

New Faces in Old Places:
The Making of Canadian Foreign Policy
Charlotte Gray

Foreign policymaking in Ottawa can look capricious to outsiders. Never was its unpredictability more evident than in August 1991. That was the month of the failed *putsch* in Moscow. For 48 hours, the fate of Mikhail Gorbachev and his reforms to the Soviet Union hung in the balance, and the rest of the world held its breath.

Barbara McDougall, Canada's newly-appointed Secretary of State for External Affairs, was caught unawares. She arrived back in the capital too late for a briefing with the Prime Minister by her own officials. So she opted for bloodless pragmatism when questioned by reporters. "The Canadian government is not encouraging particularly the resistance in the Soviet Union: it's up to the Soviet people to decide on the success of the coup," the minister announced in her studied Rosedale drawl, blinking as she faced the television cameras in the foyer of the Lester B. Pearson Building, which houses her department. "But the Canadian government wants the principles of democratic adjustment in the Soviet Union to be honoured by whoever is in power."

Nothing was actually wrong with McDougall's statement. But she ignored two cardinal rules of Canadian policymaking on foreign affairs. First, her words were untouched by Canada's traditional concerns: democratic values, and human rights (for which the incompetent *putsch* leaders would have had little respect). Although such preoccupations often make Canada sound like Miss Goody-Two-Shoes at multilateral get-togethers, they are an enduring element in Canada's image at home and abroad. Canadians like their foreign policy to be value-driven, and successive governments have striven to maintain that concern with values. Now McDougall appeared to have sacrificed tradition in favour of a newer focus in our foreign policy: cold-blooded realism. A poker-faced calculation of self-interest seemed to underlie the message that Canada would do business with whoever was in charge.

Second, McDougall was out of step with the Prime Minister. In his seventh year in office, Brian Mulroney has followed the example of his predecessor Pierre Trudeau and sought an increasingly larger role on the international stage. Opportunities to play this role are abundant, since Canada belongs to more international organizations than any other country in the world. Mulroney is now a senior statesman in both the Commonwealth and La Francophonie, and the second longest-serving leader at the Group of Seven (G-7) economic summit (after President Mitterand of France). He is clearly held in higher regard outside Canada than at home.

A consummate negotiator who cajoles and bargains with finesse, Mulroney revels in the historic Canadian role of "middle power" mediator. He bridges the gulf between North and South, rich and poor, through personal diplomacy. He enjoys international issues — after all, they offer a welcome diversion from domestic difficulties. In the fall of 1991, he was a candidate for the job of Secretary-General of the United Nations, and the prospect obviously appealed to him. (However, he was always a longshot, despite the fulsome backing of U.S. President George Bush. The job went to Boutros Boutros-Ghali, the former finance minister of Egypt.) Mulroney strokes his international allies with the same relentless charm and regular phone calls that he turns on with every Tory riding chairperson in Canada. Charm pays off. At the Commonwealth meeting in Harare in October, according to one observer, "He was clearly the biggest guy in the room — and they all referred to Brian in their speeches."

The day before McDougall had made her ill-chosen comments, Mulroney had personally consulted with foreign leaders for their views and advice on responding to the Moscow coup. Although he did not go as far as Margaret Thatcher, the former British prime minister who urged the Soviet people to take to the streets to fight the junta, he had forcefully condemned the coup.

The gulf between the different reactions from Mulroney and McDougall was quickly filled. By the end of the crucial week, McDougall had met her colleagues from the North Atlantic Treaty Organization (NATO) in Brussels. She emerged from their meeting to say that Canada was fully in accord with NATO's condemnation of the coup and insistence on the restoration of Mikhail Gorbachev to power. By then, of course, the failed coup was history. Within months, so too was Gorbachev.

But the incident suggested that Canadian foreign policymaking is unsystematic. Unless the minister has a clear logic for his or her words, policy decisions risk being driven by events or by domestic politics. Short-term advantage may overtake long-term objectives. Barbara McDougall's misfortune was to face such momentous events when she was only three months on the job. Her predecessor, Joe Clark, had a better grasp of both the nuances of foreign policy and the values guiding Canada's international actions.

More specifically, the incident illustrates that, despite the External Affairs departmental machine, with its staff of 4,400 (and cogs and wheels elsewhere, including the Departments of Finance, Fisheries and Oceans, Agriculture, Environment and Energy, to mention only a few), the locus of decision-making is not always clear. "The big decisions in foreign policy," explains a senior External Affairs official, "are usually made by a bunch of guys sitting around a table in the Langevin Block [the Prime Minister's Office]." During 1991, there were plenty of big decisions to take. Momentous events unfolded, among them the Gulf War, the dissolution of the Soviet Union, the start of trilateral trade talks with Mexico and the U.S., and civil war in Yugoslavia. But there were also significant shifts in the balance of power around that table, which will have a lasting impact on the management of Canada's foreign policy during the 1990s.

A Triangular Balance

First, the people. The year opened with Joe Clark, the former prime minister, as Secretary of State for External Affairs — a post he had held since the start of the Mulroney regime. De Montigny Marchand, a smooth career diplomat in the traditional mould, was the recently appointed Under-Secretary. Clark's record in the portfolio since his appointment in 1984 was one of low-key activism. "Where can Canada make a difference?" he frequently asked advisers. His answer usually directed him towards the Third World. His priorities included human rights (particularly in South Africa), promotion of links with the Association of South-East Asian Nations (ASEAN) countries, and attention to Canada's role as a peacekeeper. He also appointed several women as heads of mission — a belated step towards gender parity in External's old boys' club.

To the frustration of the department, however, there were many issues involving Canadian interests that Clark shirked. During the late 1980s Canada was slow to establish relationships with the nations of Eastern Europe as they threw off Soviet shackles. Security questions, and Canada's role in NATO, did not engage the minister: he frequently missed NATO foreign ministers' meetings. Clark was consistently reluctant to take up economic or trade issues: in a much-quoted remark, he admitted he once had to make a choice between studying French or economics, and chose the former.

However, Clark earned kudos at home and abroad for his dogged promotion of traditional Canadian values: moderation, compromise, and social justice. Canadians admired the way he handled the relationship with the Prime Minister, given the two men's lifelong political rivalry. Clark and Mulroney had different views on the Middle East (the Prime Minister was more sympathetic to the Jewish lobby than Clark) and on the bilateral relationship with Washington (Clark was less supportive of the U.S. invasion of Panama than Mulroney). During the Gulf War, Clark was a dove, anxious to keep some distance between Ottawa and Washington and reluctant to commit Canadian forces. Mulroney, on the other hand, was a hawk, committed to quick multinational action, under U.S. leadership, against Saddam Hussein.

But Clark successfully contained his personal differences with the Prime Minister. As the Mulroney years rolled by, Clark established himself as a pillar of consistency and small virtues on the political landscape. His stature allowed him to pursue his activities out of the limelight. He ignored much of Ottawa's Cuisinart of committees through which policy is usually processed. The cabinet committee on defence and external affairs, which the Secretary of State for External Affairs chairs, rarely met. Clark's departmental officers saw their minister only sporadically. Policy development in those areas on which he chose to focus was a one-man affair.

Nevertheless, Clark was clearly the lead minister in a department that, since 1982, has had a triad of ministers at its apex. Alongside the Secretary of State for External Affairs is the Minister for International Trade and the Minister for External Relations and International Development.

The role of the Minister for International Trade has expanded steadily since the merger of the trade and foreign policy bureaucracies in 1982. In the early 1980s, the trade minister was clearly the junior partner, primarily serving the needs of the Canadian business sector. Gerald Regan and Ed Lumley, trade ministers in the late Trudeau years, spent their time on airplanes, cheer-leading for trade missions to promote Canadian exports.

Since 1984, however, trade issues have been propelled to centre-stage by the "New Right" agenda of the Mulroney government and by the pressure to compete globally. This trend has been reflected in the increasing seniority of the ministers handling the portfolio. James Kelleher, a rookie M.P., was the first Tory to be given the job. As bilateral trade talks with Washington gathered speed, Pat Carney, who had already had two major portfolios, took over. Before the Free Trade Agreement was signed in 1988, John Crosbie, a front-bench veteran, was in charge of trade.

John Crosbie did not hide his resentment that Clark's job had higher status than his own. However, Clark's preoccupations left plenty of turf for the moody intellectual from Newfoundland, who was not intimidated by economics. Crosbie concentrated on trade negotiations. He travelled extensively, leading trade delegations both west and east. A *cordon sanitaire* developed between the two ministers. Their staffs often clashed, but spats between ministerial staffers are as much a part of the Ottawa scene as Question Period theatrics.

Meanwhile, the third member of the triad is Monique Landry. Landry became external affairs minister in 1986, only two years after she was first elected to parliament. Landry is physically removed from the two senior ministers: her responsibility, the Canadian International Development

Agency (CIDA), is located in Hull, across the Ottawa River from the squat brown concrete leviathan known as the Pearson Building.

Inhibited by inexperience and a lack of fluency in English, Landry has rarely made news in the Anglophone press during her time as head of Canada's overseas development programs. In her native Quebec's press, she is lauded for the contracts CIDA has given to Quebec firms. But the hard-hearted 1980s saw a steady decline in the percentage of GDP committed to overseas aid, from a high of 0.52 percent in 1975 to only 0.44 percent in 1989. Landry, with few allies in cabinet, has been unable to arrest the slide. Her officials have been scrambling to adjust to a harsher fiscal climate.

By mid-1991, however, Landry was the only one of the three ministers who remained. Joe Clark had been press-ganged by the Prime Minister into the tough area of national politics. In May, he had been given the dubious honour of handling constitutional reform. Barbara McDougall, a Toronto minister who has been a high-flyer in the Mulroney cabinet since her election in 1984, took his place in the Pearson Building. At the same time, Michael Wilson, the anchor of the government's fiscal policy, moved over from the Department of Finance to the international trade portfolio, replacing John Crosbie. Wilson was also appointed Minister for Industry, Science and Technology.

The simultaneous arrival of McDougall and Wilson on the ninth floor of the Pearson Building signalled a re-examination of priorities. McDougall and Wilson share an economic orientation. Both came to politics from Bay Street, although Wilson had operated at more stratospheric levels. Neither shirks attendance at high level international meetings ("You'd be amused to see the way heads swivel at a meeting of foreign ministers, when a self-possessed woman in a short skirt and black stockings joins them. It's done something for Canada's image . . ." one official confided). Both have held senior economic portfolios in government: Wilson as Finance Minister, McDougall as Minister of Employment and Immigration.

However, Michael Wilson's appearance on the ninth floor further distorted the delicate triangular relationship between the lead ministers. Wilson has considerably more political experience and *gravitas* than Barbara McDougall, although nominally she is the senior minister. Back in 1984, McDougall had been Wilson's junior minister at the finance department. Moreover, Wilson holds three trump cards. He has the ear of the Prime Minister. As a veteran of seven economic summits, he has a better grasp of Canada's position in the world: he quickly stepped into the big economic issues (such as Canada's relations with the former Soviet republics) that had previously been ignored. Lastly, he is in charge of trade negotiations that are crucial to Canada's economic well-being. When he is not keeping a close eye on what is going on in Geneva, at the GATT negotiating table, Wilson is in Washington, participating in the trilateral trade talks between Mexico, the U.S. and Canada.

Rivalry between the two ministers, according to insiders, is minimized by the fact that Wilson has his own departmental resources at the industry department. Wilson's two portfolios give him responsibility for both the macro and the micro aspects of trade policy. He also spearheads the government's efforts to improve Canada's productivity and competitiveness. A legendary workaholic, he divides his time equally between ministries — within ten days of his appointment, he was off on a trade mission to Saudi Arabia and Kuwait. Although the deputy minister for trade also reports to the Secretary of State for External Affairs, so far there are few signs of tension.

However, there has been a perceptible shift in power in the department. McDougall's reaction to the Soviet coup was quickly chalked up as evidence of her inexperience. When Wilson, rather than McDougall, went off to the Baltic republics the following week, it seemed that he was now the departmental heavyweight. There were instant obituaries of McDougall: one *Toronto Star* headline read: "Critics forecast short stint for McDougall." *La Presse* asked: "Barbara McDougall: futur leader ou gaffeuse chronique?" The *Ottawa Citizen* suggested: "Adrift in External Affairs: McDougall struggles to save face as the PM seems to take over."

By the end of the year, McDougall had recovered from her shaky start. She applied herself to Canada's participation in all the international clubs, a course that endeared her to multilateral-minded bureaucrats. ("As a middle power, our interests have always been best served by strengthening the international machinery," explains a senior External officer, using a mantra that has not changed since the days of Lester B. Pearson himself.)

McDougall is an assiduous attender of NATO meetings. At her maiden speech in October at the United Nations, she endorsed the idea that the UN should seize the opportunity to foster world peace and security — a familiar Canadian theme. The same month, she participated in the effort by the Organization of American States (OAS) to restore deposed leader Jean-Bertrand Aristide to power in Haiti. Backed by the Prime Minister, she has pushed for a UN peacekeeping mission to Yugoslavia. The proposal initially met with derision at the UN and in Europe, but within months had been translated into action.

McDougall has stayed out of trouble largely by sticking close to the Prime Minister's side. However, the cautious pragmatism that is her hallmark is now proving to be a hindrance. The Department of External Affairs needs more than a technician at the helm; international issues require a creative intellect. So far, she has given little indication that she is really engaged by issues that do not affect her Toronto voters.

Nevertheless, the reason why McDougall was savaged by the press for her gauche reaction to the Soviet coup was that, in media eyes, she had already stumbled. Her reputation had been scarred by her role in the Al Mashat Affair, which shook Ottawa in the spring of 1991.

Mohammed Al Mashat is the former Iraqi Ambassador to the United States who was admitted to Canada in March 1991, under a minister's permit. When news of Al Mashat's arrival leaked into the press, there was uproar. Why had a henchman of Saddam Hussein been fast-tracked into the country? The Prime Minister's Office provoked a still louder outcry with a clumsy effort at damage control. In a confidential meeting in May, a huddle of ministers and senior mandarins decided to name an aide to Joe Clark, and an External Affairs officer, as the people responsible for the decision. The affair became a *cause célèbre* when a parliamentary committee discovered that these people had written their apologies on orders from their superiors.

The Al Mashat Affair called into question the cherished principle of ministerial responsibility — the Westminster doctrine that civil servants are accountable to their ministers, who, in turn, are accountable to parliament. At the time, Gordon Robertson, who served as Clerk of the Privy Council between 1963 and 1975, said,

> This episode is the most damaging thing that has happened to the public service in the 50 years with which I have been associated with it. The issue could not have been handled worse. The distrust between public servants will severely impair confidence. What public servant will take the onus of decision-making if he thinks his minister will denounce what he did and name him in public? He'll just send every decision upstairs, and overburdened ministers will make hasty decisions on inadequate evidence.

The affair certainly damaged the reputation of Barbara McDougall, who was Minister for Employment and Immigration at the time Al Mashat entered the country, and was widely viewed as the author of the disastrous "damage control" strategy. When she mishandled the Moscow coup only two months after the parliamentary inquiry, she found few friends within Ottawa or the press corps rushing to her defence.

The Al Mashat Affair also eroded morale in the Department of External Affairs. The corridors of the Pearson Building have echoed with grumbles for years. Endless reorganizations, triggered by the merger with the trade department a decade ago, plus wrenching personnel cutbacks, have bred dismay and frustration. The Al Mashat Affair dealt a blow to departmental collegiality. It likely contributed to the fact that, by the year's end, the department had a new deputy minister. De Montigny Marchand, who had colluded in the decision to put the blame for the Al Mashat blunder on two of his subordinates, was posted to Italy. He was replaced by Reid Morden, an affable rolled-up-sleeves administrator who has never served as a head of post abroad. Morden's previous job had been to crack the whip at the Canadian Security and Information Service (CSIS). He arrived in the Pearson Building with a mandate to improve departmental management.

So, within a few months, two of the three ministers and the lead deputy minister in the Department of External Affairs had changed. Among the ministers, only Monique Landry remained, and among the deputies, only Don Campbell, the long-time deputy trade minister. The sum total of all these comings and goings is a shift in focus, from political-diplomatic to economic. The operative question is no longer the simple one: "Where can Canada make a difference?" Now, according to senior officials, priorities are more likely to be established on the basis of national self-interest.

Two-Tract Policy

But Canadians do not want to relinquish the Boy Scout role. They do not want to think of the world in terms of rival trading blocs, with the North bullying the South into sticking to the North's rules. The Mulroney government has been burnt by the bitterness of the debate on bilateral free trade and by the poor response to Michael Wilson's competitiveness agenda. So the current North American trade talks are underplayed in public.

Instead, a different (although parallel) foreign policy makes headlines, with Mulroney as its star. One side-effect of Canadian involvement in the Gulf War was an unanticipated (and short-lived) surge in patriotism and support for Ottawa. Once Canadian troops were engaged in military actions in Iraq in January 1991, public opinion rallied around the flag. After the war, the government's popularity sank to new lows. But the lesson that overseas adventures could build popularity at home had not been lost on political strategists in the Prime Minister's Office. Since early fall, the Prime Minister has toiled to boost his image as a high-profile player on the international stage.

On September 29, in a major foreign policy address at Stanford University, Brian Mulroney outlined a radically activist approach to post-Cold War diplomacy. He called for a wide range of measures to assist the Soviet Union and its newly independent republics. He also spoke in favour of international intervention in the internal strife of sovereign states. Canada favours, he suggested, "rethinking the limits of national sovereignty in a world where problems respect no borders."

Mulroney tied this new approach to Canadian values. "There is no map to the future, no instruction book to the new world order," he said, speaking from a text that the Department of External Affairs and the

Prime Minister's Office had laboured over together for weeks. "We have only our values and the hard-earned lessons of the past to go on."

The first chance to put this new, value-driven activism into practice came quickly, with the overthrow of Haitian president Jean-Bertrand Aristide in a military coup. Mulroney expressed outrage and immediately sent Barbara McDougall to the OAS with a proposal to restore Aristide through diplomatic efforts. She flew to Port-au-Prince as part of the OAS mission, to meet with the leaders of the military coup and persuade them to restore Aristide to power.

Human rights issues have been a priority for the Prime Minister since 1984, as can be seen from his continual insistence on economic sanctions against South Africa, in the teeth of Mrs. Thatcher's opposition. But now, with McDougall at his side, he turned up the volume. At the October Commonwealth meeting in Harare, the Prime Minister announced, "We shall increasingly be channelling our development assistance to those countries which show respect for fundamental rights and freedoms." Despite a cool response in Harare, Mulroney made the same argument for linkage between foreign aid and respect for human rights at the fourth summit of La Francophonie in Paris in November.

Mulroney's crusade has had a warm reception at home. It reminds Canadians of their altruistic image abroad, at a time when they are enmeshed in a mean-spirited, divisive constitutional debate and Mulroney's personal popularity is at its nadir. However, his human rights rhetoric could not shield him from a cynical reaction to Canada's hasty recognition of an independent Ukraine in November. The decision to recognize the new republic was regarded as crassly political — driven by the presence of one million Canadians of Ukrainian origin, rather than by any altruistic concern for the newly emerging republic.

The Process

How do these different themes and directions in Canadian foreign policy fit together — if, indeed, they do?

The Department of External Affairs went to considerable lengths in 1991 to shape a framework for its foreign policy objectives in a world freed from superpower rivalry. The department deliberately spurned the vehicle of a White Paper for such a review. White Papers are great favourites of new ministers, who want to demonstrate how their foreign policy will differ from that of their predecessors. But a White Paper implies a dramatic discontinuity from previous policy, although Canadian interests remain roughly the same whichever government is in power. Instead, argued policy analysts in the Department of External Affairs, a more appropriate instrument would be a framework document of themes and priorities.

The document could then be updated annually, explained its chief author, Howard Balloch (then director of the department's policy planning staff), to revalidate directions and make course adjustments. Such a document would articulate the policy base for major issues faced by government, such as the allocation of diminishing aid funds. It would also integrate domestic policy with foreign policy: Canada's environmental programs, for instance, could be linked to UN environmental programs.

The policy planners started work on the document in mid-1990, with the approval of the then minister Joe Clark. The Gulf War temporarily derailed the exercise, but by mid-1991, a draft was circulating through different departments.

By now McDougall had succeeded Clark, and was developing her own style in the portfolio. The proposed policy document appealed to her as a way of managing the competition between the interests within government and between Canada's interests abroad. Less confident in her portfolio than Clark, McDougall proved a more diligent chair of the cabinet committee on defence and external affairs. The difficult decisions facing the committee's members required a more rigorous analysis than Clark had ever provided.

For example, since the February 1991 budget, all Canada's international financial assistance (including both overseas development programs and assistance to Eastern Europe) now comes from one budgetary envelope. This means that the Minister for External Relations must defend the overall size of the envelope in pre-budget discussions, then negotiate with sharper elbowed colleagues at Finance and Trade for CIDA's share of a shrinking pie. What principles should be reflected in resource allocations? Debate on External's draft paper was, according to Balloch, "extensive."

The paper was finally released to the public in December 1991, under the title "Foreign Policy Themes and Priorities." It attempted to tie together the different elements in current foreign policy into a coherent package. Much of the paper reads like a catalogue of everything successive foreign ministers have ever cared about — peacekeeping, refugees, multilateralism, technology spread, arms control, and human rights. However, all serious policy documents, whether White Papers or departmental briefing notes, contain new buzzwords. "Good governance" was the novel theme in the 1991 paper. Countries committed to good governance (i.e., democratic practices and respect for human rights) are the countries most likely to receive Canadian assistance in the future.

The document's emphasis on common values reflected domestic *angst*, and echoed Mulroney's speeches. At its launch, McDougall said: "The very existence of Canada — its languages, its cultures, its values, its tolerant spirit, its standard of behaviour — has represented an independent voice and has constituted something different, something special, for the larger world. By freely forging a united nation based on respect for diversity, Canadians bring a special sensitivity to other problems in the world."

The values underlying Canadian foreign policy are described at length: the spirit of moderation, compromise, the rule of law, and social and economic justice. The paper outlines Canadian interests abroad: security, prosperity and a rule-based international order. It points out that new threats to security, including environmental degradation, proliferation of weaponry, and international migration, have replaced the old Cold War threat. The importance of foreign investment and liberalized trade to Canada's prosperity is emphasized, particularly where they involve our relations with our three key trading partners, the U.S., the European Community, and Japan. Finally, the paper draws a connection between foreign policy and domestic issues — "national unity, competitiveness and sustainable development." The importance of integrating foreign policy with the pressing domestic agenda "has never been higher."

The authors of the paper, perhaps naively, were surprised when media comment on their work focused on the link they had made between a value-driven foreign policy and national unity. McDougall herself drew attention to other objectives, including a greater peacekeeping role, liberalized trade, and "good governance," as a measure of a country's eligibility for Canadian aid. The domestic implications of Conservative foreign policy are important in the short-term. In the long-term, it is the proposed changes to the way Canada does business with the rest of the world that will be more significant. The paper reflects the Conservative government's determination to articulate Canadian interests abroad more clearly, and to focus more closely on trade and conditional aid, at the expense of traditional diplomacy and development aid.

New Directions

So with new faces, and a new annual process, what are the foreign policy themes for the 1990s?

Officials in different departments all mention different objectives — External Affairs officers mention human rights; trade officers target successful outcomes at GATT and NAFTA; senior members of the Department of Finance talk about global economic stability. But all agree that, for a trading nation like Canada, the need to maintain a strong economy in a rapidly changing world is crucial. Even "good governance," which sounds so altruistic at first mention, is about more than promoting democracy. "Democracy goes hand-in-hand with economic growth and free trade," explains an External Affairs mandarin. "And we argue that the benefits of development go hand in hand with democracy." Democratic nations are more likely to adhere to international trading rules, and less likely to provoke turbulence of the Gulf War type.

Continued membership of the G-7 is key to Canada's future, argue policy-makers within government. "It gives us an *entrée* into the biggest sandbox, and allows us to play on the big issues," explains a senior finance bureaucrat. But our membership is threatened from several directions. Constitutional dislocation would take us out of the big leagues. And as three megatrading blocks emerge — North America, Europe, and Japan — Canada's status as Uncle Sam's junior partner will be confirmed.

The prospect of being elbowed out of the G-7 (or the "directorate," as External staff nickname it) appals foreign affairs buffs. Meanwhile, G-7 business keeps Ottawa busy. In the fall of 1991, for example, a group of senior officials from the G-7 countries began work on restructuring the West's relations with the emerging Soviet republics. David Dodge, from the Department of Finance in Ottawa, spent long weeks in Moscow and other capitals, as part of the team.

The fact that it was an official from the Department of Finance, rather than an emissary from the Pearson Building, illustrates the diffusion of responsibility for action, as well as decisions, on foreign policy. The Department of External Affairs prides itself, with justice, on its strategic thinking, but increasingly the tools for carrying out its strategies are to be found elsewhere. For example, sanctions against Yugoslavia involve a ban on import and export licenses imposed by the Department of Trade, and a change in the Department of Finance's bilateral tariff agreements with Yugoslavia.

This dispersion of issues and bureaucratic responsibility means that other parts of the government are challenging ever more strongly External Affairs' control of the foreign policy agenda. Nowhere is this more evident than in the role of the Department of Finance — the temple of Tory free market theology. While trade officials within the Pearson Building concentrate on the nitty-gritty of GATT or NAFTA negotiations, it is more likely that Finance officials will be dealing with the big picture. ("Those trade guys are so narrow," grumbles a Finance official. "They'll ask for yet another meeting on yogurt quotas, but they'll never stand back and ask where does this sit in the government's overall economic agenda.") Despite popular loathing of the FTA, evident in opinion polls and a raft of critical books by authors such as Mel Hurtig, the confidence of the government and the Department of Finance remains undimmed. "We've got to make it work and ensure that irritants don't sour the climate," explains the official. "When the economy starts growing again, people will realize it was the right step."

This was the case when Wilson was in the Finance portfolio, pushing the Free Trade Agreement with the U.S. It is doubly true now that Wilson is in the Trade portfolio and Don Mazankowski, another continentalist free trader, has taken over Finance. While Mulroney and McDougall have taken public ownership of popular themes such as peacekeeping and good governance, the strongest ministers in cabinet are keeping tabs on multilateral economic co-operation. Their goal, as spelled out in the clunky prose of the framework paper, is to "pursue completion of a balanced and comprehensive multilateral trade negotiation (MTN) and NAFTA, the latter to protect FTA gains and construct a key building block for hemispheric trade and investment." In the Darwinian world of rival trading blocs, Canada must perform or perish.

How do Canada's commitment to development aid to the Third World and the Prime Minister's commitment to human rights fit into the bottom-line thinking of the 1990s? Poorly. The tension between Canada's aid and trade policies was bleakly highlighted in December. Ottawa announced it was cutting off $30 million in aid to Indonesia, one month after 100 unarmed pro-independence demonstrators were slaughtered by Indonesian troops in East Timor; however, it is 16 years since such atrocities began, with the invasion of East Timor by Indonesia in 1975. Since then, an estimated 200,000 people have died in East Timor. But Ottawa has been reluctant to act, because Indonesia is one of Canada's biggest trading partners in Southeast Asia.

CIDA has been in flux for some time. The agency assists more than 150 countries, with strong emphasis on 36 of them. Dwindling resources have eroded its *raison d'être*. Its current president, Marcel Massé, has indicated that he wants CIDA to conform more closely in its program criteria to the approach of the International Monetary Fund. This approach (which had already been adopted by both the U.K. and France) makes development assistance dependent on economic restructuring. "Deserving" recipients will reduce the role of government in economic planning (food subsidies, for example, are frowned on) and move towards a free market aimed at bolstering exports and attracting foreign investment. Massé himself used to work at the World Bank, the IMF's Washington neighbour.

Massé's tough-minded approach did not go down well with church groups and non-governmental agencies, which pointed out that every year since 1984 has seen a net flow of capital away from developing countries to developed ones. "Restructuring," they argue, "is a euphemism for insidious recolonization."

But other pressures on CIDA pull the organization in the opposite direction. In November, a report commissioned from the Montreal-based consulting firm SECOR said that CIDA uses its $2 billion aid budget to help too many countries and spends too much on administering its programs. One issue raised is whether it would be more efficient for Canada to deliver a larger percentage of its aid through multilateral organizations such as the World Bank. The aid community deplores this idea, on the grounds that programs would lose their Canadian flavour. However, the Department of Finance argues it would make sense, and give us credit where we could obtain the greatest benefit — in multilateral circles and in Washington.

A Smaller Role, A Closer Focus

In the jigsaw of personalities, issues and priorities within Ottawa's tight little world, it is easy to lose sight of the forces beyond our borders that are diminishing our role. With the end of the Cold War, there is no call for intermediaries between the U.S. and the Soviet Union — a role that Trudeau played to some effect. As the Central American countries settle down to an uneasy peace, the "Good Guy" act that Clark adopted is *passé*. As international concern for the underdeveloped world ebbs, Canada scuttles toward the safety of the multilateral umbrella, abandoning the missionary roots of its original sandalled aid workers. And as the world's economic order reassembles along different fault lines, the logic of Canada's membership of the G-7 is less and less obvious.

There are still opportunities ahead. A reformed and relevant United Nations would offer Canada the chance to continue its historic mediator role, particularly as the world's leading peacekeeper. As environmental concerns move up the international agenda, Canadian expertise and commitment may be of increasing value. Policymakers in the Department of External Affairs are monitoring such developments, seeing which niches Canada may fill in the future. The ninth floor of the Pearson Building remains the locus of long-term policymaking, even though short-term decisions may be taken and implemented in other government buildings.

Joe Clark's question for the 1980s was, "Where can Canada's presence make a difference?" Today's policymakers have given the question a new twist — less selfless, perhaps, but a more accurate reflection of Tory thinking. Their concern is: where can Canada's presence make a difference to Canada?

3

The New Canadian Embassy in Tokyo: Ambassador Extraordinary

Raymond Moriyama

A Wonderful Opportunity

Receiving the commission to design the new Canadian Embassy in Tokyo was an unimaginable joy for a second-generation Japanese Canadian.

Our firm had already designed two projects that, each in its own way, acknowledged the connection between the peoples of Japan and Canada. Completed in 1964, the Japanese Canadian Cultural Centre in Toronto signified the readiness of the Japanese Canadian community to re-enter Canadian life after the years of internment and to take its place within the cultural mosaic. The Goh Ohn Bell, built in 1977, was an expression of gratitude from Ontario's Japanese Canadians to the people of Ontario celebrating the Japanese community's centenary in Canada. Both were gestures between Japanese Canadians and the larger Canadian community.

The opportunity to reach across the seas, to grasp firmly the hand of my ancestors, carried with it an intensely personal spiritual significance that I had not yet encountered in architecture. The project became more than the opportunity to design a fine building. It was a chance to create an edifice that would represent Canada to the Japanese and bring Canadians and Japanese together.

As a founding member of the Asia Pacific Foundation of Canada, I was aware of the importance of the Pacific Rim, Japan, and the other Asian countries to Canada's economic future. I believed that this project could become a window through which the people of these countries could view Canada as a potential business partner.

Fortunately for Canadians, Canada's first Minister to Japan, Sir Herbert Marler, had acquired in 1932 a property in the prestigious Akasaka district during a temporary drop in the yen. Its reputation as the home of a fierce samurai ghost kept Japanese buyers away. (Soon after the Marler purchase the samurai ghost supposedly departed to join two beautiful female ghosts at the bottom of a well next to the Official Residence.)

Now, in Tokyo's most desirable neighbourhood, the land is among the most expensive in the world. How expensive? Imagine a piece of property situated across from Buckingham Palace, along the Champs Elysées, and on Times Square. This property is even more expensive than that!

Once the home of the Viscount Tadatoshi Aoyama, last feudal lord and daimyo of the Sasayama clan, the property is now the setting for the Official Residence, an imposing structure which occupies the southeast portion of the L-shaped site. Along the northern edge of the property is Aoyama dori, a busy eight-lane thoroughfare lined with offices, fashionable boutiques, and cultural institutions. Directly opposite are the beautifully treed Akasaka Imperial Grounds. Set within the Grounds is the Akasaka Palace (the state guest house), on axis with the Embassy site, and the home of the Prince and Princess Takamado, directly in front of the Embassy. Adjacent is the Takahashi Memorial Park. To the south is a mix of low-scale residential, commercial, and professional buildings; to the west, low-scale residential buildings. An aerial view shows the neighbourhood as a small oasis of greenery amid the dense building fabric of the city. We could not have asked for a more magnificent site.

Challenges to Meet

The list of physical requirements presented to us included the offices for the Embassy, public facilities (library, art gallery, theatre, exhibition area, and reception room), and underground parking. A second phase on the southwest portion of the site would provide living quarters, fitness facilities, and parking for Canadian personnel. The Official Residence and adjoining garden would be retained.

While these basic requirements were not unusual, challenges were imposed by the site, program, local regulations, surrounding urban context, and the gaze of the Japanese eye. How, I wondered, could we create an ambience that would suit the Japanese as well as Canadians?

The Canadian Government had a brilliant idea! It issued a proposal call to Canadian developers to see if the project could be built without cost to the Canadian people. There was no response. The proposal call was then issued in Tokyo, and twenty-eight proponents responded. The commission was awarded to a consortium consisting of Shimizu Corporation and the Mitsubishi Trust and Banking Corporation, which would provide the $200 million project at no cost to Canadians except for furnishings and security equipment. A surplus portion exceeding the Embassy's space requirements would be leased to tenants for a prescribed period of time, enabling the consortium to recover its design, construction, and financing costs.

This financial strategy required a design for short-term dual occupancy. It also called for two distinct entrances, one for the Embassy and one for the surplus portion, both with the prestigious Aoyama dori address. It necessitated a maximum floor area for the surplus portion: the greater the leasable area, the sooner would the surplus portion revert back to Canada. Yet the spatial requirements of the Embassy had to be met. (The Embassy portion would belong to Canada from the very beginning.) In short, a delicate balancing act was required. And finally, because we were commissioned as architects by Shimizu Corporation rather than by Canada, the working relationship required a great deal of diplomacy, trust, understanding, and a pragmatic application of phenomenology to work smoothly.

The site's special location brought its own set of problems. We were all eager to please the Embassy's neighbours, including the Prince and Princess Takamado. (When the Prince, the Honorary Chairman of the Canada Japan Society, and the Princess previewed the final design they jokingly suggested that a bridge be built connecting it to the Palace! Of course, we were thrilled!)

Tokyo's stringent sun shade regulations restrict building envelopes considerably. In this case, the site's proximity to Takahashi Memorial Park and the Akasaka Imperial Grounds imposed even greater limitations on the Embassy. The new building could only cast a shadow on the Imperial Grounds and the Park to a depth of ten metres and for no more than two hours per day. This greatly reduced the allowable mass of the building.

By giving up part of the site to provide public open space, the Canadian Government could have gained increased density and dispensation for the shadow envelope. It decided to forego such bonuses for security reasons and as a sign of respect or *enryo*, a concept of great importance to the Japanese. Although this decision made our task more difficult, I applauded such sensitivity. As a gesture of *enryo* to the Akasaka Imperial Grounds, the north-facing roof slope follows an even more acute angle than that allowed.

With any Embassy structure, security is a prime issue. Points of entry and exit must be controlled. The building itself must be impenetrable, and, in a dual-use building, security tends to become more complicated (or simpler, as we shall see).

Working closely with Shimizu we approached the initial schematic design phase determined to resolve these four major challenges: security, a restricted building envelope, dual occupancy, and, most important of all, the creation of an architectural symbol for Canada.

The new Embassy shares one of the most expensive sites in the world with the Official Residence, built in 1933 by Sir Herbert Marler, Canada's first Minister to Japan.

The Embassy sits within an oasis of greenery in downtown Tokyo.

1. Three symbols fundamental to oriental culture — earth (*chi*), people (*jin*), and heaven (*ten*) — appear in a traditional Japanese Ikebana diagram.

2. The symbols for earth, people, and heaven are the bridge between the two countries.

The Embassy's theatre was inspired by seventeenth-century open-air Noh theatre.

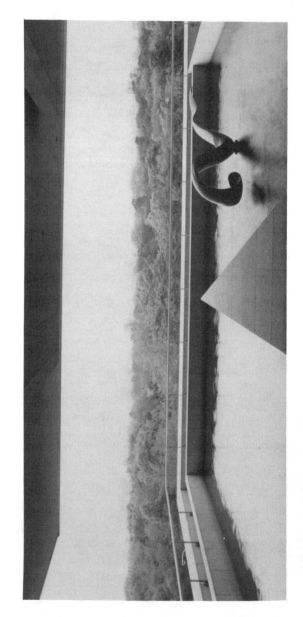

Seen from the Canada Garden, the treetops of the Akasaka Imperial Grounds and Takahashi Memorial Park stretch out a compelling lush green carpet.

A traditional Japanese garden, a place of serene and timeless beauty, offers a sharp contrast to the rugged Canada Garden.

The Embassy Library is the largest Canadian research library in Asia.

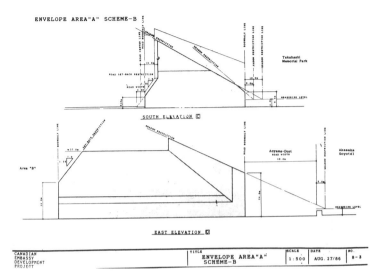

ENVELOPE AREA "A" SCHEME-B

SOUTH ELEVATION

EAST ELEVATION

CANADIAN EMBASSY DEVELOPMENT PROJECT	TITLE ENVELOPE AREA "A" SCHEME-B	SCALE 1 : 500	DATE AUG. 27/86	NO. 8-3

Tokyo's stringent sun shade regulations restricted the shape of the building considerably.

Symbol of Canada

We produced almost forty alternatives. Almost all of them focused on two major themes — Canada as characterized by vast open spaces and expansive landscapes, and the mild, good-mannered, open nature of its people. Our thoughts ran to images of mountains, trees, plains, and water. At the same time, we were searching for an appropriate symbol for the good will between the two countries. Many people refer to an embassy building as a bridge between nations. But, in my mind, people are the bridge, and the embassy is a friendly but powerful abutment, supporting the forceful flow from shore to shore. This metaphor provided the basis for our design; our next challenge was to find an architectural expression for these ideas.

The solution which most successfully addressed all issues was an eight-storey building split in half horizontally. How did we arrive at this solution? To understand better the meaning of a meeting place for Canada and Japan, we developed a diagram to illustrate the two countries. For us, Canada evokes images not only of nature but of industry — transportation, communications, manufacturing, and high technology. Our diagram, therefore, illustrates Canada's natural heritage and industrial spirit, with the Canadian people as the link between the two.

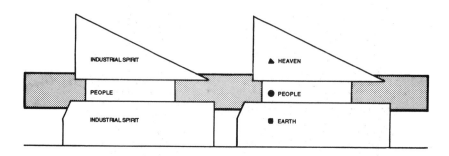

The people of Canada and of Japan are the bridge between the two countries.

Three Japanese Symbols

To represent Japan, we drew inspiration from the three symbols which are fundamental to Japanese culture — earth, people, and heaven, symbolized by the square (chi), circle (jin), and triangle (ten) — and which are articulated visually in Ikebana, the traditional Japanese art of flower arrangement.

The common element in our two diagrams, which bridges Canada and Japan, is people, the people of Canada and the people of Japan.

Our horizontally split building is divided into three symbolic components. The three-storey rectilinear base (the surplus commercial portion), built of stone, with square windows, represents earth. (Windows facing southeast are narrowed to minimize views of the Ambassador's residence.) The glass-enclosed roof sheltering the upper four floors (and the Embassy offices), and shaped by the sun shade laws, is triangular in profile and recalls the Japanese symbol for heaven. (Viewed from the balcony of the Akasaka Palace, the state guest house, the roof appears as a glass triangle floating above the trees. No guest will miss this symbol of Canadian spirit!) In the middle is the fourth floor, the meeting place of the people of the two countries, where experiences and thoughts can be exchanged high above the trees overlooking the Park.

The horizontal split works not only symbolically but functionally as well. It provides a simple approach to the dual functions of Embassy and surplus commercial space. The upper five floors are used by the Embassy. The lower three floors constitute primarily the surplus portion. With the surplus portion occupying the lower storeys, security is simplified: penetration directly into the Embassy from the outside is almost impossible.

In spite of strict security requirements, we sought to avoid any suggestion of exclusivity or restriction. Instead, we wanted the building to express the good relations between Canada and Japan, the special open communications which the two countries enjoy. The building is so designed that security levels rise as one moves upward. Public, low-security spaces such as the theatre, art gallery, and reference library are located on the lower levels. The Immigration Department requires public accessibility and is located at the rear of the second floor. Administration and consular offices occupy the fifth, sixth, seventh, and eighth floors and are accessed only by a single security checkpoint at the fourth floor.

Separate entries to the surplus office space and the Embassy are located on prestigious Aoyama dori. Here, Canadian artist Gar Smith has created a three-part work of art that underlines the metaphor of Ikebana and the relationship of earth, people, and heaven. A cast bronze, seventy-foot-long bow with a bark-like finish is suspended along the front of the building to gently command attention on the busy street. Below is a long narrow pool of water. Inside the lobby for the surplus office space is suspended the third component — another bow of similar size and shape but with a rock-like finish. A directional element, it leads visitors over a pedestrian bridge to the elevators. Both suspended pieces have internal electronically activated hammers but they also whistle softly with the wind. Hung low, they can be used as tuning forks by passers-by.

The Commonality of Sensory Experience

Gar's work is just one example of how the building calls into play all five senses. Regardless of cultural heritage, all peoples share the sensations of hearing, taste, smell, touch, and sight. The five senses are an important fundamental cross-cultural tie. Visitors entering the Embassy progress from Aoyama dori down a winding path where fragrant and colourful shrubs are in bloom year-round. (Recognizing the site's uniqueness as a natural habitat, the Municipality of Tokyo prohibited any changes that would affect the environment in the adjacent park. Environmental impact was measured by insect count. Trees could not be destroyed; the water table could not be altered. Otherwise, insects would disappear or die.)

Working with the land engages the senses and appeals to people world-wide. Artist Warren Carther employed this idea in a stained glass wall at the ground floor entry. Warren discovered in aerial photographs of Canadian prairie farmlands that the patterns created by farm machinery resembled those in the raked stone and gravel of Japanese dry landscapes. Those same patterns echo in the sandblasted, soft, yellows, blues, and greens of his wall.

References to nature continue at the lower level, where culture (theatre, art gallery, and library) nestles within the earth. In the theatre human emotions are played out under metallic branches and leaves that sparkle below the "stars" of a fibre optic ceiling. Our inspiration for the

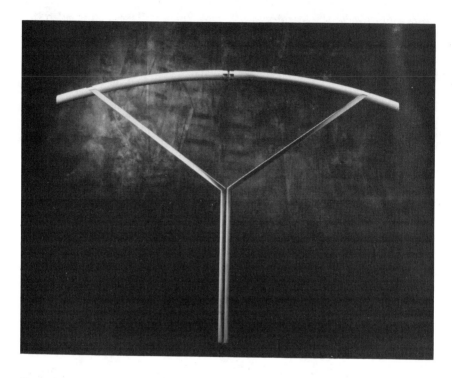

Bow-shaped door handles at the theatre entrance aim towards the heavens.

theatre's design came from Noh theatre where, on a late seventeenth-century October evening, actors performed under open skies in the glow of torchlight.

Lately I have become fascinated by the bow and arrow as ancient symbols of parents and offspring, of present and future. It seems natural then that at the lower "cultural" level, bow-shaped door handles at the theatre entrance should aim towards the heavens.

Meeting Place of the People

At the fourth floor is the official entrance of the Embassy and the symbolic and literal meeting place of the people. Again, all five senses are engaged on the journey from the outside world into the inner sanctum or *oku*. Visitors to the Embassy are swept upwards on a four-storey-high outdoor escalator through the trees of Takahashi Park. At the top of the escalator the open air Canada Garden unfolds.

At the same height as the neighbouring treetops, the Canada Garden gives the feeling of space that is so abundant in Canada and has such

"SLICE OF CANADA"

The fourth floor Canada Garden leads visitors on a symbolic journey from the Atlantic, across the Canadian Shield, to the Canadian North, over the Rockies, to the Pacific.

a powerful impact on Japanese visitors. The Garden's low cantilevered overhang compresses the vertical space, thus emphasizing the sense of horizontal space even further. (It also provides a sheltered outdoor gathering place.)

Clearly visible beyond the glass walls that contain the entry lobby and exhibition area, the Canada Garden underlines a contrast between the two cultures that extends even to physical geography. To the west visitors view the serene and timeless beauty of a traditional Japanese garden. To the east is the rugged Canadian landscape characterized by the Canadian Shield. Beyond, the treetops of the Akasaka Imperial Grounds and Takahashi Memorial Park spread out a compelling lush green carpet that stretches the boundaries of the building and visually pulls visitors beyond its edge, almost inviting them out for a stroll!

Visitors begin their tour of the Garden at Canada's Atlantic coast. Artist Ted Bieler's series of dramatic, bronze sculptural elements emerge from a reflecting pool to symbolize the wave of communication which closes the vast geographic gap between the two cultures. The story of the Canadian Shield unfolds around the perimeter of the fourth floor, depicting the forests, lakes, prairies, mountains, and rivers from which the Canadian experience is drawn.

The Inuit, descendants of the first inhabitants of the Shield, have a special representation of the Shield and the people who settled it — the Inukshuk. This human image, shaped from the rocks of the Shield, was created for the Canada Garden by Inuit artist Kananginak Pootoogook. The Embassy Inukshuk represents the Canadian Arctic and, like some oriental figure, points to both heaven and earth.

Along the northern edge of the terrace rise three triangular stone mounds representing the Rockies. The Wave, a bronze sculpture by Maryon Kantaroff, emerges from a pool of water, a symbol of the invisible vibrations that link the two cultures. Finally, the Shield disappears below the water's surface and Canada is left behind. Visitors are led across the Pacific via a series of stepping stones, through a stone portal and into a Japanese garden, to begin the journey anew.

The Embassy as Ambassador

Earlier I discussed my vision of the Embassy as a friendly abutment, supporting the bridge of people between the two countries. Now, less than one year after the Embassy's official opening, I am pleased to see that my vision is already becoming a reality.

For our firm, the nine-year process (from the initial competition to the design process and finally to construction) has been tremendously gratifying, especially at the level of human relationships. We have made good friends in Japan and in Canada. We have reached a special understanding with the people at the Shimizu Corporation and the Mitsubishi Trust and Banking Corporation. Working intimately as a team, we have established a friendship that far surpasses even the best of client/architect relationships.

The Embassy itself has become a valuable tool in international relations. Stories about the Embassy and Canada's genius in achieving a $200 million development at no cost have appeared in newspapers around the world. London's *The Independent* headlined the Embassy as a "Canadian Jewel in a Japanese Setting"[1] that "cost its government nothing." An article in the rather conservative *Japan Financial Times* is my favourite. Under the headline "Embassy — You must be joking!" is a photograph of Tokyo office workers lunching in the Canada Garden.[2]

In a year when Canada is viewed internationally as a country beset with constitutional and economic problems, the building of the Embassy is a welcome positive note in the media. Canada is and must be perceived as an active participant, even a leader, in the new alliance of the Pacific Rim countries. And the Embassy and its publicity are letting Canadians know that they should be proud of their country's role.

The Embassy's art gallery, theatre, and fourth floor exhibition and reception area are already being used for events that support Canada's trade, investment, tourism, and cultural objectives in Japan. The Embassy library is the largest Canadian research library in Asia. Whether visiting the library, or attending a trade show, exhibition opening, or dance performance, the Japanese will see that we Canadians are open and accessible, that we are ready to reach out to another culture, that we are willing to bow, shake hands, and make a deal.

One of the joys of being an architect is the surprise and wonder of watching how a building comes to life — it's almost like being a parent! To be completely honest, I did not anticipate that the Embassy would fulfil its role as ambassador so well. I am enormously pleased that it has exceeded our expectations. But I can see that Canada must continue to nurture the Embassy, supplying it with the staff and funds that will help it reach its full potential. The Embassy and Canada's relationship with the Pacific Rim countries have not yet reached their adolescence. There is still a lifetime of growth ahead.

Notes

1 Tim Jackson, "Canadian Jewel in a Japanese Setting," *The Independent* [London, UK], July 10, 1991.
2 "Embassy — You must be joking!," *Japan Financial Times* [Tokyo], May 21, 1991.

4

La dimension internationale dans le débat sur l'avenir constitutionnel du Canada

Ivan Bernier

Dans une récente étude préparée pour le compte du Canadian-American Center de l'Université du Maine et intitulée "If Canada Breaks up: Implications for U.S. Policy," le professeur Joseph T. Jockel conclue son propos en affirmant:

> As they contemplate the possibility of a future politically apart, English Canadians and Quebeckers have necessarily considered what this could mean for their relations with the U.S. In 1992 the U.S. government may be forced to turn to this agenda as well.[1]

Malheureusement, force est de reconnaître qu'à ce jour le débat sur l'avenir constitutionnel du Canada n'a pas donné lieu à une étude sérieuse des répercussions internationales des principaux scénarios envisagés pour résoudre la crise actuelle. On retrouve bien, ici et là, des allusions au fait que dans un contexte de globalisation des marchés et d'internationalisation de l'économie, il serait pour le moins paradoxal que le Canada évolue vers une forme de balkanisation plus ou moins prononcée. Récemment aussi, diverses études sont apparues qui affirment qu'advenant la séparation du Québec, les États-Unis profiteraient certainement de la demande d'adhésion de ce dernier à l'Accord de libre-échange pour lui imposer de nouvelles conditions d'entrée, tout en soulignant, par la même occasion, qu'un Québec indépendant aurait à assumer, en tant que partie à l'Accord de libre-échange et membre du GATT, des obligations auxquelles il échappe présentement en tant que province.[2] Mais ces propos, dont l'objectif politique est assez évident, disent peu finalement sur les implications, pour la politique étrangère canadienne, d'un Québec indépendant et rien du tout sur les implications d'autres solutions envisagées, telles que le statut quo, le fédéralisme décentralisé et le fédéralisme asymétrique. En d'autres termes, dans la mesure où l'on s'intéresse à la dimension internationale dans le présent débat sur l'avenir du Canada, c'est très manifestement dans le but de dissuader les Québécois d'opter en faveur de l'indépendance.[3] Que l'on soit d'accord ou non avec cet objectif, celui-ci est trop restreint pour que l'on s'en satisfasse. En réalité, ce qui importe par-dessus tout à ce stade-ci du débat sur l'avenir constitutionnel du Canada, c'est de saisir toutes les conséquences des divers choix qui se présentent à nous, ce qui inclue, évidemment, leurs conséquences internationales. Quel que soit le choix qui sera effectué en dernier ressort, celui-ci sera d'autant plus valide qu'il aura été fait en toute connaissance de cause.

Pour avoir une vue globale de la situation donc, il faut d'abord prendre en considération l'ensemble des hypothèses envisagées, chacune ayant ses conséquences propres. Ces hypothèses, nous les ramènerons pour les fins de la discussion à trois. Il s'agit d'abord du fédéralisme renouvelé, dont le prototype par excellence est le réaménagement constitutionnel mis de l'avant par le gouvernement fédéral dans ses propositions de septembre 1991. Dans cette première hypothèse, le Canada demeure uni, le partage des compétences n'est modifié qu'à la marge — ce qui exclut donc la possibilité d'une décentralisation majeure — et il n'est pas question d'asymétrie formelle, même si en pratique les possibilités d'asymétrie administrative entre les provinces demeurent assez nombreuses. La seconde hypothèse, on peut la qualifier de fédéralisme décentralisé, reprenant à cet égard l'expression utilisée par le Conseil économique du Canada dans son dernier exposé annuel.[4] Cette hypothèse fait place à une décentralisation relativement prononcée en matière de partage des compétences et peut même admettre une certaine asymétrie; elle maintient encore le Canada uni économiquement et politiquement avec cependant un rôle accrue des provinces dans les décisions centrales. La dernière hypothèse, enfin, celle de la séparation du Québec, parle par elle-même; elle englobe à la fois l'indépendance pure et simple et ce qu'il est convenu d'appeler la souveraineté-association.

L'actualisation de chacune de ces hypothèses, ainsi que mentionné précédemment, est susceptible d'entrainer des répercussions, plus ou moins prononcées selon le cas, dans le domaine international. Deux types de répercussions retiendront en particulier notre attention. Il y a d'abord les répercussions sur le processus même de formulation de la politique étrangère canadienne. Suivant le degré de complexité du processus décisionnel retenu, le niveau de décentralisation des compétences législatives et la plus ou moins grande fragmentation de la représentation extérieure, la politique étrangère canadienne en ressortira plus ou moins affectée au plan de sa formulation. Il y a ensuite les répercussions sur le contenu de la politique étrangère canadienne. Celle-ci devra tenir compte des contraintes et attentes internes ainsi que des réactions, réelles ou appréhendées, des partenaires étrangers. Déjà on constate que l'incertitude actuelle relativement à l'avenir constitutionnel du Canada a eu un impact sur la politique étrangère canadienne: des démarches sont entreprises pour calmer les appréhensions des pays étrangers et ce n'est manifestement pas par hasard que certains chefs d'Etat se sont déjà prononcés ouvertement en faveur du maintien d'un Canada uni. S'il est manifeste que c'est l'hypothèse de la séparation du Québec qui préoccupe par-dessus tout et qui risque d'affecter le plus en profondeur la politique étrangère canadienne, il ne faut pas en conclure pour autant que les autres hypothèses n'auront pas de répercussions. Dans la mesure enfin où les remarques qu'on peut formuler sur ces répercussions sont fonction de développements à venir, elles ne peuvent faire autrement que d'avoir un certain caractère spéculatif; elles seront justifiées essentiellement par notre propre interprétation des intérêts mis en cause par ces développements.

Ceci étant dit, voyons maintenant chacune des trois hypothèses mentionnées précédemment, en commencant par la plus simple, celle du fédéralisme renouvelé. Suivront ensuite l'hypothèse du fédéralisme décentralisé et en dernier lieu celle de la souveraineté du Québec.

Le fédéralisme renouvelé

À première vue, une modification de la constitution canadienne qui conserverait dans l'ensemble les grandes lignes du système fédéral actuel, une modification du type de celle mise de l'avant par le gouvernement fédéral dans ses propositions constitutionnelles de septembre 1991, ne semble guère susceptible d'affecter substantiellement la politique étrangère canadienne. Pour reprendre les termes de Denis Stairs dans une étude de 1982 sur le même sujet, un tel type de modification "would have, at most, a negligible effect on the international environment within which Canadian foreign policy is conducted and to which it must respond."[5] De fait, il est difficile de voir comment les États étrangers pourraient considérer un tel changement autrement que comme une question purement interne ne concernant que le Canada.

Néanmoins, il est possible que le processus même de formulation de la politique étrangère canadienne ressorte quelque peu affecté par un tel type de changement, ne fût-ce qu'au plan des délais exigés pour réaliser un accord sur une politique donnée. Il est intéressant de constater à cet égard que l'une des rares references au domaine des relations internationales que l'on retrouve dans les propositions fédérales de septembre 1991 porte précisément sur cette question. Parmi les principes qu'il énonce relativement à la réforme du Sénat, en effet, le gouvernement fédéral propose que, "dans le cas des questions d'importance nationale, comme la défense nationale et les relations internationales, le Sénat dispose d'un véto suspensif de six mois. Après l'expiration d'un véto suspensif, la Chambre des communes devrait adopter de nouveau le projet de loi visé par ce véto pour qu'il devienne loi."[6] Il faut comprendre ici que si le Sénat ne peut retarder indûment l'adoption d'un projet de loi touchant aux relations internationales ou à la défense, il pourrait malgré tout ralentir le processus, surtout si l'on envisage la possibilité d'un va-et-vient entre la Chambre des communes et le Sénat. Il ressort aussi du document fédéral que si le gouvernement du Canada est disposé à reconnaître la compétence exclusive des provinces dans un certain nombre de domaines où elles sont déjà fortement présentes, il n'est pas prêt pour autant à abdiquer ses responsabilités en matière de relations internationales dans les domaines en question. Cette réserve fait bien ressortir le souci des autorités fédérales de préserver dans toute la mesure du possible la marge de manoeuvre que leur reconnaît la constitution actuelle dans le domaine des relations internationales. Cette dernière préoccupation se comprend particulièrement bien lorsqu'on considère que dans l'état actuel du droit constitutionnel canadien, le gouvernement fédéral ne peut mettre en oeuvre que les engagements internationaux qui relèvent de sa propre compétence. Toute modification au partage des compétences, même mineure, est donc susceptible d'affecter sa liberté d'action. Enfin, on retrouve dans le document intitulé "Le fédéralisme canadien et l'union économique: partenariat pour la prospérité"[7] une liste d'entraves existantes à la libre circulation des biens, des services, des personnes et des capitaux, liste qui inclue des sujets manifestement liés aux engagements actuels où à venir du Canada dans le domaine du commerce international, telles les pratiques provinciales concernant les vins, les spiritueux et la bière ou encore les offices de commercialisation des produits agricoles. On perçoit bien , à la lecture de ces dernières remarques, que le gouvernement fédéral n'est pas satisfait de l'ambiguité actuelle de la constitution sur la question du pouvoir de mise en oeuvre des traités; mais rien n'est suggéré concrètement pour pallier à cette difficulté.

De fait, il est quelque peu surprenant de constater que l'une des critiques les plus souvent formulées à l'encontre du statu quo constitutionnel dans le domaine de la politique étrangère, à savoir l'absence d'un pouvoir complet de mise en oeuvre des traités au plan fédéral, n'est pas abordée dans les récentes propositions fédérales.[8] Le Rapport de la Commission royale d'enquête sur l'union économique et les perspectives de développement du Canada, encore en 1985, n'hésitait pas à affirmer que cette lacune constitutionnelle gênait sensiblement l'aptitude du Canada à passer des ententes efficaces et exerçait des contraintes sur sa participation à la vie internationale. Mais, en même temps, il rejetait la notion de "pouvoirs illimités du gouvernement fédéral dans la passation et l'application de traités ayant des clauses débordant la juridiction fédérale," pour suggérer plutôt des mécanismes axés sur la collaboration intergouvernementale, comme par exemple l'institutionalisation du mécanisme de consultations développé durant les négociations du Tokyo Round.[9] Mais même dans ce domaine du commerce international, qui semble bien devoir occuper une place primordiale dans la conduite de la politique étrangère canadienne dans les années à venir, rien n'a encore été décidé concernant la mise en place d'une telle structure permanente de collaboration fédérale-provinciale, laquelle est pourtant demandée par les provinces depuis plusieurs années déjà, comme si un changement aussi modeste comportait des dangers majeurs.[10] Faut-il en conclure que le partage des compétences dans le domaine des relations internationales est une question trop délicate au plan politique pour que l'on s'y attaque de front?

Le fait est que le seul développement qui s'est produit dans ce domaine a pris place carrément en marge du partage des compétences. Au début des années soixante, en effet, le gouvernement d'Ottawa, se trouvant confronté à une volonté manifeste du gouvernement québécois de s'affirmer au plan international dans les divers domaines relevant de sa compétence, réagit en faisant valoir que toutes les activités internationales d'une province devaient se dérouler sous l'autorité fédérale. La controverse prit rapidement l'allure d'un débat constitutionnel, avec la publication de deux études du gouvernement fédéral sur le droit des provinces d'entretenir des relations avec l'étranger,[11] suivie de la publication d'un document de travail québécois sur le même sujet. Puis les évènements se bousculant, elle se transporta ensuite sur le terrain, avec ce qu'il est convenu maintenant d'appeler la guerre des drapeaux. Mais graduellement, avec le temps, un modus vivendi s'installa. Le droit du gouvernement québécois d'entretenir des relations et de conclure des ententes avec des gouvernements étrangers fut implicitement reconnu, le Québec étant même admis à siéger à titre de gouvernement participant à l'Agence de coopération culturelle et technique ainsi qu'aux Sommets francophones. Le Québec, par ailleurs, n'a pas été la seule province à s'ouvrir à l'international; à l'instar de cette dernière province, l'Ontario, l'Alberta et la Colombie Britannique en particulier n'ont pas hésité à développer leurs relations avec l'étranger. À un point tel, en fait, que la participation des provinces aux relations internationales est devenue chose admise maintenant et ne soulève pratiquement plus de problèmes: le débat constitutionnel a simplement cédé la place à la réalité.

Il n'en va malheureusement pas de même de la question du partage des compétences en général et plus spécialement de la question du statut du Québec. L'hypothèse du fédéralisme renouvelé demeure ancrée fondamentalement dans une conception du Canada et du rôle du gouvernement central qui laisse peu de place à la décentralisation des pouvoirs et encore moins à la reconnaissance d'un statut particulier pour le Québec. Si cette conception devait l'emporter dans la présente ronde de négociations constitutionnelles, il n'est pas impossible que cette victoire soit éphémère et débouche sur une nouvelle controverse constitutionnelle encore plus virulente, ce qui ne pourrait manquer d'avoir des effets importants sur la conduite de la politique étrangère canadienne. En d'autres mots, si la solution proposée ne va pas au fond des problèmes, elle risque d'être illusoire. Illusoire si elle persiste à faire du Québec une province comme les autres. Illusoire si elle n'arrive pas à définir un statut d'autonomie réelle pour les autochtones. Illusoire si elle ne s'attaque pas de façon fondamentale au problème de l'aliénation des provinces de l'ouest. Les années qui viennent à cet égard seront cruciales. Il suffit d'imaginer à Ottawa une Chambre des communes particulièrement divisée, avec une quarantaine de députés du Bloc québécois et possiblement davantage du Reform Party, un gouvernement du Parti québécois à Québec, des partis politiques traditionnels épuisés et des leaders autochtones de plus en plus organisés et actifs, pour comprendre que le gouvernement du Canada, occupé à sauver les meubles, n'aura guère de temps pour les grandes entreprises internationales.[12] Dans un tel scénario, il faut envisager un déclin important de l'influence canadienne au plan international. Les propos récents de Hampson et Maule, suivant lesquels que le Canada "is in real danger of losing the places that it has worked so hard to secure because of its problems at home and because continuing internal dissension is making its partners nervous" n'en seraient alors que plus vrais.[13]

Le fédéralisme décentralisé

Qu'en est-il maintenant de l'hypothèse du fédéralisme décentralisé? Celle-ci, nous l'avons vu au début, fait reference à une décentralisation majeure des compétences législatives du Parlement fédéral aux provinces, du type de celle mise de l'avant dans le Rapport Allaire adopté par le Parti libéral du Québec en janvier 1991.[14] Elle peut valoir pour l'ensemble des provinces, ce qui est l'hypothèse retenue par le Rapport Allaire, ou ne valoir que pour une seule province — en l'occurence le Québec — ce qui nous ramène au fédéralisme asymétrique avec statut particulier pour le Québec. Parce qu'elle est perçue comme dépouillant le Parlement fédéral d'une partie importante de ses pouvoirs, l'hypothèse du fédéralisme décentralisé, dans sa variante symétrique, est très largement rejetée par le reste du Canada, qui n'y voit qu'une simple étape vers le démantèlement final du pays. Appliquée au seul Québec, l'hypothèse n'a jamais vraiment été examinée à son mérite, le reste du Canada y voyant une atteinte au principe intangible de la symétrie. C'est pourtant celle qui répondrait, vraisemblablement, aux attentes du plus grand nombre de Québécois.

Même si le fédéralisme décentralisé ne semble pas appelé pour le moment à un avenir très brillant, l'hypothèse mérite quand même d'être envisagée, car il n'est pas exclue qu'un changement d'attitude se produise dans les mois à venir, surtout s'il devenait très évident que le Canada s'achemine vraiment vers sa désintégration. Voyons donc quelles pourraient être les conséquences de cette hypothèse dans le domaine des relations internationales, en partant d'abord de la variante symétrique.

L'hypothèse d'une décentralisation importante des pouvoirs du fédéral vers l'ensemble des provinces — on peut écarter dès maintenant l'hypothèse d'une confédération des régions qui apparaît peu crédible — serait vraisemblablement considérée par les gouvernements étrangers comme une question purement interne concernant exclusivement le Canada, une question sur laquelle ils n'ont pas à se prononcer. Ceci apparait d'autant plus plausible que la politique commerciale et la politique de défense continueraient dans cette hypothèse à relever du pouvoir fédéral: même le Rapport Allaire, qui représente le projet le plus extrême en matière de décentralisation, ne propose pas de changements à cet égard. Ce qui ne veut pas dire que cette décentralisation ne soulèverait pas certains problèmes aux yeux des gouvernements étrangers. Dans la mesure, en effet, où elle dessaisit le Parlement du Canada d'une part substantielle de ses compétences, elle contraint ces derniers, ou bien à traiter avec un gouvernement canadien trop souvent impuissant à s'engager à fond, ou bien à traiter, directement ou indirectement, en fonction du partage des compétences, avec des gouvernements provinciaux poursuivant chacun leur intérêt propre. Il peut devenir tentant alors pour ces gouvernements étrangers de chercher à profiter de la division interne au Canada pour faire triompher un point de vue favorable à leurs propres intérêts. Mais, plus souvent qu'autrement, ils auront à se plaindre de la complexité et de l'incertitude entourant la conduite de la politique étrangère canadienne. Et si l'on s'en remet à certaines décisions récentes du GATT concernant, entre autres, les agissements des monopoles provinciaux sur les alcools, ou encore si l'on se fie aux plus récents débats concernant les systèmes canadiens de gestion de l'offre dans le domaine agricole,[15] ces interlocuteurs ne seront pas très portés à excuser le Canada pour son incapacité à assumer la totalité de ses engagements en raison de ses difficultés constitutionnelles. Même si les pays étrangers acceptaient par ailleurs de traiter directement avec les provinces, ce qui suppose au préalable une décentralisation du treaty-making power correspondant globalement au partage des compétences, il n'est pas dit qu'ils renonceraient par le fait même à tenir le gouvernement fédéral responsable pour les engagements de ces dernières.

Au Canada même, une telle hypothèse obligerait à développer des mécanismes de collaboration nettement plus élaborés entre le gouvernement fédéral et les provinces. Dans le domaine de la politique étrangère plus particulièrement, il faudrait institutionaliser et élargir les mécanismes de coordination fédérale-provinciale déjà en place dans le secteur des relations économiques internationales, sous peine de nager dans la pure confusion. Le danger, toutefois, comme le fait remarquer Denis Stairs, est qu'un tel développement "can lead, in short, to a condition of 'coordination overload' that can seriously damage the capacity of the foreign service to respond with maximum tactical effectiveness to external needs and capacities."[16] Ultimement, il n'est même pas évident qu'une plus grande unité d'action en ressortirait. Ainsi, souligne Caroline Pestieau, "Canada would face constant problems in maintaining a united front in international economic negotiations, and as a result these might well be conducted on an incremental rather than an over-all basis, with the consequent danger of a sell-out of Canada's bargaining advantages."[17] Manifestement, l'hypothèse d'un fédéralisme décentralisé à l'ensemble des provinces aurait un impact considérable sur la conduite de la politique étrangère canadienne.

La situation serait différente, toutefois, si la décentralisation se limitait à la seule province de Québec. Pour les pays étrangers, en particulier, le fait de ne pas avoir à composer avec onze gouvernements mais bien plutôt avec un gouvernement fédéral et un gouvernement provincial disposant d'une plus grande marge d'autonomie enlèverait beaucoup de l'incertitude et de l'incohérence susceptible de résulter de la multiplicité des intervenants. À l'intérieur même du Canada, comme le souligne encore Stairs, "because a smaller portion of the total store of national ressources would be affected, and because consultation and co-ordination might more easily be arranged with one provincial government than with ten, the difficulties of the system could even be substantially less significant and procedurally more manageable than those associated with reformed federalism." Du point de vue du droit international, enfin, même la reconnaissance d'un statut limité à une province n'entrainerait pas de difficultés insurmontables. Ceci dit, il ne fait pas de doute qu'un développement de cette nature aurait quand même un certain impact sur la conduite de la politique étrangère canadienne. Dans les domaines de compétences spécifiquement attribués au Québec, le gouvernement fédéral devrait dorénavant rechercher un appui avant de s'engager internationalement. Et si le Québec devait chercher à s'engager directement au plan international dans les nouveaux domaines relevant de sa compétence, comme on peut s'y attendre, il faudrait nécessairement prévoir un mécanisme de co-ordination pour éviter la mise en place de politiques contradictoires au plan international. Rien ne garantit par ailleurs que cette coordination serait toujours facile.

La véritable difficulté, toutefois, avec cette hypothèse d'un fédéralisme asymétrique, qui reserverait certaines compétences bénéficiant à une seule province, est qu'elle va directement à l'encontre d'un principe considéré comme immuable au Canada, qui est celui de l'égalité de statut des provinces. Si on laisse de côté le Québec, en effet, la position officielle de toutes les autres provinces, telle qu'énoncée verbalement et par écrit par leurs gouvernements, et souvent confirmée par des commissions constitutionnelles, vent que le caractère distinct du Québec ne saurait se transposer dans un quelconque statut particulier qui reconnaîtrait à cette province des compétences dont les autres provinces ne jouiraient pas.

Cette vision est à ce point ancrée que l'on va jusqu'à affirmer que même la séparation serait préférable à l'octroi d'un statut particulier. En pratique, il est vrai qu'un tel statut soulèverait des problèmes assez complexes en ce qui concerne la représentation québécoise au sein des institutions centrales. Mais il n'est pas évident que ces difficultés soient insolubles; la meilleure preuve en est que les propositions constitutionnelles présentement sur la table laissent entrevoir la possibilité de statuts particuliers définis administrativement à partir d'arrangements négociés à la pièce. Ce qui est davantage en cause, semble-t-il, c'est toute la symbolique d'une reconnaissance non-équivoque de la spécificité du Québec, avec en arrière plan l'image d'un Canada parlant avec deux voix.

Une autre difficulté non-négligeable avec cette hypothèse d'un statut particulier pour le Québec est qu'elle pourrait très bien ne constituer qu'une solution temporaire, une étape vers l'indépendance pure et simple du Québec. Exclure cette possibilité c'est effectivement se leurrer. Tant et aussi longtemps qu'un tel arrangement n'aura pas fait ses preuves, les gouvernements étrangers demeureront plutôt ambivalents à l'égard du Canada, incertains de son futur à long terme. Mais les autres hypothèses envisagées, à savoir le fédéralisme renouvelé et l'indépendance du Québec, font également naître des incertitudes. Si l'on suppose que l'indépendance est la solution la moins acceptable, le problème revient alors à choisir entre deux hypothèses qui comportent toutes les deux un facteur d'imprévisibilité. La première, celle du fédéralisme renouvelé, fait l'objet de débats depuis près de trente ans et semble plus loin d'une solution que jamais. La seconde n'a jamais vraiment été examinée de façon concrète et objective. Faut-il continuer à l'écarter? Certains, comme le Conseil des Canadiens, commencent à croire que le temps est venu de changer d'attitude sur cette question.[18]

L'indépendance du Québec

L'indépendance du Québec, envisagée telle quelle ou encore assortie d'une forme quelconque d'association économique avec le reste du Canada, propose une réponse aux problèmes constitutionnels du Canada qui, contrairement aux deux précédentes, ne peut laisser les pays étrangers indifférents sous prétexte qu'il s'agit d'une affaire purement interne au Canada. Au strict minimum, ils auront à se prononcer, explicitement ou implicitement, sur la reconnaissance du nouvel État Québécois. L'indépendance de ce dernier se confirmant, ils voudront en outre clarifier ce qu'il advient des engagements qui les lient présentement au Canada. Enfin, les États-Unis, seul État partageant une frontière avec le Canada, verront là un potentiel d'instabilité qu'ils voudront certainement minimiser dans la mesure du possible. Quant au Canada, cette hypothèse aura forcément un impact majeur sur sa politique étrangère. Il devra dans un premier temps redéfinir ses rapports avec le nouvel État Québécois, en particulier au plan politique et au plan économique. Il devra redéfinir ensuite ses rapports avec l'extérieur en fonction des changements intervenus sur son propre territoire. À moins qu'il ne parvienne rapidement à un accord avec le Québec sur le maintien de l'actuelle union économique, le Canada risque fort de sortir d'un tel exercice avec une influence passablement diminuée au plan international, d'autant plus que sa propre survie à moyen et à long terme sera loin d'être assurée. Le Québec, enfin, cherchera à éviter l'isolement économique et politique en concluant le plus rapidement possible une entente de portée économique avec le reste du Canada, en devenant partie à l'Accord de libre-échange entre le Canada et les États-Unis et membre des grands organismes internationaux à vocation économique, comme le GATT et le Fonds monétaire international, et enfin en établissant des liens diplomatiques formels avec les États où il est déjà représenté. Tels sont les principaux développements que l'on peut envisager à la suite d'une déclaration d'indépendance du Québec, développements sur lesquels il nous faut maintenant revenir pour les analyser plus en détail.

À partir du moment où la souveraineté du Québec sera acquise dans les faits, ou, si l'on veut, à partir du moment où elle ne sera plus contestée sérieusement sur le terrain, les gouvernements étrangers, à court ou à moyen terme, n'auront vraisemblablement d'autre choix que de reconnaître le nouvel État. S'il advenait toutefois que malgré un referendum favorable à l'indépendance, le gouvernement du Canada s'oppose ouvertement à la sécession du Québec et prenne des mesures pour affirmer son autorité, la vaste majorité des États étrangers adopteraient alors une attitude prudente, préférant attendre que la situation se clarifie. Les mesures en question pourraient être des mesures légales, des mesures économiques et ultimement des mesures militaires. Divers scénarios ont même été proposés qui envisagent la possibilité d'un conflit armé entre le Canada et le Québec. Mais tout en admettant que la séparation du Québec ne pourra se réaliser sans quelques sérieux accrochages sur des questions comme la succession aux dettes, la délimitation du territoire ou le statut des autochtones, la plupart des observateurs écartent le recours à la violence comme moyen de régler la question, non pas que la chose soit impossible, comme le montre bien le cas de la Yougoslavie, mais parce qu'une telle solution serait totalement inacceptable à la population canadienne prise dans son ensemble. Pendant toute cette période, on peut présumer que l'essentiel de la diplomatie canadienne sera tournée vers des actions destinées à convaincre les gouvernements étrangers de ne pas reconnaitre le nouvel État Québécois. Mais ce qui comptera en définitive sera l'exercice effectif du pouvoir sur le territoire du Québec: si le gouvernement québécois démontre qu'il est bien en contrôle, si les chances d'un retour à l'état prévalant avant la déclaration d'indépendance s'amenuisent avec le temps, il y a tout lieu de croire que les autres États en viendront à reconnaitre le Québec. La reconnaissance récente par le Canada et par plusieurs autres États de la Slovénie et de la Croatie offrirait vraisemblablement le précédent le plus pertinent à l'analyse de cette question.[19] En tout état de cause, une telle période d'incertitude ne saurait durer très longtemps.

Une fois l'indépendance du Québec acquise, une des toutes premières questions qui se soulèvera sera celle de la succession du nouvel État aux traités du Canada. La position du droit international sur la question, bien que laissant place à une grande flexibilité, est suffisamment arrêtée pour que l'on envisage un règlement relativement rapide de la question. Il est clair, par exemple, que le Québec devra prendre entièrement à sa charge, en ce qui le concerne, les engagements du Canada relatifs à la délimitation de la frontière avec les États-Unis. Ensuite, il devra faire connaitre dans les meilleurs délais son intention de succéder ou non aux traités multilatéraux et bilatéraux du Canada, pour autant évidemment que ceux-ci soient applicables au Québec: la règle ici sera celle dite de la table rase, c'est-à-dire que le Québec sera considéré comme non lié à moins qu'il manifeste son intention de l'être.[20] S'agissant enfin des organisations internationales dont le Canada est membre, le Québec devra faire une demande d'admission conformément aux dispositions de chaque traité constitutif concerné. Ce scenario assez simple se complique, toutefois, dès que l'on prend en considération la dimension politique de la question. Le meilleur exemple en est le débat qui s'est développé récemment autour de la question de l'accession du Québec à l'Accord de libre-échange entre le Canada et les États Unis.

Déjà le gouvernement fédéral, par la voix du Premier Ministre, a averti que l'Accord de libre-échange ne sera pas automatiquement transféré au Québec: "Un Québec indépendant," a-t-il affirmé, "ne débarquerait pas en grande pompe à Washington dans le sillage du Canada: et les États-Unis ne leur accorderaient pas tout ce qu'il veut seulement parce qu'il aurait déjà fait partie du Canada."[21] Ces propos prennent appui sur le constat fait par certains commentateurs que diverses pratiques du Québec en matière de politiques d'achat, d'octroi de subventions et de politiques de stabilisation des prix ne répondent pas aux attentes américaines en matière de réglementation du commerce. Au dire de Courchene, même le modèle de concertation économique que représente le concept de "Québec Inc.," assimilable à certains égards au Keiretsu japonais, serait menacé, les Américains ne voulant surtout pas voir ce modèle se reproduire en Amérique.[22] Mais le discours, tout menacant qu'il soit, cache mal le fait qu'en définitive il reviendra aux États-Unis de décider si l'Accord doit être étendu ou non au Québec et à quelles conditions. Or pour le professeur Jockel, qui s'est penché sur la question dans son étude récente sur les réactions américaines à une éventuelle séparation du Québec, "It would be astonishing if the U.S. did not respond favorably to a Quebec proposal to continue free trade arrangements after the province became sovereign."[23] De même, pour Robert L. Pfaltzgraff, Jr., président de l'Institute for Foreign Policy Analysis et professeur à la Fletcher School of Law and Diplomacy, "It is widely assumed that the United States would extend the FTA to an independent Quebec, just as it would be expected that Quebec would have continued access on the same terms to the remainder of Canada."[24] Il n'est sûrement pas impossible que les États-Unis profitent de l'occasion pour obtenir des concessions supplémentaires relativement à certains comportements du gouvernement québécois.[25] Mais outre le fait que les États-Unis pourraient très bien trouver le Canada en défaut sur les même points, et considéreraient difficile dès lors de discriminer ouvertement à l'encontre du Québec, il n'est pas exclu aussi qu'interprétant leur intérêt dans un sens large ils choisissent d'abord d'assurer la stabilité politique et économique à leur frontière nord avant de chercher à arracher un maximum de concessions du Québec. En réalité, tout ce débat sur l'accession du Québec à l'Accord de libre-échange ne démontre en définitive qu'une seule chose: l'Accord en question, en ouvrant au Québec l'accès au vaste marché américain, a clairement donné à l'hypothèse de l'indépendance du Québec une crédibilité au plan économique qu'elle n'avait pas nécessairement auparavant. La réaction canadienne à cet égard n'a rien de très surprenant. Ce qui étonne davantage, c'est qu'en suggérant à toute fin pratique aux États-Unis de profiter de la demande d'accession du Québec à l'Accord pour en soutirer de nouvelles concessions, le Canada se trouve en quelque sorte à affaiblir sa propre position. Les conséquences dans certains cas pourraient être considérables. Ainsi, Wonnacott a bien fait voir que toute négociation relative au Pacte automobile entre le Québec et les États-Unis entrainerait par la force des choses une renégociation du même accord entre le Canada et les États-Unis: le Canada, en effet, ne serait plus en mesure alors de livrer à son partenaire américain le territoire québécois, ce qui constituerait une modification substantielle de la portée de ses engagements.[26] Les États-Unis, ajoute Wonnacott, pourraient alors sauter sur l'occasion pour mettre tout simplement fin au Pacte automobile. Dans un tel contexte de revision des arrangements existants, il n'est pas impossible que le reste du Canada, déjà pas très favorable à l'Accord de libre-échange, décide tout simplement que l'heure est venue de mettre fin à ce dernier.

Si les États-Unis en tout état de cause n'ont rien à craindre au plan économique de la division du Canada, il est possible, en revanche, qu'ils ressentent davantage la perte d'influence du Canada sur la scène internationale. C'est ce que suggère à tout le moins Jockel, qui écrit à ce sujet: "In world affairs, the more significant problem for the U.S. arising from Quebec sovereignty would not be the kinds of foreign policies a sovereign

Quebec and a diminished Canada would pursue. Rather, it would be the potential loss, at least in the short run, of a confident, influential, and constructive Canadian role."[27] Le même point de vue est également développé par Robert Pfaltzgraff qui écrit à ce sujet: "Overall, the future role of Canada in world affairs, with interests that are similar and parallel to (as well as compatible with) those of the United States would inevitably be diminished by the disintegration of Canada. A truncated Canada would have neither the resources, the international standing, nor the political will to take an active part as at present in world affairs."[28] Cette perte d'influence découlant de la séparation du Québec est également notée par Stairs.[29] Le fait est que dans le domaine économique, par exemple, le Canada sans le Québec pourrait très bien voir son statut de membre du Groupe des 7 rapidement remis en cause.[30] Et il est difficile de voir comment l'influence remarquable qu'il a exercée jusqu'à maintenant à l'intérieur du GATT pourrait se maintenir au même niveau. Sur un plan plus régional, le Canada verrait forcément sa relation privilégiée avec les États-Unis modifiée par l'apparition d'un nouveau partenaire, et — à supposer qu'un accord de libre-échange nord-américain soit conclu — il pourrait même constater avec le temps que cette relation privilégiée n'existe tout simplement plus. Au sein de l'ONU, son rôle deviendrait nettement plus effacé, sa capacité en particulier d'oeuvrer pour le maintien de la paix étant, par la force des choses, ramenée à des dimensions plus modestes. Enfin la participation du Canada à La Francophonie ferait sans doute l'objet d'une réévaluation sérieuse, et, sans être totalement abolie, pourrait facilement recevoir une attention nettement moindre. Mais il ne faut pas non plus exagérer les conséquences d'un tel développement. Contrairement à ce que l'on pourrait croire, par example, le statut du Canada au sein du Fonds monétaire international ne serait pas substantiellement modifié; même sa quote-part, malgré son importance diminuée au plan économique, demeurerait ce qu'elle est présentement.[31] En outre, s'il devait se produire que le Canada et le Québec en arrivent à une entente pour le maintien de l'actuelle union économique, les répercussions sur la politique étrangère canadienne pourraient avoir une importance moindre que celle envisagée dans les pages précédentes.

Dans le domaine de l'aide au développement et de la coopération internationale, l'effort actuel du Canada manifestement ne pourrait être maintenu. Coupé d'une part substantielle de ses revenus, le Canada serait amené par la force des choses à réévaluer sa politique d'aide au développement. Le budget total de l'aide serait très certainement amputé, l'ACDI paraissant devoir être la principale perdante de ce point de vue. Pour ce qui est du Québec, on peut douter que celui-ci cherche immédiatement à prendre la relève du gouvernement fédéral dès son accession à l'indépendance. D'abord parce qu'il ne serait pas équipé administrativement parlant pour ce faire. Ensuite et surtout parce que les premières années de l'indépendance risquent de grever de façon sensible la capacité financière du nouvel État, ce qui ne pourrait faire autrement que de limiter sa capacité de s'impliquer dans le domaine de l'aide au développement.

Une question qui aurait certainement préoccupé les États-Unis et leurs alliés il y a quelques années est celle de la place d'un Canada divisé dans le système occidental de défense et de sécurité. Mais la menace soviétique n'existe pratiquement plus et le désarmement est devenu le nouveau mot d'ordre du jour. Reflétant directement ces développements, le budget des forces armées canadiennes va en diminuant et la présence militaire du Canada en Europe n'aura plus bientôt qu'un caractère symbolique. Dans un tel contexte, il est difficile de voir comment l'indépendance du Québec pourrait modifier sérieusement le système occidental de défense et de sécurité, d'autant plus qu'un Québec indépendant, si l'on se fie aux déclarations émanant du Parti Québécois, assumerait sa part des engagements du Canada à titre de membre de l'OTAN et de NORAD. La création de forces armées québécoises pourrait peut-être occasionner certains problèmes de coordination, particulièrement dans le domaine de la défense aérienne,[32] mais rien qui doive être considéré comme vraiment très sérieux. La conséquence la plus radicale d'un tel changement pour le Canada comme pour le Québec, suggère Jockel, pourrait bien être la suppression pure et simple de NORAD, les États-Unis se considérant en mesure dorénavant d'assurer leur propre sécurité de façon indépendante à partir de leur territoire.[33] En ce qui concerne les industries de la défense, enfin, le Québec serait sans doute intéressé à succéder au Canada pour ce qui est des accords sur le partage du développement industriel pour la défense et la production de la défense; mais avec des dépenses pour la défense québécoise vraisemblablement peu élevées, font remarquer McCallum et Green, il est douteux que les États-Unis acceptent le maintien du statut quo dans ce domaine.[34]

Dans l'ensemble, comme on peut le constater, la séparation du Québec ne menacera pas de façon importante les intérêts américains et étrangers. Ce n'est donc pas de l'étranger que viendront les problèmes, si problèmes il doit y avoir. Les vraies difficultés, on s'en doute bien, se soulèveront plutôt lorsque viendra le temps de définir les nouveaux rapports entre le Québec et le Canada. Cette question risque effectivement de consommer une énergie considérable, tant du côté québécois que du côté canadien, car les solutions ne seront pas toujours évidentes. Si, au surplus, les négociations se déroulent dans un climat d'acrimonie, cela pourrait même rendre assez difficile la négociation d'une union économique Québec-Canada. Certains vont même jusqu'à suggérer qu'il serait surprenant que le Québec réussisse à obtenir du Canada mieux qu'une simple union douanière.[35] Mais les coûts d'un désaccord sur cette question cruciale seraient tels, pour l'un comme pour l'autre, qu'ils semblent pratiquement condamnés à s'entendre. Le Québec, par exemple, pourrait avoir à supporter une baisse importante de son niveau de vie s'il se retrouvait isolé économiquement. Quant au Canada, c'est sa survie même en tant qu'État qui pourrait être remise en cause s'il ne réussissait pas à maintenir l'union économique canadienne.[36] Ensemble, en revanche, ils pourraient encore prétendre exercer une certaine influence au plan international. Mais une analyse de cette nature suppose nécessairement que la raison l'emportera. À moyen ou à long terme, cela, effectivement, apparait inévitable. À court terme, par contre, les émotions, qui commencent déjà à se manifester de façon parfois virulente, pourraient temporairement l'emporter, créant une situation de tension et d'instabilité au nord de la frontière américaine. Certains commentateurs ont même développé des scénarios qui envisagent le recours à la force armée de la part du Canada. Si la situation devait effectivement évoluer dans ce sens, alors, et alors seulement, il n'est pas interdit de penser que les États-Unis utiliseraient un des nombreux moyens à leur disposition pour convaincre le Canada et le Québec de s'entendre.

Conclusion

Au terme de cette analyse, qui ne prétend pas faire justice à la complexité des problèmes soulevés, il est certaines constatations qui ressortent de façon plus manifeste.

La première est que le débat sur l'avenir constitutionnel du Canada n'intéresse les gouvernements étrangers que dans la mesure où il risque de déboucher sur l'indépendance du Québec. Les autres options peuvent affecter le processus de formulation de la politique étrangère canadienne et peut-être même la capacité du Canada de s'engager internationalement, mais pour l'essentiel il s'agit là de questions qui ne concernent que le Canada. La réforme du Sénat et de la Chambre des communes, le statut des autochtones, l'affirmation de l'identité canadienne dans la constitution et même l'union économique sont des questions qui ne touchent que de très loin leurs intérêts. La vraie, la seule question à leurs yeux, est de savoir ce qu'il adviendra du Canada dans les années à venir.[37]

La seconde constatation est que l'hypothèse du fédéralisme renouvelé, la moins susceptible à première vue de modifier de façon importante la conduite de la politique étrangère canadienne, pourrait malgré tout déboucher sur une diminution majeure de l'influence canadienne au plan international, si elle ne s'attaque pas aux causes profondes des problèmes, et au premier chef à la question du Québec. Il suffit d'imaginer le Canada aux prises avec les mêmes menaces de démembrement dans cinq, dix ans ou quinze ans, replié de plus en plus sur ses problèmes internes, pour se rendre compte jusqu'à quel point cette conjoncture pourrait changer, à moyen terme, la politique étrangère canadienne.

La troisième constatation est que le fédéralisme décentralisé, particulièrement dans sa version débouchant sur un statut d'autonomie prononcée pour le Québec, n'a toujours pas reçu l'attention qu'il mérite à titre de solution de compromis. Lorsqu'on considère que ce type de solution ne toucherait que très incidemment les gouvernements étrangers et que son impact sur la conduite de la politique étrangère canadienne demeurerait relativement modeste, ce manque d'attention est pour le moins surprenant. Mais peut-être faut-il admettre qu'en cherchant à reconcilier au sein d'un même État deux identités nationales, l'une canadienne, l'autre québécoise, cette solution se fixe une tâche impossible.

La quatrième et dernière constatation est que si le Québec devait ultimement se séparer, le gouvernement américain, de même que la vaste majorité des autres gouvernements, évalueraient la situation de façon pragmatique, en laissant de côté leurs sentiments généralement favorables à l'endroit du Canada. Déjà en 1976, à la veille de l'élection du Parti Québécois, John Holmes déclarait: "Faced with a fait accompli, Washington would have to live with a state of Quebec and pursue its special interests."[38] Les développements récents en Union soviétique et en Yougoslavie ne font que confirmer la justesse de cette analyse.

Mais au delà de ces constats, ce qui ressort par-dessus tout de ce rapide examen, c'est que les considérations de relations internationales et de politique étrangère, si elles doivent être considérées dans le présent débat constitutionnel, ne peuvent dicter en elles-mêmes le choix d'une solution. Il est clair que la survie du Canada ne sera pas assurée par les autres. C'est aux Canadiens et aux Québécois, et à eux seuls, qu'il revient de décider de leur avenir.

Notes

1 Jockel, Joseph T., *If Canada Breaks Up: Implications for U.S. Policy*, Canadian-American Public Policy, Number 7, September 1991 (The Canadian-American Center, the University of Maine).

2 Voir, entre autres, les propos de G. Ritchie, R.J. Wonnacott et R. Lipsey dans *Broken Links: Trade Relations after a Quebec Secession* (Toronto: C.D. Howe Institute) 1991.

3 Particulièrement révélateur à cet égard est l'éditorial du *Globe and Mail* en date du 16 novembre 1991, qui introduit ainsi la récente étude de l'Institut C.D. Howe: "Driving one more nail into the coffin of the idea that a sovereign Quebec can have its cake and eat it too, the C.D. Howe Institute this week released a book entitled Broken Links: Trade Relations after a Quebec Succession" [sic].

4 Conseil économique du Canada, *Un projet commun. Aspects économiques des choix constitutionnels*, Vingt-huitième Exposé annuel, 1991, pp. 83 et suivantes.

5 Stairs, Denis, "Foreign Policy," dans S.M. Beck, et I. Bernier, *Canada and the New Constitution; The Unfinished Agenda* (Montréal: L'Institut de recherche politique, 1982), vol. 2, p. 161.

6 Gouvernmement du Canada, *Bâtir ensemble le Canada, Propositions* (Ottawa: Approvisionnement et Services Canada, 1991), p. 54.

7 Gouvernement du Canada (Ottawa: Approvisionnements et Services Canada, 1991), pp. 19–20.

8 Voir entre autres sur cette question Donald C. Story, "Government — A 'Practical Thing': Towards a Consensus on Foreign Policy Jurisdiction," dans R.B. Byers et Robert W. Reford, eds., *Canada Challenged: The Viability of Confederation* (Toronto: Canadian Institute of International Affairs, 1979), p. 124.

9 Gouvernement du Canada, Commission royale sur l'union économique et les perspectives de développement du Canada, *Rapport* (Ottawa: Approvisionnement et services Canada, 1985), vol. 3, p. 171.

10 Voir sur cette question Ivan Bernier et André Binette, *Les provinces canadiennes et le commerce international* (Ottawa: Institut de recherches politiques et Québec: Centre québécois de relations internationales, 1988).

11 Les études en question, publiées toutes les deux par le Secrétariat d'État aux Affaires extérieures, s'intitulent *Fédéralisme et relations internationales et Fédéralisme et conférences internationales sur l'éducation* (Ottawa: Imprimeur de la Reine, 1968).

12 Dans *Éloge d'un fédéralisme renouvelé*, Thomas Courchene, dont la conception du fédéralisme renouvelé est beaucoup plus proche du Rapport Allaire et du fédéralisme décentralisé, décrit un scénario où le Québec demeure partie du Canada mais sans s'être véritablement reconcilié avec le reste du Canada; ce dernier, avertit-il, "risque d'avoir à se contenter d'un Canada encore plus enchevêtré avec le Québec, surtout si les Québécois continuent de 'voter en bloc' ou, de manière équivalente, de voter pour le 'Bloc'": Courchene, Thomas J., *Éloge d'un Federalisme renouvelé* (Toronto: C.D. Howe Institute, 1991), p. 86.

13 Fen O. Hampson et Christopher J. Maule, "After the Cold War," dans *Canada Among Nations 1990–1991: After the Cold War*, Hampson et Maule, ed. (Ottawa: Carleton University Press, 1991), p. 2.

14 Parti libéral du Québec, Comité constitutionnel, *Un Québec libre de ses choix* (Québec, 12–28 janvier 1991), communément appelé "Rapport Allaire" du nom de son président, Jean Allaire.

15 Voir, par exemple, "Canada can't get any sympathy," *The Globe and Mail*, Toronto, 30 novembre 1991, p. B-3.

16 Stairs, p. 165.

17 Pestieau, Caroline, "External Economic Relations and Constitutional Change," dans S.M. Beck et I. Bernier, vol. 2, p. 241.

18 Voir, par exemple, "Les nationalistes canadiens- anglais découvrent les vertus d'un Québec autonome dans la structure fédérale," *Le Devoir*, Montréal, 30 novembre 1991, p. A-5.

19 *La Presse*, Montréal, 16 janvier 1992, p. B-7.

20 Même si la Convention de Vienne sur la succession d'États en matière de traités suggère à son article 34 qu'en cas de sécession il y a continuité de

plein droit des traités de l'État prédécesseur, il est loin d'être évident que cette règle codifie la coutume internationale; or comme la Convention n'est pas en vigueur et n'a pas été signée par le Canada, il y a lieu de croire que la norme qui s'applique est plutôt celle de la table rase, qui est plus conforme à la pratique antérieure.

21 Voir "Mulroney prédit de sombres lendemains d'indépendance," *Le Devoir*, Montréal, 2 décembre 1991, p. 1.

22 Voir Courchene, pp. 33–34.

23 Jockel, p. 24.

24 Pfaltzgraff, Robert L. Jr., "Canada and the United States: Issues for the 1990s," dans W.C. Winegard, J.E. Carroll, D. Leyton-Brown, M. Slack, J.J. Sokolsky, et R.J. Pflatzgraff Jr., *Canada and the United States in the 1990s: An Emerging Partnership*, Institute for Foreign Policy Analysis, Inc. et Brassey's (US), Inc., 1991, p. 86.

25 Voir en particulier sur cette question Gordon Ritchie, "Putting Humpty Dumpty Together Again: Free Trade, the Breakup Scenario," dans G. Ritchie, R.J. Wonnacott, W.H. Furtan, R.S. Gray, R.G. Lipsey, R. Tremblay, *Broken Links, Trade Relations after a Quebec Secession* (Toronto, C.D. Howe Institute, 1991), p. 1.

26 Ronald J. Wonnacott, "Reconstructing North American Free Trade following Quebec's Separation: What Can Be Assumed?", dans *Broken Links*, pp. 20–31.

27 Jockel, p. 28.

28 Pfaltzgraff, p. 88.

29 Stairs, p. 181.

30 Charles F. Doran, "America at Century's End," in Canadian Institute of International Affairs, *Behind the Headlines*, Volume 49, No. 2 (Hiver 1991–1992): 9–15.

31 Voir à ce sujet les propos très clairs de Joseph Gold dans *Membership and Nonmembership in the International Monetary Fund* (Washington: International Monetary Fund, 1974), p. 479.

32 Jockel, p. 35.

33 Jockel, p. 35. Pour une analyse plus poussée de la dimension continentale de la défense stratégique des États-Unis, voir Arthur Charo, *Continental Defense: A Neglected Dimension of Strategic Defense* (Lanham, Maryland: University Press of America, 1990).

34 John McCallum et Chris Green, *Une rupture à l'amiable* (Toronto: Institut C.D. Howe, 1991), p. 34.

35 Voir sur cette question Ritchie, pp. 5–6.

36 Les scénarios sur la désintégration possible du Canada ne manquent pas non plus. Voir par exemple Thomas J. Courchene, *Éloge*, pp. 79ff.

37 Pfaltzgraff écrit par exemple à ce sujet: "Undoubtedly, the most important issue to confront Canada-U.S. relations in the years ahead will be Canada's future as a State," Pfaltzgraff, p. 84.

38 Holmes, J.W., *Canada: A Middle-Aged Power* (Toronto: McClelland and Stewart, 1976), p. 284; cité dans Jockel, p. 39.

The New
Multilateralism

5

The New Multilateralism and Evolving Security Systems

David A. Welch

> The lapidary approach to the building of institutions is eternal. There is no 'solution' at the end, no framework that will guarantee perpetual peace. The experimentation must go on and on.
>
> –John W. Holmes[1]

International relations theorists currently offer two starkly different visions of the post-Cold War world. One school of thought — structural realism — warns that the breakdown of bipolarity heralds a return to the chronic instability and violence characteristic of the multipolar systems of the first half of the twentieth century, that led to two devastating world wars and the most severe economic depression in modern times. While the world may escape similar calamities in the coming years, there are nonetheless, according to this view, grounds for serious concern. The collapse of Soviet power has unleashed the destructive forces of nationalism in Eastern Europe, and dissolved the strongest bond uniting the western Great Powers: fear of Soviet attack. At the same time, the less spectacular but nonetheless unmistakable decline of the United States — economically if not militarily — has undercut Washington's ability to maintain harmony from Tokyo to Bonn.[2] In the future, large and small states, old and new, may mount serious challenges to the economic and political status quo. Moreover, the uncertainty and fluidity of a world without Cold War constraints will undermine trust and heighten fear. Many features of the old world order were inherently undesirable — the domination of the superpowers within their respective blocs, the balance of nuclear terror, ideological polarization, and an unprecedented militarization of peacetime economies — but realists credit these features with preserving an unusually long and stable peace.[3]

In contrast, a second school of thought is optimistic that the end of the Cold War signals a new era of peaceful international co-operation that will at last enable states to address a broad range of deferred problems requiring concerted action on a global scale: regional conflict, injustice, hunger, poverty, disease, and environmental degradation. A wide variety of arguments has been advanced to justify this optimism. Some argue that the growing interdependence and institutionalization of world affairs increasingly inclines states towards co-operation and collective responses to international problems. Others argue that the spread of democracy and the decline of militarism will increasingly force governments to devote greater attention and resources to welfare issues. Still others maintain that the globalization of travel and telecommunications has increased the awareness and sensitivity of peoples with respect to other cultures and to cosmopolitan issues. A fourth group insists that leaders have learned the lessons of 1914, 1929, and 1939, and will successfully avoid similar mistakes. Finally, others argue that the development of nuclear weapons has itself revolutionized state and societal attitudes towards war, and rendered major wars too costly to fight (and thus to risk).[4]

Common sense, which would suggest that the coming age will be neither dark nor golden but merely a different shade of grey, should not be permitted to obscure the starkness and the beauty of the theoretical dispute, because the state of international relations theory is the best indicator we have of how well we understand the forces behind international politics. The crux of the debate on this point is the issue of co-operation; the central question is whether — and under what conditions — co-operation between states is possible. In policy circles, the question is most often phrased in terms of the future of "multilateralism." Even before the end of the Cold War, pessimists began to toll the bells of doom, taking their cue from Lester Thurow's 1988 variation on Nietzsche: "GATT is dead." More recently, the United Nations' successful liberation of Kuwait reinforced the optimists' contention that "the new multilateralism" was alive and well.

The present chapter, and the three that follow it, explore the meaning and prospects of "the new multilateralism" across a range of prominent issues on the global agenda. This chapter explores the concept of multilateralism, and attempts to determine whether its present manifestation is indeed new and significantly different. It does so inductively, by looking at evolving post-Cold War security systems, and by examining Canada's roles and interests in them.[5] The chapter argues that there is indeed a new multilateralism, and that the optimists' case is well-founded, if perhaps overstated. But while we can expect global security increasingly to rest on multilateral foundations, the robustness and effectiveness of the new multilateralism will vary from region to region and from issue to issue; it will depend upon the collective ability of the Great Powers to maintain it; and it will face enough strains and challenges to moderate the enthusiasm of the most optimistic. Canada is, and will continue to be, among its strongest supporters, and will play an increasingly important moral and material role in maintaining it.

Multilateralism: Old and New

Robert Keohane defines multilateralism as "the practice of co-ordinating national policies in groups of three or more states, through ad hoc arrangements or by means of institutions."[6] In common parlance, multilateralism is variously contrasted with unilateralism, bilateralism, and regionalism. Immediately conceptual difficulties arise, since only the first contrast is theoretically or practically interesting (only unilateralism implies an *absence* of co-operation; little of importance hangs on a distinction between two-party and three-party co-operation; and regionalism merely implies multilateralism within a restricted geographical domain). To complicate matters further, some use the term "plurilateralism" to distinguish small-group, regional, or task-specific multilateralism from broadly-based or universal multilateralism,[7] and others treat particularly successful collectivities as unities (as in "EC unilateralism").[8] To simply and clarify matters, since *co-operation* among states is what is of key interest here, I propose to deny the bilateral/multilateral distinction, to reserve the use of the term "regionalism" for cases where groups of states that succeed in co-operating regionally *fail* to co-operate with other such groups, to set aside the word "plurilateralism" as unnecessarily refined for present purposes, and to rule phrases like "EC (European Community) unilateralism" out of court altogether.

Multilateralism as defined by Keohane is at least as old as the system of sovereign states itself. If there is a "new" multilateralism, however, it might be distinguished from the old in one or more of the following ways:

1. By *degree*:
   Is the new multilateralism different because states increasingly pursue their interests multilaterally rather than unilaterally?

2. In terms of the prevailing *institutions*:
   Is the new multilateralism different because a new set of institutions and regimes now regulate international politics?

3. In terms of the *processes* of multilateral interaction:
   Do states co-operate to maintain order in innovative ways?

4. In terms of *context*:
   Is the new multilateralism new simply because the Cold War no longer dominates international politics?

5. In terms of *attitude*:
   Does "the new multilateralism" denote a renewed faith on the part of leaders in the efficacy and value of co-operation?

The simple answer to all of these questions is a qualified "yes," as an examination of evolving security systems will show. The new multilateralism denotes a diverse set of qualitative, quantitative, institutional, procedural, contextual, and attitudinal changes. Some of these changes may be durable and lasting, while others may not; some may be cyclical, others linear. But few periods of international politics have witnessed change on so many dimensions at once, and this may account for both the attention the new multilateralism has attracted, and the inherent difficulty of pinning the concept down. It is, however, important to bear in mind its evolutionary nature. Co-operation generally proceeds by fits and starts, through trial and error. One cannot know whether the process has a stable end-point, much less describe one. One cannot even be certain that it will succeed. Structural realism suggests that it will not. Recent trends and events, however, provide ground for guarded optimism.

The Multilateral Impulse

Perhaps the purest example of multilateralism is collective security, in which a number of states agree to regard an attack against one as an attack against all and credibly commit themselves in advance to respond to aggression.[9] According to Kenneth Thompson, three conditions must obtain for collective security to succeed: 1. no single state can predominate (i.e., all states must be supportive of collective action); 2. there can be no revisionist power (i.e., the major powers in the system must have compatible views of an acceptable world order); and 3. the major powers must enjoy "a minimum of political solidarity and moral community" so that they can trust one another not to renege on their commitments.[10] The failure of the League of Nations to respond to Italian aggression in Ethiopia and Japanese aggression in Manchuria may be traced to the absence of the second and third conditions, as may the failure of the United Nations for most of its history to live up to its founders' expectation that it would function as a robust collective security organization. In 1991, however, all three conditions obtained, and the United Nations mounted a successful collective security operation against Iraq.[11]

The Persian Gulf War is instructive because it starkly demonstrates that states with quite different but complementary interests may have overwhelming incentives to co-operate in thwarting aggression. Some, such as Saudi Arabia, the smaller Gulf states, and Israel, were threatened directly by the menace of Iraqi military power. Others, such as the states of western Europe and Japan, depended heavily on Persian Gulf oil and would have been vulnerable to Iraqi manipulation of prices and supplies if Saddam Hussein had retained control of Kuwait's vast reserves. There were still others, such as the United States, Canada, and the Soviet Union, whose primary interest lay simply in denying Iraq the fruits of aggression, so as to avoid a precedent that would encourage other challenges to world order.[12] These interests could only be furthered co-operatively. The United States was the only country in the world capable of projecting sufficient force into the region to ensure a military success; but while

American participation was necessary, it was not sufficient. The United States relied on the material co-operation of Saudi Arabia to stage the movement of its forces, the diplomatic co-operation of Egypt and Syria to avoid a pan-Arab anti-American backlash, the logistical co-operation of the North Atlantic Treaty Organization (NATO) to move its forces to the Gulf, the restraint of Israel to prevent Saddam Hussein from endangering the coalition by triggering a diversionary Arab-Israeli conflict, and the co-operation of the Soviet Union, China, and as many other members of the UN as possible, to bolster the legitimacy (and thus the future deterrent value) of the international response. Not least importantly, given the economic strains on a superpower in decline, the United States required the financial co-operation of Kuwait, Saudi Arabia, the United Arab Emirates, Germany, Japan, and Korea, to help defray the enormous costs of a large-scale, "high-tech" military operation half-way around the globe.[13]

While the incentives to co-operate against Iraq were powerful enough to stimulate the creation of an ad hoc opposing coalition, it is instructive to note that co-operation itself was made considerably easier by the prior existence of multilateral institutions, several of which played vital roles, either overtly or behind the scenes. The UN provided not only a well-defined set of procedures for responding to aggression that enjoyed widespread legitimacy (primarily through Security Council resolutions that became progressively more demanding), but also a venue and a variety of communication channels to facilitate both diplomacy with Iraq and the co-ordination of an international response. The Western European Union (WEU) provided a useful umbrella for some of its member countries' contributions to the war effort, as an alternative channel to NATO, whose "out-of-area problem" proved to be politically sensitive.[14] The European Community (EC) threw its collective weight into diplomatic efforts to resolve the crisis, and provided an effective channel for much-needed financial support. NATO played a series of crucial roles, even though it did not participate in the war as such. It co-ordinated allied deployments and operations through its Defence Planning Committee, deployed the ACE mobile force (Air) to Turkey, and supplied logistical support, bases, and air traffic control for forces en route to the Gulf. Years of multinational co-operation in NATO greatly enhanced the coalition's effectiveness on the battlefield, primarily as a result of joint training and standardization.[15] While the United States conceivably could have cobbled together a multinational response to Iraqi aggression in the absence of these institutions, undoubtedly it would have had vastly greater difficulty in doing so. Indeed, it is easy to imagine that it would have failed.

The Gulf War experience illustrates how institutions and regimes promote and facilitate international co-operation by legitimizing and delegitimizing certain types of actions, reducing transaction costs, facilitating negotiations and linkages, improving information flows, extending the shadow of the future, enhancing the value of reputation, and reducing incentives to cheat, free ride, or defect.[16] They are therefore useful vehicles for the pursuit of state interests. But they are (or can be) much more. There is strong evidence to suggest that institutions and regimes can also reshape states' conceptions of their national interest — and their perceptions of the threats and dangers that they face — in ways that can enhance stability and mutual security, even between adversaries.[17]

Not all states, however, perceive multilateralism to be in their national interest, and not all states seek co-operation. For example, revisionist powers, intent on overthrowing or radically changing the international order, cannot be expected to co-operate in its preservation. For several years after the Russian Revolution, the Soviet Union actively pursued revision, as did Germany under Hitler. Even a status quo power may be expected to resist the multilateral impulse if it perceives a trend toward multilateralism contrary to its self-concept as a great power or to its traditional freedom of action. India, for most of its history as an independent state, and the United States at various times in its history (most obviously during Ronald Reagan's first term as president), have both fallen into this category.[18] The fates of all of these countries are instructive. Even the Reagan administration, instinctively suspicious of multilateralism and openly hostile to many international organizations and regimes such as the UN, UNESCO, the International Monetary Fund (IMF), and the nuclear non-proliferation regime,[19] gradually discovered the high price of unilateralism and indifference and increasingly began to support these and other multilateral bodies and initiatives.[20]

That even Reagan would eventually embrace multilateralism is not surprising in view of American decline. Britain found in the early part of the twentieth century that co-operation permitted a gradual and peaceful adjustment of capabilities and commitments in a time of increasingly strained resources.[21] But burden-sharing is only one of many functions served by multilateralism, and even rising powers may perceive that their interests are best served through international co-operation. Smaller states and middle powers may feel more secure co-operating with much larger states in a multilateral setting, where there is strength in numbers.[22] Ascendant states may attribute their rise to, and conceive their welfare to depend upon, a stable international order threatened by a breakdown of multilateralism.[23] And states of all sizes and trajectories may conclude that certain problems requiring collective action are simply too important to leave unaddressed.

My use of the word *may* is deliberate. They also *may not*. Not all states decline gracefully (France did not); not all small or middle powers embrace multilateralism (Albania, Mexico, and Brazil did not); not all ascendant states perceive a strong, basic interest in multilateralism (Nazi Germany did not); and numerous pressing collective action problems, such as global warming and deforestation, have yet to be addressed by the international community as a whole. But the proliferation of international institutions and regimes, coupled with rising global interdependence across a broad range of issues, suggests that the incentives for co-operation are growing stronger. If indeed co-operation breeds co-operation, there may be a ratchet effect to multilateralism that justifies a skeptical reply to fears that the post-Cold War world will increasingly resemble a Hobbesian state of nature.

Evolving Security Systems

Collective security is not the only form which co-operation can take in the security realm; concerts,[24] collective defence, confidence and security building measures (CSBMs, such as prior notification and observation of troop movements and military exercises), arms control agreements, and measures to improve crisis prevention and management, all represent varieties of security "regimes." And possibly, as the preceding paragraph suggests, it may not be appropriate to speak of armed conflict as the only — or even the most important — modern security threat. Indeed, the government of Canada has begun to speak of "new" security threats such as economic underdevelopment, environmental degradation, and political oppression.[25] Owing to space constraints, the following analysis will focus on the full range of security regimes, but primarily on the traditional security threats (varieties of armed conflict), intending no slight to the many other pressing global problems that collectively constitute "the new security agenda."

It is natural to begin exploring evolving security systems by looking at the major institutions that may legitimately claim a role in the management of world order. These include the UN, the Seven-Power Summit, the Conference on Security and Co-operation in Europe (CSCE), the European Community/Western European Union (EC/WEU), and NATO. Also important are a variety of regimes intended to halt the spread of nuclear, chemical, and biological weapons, as well as advanced missile technologies. Of each we can ask questions about its strengths, weaknesses, and prospects, in an attempt to refine our understanding of the new multilateralism in security and gauge its likelihood of success.[26]

The United Nations

Despite its recent collective security action in the Persian Gulf, the UN's chief value and greatest likely future contribution lie in the broad range of less dramatic services it performs for the world community. The UN employs 15,000 people world-wide and spends $3 billion dollars annually to alleviate poverty, suffering, and improve standards of living.[27] Its main post-war security function — peacekeeping — has been remarkably successful in moderating international conflict, and is in the process of being supplemented by ambitious state-building operations, such as election monitoring, civil policing, and resettling refugees, that have achieved particularly notable successes in Namibia and Central America.[28] Three striking developments in 1991 indicate that the UN is becoming increasingly active in these and related roles: 1. its *de facto* trusteeship over a defeated Iraq, including its supervision of sanctuaries for Kurdish refugees near Iraq's Turkish border and its strict management of Iraqi trade;[29] 2. its aggressive enforcement of the cease-fire provisions calling for the destruction of Iraq's unconventional arsenal and production facilities; and 3. its mandate to oversee Cambodia's transition to democracy by 1993 (see Chapter 6). These various activities constitute significant interventions in the domestic affairs of states, and would appear to signal the willingness of the world community to diminish the prerogatives of state sovereignty for the purpose of enabling the UN to promote order and other values, such as human rights, more effectively.[30]

Although the UN has carved out a number of limited sectors that collectively represent an important contribution to international order "in the field," it suffers from a series of structural and procedural weaknesses that undermine its ability to play a lead role in international governance. The distribution of power within the UN itself, for example, is becoming increasingly anachronistic. While Russia may seem the logical successor to the Soviet Union on the Security Council, its status as a Great Power — even militarily — is open to doubt, and it is difficult to justify Russia's having both a permanent seat and a veto when Japan and Germany have neither. Europe's economic and (presumable) political integration raise the further question of a European Community seat, and whether it should supersede the French and British seats. Meanwhile, "regional" powers such as Brazil and Nigeria continue to argue behind the scenes for permanent representation. A failure to adjust Security Council representation to reflect changing global realities threatens to undermine the organization's legitimacy. Meanwhile, the current Security Council does not enjoy the "minimum of political solidarity and moral community" necessary to make it effective on highly politicized security issues: the People's Republic of China continues to play the pariah, resisting pressure to improve its human rights performance and to take a more responsible attitude toward arms exports. Since the other four veto powers cannot rely upon China to co-operate fully, they are inclined to put their faith in other bodies for the collaborative maintenance of world order.

Equally problematic is the attitude of the United States, which has repeatedly criticized the UN, particularly the General Assembly, for being a forum in which member states vent their anti-Americanism, and which has dragged its feet on paying its assessments in order to register its disapproval. Many UN delegations resented the United States' high-handed treatment of the organization during the Gulf War, feeling that it had bullied the organization into endorsing its leadership role and its policies.[31] Yet the UN acknowledges its ultimate dependence upon the United States. As one senior UN official remarked, "The truth about this place is that unless the U.S. is actively involved in it, nothing much that is real happens here."[32] Notwithstanding a good deal of "new world order" rhetoric, the United States has given no indication that it considers the UN the centrepiece of that order. New York was the final stop on the Bush administration's diplomatic itinerary after August 2, 1990, not the first; Washington carefully orchestrated its response to the Iraqi invasion of Kuwait with its Gulf partners, its NATO allies, and the remaining members of the G-7 Summit, before it turned its attention to securing the appropriate Security Council authorizations. Knowledgeable observers have few doubts that if those authorizations had not been forthcoming, the United States and its major coalition partners would have acted against Iraq notwithstanding. Aware of this — and conscious of the fact that Iraq's invasion of Kuwait constituted the clearest possible violation of the UN Charter (never before had one state invaded, conquered, and annexed a UN member) — the UN appreciated that had it failed to act, it would have consigned itself to political irrelevance. It therefore had no choice but to endorse the American response.[33] But since such clear-cut violations of the Charter are so rare, the UN will have few opportunities to demonstrate such unity and firmness again. Even in the post-Cold War world, therefore, the UN is unlikely to play an important collective-security role. Much of the enthusiasm about the possibility that the end of the Cold War would finally permit the UN to function as its founders anticipated would therefore seem misplaced. However, the UN has discovered new functions and unforeseen comparative advantages, and will continue to play an important role in the maintenance of world order by providing states with a valuable institutional forum for bargaining and negotiation, and by providing humanitarian, peacekeeping, and state-building services to the world community at large.

The Seven-Power Summit

Since 1975, the leaders of the western world's largest economies have met annually to discuss the great issues of the day.[34] Originally intended to be a one-time, low-key meeting to discuss the arcana of macroeconomic policy, the Summit quickly became a regular, highly visible event whose agenda has steadily broadened and deepened (particularly since 1979) to include the full range of issues of international concern, including the high politics of East-West relations, arms control, regional conflict, terrorism, and international public order.[35] Many of those (particularly in the Third World) who had hoped that the end of the Cold War heralded the rebirth of the UN as the primary organ for international governance now fear that "the new world order" more closely resembles a concert of the Great Powers, and see the G-7 Summit as its most obvious institutional expression.

Scholarly assessments of the role and importance of the Summit as an institution differ substantially. John Kirton considers the Summit an "embryonic international concert" that plays a leading role in the maintenance of world order. According to Kirton, the Summit is able to do so because it has four crucial advantages: 1. a greater concentration of power than any rival body — in particular, the five permanent members of the UN Security Council or the "Berlin Dinner" four of NATO (the United States, Britain, France, and Germany); 2. constricted participation, such that the Summit constitutes a minimum necessary winning coalition for international governance; 3. common purpose among its members; and 4. political rather than bureaucratic control, because of its minimal institutionalization.[36] These characteristics ensure that the G-7 can set its own global agenda, enforce the implementation of its agreements, and respond to a broad range of challenges flexibly and decisively.

The assessment of Putnam and Bayne is much more restrained:

> One common misunderstanding of summitry must be avoided. The popular press, encouraged by enthusiastic government press agents, sometimes has cast the summit as a kind of grand assizes of the Western world, a supranational forum in which decisions on the great problems facing the industrial democracies are collectively rendered by the world's leaders. This image evokes a unity of purpose and a decisiveness of collective action that is inappropriate for this or any other international forum. "You can't expect spectacular decisions from a meeting like that," says one of the founding summiteers. "It's naive to believe that that is possible."[37]

Among the factors that limit the Summit's influence, according to Putnam and Bayne, are its political subtext, which is largely domestic, and the many struggles between Summit members lurking just beneath the surface.[38] France and the United States, for example, struggled to control the membership, format, and agenda of the Summit itself (the United States appears to have won a decisive victory in this battle at the 1990 Houston summit).[39] Other struggles emerge from time to time on specific issues of policy. At the 1991 London summit, for example, the United States, Canada, and Japan strongly resisted German, French, and Italian pressure to provide massive financial support for Mikhail Gorbachev's efforts at Soviet economic reform.[40] This particular dispute reflected differing national interests or perceptions of stakes; being on the front lines of political instability in Europe, the three continental Summit members were clearly more willing to take financial risks to reduce the dangers of

Soviet economic and political collapse than were the three non-European members. Moreover, Japan's uncharacteristically strong stand against increasing the lending capacity of the European Bank for Reconstruction and Development (so that it might provide the Soviet Union with much-needed liquidity) stemmed primarily from its desire to exert leverage on the Northern Territories issue.[41] In this instance, Japan simply refused to subordinate its national interests to those of the other members of the group.[42] Putnam and Bayne's argument that the Summit has at best had mixed success in co-operation, for which American agreement appears to be a necessary but not sufficient condition, also casts doubt on the supposition that its unity of purpose is adequate to enable it to function as a true concert.[43] Last — but perhaps not least — the fact that the summiteers meet only briefly once a year suggests that they can give certain issues but cursory treatment (the group discussed environmental questions for all of ten minutes in London);[44] the efficacy of the group's management of international crises will depend heavily upon the timing of events. Thus the G-7, *qua* Summit, played no role at all in the conflict with Iraq, because the entire affair fell between two meetings.

While it would obviously be prudent neither to overstate nor to understate the Summit's importance, understatement seems to be the more likely error. The annual meetings of heads of state and government are less important, in the long run, than the strength of the personal relationships the summiteers develop over the course of the years through their membership in the club. It is natural for the G-7 heads to consult with one another frequently and extensively, both bilaterally and multilaterally, on a broad range of issues. Their ministers of finance and foreign affairs are in similarly close contact throughout the year, as are their personal representatives (or "sherpas"). The G-7 process has instituted and reinforced norms of consultation, deliberation, and outward unity that are the essential hallmarks of an international concert. Thus, while the Iraqi invasion of Kuwait was never on the agenda of a G-7 *summit*, the G-7 heads, in effect, orchestrated the global response. The G-7 obviously falls short of complete consensus on various issues, and is clearly constrained by disagreements or conflicts of interest within the group (Paris, for example, attempted to play an independent diplomatic role at various points in the Gulf crisis, much to Washington's chagrin). Yet its members place a very high value on their membership, and have thus far proven unwilling to permit their disagreements to jeopardize either the institution itself or the global perception that it is an institution of consequence. It has succeeded in bringing about a degree of Great Power consensus and co-operation that is unprecedented in this century, and that more closely resembles the nineteenth century Concert of Europe than any subsequent international institution or regime. Barring an unforeseen and unlikely rupture, we may therefore expect it to play a leading role in the shaping of the international order in the years to come.

The CSCE

The CSCE is the only organization with a security function whose members include all the states of Europe, in addition to the United States and Canada. As a decision-making body, it has the advantages of a clear mandate and unparalleled legitimacy (since all states potentially subject to its actions and decisions are also members). But it also has two crucial disadvantages: 1. nascent, functional institutions and procedures that are as yet poorly developed; and 2. a paralyzing unanimity rule.

As a security organization, the CSCE has three functions: managing the negotiation and implementation of CSBMs; providing a forum and umbrella for disarmament negotiations; and peacefully settling disputes. In the first and second, it has already achieved notable success. The CSCE proved extremely useful in the de-escalation of tensions between NATO and the Warsaw Pact, and oversaw the conclusion and implementation of the 1990 Conventional Forces in Europe (CFE) agreement. At the Paris summit of November 19–21, 1990, the CSCE sought to formalize and institutionalize its chief functions by arranging for regular political consultations between heads of state or government, foreign ministers, and senior foreign office officials; organizing a secretariat in Prague; establishing an Office for Free Elections in Warsaw; and creating a Conflict Prevention Centre (CPC) in Vienna.[45] In Valetta (January 15–February 8, 1991), the CSCE began to detail precise mechanisms for peacefully settling disputes.[46]

The Yugoslav civil war, however, starkly illustrated the limits and weaknesses of the CSCE as a comprehensive security organization. Although the CSCE held a special emergency meeting in Prague to deal with the crisis, and although the CPC mechanism was invoked, the organization failed to affect the course of the conflict and quickly lost the diplomatic initiative, first to the EC and then to the UN. Largely a victim of its own unanimity requirement, the CSCE also seemed paralyzed by a particularly acute collective action problem. Its members could not muster the political will to devote significant resources to a problem that as yet posed only a *potential* international security threat. Indeed, many of them (particularly the newly independent Baltic states and the former members of the Soviet bloc) had no resources to spare, and faced dire domestic political problems of their own, many of which were partly or largely a function of precisely the same pressures as those that were rending Yugoslavia.

The CSCE seems best suited to a secondary role in the maintenance of European security, acting as an agent for another principal or set of principals. Its great successes in confidence- and security-building and arms control, for example, were achieved at the behest of NATO and the Warsaw Pact. The Great Powers have few incentives to allow the CSCE to play a larger role. The organization is too unwieldy and too constrained procedurally to enable them to exercise within it the same degree of influence available to them in other fora.[47] In an agency role, however, the CSCE's comprehensive regional membership gives it an attractive and unparalleled legitimacy. The Great Powers therefore gain if the CSCE succeeds in serving regional functions they conceive to be in their interest, but lose little if the CSCE fails to play an autonomous role in the maintenance of regional security (since the Great Powers have a variety of alternative multilateral structures available to them). Indeed, in a perverse way, the CSCE may have systemic value as an organization that may be set up to fail in circumstances warranting some kind of international response, in which, however, there is not justification either for a major commitment of resources or for a potential disruption of those institutions and regimes in which the Great Powers invest a greater proportion of their political capital.[48]

The EC and WEU

As the European Community moves toward political union, it will inevitably take on greater responsibility for the maintenance of European security. In anticipation of that eventuality, on October 14, 1991, France and Germany proposed the creation of a European defence force, crystallized around the WEU, that would eventually become an integral part of the European Union. Britain, Italy, the United States and Canada reacted coolly to the proposal, on the ground that it would usurp the functions of NATO. The dissenters preferred to maintain the WEU as an autonomous body with connections to NATO and the EC, but independent of both. The proposal prompted President Bush to proclaim in no uncertain terms, "If your ultimate aim is to provide independently for your own defence, the time to tell us is today."[49]

It is too early to tell what form the European Community's security provisions will take, or how effective they will be, if the EC succeeds in attaining meaningful political union. The WEU — all of whose members belong to the EC — would appear to be the logical nucleus of a collective security organization or collective defence force. But before the future of the WEU becomes clear, the fate of NATO must be settled. While France would like to see the WEU largely replace NATO, in keeping with its longstanding resentment of American hegemony and its desire to play the lead role in the drama of European unification, there is no European consensus on this point. In the meantime, while being careful not to put pressure on NATO, the EC is making its first attempts to play an independent security role, and seems comfortable experimenting with the WEU as its collective military arm. Thus, the EC took the lead in orchestrating the international response to the Yugoslav civil war, brokering more than a dozen unsuccessful cease-fires before dispatching a humanitarian convoy, protected by warships of the WEU, to provide relief for the beleaguered Adriatic port of Dubrovnik.[50]

NATO

NATO was formed in 1949 to defend Western Europe against Soviet invasion. With political change in the Soviet Union and Eastern Europe, the Soviet military threat vanished, and along with it NATO's stated *raison d'être*. On July 1, 1991, the Warsaw Pact voted itself out of existence, and five days later NATO declared the Cold War over.[51]

To many, the end of the Cold War implies the end of NATO. The alliance's effort to articulate a new rationale for its continued existence has been widely perceived as an identity crisis heralding the organization's ultimate demise. Indeed, NATO's most dramatic response to the new post-Cold War era has been the announcement of significant force reductions, including the phased withdrawal of more than a quarter of a million foreign troops from Germany by 1997, and a total reduction of 750,000.[52] Little imagination is required to extrapolate from this trend the ultimate dissolution of the alliance, particularly if the EC succeeds in building an alternative security apparatus to take its place.

It is doubtful, however, whether any alternative organization could fully take NATO's place, at least for the foreseeable future. NATO is, quite simply, the most successful military alliance — and possibly the most successful international organization — in history. While its original purpose may have been to deter and defend against a Soviet attack, its members quickly discovered that it served a broad range of useful — indeed, vital — purposes. On this theme, Manfred Wörner writes:

> The Alliance has evolved over the years into a political commonwealth of like-minded and equal nations sharing common values and, increasingly, common interests.
> The Treaty of Washington of 1949 nowhere mentions the Soviet Union but stresses instead the need for a permanent community of western democracies to make each other stronger through cooperation, and to work for more peaceful international relations. The alliance has played a major role in reconciling former adversaries, such as France and Germany, in counteracting neo-isolationism within the world's greatest power and in promoting new standards of consultation and cooperation among its members. All these elements would still have been fundamental to security and prosperity in Europe even in the absence of the post-war Soviet threat.[53]

NATO has bound Europe and the United States closely together; it has amplified the ability of its lesser members to exert some degree of influence over the conduct and policies of its larger members, affording them some measure of safety against Great Power unilateralism; it has transformed and pacified relations between its members by acting in the first instance as a giant confidence- and security-building measure, and later as a powerful vehicle for the incubation of Atlanticist attitudes and attachments; and it has proven its value to global security time and again by stabilizing Western Europe and facilitating the military operations of its members even in "out-of-area" conflicts such as the 1962 Cuban missile crisis, the 1982 Falklands/Malvinas war, and the 1991 Persian Gulf War. It is a testament to NATO's success and its importance that the former members of the Warsaw Pact, far from demanding the dissolution of NATO, actively sought membership.

Until a viable alternative structure can be identified, NATO will continue to exist and to perform a broad range of security functions. It is clear that NATO has a role to play and that it faces a series of important latent threats. While the Soviet Union and its former allies no longer constitute a serious menace, ethnic violence and political instability in Eastern Europe increasingly threaten to spill across borders, and NATO stands as an important firebreak against their unchecked spread. Moreover, the dissolution of the Soviet Union raises the possibility that Soviet nuclear weapons will fall into the hands of groups either willing to use them, or unable to control them.[54] To help guard against these two chief dangers, NATO has adopted a new strategic concept emphasizing rapid response to conflicts wherever they may occur, and has downgraded its emphasis on nuclear weapons.[55] In addition, at their November 1991 summit, NATO leaders offered associate status to the Soviet Union, the East European countries, and the Baltic states, inviting them to participate annually in joint ministerial meetings, and in meetings of a co-operation council composed of ambassadors and military representatives, to address potential security threats.[56]

NATO will undoubtedly face difficult challenges in the years ahead. Particularly sensitive will be the question of foreign bases in Germany once the last unit of what used to be the Soviet Red Army pulls out of the territory of the former German Democratic Republic. Unless NATO moves toward a general policy of multinational bases in all NATO countries, Germans may well interpret the continued presence of foreign troops on their soil as a sign that the alliance considers German resurgence to be the real danger to European security.[57] But despite some degree of public uncertainty over the future role and importance of NATO, none of the leaders of NATO's core group has expressed any desire whatsoever to dissolve or weaken the organization.[58] Given its remarkable achievements and the unclear prospects for the future, this should hardly be surprising.

Non-Proliferation Regimes

The Persian Gulf War and its aftermath dramatically demonstrated the potential dangers of a world in which nuclear, chemical, and biological weapons, as well as the means to deliver them over considerable distances, proliferated. Many of the states exerting the greatest efforts to obtain unconventional military arsenals — such as North Korea, Pakistan, Libya, and (until 1991) Iraq — have demonstrated an historical willingness to use force to achieve their goals, and harbour unresolved grievances toward their neighbours. Their attempts to acquire such arms pose a threat to regional stability not only because they might be tempted under certain circumstances to use these weapons, thus crossing psychologically significant escalation thresholds, but also because their efforts might trigger preemptive military action.[59]

The international community's best defence against the proliferation of nuclear weapons, chemical weapons, biological weapons, and delivery systems is a series of non-proliferation regimes intended primarily to obstruct the flow of certain arms, components, technologies, and materials to pariah states. Most notably, these include the nuclear non-proliferation regime, embodied in the 1968 Nuclear Non-Proliferation Treaty and overseen by the International Atomic Energy Agency (IAEA), as well as by the twenty-six members of the Nuclear Suppliers' Group (NSG); the 1972 Convention on Biological Weapons; the Australia Group of twenty major chemical-producing states; the seventeen-member Co-ordinating Committee (COCOM), whose mandate was originally to restrict the flow of sensitive technologies from the West to the former East bloc; and the sixteen-member Missile Technology Control Regime (MTCR), created in 1987 after four years of difficult negotiations by the G-7.[60] The Persian Gulf War also renewed international interest in restrictions on conventional arms transfers, both to avoid the destabilizing effects of Third World arms races and to encourage Third World regimes to devote a greater proportion of their resources to welfare issues.[61] To this end, Canada obtained the CSCE foreign ministers' endorsement of its call for greater "transparency" of arms sales in June 1991, signalling for the first time the willingness of some of the world's largest arms suppliers to accept at least minimal constraints on their exports.[62]

The success of these various non-proliferation efforts will ultimately depend upon the unity of purpose of those states which collectively monopolize the knowledge, skills, and resources needed to build the weapons in question. To some extent, the genie is already out of the bottle. Iraq proved in 1991 to be much closer to a nuclear weapon than had been suspected by the outside world prior to the outbreak of the Gulf War. The testimony of an apparently knowledgeable North Korean defector indicates that Pyongyang is likewise further advanced than had previously been thought. Pariah states such as Libya and Iran already possess chemical weapons, and both China and North Korea have shown little inclination to co-operate in restricting the export of first-generation ballistic missiles (such as the Soviet-designed SS-1 or "Scud") to unpredictable states such as Syria and Iraq. Even France has been reluctant historically to restrain its export of nuclear technologies, and all major Powers — including such enthusiastic supporters of the NPT as the United States, Britain, and the Soviet Union — have proven more than willing to sell conventional arms in Third World markets. Nevertheless, the developed world has of late expressed a greater interest in halting the spread of weapons of all kinds, and has at its disposal both the institutional mechanisms (the G-7, IMF, NATO, and UN, in addition to the various specific non-proliferation regimes) and the collective capability to reduce the rate at which proliferation occurs and to enforce norms against the use of such weapons if non-proliferation efforts fail. The only question is whether these states will muster the political will necessary to do so.

Canada and the New Multilateralism

> We are not a great power. We cannot impose order or ignore it. We have no choice but to build it with others — co-operatively.
>
> –Joe Clark[63]

As the foregoing discussion indicates, the post-Cold War world's most significant evolving security systems are heavily Eurocentric or Atlanticist in their orientation. Collectively, they constitute the means by which the largest states in the developed world can attempt to define and maintain an international order to their liking. Whether or not they do so will depend less upon the collective resistance of the rest of the world (which essentially lacks both the resources and unity of purpose necessary to break the shackles of a *Pax Potentium*) than upon the ability of the Great Powers to transcend their historic parochialisms and rivalries. However, the complexity of European security systems should not be permitted to obscure successful multilateral responses to security problems in other parts of the world (such as the noteworthy 1987 success of five Central American nations at Esquipulas, bringing an end to the Nicaraguan civil war).[64] Nor should we lose sight of the fact that a new world order that amplifies the differences of interest between North and South will in the long run be less effective in promoting and maintaining global security than an order that narrows them. The new multilateralism in security will, therefore, prove more durable, more valuable, and more successful if it includes strong institutional bridges between regional subsystems, and between North and South. Canada's role and interest in the new multilateralism may be understood in this light. Its strong support for multilateralism follows from the premises that stability breeds stability, that order breeds order, and that unilateralism and self-help are inconsistent with both. It rests upon a deeply-entrenched conviction that Canada's core interests lie in a stable, orderly, rule-governed international environment.

For much of the postwar period, Canada's interest in multilateralism stemmed largely from its fear of a capricious and overbearing southern neighbour; it was attracted to multilateralism out of a sense of weakness and of its vulnerability to the actions of a particular state, and it sought refuge in the safety of numbers. Brian Mulroney's early foreign policy, known by the label "renewed internationalism," fell within this tradition. But as the labels changed, so did the driving concern. "Constructive internationalism" was less a defensive response to the United States than a concern with preserving a stable international order more broadly understood.[65] "Co-operative security" completed the evolution.[66] By 1991, Canada was fighting a war in the Persian Gulf for its own good reasons: to defend an international order thought to be vital to Canada's well-being.[67]

Canada's interest in a stable international order stems from two crucial facts: 1. thirty percent of Canada's GNP depends upon international trade; and 2. there are no serious threats to Canada's physical security that Canada can defend itself against, no matter how many resources it devotes to the task. The gravest of these (and the only plausible one, if one discounts the likelihood of American invasion) is the nuclear threat.[68] Canada, therefore, has an important interest in peaceful change in the former Soviet Union, including the maintenance of strong central control of nuclear weapons; effective non-proliferation; the peaceful management and resolution of international disputes, particularly in economically vital regions such as the Persian Gulf; and progress toward addressing the full range of social, economic, and environmental problems on the global agenda that might constitute future security threats if they disrupt the smooth operation of the world economy and trigger violent conflicts, wholesale migrations, and intensified competition for resources.

Diplomacy — not military force — will be the most important instrument for preserving security as Canada conceives it in the new international environment. Accordingly, Canada seized the opportunity in 1991 to conduct a sweeping defence review resulting in a decision to close two bases in Germany by 1995, redeploying two squadrons of CF-18 fighters and 5,500 of 6,600 military personnel to Canada; to reduce Canada's regular armed forces from 84,000 to 76,000; to reduce the civilian work force from 33,000 to 32,000; and to increase the size of the reserves from 44,000 to 65,000. These measures were in keeping with those of most of Canada's NATO partners, and in no way signalled a diminution of Canada's support for the alliance. Instead, the savings realized from these measures

($11 billion over fifteen years from German base closings alone) were intended to enable Canada to improve the quality of its armed forces and their ability to perform peacekeeping and enforcement functions around the globe while keeping the overall defence budget under control.[69] They were therefore consistent with NATO's analysis of the new threats to European security, and with NATO's new emphasis on rapid and flexible responses to localized conflicts.

But while a leaner Canadian Armed Forces might be better suited to the military realities of a post-Cold War era, neither deterrence nor collective security will in future play as prominent a role in maintaining international security as they have done since 1945. In the first place, armed conflict is becoming increasingly diffuse, subsystemic, and intra-state in origin. As such, it cannot easily be handled by traditional collective security organizations. Accordingly, we are witnessing a process of creative institutional adaptation, often (but not always) regionally based, that renders the new multilateralism both complex and eclectic. No single institution is charged with responsibility for dealing with international conflicts, and no single international conflict is dealt with by one institution alone. Secondly, "the new security agenda" lends itself less easily to the diplomacy of violence than the diplomacy of persuasion. The use of force might have been an appropriate response to Iraq's invasion of Kuwait; would it also be an appropriate response to Brazil's deforestation of the Amazon?

Together, these two considerations present Canadian foreign policy with both a challenge and an opportunity. Joe Clark writes:

> The real art in managing current international relations, resides in skilful deployment of resources among all the available channels. . . . In the current world, Canada has to be adept — as a considerable power — in forming *fluid, issue-specific* working relations with other countries. It has to draw upon its wealth of affiliations, forming coalitions of common cause as the need arises. This means targeting the most appropriate organizations and being very clear about its agenda. Perhaps the newness of the 'New Internationalism' resides partly in this — the unprecedented imperative for multiple but highly selective alternatives, the weaving of coalitions in an increasingly complex web of institutions.[70]

But the complexity of that web is the very ground of its power and stability. As our tour of evolving security systems indicates, the primary institutions that claim a role in international governance vary widely in size, structure, and process; they have characteristic strengths and weaknesses; they have comparative advantages and disadvantages; and together, they constitute a robust complex that contains redundant elements whose diplomatic virtues are analogous to the military virtues claimed for a strategic nuclear triad. The G-7 acts increasingly as a global board of directors, shaping the international agenda, setting broad policy directions, and elucidating basic principles of order. The UN delivers a range of crucial services, including conference facilities, peacekeeping, and state-building. NATO provides military security for Western Europe, and the infrastructure for effective policing of the entire globe. The EC, WEU, and CSCE are gradually taking on a range of security functions in Europe, as principal and agents respectively. It is unlikely that all of these systems will fail simultaneously and catastrophically; if effective international action is blocked in one forum, it may go forward in another; a dissenter or free rider may find itself outflanked and left behind as responsibility shifts to other institutions in which it has significantly less influence, thereby providing incentives not to dissent or free ride in the first place. In short, the new multilateralism represents a quantum change from early conceptions of international order emphasizing the central, largely unsupported role of broadly multilateral, highly formal institutions such as the League of Nations and the UN.

The foregoing institutions, of course, do not exhaust the relevant list. At the end of 1991, for example, the Organization of American States (OAS) and La Francophonie took steps to use economic pressure to force a Haitian military junta to restore deposed President Jean-Bertrand Aristide to power.[71] These bodies, too, have a role to play in the new multilateralism. Their willingness to intrude into what just a few years ago would have been considered a purely internal matter illustrates again the erosion of state sovereignty in the new international order, and strongly indicates that the post-Cold War world is more sensitive to the potential international security implications of desperate domestic conditions. The OAS, the Commonwealth, and La Francophonie are among those institutions that have not developed into security organs traditionally conceived; but as the world grapples with "the new security agenda," they will play increasingly important roles as precisely those bridges between regional subsystems, and between North and South, needed to prevent the exacerbation of disparities and tensions on these dimensions. Canada, as one of the best-connected countries in the world, expects to play an increasingly important role in keeping those bridges in repair.[72]

Notes

The author would like to acknowledge the helpful assistance of Richard Burgess, David Dewitt, David Haglund, John Kirton, Albert Legault, Robert Matthews, Arthur Rubinoff, and the participants in the *Canada Among Nations* authors' workshop at Carleton University, December 5-6, 1991.

1 "Conclusion: Security and Survival," in John W. Holmes, ed., *No Other Way: Canada and International Security Institutions* (Toronto: Centre for International Studies, 1986), pp. 149–50.

2 For a detailed analysis and documentation of American decline, see John Kirton, "America's Hegemonic Decline and the Reagan Revival," in David Flagherty and William McKercher, eds., *Southern Exposure: Canadian Perspectives on the United States* (Scarborough, Ont.: McGraw-Hill Ryerson, 1986), pp. 42–61. Contra the decline thesis, see Joseph S. Nye, *Bound to Lead: The Changing Nature of American Power* (New York: Basic Books, 1990).

3 The now classic realist analysis is John Mearsheimer, "Back to the Future: Instability in Europe After the Cold War," *International Security*, Vol. 15, No. 1 (Summer 1990): 1–56. See also John Lewis Gaddis, "The Long Peace: Elements of Stability in the Postwar International System," *International Security*, Vol. 10, No. 4 (Spring 1986): 99–142. The clearest articulations of the theory undergirding this analysis are Kenneth N. Waltz, *Theory of International Politics* (Reading, Mass.: Addison-Wesley, 1979); and Joseph Grieco, "Anarchy and the Limits of Cooperation: A Realist Critique of the Newest Liberal Institutionalism," *International Organization*, Vol. 42, No. 2 (Summer 1988): 485–507.

4 The literature on each of these claims is vast. A recent optimistic analysis may be found in Stephen Van Evera, "Primed for Peace: Europe After the Cold War," *International Security*, Vol. 15, No. 3 (Winter 1990/91): 7–57. For an overview, historical background, and analysis of a range of these arguments, see David Welch, "Internationalism: Contacts, Trade, and Institutions," in Joseph S. Nye, Jr., Graham T. Allison, and Albert Carnesale, eds., *Fateful Visions: Avoiding Nuclear Catastrophe* (Cambridge, Mass.: Ballinger, 1988), pp. 171–96.

5 My justification for treating the subject inductively is the unsatisfactory record of deductive approaches. Robert Keohane writes:

> A good deal of thinking has already been done about multilateral institutions, although we hardly have well-specified theories. Approaches that could be useful for explaining variations among issue-areas and multilateral institutions include: neorealist arguments stressing relative state capabilities; arguments about interdependence and domestic politics, separately or together; contractual theories emphasizing responses to externalities, uncertainty, and transaction costs; and models of organizational adaptation and learning. None of these perspectives has established itself as superior, but all contain promising elements.

"Multilateralism: An Agenda for Research," *International Journal*, Vol. 45, No. 4 (Autumn 1990): 763.

6 Keohane, "Multilateralism . . . ," p. 731.

7 Rt. Hon. Joe Clark, "Canada's New Internationalism," in John Holmes and John Kirton, eds., *Canada and the New Internationalism* (Toronto: Canadian Institute of International Affairs, 1988), pp. 8–9.

8 See, for example, Michael A. Samuels, "The Decline of Multilateralism — Can We Prevent It?" *The World Today*, Vol. 46, No. 1 (January 1990): 7.

9 For sources on collective security, see Charles A. Kupchan and Clifford A. Kupchan, "Concerts, Collective Security, and the Future of Europe," *International Security*, Vol. 16, No. 1 (Summer 1991): esp. 118–19 n. 11.

10 Kenneth Thompson, "Collective Security Re-examined," *American Political Science Review*, Vol. 47, No. 3 (September 1953): 758–63, 761; see also Kupchan and Kupchan, pp. 124–25.

11 The successful UN operation in Korea (1950–1953) would seem to represent a counterexample demonstrating that Thompson's conditions are not strictly necessary. However, given the rather unusual circumstances under which the UN approved collective action (the Soviet Union had foolishly boycotted the Security Council in protest of the UN's failure to seat the People's Republic of China, and was unable to exercise its veto), the case should not be permitted to obscure Thompson's point that the absence of one or more of these conditions will make the smooth functioning of a collective security regime problematic.

12 See generally Martin Rudner, "Canada, The Gulf Crisis and Collective Security," in Fen Osler Hampson and Christopher J. Maule, eds., *Canada Among Nations 1990–91: After the Cold War* (Ottawa: Carleton University Press, 1991), pp. 241–80.

13 The Gulf War dramatically illustrated the increasing marginal utility of technological advantages in war; it proved to be one of the most one-sided conflicts in history despite approximate numerical parity between the belligerents. Technological advantages, however, come at a high cost (a single Tomahawk missile, for example, costs $1.35 million). On the eve of war, the Congressional Budget Office estimated that the war would cost between $17 billion and $35 billion in FY 1991, and could ultimately cost between $28 billion and $86 billion. "The Price Tag of War," *Congressional Quarterly Weekly Report*, Vol. 49, No. 3 (January 19, 1991): 186. The coalition partners of the United States delivered or pledged a total of $58 billion in cash or supplies to help defray American expenses. In addition, the EC, Japan, Korea, and the countries of the Persian Gulf pledged more than $14 billion in support to other coalition partners — primarily Egypt and Turkey — and to Jordan. *Journal of South Asian and Middle Eastern Studies*, Vol. 14, No. 3 (Spring 1991): 86.

14 As a defensive alliance whose strictly defined geographical coverage did not include the Persian Gulf, NATO could not take the lead in liberating Kuwait without inviting domestic dissent in NATO countries and violating one of the tacit conditions under which the Soviet Union had consented to a unified Germany's membership in the alliance: namely, that NATO retain its defensive scope and character. The WEU — a far less visible organization operating under less stringent constraints — proved a useful surrogate, since all of its members were also members of NATO (Belgium, France, Germany, Great Britain, Italy, Luxemburg, the Netherlands, Portugal, and Spain).

15 William H. Taft, IV, "European Security: Lessons Learned from the Gulf War," *NATO Review*, Vol. 39, No. 3 (June 1991): 8.

16 See Robert O. Keohane, *After Hegemony* (Princeton: Princeton University Press, 1984), pp. 244–45.

17 See Joseph S. Nye, Jr., "Nuclear Learning and U.S. Security Regimes," *International Organization*, Vol. 41 (Summer 1987): 371–402. Nye's argument suggests that regimes are capable of transforming competitive, zero-sum security relationships into partially co-operative, positive-sum games.

18 See Arthur G. Rubinoff, "The Multilateral Imperative in India's Foreign Policy," *The Round Table*, No. 319 (July 1991): 313–34; and Robert O. Keohane and Joseph S. Nye, Jr., "Two Cheers for Multilateralism," *Foreign Policy* No. 60 (Fall 1985): 148–67.

19 As a candidate, Reagan had once said halting nuclear proliferation was not "any of our business." Keohane and Nye, "Two Cheers for Multilateralism," p. 149.

20 *Ibid.*

21 Particularly noteworthy in this regard are the Anglo-Japanese alliance (1902) and British appeasement of the United States, which together enabled Britain to lighten the burden of defending distant possessions and devote greater effort to maintaining her margin of naval superiority over the burgeoning German High Seas Fleet. See Aaron L. Friedberg, *The Weary Titan: Britain and the Experience of Relative Decline, 1895–1905* (Princeton: Princeton University Press, 1988), pp. 177, 188, 299.

22 This was one of Canada's major early incentives to join NATO: "Canada strove to build a multilateral framework in which it could more safely co-operate with its sometimes overpowering neighbour, the United States." Gerald Wright, "NATO in the New International Order," *Behind the Headlines*, Vol. 36, No. 4 (April 1978): 4. Or, as John Holmes puts it, NATO is Canada's "most likely means of control over United States strategic policy and of differing with them, if need be, in company." John W. Holmes, *Life With Uncle: The Canadian-American Relationship* (Toronto: University of Toronto Press, 1981), p. 92. See later justification by the Department of External Affairs of Canada's commitment to NATO; namely, that membership provides an important *entrée* into Europe's evolving political and economic union. Canada, Department of External Affairs, "Canada and NATO," Reference Paper 77 (Ottawa: Minister of Supply and Services Canada, 1977).

23 Japan would seem to be the obvious illustration. See Richard Rosecrance, *The Rise of the Trading State* (New York: Basic Books, 1986).

24 On concerts, see Kupchan and Kupchan.

25 Department of External Affairs and International Trade Canada (DEAITC), statement 91/32, "Notes for Remarks by the Honourable Barbara McDougall, Secretary of State for External Affairs, at the Conference on Security and Co-operation in Europe (CSCE), Council of Ministers Meeting, Berlin, Germany, June 19, 1991." John Kirton adds, *inter alia*, terrorism, drugs, and AIDS. "Managing the New Security Challenges: The Seven Power Summit as International Institutional Reinforcement, Rival and Replacement," draft paper prepared for a conference on "Canada and International Governance," Centre for International Relations, Queen's University, Kingston, Ontario, November 13–14, 1991, pp. 4–6.

26 For background, see John Halstead, "A New Order in Europe: Evolving Security Systems," in Hampson and Maule, eds., *Canada Among Nations 1990–91*, pp. 145–65.

27 Colin MacKenzie, "UN Still far from utopian dream," *The Globe and Mail* (Toronto), May 8, 1991.

28 Fen Osler Hampson and Christopher J. Maule, "After the Cold War," in Hampson and Maule, eds., *Canada Among Nations 1990–91*, p. 11.

29 More than 21,000 troops from Britain, France, the United States and the Netherlands were deployed in northern Iraq at the height of the emergency, alongside a handful of UN security guards from Geneva. *The Globe and Mail*, June 22, 1991. The UN largely maintained its economic blockade of Iraq, but in August 1991, the Security Council permitted Iraq a one-time $1.6 billion sale of oil to purchase food and medicine. *The New York Times*, August 8, 1991.

30 The Soviet Union proposed in March 1991 that the UN sponsor "preventive" peacekeeping deployments to act as trip-wire deterrents in areas of potential conflict, as a means of preventing situations like that which arose in the Persian Gulf; but the proposal raises serious moral and operational questions that seem destined to derail it. Two problems seem particularly acute: first, the Soviet proposal called for a preventive deployment in response to a *unilateral* request, which could undermine the traditional neutrality of UN peacekeeping operations; and second, the rapid insertion of third-party forces into a potential battlefield zone would be extremely difficult and would seem to expose the soldiers involved to an unreasonable degree of risk. Cf. David B. Dewitt, "The Role of Institutions in International Security: The UN and a New Security Agenda," draft paper presented at a conference on "Canada and International Governance," Centre for International Relations, Queen's University, Kingston, Ont., November 13–14, 1991; and *The Globe and Mail* editorial, "Toward a new United Nations (1)," March 25, 1991.

31 Douglas Roche, "U.N. seeks to avoid further U.S. control," *The Toronto Star*, May 28, 1991.

32 Gwynne Dyer, "A Reborn U.N.," *The Toronto Star*, November 17, 1990.

33 Seemingly unaware of the irony, Joe Clark asked a Chateau Laurier audience,

> Under what possible circumstances would any great power in the future bother with a body which proved itself incapable of following through on its own decisions? The United Nations cannot cry foul and then cry wolf. Other organizations have done that and they have failed. The League of Nations cried foul and then cried wolf. And it collapsed and with that collapse came conflict.

DEAITC statement 91/05, "Peacekeeping and Peacemaking: The Persian Gulf Crisis and Its Consequences," Notes for a speech by the Secretary of State for External Affairs, the Right Honourable Joe Clark, to the Seventh Annual Seminar, Conference of Defence Association Institute, Chateau Laurier Hotel, Ottawa, January 24, 1991, pp. 2–3. In the days of the League of Nations Canada was one of the members most ready to cry wolf; see C.

P. Stacey, *Canada and the Age of Conflict*, Vol. 2 (Toronto: University of Toronto Press, 1981), pp. 179–90.

34 The original participants included Britain, France, Germany, Italy, the United States, and Japan. Canada joined the group in 1976, and the EC in 1977.

35 See especially Robert D. Putnam and Nicholas Bayne, *Hanging Together: Cooperation and Conflict in the Seven-Power Summits*, rev. ed. (Cambridge, Mass.: Harvard University Press, 1987), pp. 241–46; and John J. Kirton, "Introduction: The Significance of the Seven-Power Summit," in Peter I. Hajnal, ed., *The Seven-Power Summit: Documents from the Summits of Industrialized Countries 1975-1989* (Millwood, NY: Kraus, 1989), p. xxvi.

36 Kirton argues the case most forcefully in "Managing the New Security Challenges."

37 Putnam and Bayne, *Hanging Together*, pp. 18–19.

38 Putnam and Bayne, passim., esp. pp. 276–79.

39 Kirton, "Introduction: The Significance of the Seven-Power Summit," p. xxxii. Kirton argues that Houston's Political Declaration, "Securing Democracy," and its "Statement on Transnational Issues," "marked the emergence of the Summit as a major, fully global, security institution and the end of French resistance to this evolution." Notably, the United States finally secured at Houston French acquiescence to the Non-Proliferation Treaty. In Holmes and Kirton, *Canada and the New Internationalism*, p. xv.

40 *The Manchester Guardian*, July 21, 1991.

41 *The Financial Post* (Toronto), July 24, 1991.

42 The failure of the hard-line coup in August and the Soviet Union's deepening economic crisis finally prompted the G-7 to offer a significant financial package in November, indicating that the group is able to transcend its differences and agree on concerted action in situations perceived to be acute. The package included U.S. $3.6 billion in debt relief through 1992, $18–$20 billion in short-term credits, a conditional $1 billion loan, and shipments of food and medicine. "G7 Presents Aid Package to Soviets," *The Globe and Mail*, November 20, 1991; "G7 Nations Sign Soviet Aid Program," *The Globe and Mail*, November 22, 1991.

43 Putnam and Bayne, pp. 272–73.

44 *The Toronto Star*, July 20 and 21, 1991.

45 Victor-Yves Ghebali, "The CSCE in the Post Cold-War Europe," *NATO Review*, Vol. 39, No. 2 (April 1991): 9.

46 These represented a slight relaxation of the organization's unanimity rule, since the CSCE agreed that its conflict-prevention mechanisms could be invoked at the request of any twelve members. However, any decisions of the CSCE would still require unanimity, and no decision could be imposed against a member's will. *The Financial Times* (London), June 21, 1991.

47 The waning interest of the United States in the United Nations through the 1970s and 1980s may be understood similarly.

48 If this line of argument is correct, then the Great Powers have no interest in recasting the CSCE as a concert-based collective security organization, as Kupchan and Kupchan suggest (pp. 114–61).

49 *The Financial Times*, November 8, 1991. See also *The New York Times*, October 26, 1991; *The Financial Times*, November 8, 1991; and Peter Schmidt, "The Evolution of European Security Structures: Master Plan or Trial and Error?" draft paper prepared for a conference on "Canada and International Governance," Centre for International Relations, Queen's University, Kingston, Ont., November 13–14, 1991.

50 *The Globe and Mail*, November 5, 1991; November 20, 1991.

51 "London Declaration on a Transformed North Atlantic Alliance," July 6, 1991 (NATO Press Service).

52 *The New York Times*, May 29, 1991; June 9, 1991; David G. Haglund, "Bound to Leave? The Future of the Allied Stationing Regime in Germany," draft paper prepared for a conference on "Canada and International Governance," Centre for International Relations, Queen's University, Kingston, Ont., November 13–14, 1991.

53 Manfred Wörner, "The Atlantic Alliance in the New Era," *NATO Review*, Vol. 39, No. 1 (February 1991): 5.

54 For this reason, NATO has made adequate safeguards over the Soviet arsenal a condition of economic aid. *The Globe and Mail*, November 8, 1991.

55 NATO's defence ministers agreed in May 1991 to establish a Rapid Reaction corps consisting of two British and two multinational divisions, for which the United States would provide airlift capability. *The New York Times*, May 29, 1991; June 9, 1991. In response to President Bush's September arms control initiative, NATO agreed to reduce its tactical nuclear arsenal from 3,500 warheads to 700. *The Globe and Mail*, October 21, 1991.

56 The first such meeting was scheduled for Brussels on December 20, 1991. *The Financial Times*, November 8, 1991.

57 See Haglund.

58 Only France, Portugal, and Spain have publicly questioned the value of NATO in the post-Cold War world. France is a peripheral member, since its forces are not part of NATO's integrated command structure; Portugal and Spain are peripheral members because of their geographic location and relatively minor contributions to the alliance.

59 Both of these dynamics are evident in the relationship between Israel and Iraq. In 1982, to pre-empt Iraq's nuclear program, Israel attacked and destroyed Iraq's Osirak nuclear reactor. There is also circumstantial evidence that in the Persian Gulf War Israel contemplated a nuclear response to a possible Iraqi chemical attack. See David A. Welch, "The Politics and Psychology of Restraint: Israeli Decision Making in the Gulf War," *International Journal*, forthcoming.

60 For a thorough discussion of the MTCR and its location in the constellation of non-proliferation regimes, see Albert Legault, "Le régime RCTM: un ou plusieurs régimes?" draft paper prepared for a conference on "Canada and International Governance," Centre for International Relations, Queen's University, Kingston, Ont., November 13-14, 1991 (reprinted by *La Fondation pour les études de défense nationales*, Paris, February 1992).

61 For background, see Thomas Ohlson, ed., *Arms Transfer Limitations and Third World Security* (New York: Oxford University Press, 1988).

62 *The Globe and Mail*, June 21, 1991.

63 DEAITC statement 91/01, "Notes for a Speech by the Right Honourable Joe Clark, Secretary of State for External Affairs, at a Meeting of the Senate Finance Committee, Ottawa, January 14, 1991," p. 5. Cf. Joel J. Sokolsky, "Canada in NATO: The Perceptions of a Middle Power in Alliance," *The Fletcher Forum*, Vol. 4, No. 2 (Summer 1980): 205.

64 See Tim Draimin and Liisa North, "Canada and Central America," in Maureen Appel Molot and Fen Osler Hampson, eds., *Canada Among Nations 1989: The Challenge of Change* (Ottawa: Carleton University Press, 1990), pp. 225–43.

65 John Kirton, "Canada's New Internationalism," *Current History*, No. 87 (March 1988): 101–04, 134.

66 "Co-operative security" refers to a non-institutional dialogue "as a regional or sub-regional multilateral exercise that brings together a relatively small number of countries that share geography and have common interests." DEAITC statement 91/17, "Notes for a Speech by the Right Honourable Joe Clark, Secretary of State for External Affairs, to the Colloquium on North Pacific Co-operative Security Dialogue in Victoria, British Columbia, April 6, 1991," pp. 5–6.

67 See Canada, Office of the Prime Minister, "Speaking Notes for Prime Minister Brian Mulroney, Press Conference, National Press Theatre, September 14, 1990;" DEAITC statement 91/01, p. 2.

68 See Joe Clark, "Canada's Stake in European Security," *NATO Review*, Vol. 38, No. 5 (October 1990): 2; and Canada, DEAITC Statement 91/01, p.6.

69 The review postponed the politically sensitive question of base closings in Canada, calling for the Minister's Advisory Group on Defence Infrastructure to report in May 1992. Department of National Defence (DND), "Backgrounder: The Minister's Advisory Group on Defence Infrastructure," September 1991; DND, "Address: Statement by the Honourable Marcel Masse, Member of Parliament for Frontenac and Minister of National Defence, at the National Press Theatre, September 17, 1991."

70 Clark, "Canada's New Internationalism," p. 4. Holmes and Kirton define "the new internationalism" as "all those international institutions and groupings that have sprung to life, within or outside the United Nations galaxy, during the past decade and a half, at a time when the old internationalism based on the inherited institutions of the first post-war decade seemed to be in such decay." in Holmes and Kirton, *Canada and the New Internationalism*, p. x.

71 *The Globe and Mail*, November 21, 1991.

72 "There is simply no other country in the world that belongs to the particular combination of the Western summit, the Organization for Economic Co-operation and Development (OECD), the Group of 7, Quadrilateral, the North Atlantic Treaty Organization (NATO), the Commonwealth, and La Francophonie. No other major power has Canada's institutional reach." Clark, "Canada's New Internationalism," p. 4.

6

Canada, Peacekeeping and the United Nations

Gregory Wirick

The United Nations has been Canada's avocation: a calling more than a duty, an inclination no less than an interest. Beginning with the creative engagement of such well-known figures as Lester Pearson, Escott Reid and John Holmes, the gallery of Canadian politicians and diplomats who have sought to improve the United Nations (UN) system and enhance Canada's standing in it has been long and impressive.

Multilateralism has thus become a kind of code word in the Canadian political lexicon, signifying all those pragmatic virtues — e.g., conciliation, moderation, consensus- and bridge-building — which, until our latest constitutional fracas, the world assumed were part and parcel of the Canadian character. This has been no less in evidence under the Progressive Conservatives than it was under the Liberals; indeed, in the early years of the Mulroney government, Joe Clark, as External Affairs Minister, sought to draw a distinction between his own "Pearsonian" instincts and the rather glib scepticism of the Trudeau years.

Such a claim was easier to make with the accession to power of Mikhail Gorbachev in the Soviet Union and the extraordinary impact this had on international relations. Above all, the warming of superpower relations and the eventual end of the Cold War led to a virtual renaissance of the United Nations. The new-found consensus among the permanent members of the Security Council engendered a series of initiatives in several regional conflicts that previously had been impervious to attempts at resolution. Notable among them were the UN good offices mission in Afghanistan, the decolonization of Namibia and the gradual defusing of conflict in Angola, and the mediation efforts in Nicaragua, El Salvador and throughout Central America as a whole.

It was during 1991, however, that the UN became involved most spectacularly in events at the forefront of world affairs. First, the Security Council demonstrated a capacity for sustained action during the Gulf crisis and war that dispelled any lingering notions about its ineffectualness. Instead, the criticisms levelled against the UN focused either on the aggressiveness it displayed in abandoning sanctions for military action, or on its willingness to be exploited by the world's remaining superpower.

Nevertheless, the events in the Persian Gulf may yet come to represent a watershed in the history of the world organization.

Since the war, the UN has been deeply involved in efforts to restore order to the region. This has included monitoring the demilitarized zone along the Iraq-Kuwait border and clearing it of mines and other unexploded ordnance, overseeing reparations from Iraq, assisting in the protection of Kurds within the national borders of Iraq, and attempting to inspect Iraq's nuclear capacity. The significance of these endeavours can scarcely be underestimated since they represent examples of the clearest and most far-reaching intervention into the sovereignty of a member state in UN history.

In addition, the United Nations has been, and is, playing a central role in the lengthy but so far successful efforts to establish a "modus operandi" between long-time foes in the Western Sahara and in Cambodia, and to determine the subsequent governance of those territories. For this purpose it has reached deep into its basket of peacemaking and peacekeeping techniques to offer services ranging from the organization and monitoring of elections to civil administration, refugee resettlement and policing activities.

Finally, the sensitive role of the good offices of the UN Secretary-General in negotiations to secure the release of a variety of Western hostages in the Middle East, and the crucial contribution of the organization in the laborious but essential preparatory sessions leading up to the 1992 UN Conference on Environment and Development in Brazil, are two of the most visible examples both of the ubiquity and of the compelling nature of the world organization's mandate in the maintenance of international peace and security.

Canada was engaged in virtually all of these endeavours. Having participated in the multinational coalition arrayed against Iraq, Canadians also contributed to the UN Iraq-Kuwait Observer Mission (UNIKOM), to the team assessing Iraq's nuclear capabilities, and to the planning or the operations of the peacekeeping missions in the Western Sahara and Cambodia. It was a quintessentially Canadian performance: instinctively committed to the UN and a multilateral approach; anxious to be involved and helpful; fearful that non-involvement might lead to penalties of some kind or, what would be almost as hurtful to the Canadian psyche, might simply cause the country to be ignored; and finally, stretching diplomatic and military resources to the utmost. It was not necessarily a flawed policy — it may even have been the best conceivable policy — but it did beg many questions, particularly concerning the future of Canada's military in the post-Cold and post-Gulf War world.

The Gulf War and its Impact

The remarkable consensus that had developed within the UN Security Council in opposition to Iraq's aggression against Kuwait culminated in Resolution 678 of November 29, 1990, which authorized member states "to use all necessary means" to enforce previous UN resolutions demanding Iraqi withdrawal from Kuwait. It was endorsed the same day in the House of Commons by a vote of 111 to 82 over strong objections from both opposition parties. The UN resolution set January 15, 1991 as the deadline for Iraqi compliance before the international community would resort to force. As the deadline drew closer, the newly-created "ad hoc cabinet committee on the Gulf" (better known as the "war cabinet") decided to reconvene Parliament for an emergency session — also on January 15.

Once the Commons was back in session, the Prime Minister immediately moved, "That this House reaffirms its support of the United Nations in ending the aggression by Iraq against Kuwait." It was a tactic, on the government's part, that was at once calculated and sincere. By wrapping the U.S.-led coalition against Iraq in the UN flag, the government sought to garner greater public acceptance of its intention to participate in military operations. Polls suggested that Canadians were willing to accept such action insofar as it could be seen as supporting UN objectives.[1] At the same time, the Progressive Conservatives believed that Canadians had not given the government enough credit for the role it had played in moderating the U.S. approach to the gulf crisis. In an interview on the CBC radio program *Morningside*, External Affairs Minister Joe Clark said, "In August and September, the United States was very seriously considering going alone. Canada argued consistently that the United States had to come in under the UN umbrella, that if there was to be any kind of action, it had to be in the context of the United Nations. That has happened."[2]

Mr. Clark also emphasized Canada's contribution to the package of proposals UN Secretary-General Javier Perez de Cuellar took to Baghdad on January 12, particularly Canada's support for the concept of a UN peacekeeping force that would monitor the withdrawal of Iraqi and U.S. forces. The Prime Minister's letter to the Secretary-General was tabled in the House of Commons on January 15. "That package," said Mr. Clark, "was very similar to the contents of the last-minute pleas for peace made by Mr. Perez de Cuellar prior to midnight on January 15."[3]

The lengthy parliamentary debate on Canada's entry into the war featured the first appearance back in the House of Commons of the newly elected Liberal Leader Jean Chrétien, following a December by-election victory. In his inaugural speech on January 15, he proposed an amendment by adding to the government's resolution, after the last word: "through the continued use of economic sanctions, such support to exclude offensive military action by Canada at this time." More significantly, Mr. Chrétien recommended that the minute war broke out, Canadian troops should be called back — that they were there only to enforce the embargo.

Both the Liberal and New Democratic Party (NDP) amendments to the government's original resolution were defeated on January 16. The NDP had proposed a sub-amendment to that of the Liberals which deleted all the words after the word "sanctions" and substituted: "such support to exclude the involvement by Canada in a military attack on Iraq or Iraqi forces in Kuwait." The NDP sub-amendment was defeated 210–39, with the Liberals voting against it, while the Liberal amendment was defeated 134–116.

Immediately afterwards, Mr. Chrétien's position was considerably undercut by the rare appearance in the Commons (on January 16) of Mr. Chrétien's predecessor, John Turner, who argued strongly that Parliament had a duty to support the UN resolutions and, therefore, the resolution the government had proposed. The contradiction between the two Liberals may have had something to do with personalities and the antipathies aroused by several years of political infighting, but it also reflected genuine divisions with the Party as a whole.[4]

The debate continued through the actual outbreak of hostilities on January 16 at 7 PM Eastern Standard Time. It featured a host of speeches, many of them by relatively unknown backbenchers, but virtually all of them reflecting an intense and sombre consideration of the issues. In the evening session, following remarks by the Prime Minister acknowledging the latest development, Mr. Chrétien announced that "all Canadians have the obligation to stand united under the circumstances" in backing up the Canadian troops. He was followed by NDP Leader Audrey McLaughlin, who also indicated support for the troops, but insisted that they should only be used in humanitarian actions and not in combat.

The House finally approved of the government's main motion on January 22, just prior to adjourning again, by a vote of 217 to 47. Almost all of the Liberal MPs ultimately supported the motion, while almost all of those opposed were NDP. They were joined by four Liberals, three Bloc Québécois MPs and an independent.

The debate did not end with the decision by Parliament. Among the most vociferous opponents was the Canadian Peace Alliance, an umbrella organization of peace, women's and labour groups, which was adamantly opposed to the war and equally strongly in favour of continued economic sanctions. It felt snubbed when several government ministers refused to meet with Alliance activists in Ottawa in February. It also condemned Liberal Party "flip-flopping" over the war and praised instead the NDP's consistent anti-war stance. Although some press comment suggested that the anti-war demonstrations were far smaller than those during the Vietnam era, the movement was sufficiently galvanized into action to organize, following the war, "The Citizen's Inquiry into Peace and Security." This effort was co-sponsored by 15 non-governmental organizations including the Canadian Peace Alliance. It consisted of five commissioners[5] who donated their time so that they could travel across the country during the autumn of 1991 and then prepare a report outlining a new security policy for Canada.[6]

Somewhat more successful was the opposition of the United Nations Association in Canada (UNAC), which released a letter it had written Mr. Clark on January 16. The Association took strong exception to resolution 678, arguing that it did not fall under either of the only two articles in the UN Charter which authorized the use of armed force, articles 42 and 51. In the UNAC's estimation, the chief flaw was the Security Council's failure to assess the effectiveness of the sanctions against Iraq. It recommended that Canada should limit its involvement to sanctions enforcement, humanitarian relief for refugees and a military field hospital. Later, an Association press release insisted that this was not a "UN war" and appealed to the government to press for the early intervention of the Office of the UN Secretary-General and for an early ceasefire to the war.[7]

Partly to counter the critics who charged that the government had no ideas of its own and took all of its orders from the Americans, the Prime Minister and the External Affairs Minister gave simultaneous speeches in early February, in Ottawa and Quebec City respectively, on different aspects of postwar planning in the Middle East.[8] They recommended a regional security structure similar to that of the Conference on Security and Cooperation in Europe (CSCE): based on border guarantees, a dispute resolution mechanism and confidence-building measures. They identified the root cause of instability in the Middle East — the Arab-Israeli conflict — and the paramount need for a negotiated settlement based on Security Council Resolutions 242 and 338, describing an international conference as an important first step. Finally, they broached the idea of a "world summit on instruments of war and weapons of mass destruction." Mr. Clark would later develop the concept before the specially constituted Joint Committee of the House Standing Committees on External Affairs and on National Defence, which had continued to meet regularly during Parliament's adjournment to hear from relevant Ministers and officials on the conduct of the war.[9]

The proposal to limit the sale of high-technology arms and vastly destructive weapons following the war was passed to the UN Secretary-General on February 12. Yet the idea did not find much favour either among allies or commentators, a point which Clark later admitted himself.[10] John Hay, foreign affairs columnist in *The Ottawa Citizen*, called it the only original idea that Canada was proposing for a postwar Middle East peace and also the worst — "an idea of airy inconsequence."[11]

To explore less original ideas more fully, Mr. Clark travelled to Europe to discuss potential peacekeeping structures with his Irish and Nordic counterparts (almost all with peacekeepers in the Middle East) during the week of February 18.[12]

Meanwhile, the Gulf War moved to a speedy conclusion. Within six weeks of the opening of offensive military operations by the multinational coalition arrayed against Iraq, U.S. President George Bush ordered their suspension on February 27, declaring Kuwait liberated and Iraq's army defeated. On March 3 Iraq accepted the UN Security Council resolution 685 setting conditions for a permanent ceasefire.

Important precedents were established during the Kuwait operation which will be difficult for governments to ignore in the future. In the first place, the United States, in a matter it deemed a national security emergency, still felt it prudent to work through the United Nations. The results were a rather selective application of the collective security principles of the UN Charter, described by one observer as a "hybrid of multilateral sanction and national application of force" which cynics faulted "as a cover for nationally self-interested intervention."[13] Nevertheless, the willingness of a profoundly nationalistic country with deeply rooted unilateralist attitudes to work through the United Nations and painstakingly assemble an international coalition should not be downplayed. The result of this precedent is that it becomes harder for any government, even for Washington, to avoid taking a security issue first to the UN.

Secondly, a surprisingly comprehensive set of sanctions were imposed by the Security Council against Iraq and almost universally applied. It was the first time that the Council had ever invoked sanctions against an act of aggression, for, on the two previous occasions on which sanctions had been applied, the action had been a response to perceived threats to peace in southern Africa. Moreover the Council subsequently authorized coercive action to enforce the embargo, thereby creating yet another precedent, something it had not done with respect either to Rhodesia or to South Africa.[14]

Third, by authorizing the use of force, the UN had "bared some teeth" and shaken long-held assumptions that it had no teeth to bare or was far too cautious to show them. Bernard Wood, the head of the Canadian Institute for International Peace and Security (CIIPS), quoted approvingly another analyst who wrote, "Manifestly, the new Organization was not meant to be lacking in teeth. The absence of enforcement provisions was seen as a principal failing of its predecessor [the League Covenant]."[15]

Similar sentiments were expressed by Geoffrey Pearson, a former Ambassador to the Soviet Union and son of one of the originators of UN peacekeeping, who was quoted by Mr. Clark as writing in *La Presse*:

> My father [Lester B. Pearson] was not a pacifist. His politics were founded primarily on the importance of the United Nations in ensuring peace. But if a war were to be triggered, he believed that member states of the United Nations should take military action against the aggressor. [translated from French] [16]

In the immediate aftermath of the war, Joe Clark sought to shift attention to longer-term questions of regional peace and security by visiting the Middle East. Reporting to the House of Commons about his trip to Jordan, Israel, Saudi Arabia, Syria, Iran, Kuwait and the United States, Mr. Clark identified the Israeli-Palestinian issue as fundamental. He stressed that the next several months would "offer a real chance to resolve the most intractable conflict the world knows . . ."[17]

Peacekeeping Operations

A frequent refrain during the Gulf War was that Canada's credibility as a peacekeeper was being damaged, perhaps irreparably, by its participation in offensive operations. No less frequently, the Secretary of State for External Affairs strenuously denied this charge, emphasizing that in all of his dealings with foreign governments, including Arab ones, Canadian participation in peacekeeping following the war had been welcomed.[18]

Events themselves seemed to give the lie to opposition fears for, in April Canada was asked, and agreed, to contribute to the 1,440-member UN Iraq-Kuwait Observation Mission in the Persian Gulf, as one of 34 nations taking part in the monitoring of the ceasefire that had been established. The government dispatched 300 field engineers who were responsible, among other things, for clearing mines and dismantling fortifications.

Canadian military journalist Gwynne Dyer noted in connection with UNIKOM that, for the first time since peacekeeping had been created, the five permanent members of the Security Council were all contributing their own troops to a peacekeeping force. Dyer suggested that their joint involvement created a precedent "that could one day be of great use in guaranteeing an Israeli-Arab peace settlement that includes a Palestinian state."[19]

Still another precedent was set when the Security Council adopted resolution 688 on April 5, which condemned Iraqi repression of the minority Kurdish population in northern Iraq and the Shi'ite Muslim population in the southern part of the country, and described the resulting flow of refugees as a threat to international peace and security. It also set the rules for humanitarian relief to the Kurds and demanded that Iraq give relief organizations access to the victims. As Gwynne Dyer tartly commented, this precedent "challenges the right of a sovereign government to kill its own citizens with impunity so long as it does not disturb the neighbours."[20] In belated response to the tragic situation confronting the Kurdish refugees from Iraq, the United States, Britain and France effectively declared a portion of northern Iraq off limits to Iraq's armed forces on April 16 and began sending in thousands of their own troops in order to create safe havens for the Kurds. Thereafter, it became difficult for U.S. and other allied forces to withdraw or to be replaced by UN guards because of Kurdish fears about reprisals by the Iraqi military.

Meanwhile, in another part of the world, the UN Secretary-General had managed to work out the details of a peace plan establishing a ceasefire in the Western Sahara between Morocco, which claimed the former Spanish territory, and Polisario rebels who had been waging a guerrilla war against such an outcome since 1973. The Security Council gave formal approval on April 29 to the UN Mission for the Referendum in Western Sahara (MINURSO), a peacekeeping force of approximately 1,700 military personnel and 900 civilian staff. Its mandate was to monitor the ceasefire and oversee a referendum in early 1992 in which the people of Western Sahara would determine whether they preferred independence from or integration with Morocco.

On July 18, Barbara McDougall, the new Secretary of State for External Affairs, and National Defence Minister Marcel Masse announced that Canada had accepted the formal request of the Secretary-General to participate in MINURSO. Canada would contribute a contingent of approximately 740 troops drawn from the Canadian Airborne Regiment, the largest peacekeeping commitment Canada had undertaken since the Canadian contingent in Cyprus was augmented during the 1974 crisis there. Canada also contributed the force commander, Major-General Armand Roy, for the military component of MINURSO. The first contingent arrived on September 5 to monitor the ceasefire that took effect the following day.[21]

On June 21, the government announced that Canada would send 15 officers as observers within the military component of the second phase of the UN Angola Verification Mission (UNAVEM II). Its mandate was to verify the ceasefire and demobilization arrangements in the Angola Peace Accords signed in Lisbon on May 31 by the government of Angola and the opposition Union for the Total Independence of Angola (UNITA), which brought to an end 16 years of civil war. The first peace accords of December 1988 — between Angola, Cuba and South Africa — had resulted in the creation of the original UNAVEM force, which supervised the withdrawal of Cuban troops. UNAVEM II is being expanded from a small mission of 60 observers to a total strength of over 600, including 350 military observers, 90 police, and the remainder civilians. It is expected to remain in Angola until the country's first national, multi-party elections are held in the fall of 1992.[22]

In July, Canada made it clear it would contribute military observers to the UN Observer Mission in El Salvador (ONUSAL). The UN is conducting peace talks between the rebels and the government in an effort to end an eleven-year civil war which has claimed some 75,000 lives.

Finally, on October 23, External Affairs Minister Barbara McDougall signed the Paris Accords on Cambodia — agreements embodying a comprehensive political settlement of the Cambodian conflict at the Paris International Conference on Cambodia (PICC). Canada co-chaired the First Committee of the PICC on peacekeeping arrangements and had already accepted requests to provide military officers to the UN advance mission in Cambodia as well as officials to the UN electoral appraisal mission. These missions were to begin preparations for the UN Transitional Authority in Cambodia (UNTAC) which, as part of its peacekeeping role, will direct the administration of key aspects of the government in Cambodia to ensure that free and fair elections are held in a neutral political environment.[23]

UNTAC may find its mission daunting, as more than one commentator has observed.[24] In particular, no formal mention was made in the Paris Accords of the genocide committed by the Khmer Rouge after seizing power in 1975, but their horrifying legacy infects the hearts and minds of everyone, especially since the Khmer Rouge is now supposed to share power in the elaborate Cambodian national council. The principal document of the Accords strains mightily to provide for every contingency — the mandate of UNTAC; withdrawal, ceasefire and related measures; elections; repatriation of refugees and Cambodian displaced persons; the principles of a new constitution. But, "implementation of every provision will require good faith on the part of all" the factions — a very tall order.[25]

Cambodia demonstrates the enormously complex nature of the new peacekeeping challenges. The original conception of peacekeeping was as a limited quasi-military operation, akin in some respects to a policing action insofar as the typical requirement was for verification of a ceasefire. Recently, however, the boundaries of peacekeeping have expanded while definitions have come to embrace everything from civil administration to disaster relief. At the same time, the highly political nature of peacekeeping has been emphasized by certain conflict situations where the ceasefire appears extremely fragile and the operations, therefore, that much more perilous. For Canada, if the intention is to remain at the forefront of peacekeeping, the future challenge to be met in applying this specialized skill will be, first, to accept the risks as part of the changed realities and second, to prepare accordingly. Whether the government has really assessed these challenges is, however, still doubtful.

Reshaping the United Nations

Canadians on both sides of the debate over the Persian Gulf War could agree about one thing: the importance of trying in the war's wake to foster conditions conducive to the creation of a "new world order" — the phrase with which U.S. President George Bush had sought to elevate American war aims. Moreover, although there were differences over what precisely this new order should be, there was also a surprising amount of agreement about at least some of the necessary pre-conditions.

For one, there was increasing consensus about the need to permit the UN or other recognized international bodies to intervene in the affairs of sovereign states in certain cases, when either international security or humanitarian considerations warranted. As noted above, a precedent for such intervention was established with the Security Council and other allied involvement in protecting the Kurds. Another instance was the final ceasefire agreement with Iraq (Security Council resolution 687 of April 3), which contained a clause requiring Baghdad to destroy or surrender all its weapons of mass destruction and associated production. This meant not only research plants working on nuclear, chemical, and biological weapons, but also ballistic missiles capable of delivering such weapons over long distances. Hitherto, there had been no law against any state possessing chemical or biological weapons (though it is illegal to initiate their use in war).[26]

Locating and destroying Iraq's inventory of weapons alone is expected to require hundreds, perhaps thousands, of technical experts in a project lasting several years and a process guaranteed by the Iraqi government's obduracy to be both arduous and emotionally charged. Yet the stakes are high. Military analyst Anthony Cordesman has commented, "If we let Iraq get away with this, it will make our efforts to impose any regime over weapons of mass destruction impossible. If the UN fails, who in the region is going to sign any non-proliferation agreement and stick by it?"[27]

This theme — the importance of setting international standards of behaviour above previously untrammelled claims of state sovereignty — was addressed by a wide variety of observers.[28] In June, Liberal Leader Jean Chrétien called for "a new internationalism" which would "place human rights above the absolute right of sovereign states."[29] In September it was the turn of the Prime Minister. In a major foreign policy address at Stanford University in California, Mr. Mulroney pointed to examples of countries blocking UN arms inspections or the delivery of food to starving people and remarked, "Quite frankly, such invocations of the principle of national sovereignty are as out of date and as offensive to me as the police declining to stop family violence simply because a man's home is supposed to be his castle."[30]

Another theme was the need to reassess UN institutions, especially those involving the maintenance of peace and security, and, besides them, the entire panoply of UN agencies. In a couple of editorials on the UN's future, *The Globe and Mail* declared that it was time to take the world organization seriously again.[31] The newspaper pointed to Soviet reform proposals for, among other things, the "creation of a UN military reserve force, with troops of different countries placed under UN command," which could then be used as a deterrent in potential conflict situations. It also noted an important study by former senior UN officials, Brian Urquhart and Erskine Childers, which called for reforms in the election of the Secretary-General, as well as the term of office and the manner in which deputies were selected.[32]

In April, Allan Gotlieb, Canada's former Ambassador to the United States, wrote of the need for a reconstructed Security Council to include as permanent members Germany and Japan.[33] Later in the year, Liberal External Affairs critic Lloyd Axworthy called for a UN Charter review conference, noting that provision had been made for such an event by the Charter's original drafters in 1945, but that the rigidities of the Cold War had made any such fundamental rethinking of the world body impossible.[34]

Parliamentarians for Global Action, an international association, sponsored an Ottawa seminar in May on a new approach to UN collective security, sub-titled, "Lessons of the Gulf crisis." The Canadian chairman of the group, Warren Allmand, commented in Parliament, "What is needed is an early warning process that will provide for preventive peacekeeping. Under such a process there would be standing UN peacekeeping forces stationed in the different regions of the world which would be sent to trouble spots to deter and repel aggression such as that of Iraq against Kuwait."[35]

Other interest groups were also active. The UNAC sponsored a May seminar entitled, "For the peoples: Building the United Nations of tomorrow," for which it commissioned a series of papers on the political, economic and environmental repercussions of the Gulf War. The World Federalists of Canada were sponsoring the idea of an "independent commission on the future of the United Nations" aimed at strengthening the present Charter, reforming it to increase the permanent membership of the Security Council, establishing a UN military force, and developing a system of "enforceable law." CIIPS held a high-level workshop in July on civilian aspects of peacekeeping. One of its major conclusions was that the UN Transition Group in Namibia marked a watershed in peacekeeping, because of the "extremely political nature of the operation and its multifunctional character."[36]

There was even recognition at the G-7 Summit of leading industrialized countries of the central role a revitalized UN could play in strengthening the international order. The communiqué following the leaders' London meeting included the following passage:

> We commit ourselves to making the UN stronger, more efficient and more effective in order to protect human rights, to maintain peace and security for all and to deter aggression. We will make preventive diplomacy a top priority to help avert future conflicts by making clear to potential aggressors the consequences of their actions. The UN's role in peacekeeping should be reinforced and we are prepared to do this strongly. . . .[37]

The United Nations was also the subject of a special debate in the House of Commons on a private member's motion introduced by Conservative MP Walter McLean, the Prime Minister's special representative on African questions, who for some years has been a mainstay of Canada at the fall meetings of the UN General Assembly. Mr. McLean moved on September 19, "that the government promote a summit level meeting at the United Nations on global security, to examine ways of implementing and strengthening the United Nations peacekeeping and enforcement mechanisms."[38]

Any stocktaking of the UN's capabilities in the maintenance of international peace and security must take account of two fundamental requirements: appropriate (i.e., workable) mechanisms and adequate resources. The mechanisms have been described as diplomacy, peacemaking (i.e., the good offices of the Secretary-General), peacekeeping and collective action or enforcement. Former UN Under-Secretary General Brian Urquhart has argued that these should be treated as a kind of seamless web or continuum, one leading automatically to the other.

> For example if a peacekeeping operation gets run over by a government, like for example the peacekeeping forces in South Lebanon did in 1982, in the mandate of that peacekeeping operation that should automatically trigger collective action from the Security Council . . . . If they got trampled on, they would become a tripwire.[39]

The mechanisms for enforcement action provided for in Chapter VII of the UN Charter were clearly found wanting during the Gulf crisis. Sanctions, though almost universally demanded, then appeared to their principal sponsors to be ineffective in obtaining a quick resolution to the crisis. This shortcoming has prompted some observers to call for a reassessment or refining of the blunt instrument of sanctions — the development of "smart" sanctions.[40] As for military enforcement, Urquhart has summarized the inadequacy of UN arrangements.

> Forty years of cold war have meant . . . that the steps outlined in the Charter for providing the Security Council with standby forces to enforce its decisions have never been taken. No agreements have been concluded with member states under Article 43 to make assistance and facilities available to the Council armed forces. The Military Staff Committee, which was to assist the Council in the application of armed force, has conducted purely token meetings throughout the cold war period, and . . . is still a largely inactive body.[41]

In fact, the willingness of member states to commit themselves in advance to provide troops and facilities at the request of the Security Council for enforcement purposes has never been tested.[42]

Issues relating both to mechanisms and to resources were addressed on the eve of the 46th session of the UN General Assembly, when negotiators from 22 countries agreed on a plan to streamline the UN secretariat, increase the power of the new Secretary-General (who would be chosen later in the year) and make the organization more responsive to humanitarian disasters. The group of 22 industrial and developed countries included the United States and the other permanent members of the Security Council as well as Canada. The plan condemned the organization's cumbersome hierarchy, under which 30 to 40 top officials report directly to the Secretary-General. Instead, it proposed four major departments: political and security affairs; humanitarian and human rights issues; development and environmental questions; and management and finance. Each department would be headed by a deputy Secretary-General chosen by the Secretary-General. These four deputies would then supervise the work of about twenty undersecretaries with more tightly-defined responsibilities.[43] The plan drew from a variety of sources, but an important influence was the earlier work by Brian Urquhart and Erskine Childers.

In her first appearance before the General Assembly, External Affairs Minister McDougall touched on many of the points described above, including the importance of expanding the permanent membership of the Security Council to include all regions of the globe, the need to strengthen the Council's capacity to take preventive or anticipatory actions, and the need for all member states to respect their financial obligations.[44]

Above all, much of the impetus for reshaping the UN will depend on the energy and abilities of the new Secretary-General, Mr. Boutros Ghali, the Egyptian diplomat chosen to succeed Mr. Perez de Cuellar at the beginning of 1992. Various candidates had been mentioned, but the story of the selection process became tantalizing when it was learned in

October that Prime Minister Brian Mulroney was in contention for the post. For over a week, the rumours swirled and Ottawa political circles were abuzz with gossip. The Prime Minister's name survived at least one straw poll of the Security Council members intact, even though it was only somewhere in the middle of the pack.[45]

In the Commons, Mr. Mulroney made it clear, in response to a query from Opposition Leader Jean Chrétien on October 22, that he had not put his name on the official list of candidates. Noting the reply, Mr. Chrétien inquired the next day, "why the name of the Prime Minister has not been withdrawn from this list" and what instructions Canadian diplomats abroad had been given in relation to his candidacy. To this there was no definitive answer until October 28 when Mr. Mulroney instructed Yves Fortier, Canada's ambassador to the UN, to withdraw his name from any further consideration. With that the speculation abated. It did seem evident, however, that the Prime Minister had been sorely tempted by the possibility and that it took a flood of appeals from the party faithful to help him make up his mind.[46] Any reshaping at the United Nations would have to be done without the assistance of Brian Mulroney.

Challenges to the New World Order

There were two important challenges to the concept of a "new world order" — however sketchy that idea continued to be — which, while they did not directly concern the UN, did have significant implications for both multilateral peacemaking and peacekeeping. The Yugoslav crisis was the first to arise, as relations between the different ethnic groups deteriorated following Slovenian and Croatian declarations of disassociation from the rest of Yugoslavia in February 1991. Thereafter, tensions mounted steadily as both the European Community (EC) and the CSCE repeatedly brokered ceasefires, all of which were shortlived.

In mid-September, the External Affairs Minister signalled the government's desire to have the UN Security Council consider the matter. The Prime Minister sent an urgent letter to the UN Secretary-General on September 20, urging an emergency Council session and promising that Canada would be part of any international peacekeeping force.[47] News reports drew attention to the conflicting views of the Canadian government and the British Foreign Secretary Douglas Hurd, who happened to be visiting Ottawa at the time. He stated in an interview that he did not see any point in UN intervention unless there was a likelihood that a ceasefire would hold — the same point made in *Le Devoir* by respected military analyst Jocelyn Coulon.[48]

The issue continued to elicit anguished calls in Parliament for something to be done, especially when Serbian-led assaults were mounted against the Croatian capital of Zagreb and the port city of Dubrovnik was placed under siege. Both of the opposition external affairs critics called on the government to join with the EC in imposing sanctions against the Yugoslav government. At first, Ms. McDougall cast doubt on an economic embargo, saying that it would hurt the people it was intended to help. Later, she agreed with the Liberal critic's suggestion that she should raise with member states of the EC and the UN the issue of a humanitarian airlift of goods to the besieged people of Dubrovnik.[49] When the EC finally acted to impose a limited package of economic sanctions on November 8, Canada immediately followed suit.[50]

The other challenge, of particular concern to those who sought to include democratization in their concept of a new world order, was Haiti. This clearly involved the Canadian government which had invested heavily — at least in moral and psychological terms — in the tenuous emergence of democratic norms in Haiti that the recent election of Jean-Bertrand Aristide had seemed to promise. His unceremonious ousting in a military coup therefore came as a rude shock to the government and upset a host of plans to further the development of democratic institutions and civil society. Hence the immediacy and vigour of the government condemnation of the coup, beginning with a statement by Ms. McDougall on September 30. On October 2, she attended an emergency Foreign Ministers' meeting of the Organization of American States (OAS) in Washington, which produced a tough 11-point resolution calling for cutting all aid to Haiti and otherwise isolating it politically and economically. She also took part in an OAS mission which flew to Haiti on October 4 and met briefly with the coup leaders in an unsuccessful attempt to convince them to restore the Aristide government.

In reply to questions in the Commons, the Prime Minister revealed his sense of personal affront with his blunt statement, "We want the thugs who have usurped power in Haiti out and we want the democratically elected president back in."[51] Later, however, Mr. Mulroney qualified an earlier implication by quoting President Aristide himself as saying that military intervention would not be considered and that economic and diplomatic boycotts would be the strategy of the Haitian people.[52]

Ms. McDougall returned to the UN on October 11 to address the General Assembly on the question of Haiti. She urged UN member states to join the OAS in its efforts to restore the legitimate government in that country.[53] A few weeks later she briefed the House of Commons on how Canada was giving effect to the original OAS resolutions. These included: the halting of bilateral trade except for food exports for humanitarian reasons; suspension of all bilateral development assistance; halting of all funds, credits or advice from government agencies such as CIDA and the Export Development Corporation; halting of all assistance to exporters; instructing Canadian representatives at the multilateral development banks and the International Monetary Fund to oppose any proposals for new credits, loans or the provision of technical assistance; and introduction of legislation to freeze all assets of the Haitian government in Canada. Opposition party spokespersons essentially supported these sanctions, while expressing concern that the harsh measures could hurt the poorest people of Haiti who are the legitimate government's strongest supporters.[54]

Future Options

The disheartening news out of both Yugoslavia and Haiti demonstrated that any attempts to reshape the world order were certain to be tentative and fraught with disappointments. New mechanisms and resources are certainly needed, but with the best capabilities and the best will in the world, traditional peacekeeping is all but impossible in situations where the conflicting parties refuse to accept a ceasefire. Brian Urquhart has suggested a third category of UN intervention — something between traditional peacekeeping and large-scale collective enforcement action.

> It would be intended to put an end to random violence and to provide a reasonable degree of peace and order so that humanitarian relief work could go forward and a conciliation process could commence. The forces involved would be relatively small, representatively international and would not have military objectives as such. But, unlike peacekeeping forces, such troops would be required to take, initially at least, certain combat risks in bringing the violence under control. They would essentially be armed police actions.[55]

This is among the new approaches that the UN needs, some of which may challenge accepted notions about the nature of sovereignty and the rules of engagement in protracted conflict situations. Is there a point at which intervention by the UN or other international bodies is acceptable and even warranted, regardless of whether the contesting parties agree? These are ideas with which Canada is and should be grappling — indeed, even leading the discussion, as a country committed to and long engaged in multilateral diplomacy, the UN, and peacekeeping. Unfortunately, up to now, Canada has practically taken a back seat in this debate.

This brainstorming is urgently needed because of the rising expectations that the Canadian armed forces will face with respect to a variety of new tasks for which they are unprepared psychologically, materially, or in terms of training. Peacekeeping is far from being a new task, but its evolving nature will require considerable reorientation on the part of Canada's military, especially if it, rather than European defence, becomes the principal objective of Canada's land forces.[56]

The defence policy changes announced by National Defence Minister Marcel Masse in September reflected some awareness of the kinds of adjustment needed, although there were no dramatic alterations. The Minister postulated the need for a flexible, versatile, mobile force, providing the following strategic analysis as the rationale:

> Within a few short years, we have moved from a straightforward scenario of East-West confrontation to an ill-defined, relatively uncertain situation with respect to possible threats to security and world peace.
>
> In this strategic perspective, any military disengagement must be coupled with a new requirement for flexibility and effectiveness. . . . We believe, as do our Allies, that vigilance is still necessary, given the potential for conflict throughout the world. Thus, for example, as Moscow loosens its grip on its former satellites . . . there is a resurgence of old rivalries which . . . present serious dangers to the stability of that region.
>
> Similarly, there has been no decline in the number and the intensity of conflicts in the rest of the world, as the events in the Persian Gulf reminded us.[57]

Yet if there was an acknowledgement of the changed strategic realities, the resulting reorientation remained modest and almost grudging. It seemed to be a policy that reflected the country's meagre purse and diminished aspirations (which the recession and the constitutional morass merely served to confirm) rather than any comprehensive strategic insight. It was not quite drift, but neither was it decisive.

Nor, for that matter, will it be definitive. The changes in the post-Cold War environment are coming too fast for that. What does seem clear, however, is that the demand for peacekeeping is not about to disappear. Moreover, there could be a nice merging of interests here because, as the Canadian presence in Europe inevitably recedes with the removal of the Soviet threat, Canada will be seeking new opportunities to play a part and to have some influence on the world stage. Canada's expertise in peacekeeping and its commitment to a reformed and more effective United Nations are obviously instruments to be used. David Dewitt has argued forcefully:

> the traditional residual out-of-area commitment must now become the mainstay of our contribution to international peace and security. . . . While the Cold War may have made peacekeeping necessary, the decline of the Cold War in the absence of effective collective security makes it inevitable.[58]

Precisely because, for the foreseeable future, much of the world will remain beyond order and control, Canada should work assiduously to build a strong and dynamic United Nations, one that is capable of maintaining peace and security in all the regions of the world. That will require far more than the UN's present mechanisms or resources permit. If ever Canada had a calling, and an interest, this is the time to give expression to both of them.

Notes

1 Susan Delacourt, "MPs strike right note, pollsters Say," *The Globe and Mail*, January 17, 1991.
2 Hugh Winsor, "Canada sends 6 more jets to join task group in gulf," *The Globe and Mail*, January 12, 1991.
3 House of Commons, *Minutes of Proceedings and Evidence of the Standing Committee on External Affairs and International Trade*, Ottawa, January 21, 1991, p. 79:7.
4 Ross Howard, "Liberals plagued by split over gulf war," *The Globe and Mail*, January 23, 1991.
5 The five commissioners in the "Citizen's Inquiry" were Doug Roche, a former Conservative MP and disarmament ambassador; Iona Campagnolo, a former Liberal cabinet minister and party president; Johanna den Hertog, former president of the New Democratic Party; Jules Dufour, a Quebec geography professor and environmentalist; and Konrad Sioui, vice-chief of the Assembly of First Nations for the Quebec region. See Carol Goar, "Peace movement goes on the offensive," *The Toronto Star*, September 12, 1991. For other articles on the peace movement during the Gulf War and their links with the "Citizen's Inquiry," see also Linda Hossie and Robert MacLeod, "Peace groups growing quickly," *The Globe and Mail*, January 10, 1991; Joseph Hall, "Where are the campus protests," *The Toronto Star*, February 4, 1991; Joseph Hall, "Peace groups plan post-war strategies," *The Toronto Star*, February 15, 1991; Joseph Hall, "Peace groups unite in effort to halt war," *The Toronto Star*, February 18, 1991; and Tim Harper, "Peace group feels snubbed by Ottawa," *The Toronto Star*, February 19, 1991.
6 United Nations Association in Canada, "This is not a 'UN War,'" Press Release, February 4, 1991.
7 Chris Young, "Mulroney, Clark step into political minefield," *The Gazette*, Montreal, February 8, 1991.
8 "Canada and the Challenges of the Post-War Period in the Gulf," Notes for a Speech by the Secretary of State for External Affairs, Quebec City, February 8, 1991, #91/10.
9 Minutes of Proceedings and Evidence of the Standing Committee on External Affairs and International Trade, February 13, 1991, p. 90:22.
10 Before the House of Commons Defence Committee on March 20, Clark admitted that U.S. officials had reservations about the Canadian proposal for a world summit and described the reactions of other major powers on the UN Security Council as "sceptical."
11 John Hay, "Canada falls short on originality in Middle East peace proposals," *The Ottawa Citizen*, February 13, 1991.

12 Paul Koring, "Canada ready to oversee pullout," *The Globe and Mail*, February 19, 1991.

13 Jeffrey Laurenti, "The United Nations After the War: New Precedents and Possibilities," an address to the International Studies Association, Vancouver, March 20, 1991, p. 3.

14 Laurenti, p. 6.

15 Bernard Wood, *World Order and Double Standards: Peace and Security 1990–91* (Ottawa: Canadian Institute for International Peace and Security), p. 14.

16 Clark had quoted him before the House External Affairs Committee. See House of Commons, Minutes of Proceedings and Evidence of the Standing Committee on External Affairs and International Trade, Ottawa, January 21, 1991, p. 79:33.

17 *House of Commons Debates*, March 15, 1991, p. 18537.

18 The critics included Dalton Camp, "Canada must face the aftermath of the war," *The Toronto Star*, February 27, 1991. See also James Mennie, "Can warrior Canada be peacemaker again?" *The Gazette*, Montreal, March 2, 1991; Minutes of Proceedings and Evidence of the Standing Committee on External Affairs and International Trade, House of Commons, January 21, 1991, pp. 79:25–6; February 21, 1991, pp. 97:15ff.

19 Gwynne Dyer, "Sovereignty ebbs as Kurds go on dying," *The Gazette*, Montreal, May 2, 1991.

20 Dyer.

21 Government of Canada, "Canada contributes Largest Peacekeeping Force since 1974 to UN Operations in the Western Sahara," *News Release No. 163*, July 18, 1991; "Canadian-led contingent declares ceasefire in Western Sahara," *The Gazette*, Montreal, September 7, 1991.

22 Government of Canada, "Canada joins Angola Peacekeeping Mission," *News Release No. 146*, June 21, 1991.

23 Department of External Affairs and International Trade, "Canada signs Cambodia Peace Agreements," *News Release No. 237*, October 23, 1991.

24 John Cruickshank, "The UN's next job: mission in a minefield," *The Globe and Mail*, October 25, 1991.

25 Gérard Hervouet, "Rebirth of the Cambodian Nation," *Peace & Security* (Winter 1991/92): 15.

26 Dyer.

27 Elaine Sciolino, "The dauntingly expensive task of imposing arms control," *The New York Times*, April 28, 1991.

28 Among them were John Hay in *The Ottawa Citizen* of April 19, 1991 who wrote that the UN should "interfere decisively [in protracted conflict situations] — with force if necessary, and food." Also note Lloyd Axworthy, "Perfect chance to repair the UN Charter," *The Globe and Mail*, August 14, 1991; *The Economist*, "A New World Order," September 28, 1991.

29 Notes for a speech by the Hon. Jean Chrétien, Leader of the Liberal Party of Canada, "Pursuing a Vision: Canadian Foreign Policy and the New Internationalism," George Ignatieff Theatre, Trinity College, Toronto, June 14, 1991, p. 5.

30 Office of the Prime Minister, Notes for an Address by the Prime Minister on the occasion of the Centennial Anniversary Convocation, Stanford University, California, September 29, 1991, p. 6.

31 "Toward a new United Nations," *The Globe and Mail*, March 25 and 26, 1991.

32 Brian Urquhart and Erskine Childers, "A World in Need of Leadership: Tomorrow's United Nations," *Development Dialogue*, 1990: 1–2.

33 Allan Gotlieb, "Join the club and share the load," *The Globe and Mail*, April 1, 1991.

34 Lloyd Axworthy, "Perfect chance to repair the UN Charter," *The Globe and Mail*, August 14, 1991.

35 *House of Commons Debates*, May 22, 1991, p. 3.

36 CIIPS, Working Paper 36, October 1991, p. 8.

37 London Economic Summit 1991, "Strengthening the International Order," Political Declaration, p. 2.

38 *House of Commons Debates*, September 19, 1991, p. 2430.

39 "What Kind of World and Whose Order?" *Peace & Security* (Spring 1991): 4.

40 Bernard Wood, "From the Director," *Peace & Security* (Winter 1991/92): 16. Wood also noted, "As we grope our way toward some kind of new world order, it is now vital to get a better handle on the use of sanctions as an instrument of pressure short of military force."

41 Brian Urquhart, "Learning from the Gulf," *The New York Review of Books*, March 7, 1991, p. 34.

42 Bruce Russett and James S. Sutterlin, "The U.N. in a New World Order," *Foreign Affairs*, Spring 1991: 78.

43 Paul Lewis, "UN plan would limit U.S. power to control body's top jobs," *International Herald Tribune*, September 18, 1991; Jeff Sallot, "Ottawa supports streamlining plan for UN," *The Globe and Mail*, September 20, 1991.

44 Notes for a Statement by the Secretary of State for External Affairs to the 46th Session of the United Nations General Assembly, September 25, 1991, 91/43, pp. 3–4.

45 Graham Fraser, "Mulroney at the UN? Plausible, but unlikely," *The Globe and Mail*, October 19, 1991; "Mulroney added to list of names in line for UN post," *The Globe and Mail*, October 22, 1991; Alan Toulin, "Is Mulroney's next step likely to be UN?" *The Financial Post*, October 23, 1991; Carol Goar, "To rest of world, Mulroney's résumé isn't bad," *The Toronto Star*, October 24, 1991; Jeffrey Simpson, "If he really isn't interested, he can still 'give a Sherman'," *The Globe and Mail*, October 25, 1991; Jeff Sallot and Graham Fraser, "Mulroney pulls plug on UN race," *The Globe and Mail*, October 29, 1991.

46 Rosemary Speirs, "UN flirtation put party in peril PM was warned by Tory brass," *The Toronto Star*, October 29, 1991.

47 External Affairs, *News Release No. 189*, September 5, 1991. The government had earlier agreed, on September 5, that Canada would contribute up to 15 representatives to a 150-person mission to monitor the implementation of the most recently negotiated ceasefire by the EC.

48 "Mulroney, Hurd disagree on UN move," *The Globe and Mail*, September 21, 1991 and Jocelyn Coulon, "Mission impossible pour l'ONU," *Le Devoir*, September 16, 1991.

49 *House of Commons Debates*, October 28 and November 1, 1991, pp. 4102, 4370.

50 Paul Koring, "Sanctions imposed on Yugoslavia," *The Globe and Mail*, November 9, 1991.

51 *House of Commons Debates*, October 2, 1991, p. 3138.

52 *House of Commons Debates*, October 8, 1991, p. 3464.

53 "A Statement on the Situation in Haiti to the United Nations General Assembly by the Secretary of State for External Affairs," 91/48, October 11, 1991.

54 *House of Commons Debates*, November 4, 1991, pp. 4465–69.

55 Brian Urquhart, "Who can stop civil wars?" *The New York Times*, December 29, 1991.

56 David B. Dewitt, "Canadian Defence Policy: Regional Conflicts, Peacekeeping, and Stability Operations," Canadian Defence Quarterly, August 1991; Geoffrey Pearson, interview on CTV's *Sunday Report*, November 3, 1991.

57 Department of National Defence, Statement by the Minister, September 17, 1991, pp. 1–2.

58 Dewitt.

7

Canada, GATT, and the Future of The World Trading System

Gilbert R. Winham

The foundation of Canada's foreign economic policy is the General Agreement on Tariffs and Trade (GATT). Even though Canada has negotiated a bilateral trade agreement with its large neighbour, and is further contemplating the extension of that bilateral agreement to include Mexico, these initiatives have nevertheless been taken within the framework of the GATT. Since 1947, the GATT framework has been a solid foundation for the conduct of trade and trade policy. Whether this foundation will retain its strength depends in part on the outcome of the current GATT negotiation, the Uruguay Round.

The Uruguay Round represents a critical juncture in the evolution of the GATT as a governing regime. The GATT has made progress largely through multilateral negotiation, and negotiation serves a function akin to legislation in a domestic system. At this writing, at year's end 1991, the Uruguay Round continues to be in trouble and the risk of failure remains high. The Uruguay Round has not recovered from the breakdown of the Brussels Ministerial Meeting approximately one year ago, and negotiators are still trying to craft deals on the major issues that would pave the way for a general agreement in all areas of the negotiation.[1]

Were the Uruguay Round to fail, it is not likely (although it cannot be ruled out) that the GATT itself would go down with it. The real question is whether international trade rules will keep pace with the increasing globalization of national economies. Without the Uruguay Round, the future trade system will be less certain, less liberal, less stable, and therefore, more prone to serious disturbances. Given Canada's reliance on international trade, any serious setback to the international trade system would threaten important Canadian national interests.

Progress Report on the Uruguay Round

The United States and the European Community (EC)

The Uruguay Round has been in serious difficulty since the Brussels Ministerial meeting in December, 1990. That meeting broke down over agriculture, and largely as a result of the inadequate offer by the EC.

In retrospect, it was no surprise the EC offer would be inadequate, but what was disturbing is that there was no plan put in place to gradually improve the offer. Few thought the Brussels meeting would succeed, but what many thought was achievable was the provision of political guidance by governments to move the negotiation forward. This did not occur. Instead, what did occur dealt more with process than substance: it was a negotiation over blame, with all that includes in the way of subterfuge, innuendo and aspersions directed at personalities. The whole affair was uncharacteristic of GATT negotiations.

What was lost from sight at Brussels was that there were many other issues besides agriculture that were dealbreakers; that is, serious enough to prevent a general agreement. In services, for example, negotiators had drafted a code of conduct, but there were very few market access offers attached to the code, which led the United States to make a startling withdrawal of its offer of most favoured nation (MFN) treatment in services shortly before the Brussels meeting was to begin. In subsidies, negotiators had before them a chairman's text that was flatly unacceptable to the U.S. Congress. There was no draft at all on anti-dumping practices. In the areas of intellectual property and dispute settlement, U.S. negotiators were working in the knowledge that their private sector strongly opposed dropping unilateral measures, and this was sufficient to stall progress in those areas.

Given these obstacles to negotiation, which lay largely on the U.S. side, it was fortunate for the Americans that the Brussels meeting remained fixated on the lack of progress in agriculture. Had issues like services or intellectual property been more prominent, it is probable that blame for the failure at Brussels would have been more evenly distributed between the United States and EC. As it was, the negotiation remained focused on agriculture and the Americans won a total public relations victory. However, such unilateral victories in negotiation often carry a future cost in the form of reduced trust and co-operativeness.

In Brussels and afterwards it has become clear how much the United States and the EC dominate the Uruguay Round. For example, intellectual property has unexpectedly become a problematic issue for the United States, and consequently for the overall negotiation. One reason is that the private sector has insisted on the retention of U.S. unilateralism (especially Section 337) in intellectual property, even though the United States has lost in a GATT panel seized with the application of this legislation.[2] Even more important, however, the intellectual property issue was conceived as a demand made by the United States on developing countries, in an effort to bring their protection for copyright and patents up to Western standards. In the negotiation of this issue, developed countries (principally the EC and Japan) have sought to harmonize national laws on intellectual property, which has resulted in a series of demands for changes to U.S. legislation. This surprising development has changed the intellectual property negotiation from a North-South to a North-North confrontation, and has put the United States decidedly on the defensive. The reaction of U.S. trade negotiators and congressional staffers alike to this development can be summed up in the phrase: "we didn't get into the intellectual property negotiation to change our own laws."[3]

Developing Countries

Despite the fact that events of the past year have demonstrated the importance of the United States and the EC, the developing countries have been more assertive in the Uruguay Round than in past negotiations, and this has added the complication of more voices at the bargaining table. An indicator of the impact of developing countries on the Uruguay Round has been the extent to which their demands have influenced the progress of the negotiation. For example, from the beginning of the negotiation to the Montreal Mid-Term Review in December, 1988, Brazil and India led a coalition of developing countries which opposed the introduction of new issues such as services, into the Uruguay Round agenda. As a result, developed countries became thoroughly sensitized to developing country concerns. An even more vivid example of developing country influence was an action by five Latin American countries. They withheld consensus on the overall package negotiated at the Mid-Term Review, in response to the inability of the United States and the EC to agree on agriculture. This action would have been unthinkable in previous GATT negotiations. It demonstrates that developing countries are now unwilling to allow the GATT agenda to move forward if their own vital interests are not served in the process.

One interesting phenomenon has been the change in the positions of many developing countries since the start of the Uruguay Round. Developing countries entered the Round fearful of negotiating on services and intellectual property with the developed countries. By the time of the Brussels Meeting their position had changed, and they were prepared to negotiate these issues as part of a global package. Consequently, they will probably be the biggest losers if the Uruguay Round fails. What caused this sea change in the position of the developing world? One reason undoubtedly is that they recognized the need for a trade-off that would encourage the developed countries to liberalize trade in agriculture and textiles. A second reason is that several leading developing countries (like Brazil) have been targets of Section 301 actions by the United States, and they saw an agreement on dispute settlement and perhaps intellectual property as a means of avoiding such actions in the future.

There is an additional reason: in the late 1980s the developing countries were becoming subject to the same pressures as developed countries to attract foreign investment and to promote exports as a means of boosting domestic economic performance. For example, these pressures led India, with its large autarkic (or protected) internal market, to conduct a fundamental reassessment of its position in world trade and to drop much of its ideological opposition to services and intellectual property in the Uruguay Round. Similarly, Brazil is independently writing a new code on intellectual property in an effort to avoid the technological obsolescence that the absence of such legislation tends to perpetuate.

Agriculture and Services

By all accounts agriculture is the linchpin of the Uruguay Round. If this issue is settled, most feel the Uruguay Round can be concluded; if not, the Round is doomed. It often occurs in large-scale negotiations that attention becomes focused on a single "crunch" issue, but there is no one answer to explain why this has happened with agriculture. The cause seems to be some combination of the economic importance of agricultural exports, the political symbolism of agricultural protectionism in the large and wealthy European Community, and finally the historical continuity of agriculture as a trade problem. It should be recalled that agricultural protectionism was a major issue in the Kennedy and Tokyo Round negotiations, and that the Tokyo Round nearly collapsed over that issue, only to be salvaged by a decision of the United States and others to accept a resolution of the matter which was largely symbolic.

How has agriculture developed into such a difficult problem in GATT negotiations?[4] The reason is that agriculture is a difficult problem domestically in trading nations, and these domestic problems are simply projected onto the GATT agenda. In all countries, agricultural incomes have fallen relative to manufacturing incomes throughout the post-war period, which has caused a general exodus of population from rural to urban areas. The fact is that, due to mechanized farming, the world needs fewer farmers now than it did a generation ago. Concurrently with its economic decline, agriculture has been viewed increasingly as a social problem involving the depopulation of rural areas, while at the same time agricultural producers have been an important political force in democratic politics everywhere. In consequence, all Western nations, including the United States, have regulated agricultural production internally and have maintained protectionist regimes externally.

When the European Common Market was created in 1958, it was recognized that agriculture would be the principal test for the success or failure of European integration. The European response was to establish the Common Agricultural Policy (CAP) in 1962, which integrated agricultural policies of member countries within a highly protectionist system of internal price supports and external subsidies. Over the years the CAP cut deeply into export markets of more efficient agricultural producers, and it particularly clashed with the growing reliance of nations like the United States and Canada on agricultural exports. The EC was thus on a collision course with North America over agricultural trade, and in the past decade efficient Third World agricultural exporters, such as Argentina, have joined the ranks of countries demanding changes in the CAP.

The long-standing dispute over agriculture finally reached a climax in the Uruguay Round. The lead was taken by the Cairns Group and the United States, which jointly pressed the EC for liberalization in three areas: domestic assistance (i.e., production subsidies), market access (i.e., import barriers), and export subsidies. The initial demands of the United States were to cut production subsidies and import barriers by 75 percent and export subsidies by 90 percent over ten years. These demands were extreme, and arguably would not have been politically acceptable within the United States itself. The EC responded with an offer of a global cut of 30 percent but without specifying the action to be taken on subsidies, particularly export subsidies, which have the most negative impact on the exports of more efficient producers. At the Brussels Ministerial Meeting, a compromise was put forward by Swedish Foreign Minister Mats Hellstrom that would have required 30 percent cuts in the three areas over five years. However, it would have made the cuts from contemporary levels rather from 1986 as the EC proposed, thereby denying the EC the benefit of unilateral reductions it has already made. The Hellstrom paper failed to produce consensus in Brussels, but remained the point of departure in the negotiations following the Brussels Meeting.

The negotiations on this proposal focused on structure, such as the initial date for beginning reductions, and the length of the phase-in period. However, there never was a serious negotiation over details, nor were precise numbers ever attached to actions dealing with specific products. The reason is that even the Hellstrom proposal went much further than the EC negotiators were prepared to consider in the Fall of 1990. The Brussels Meeting demonstrated that even though further compromise was necessary for the agricultural exporters, there was still a need for major reform of agricultural policy in the EC before further progress could be made at the Uruguay Round.

Since Brussels, several events have occurred that have substantially improved the prospect for an agreement on agriculture. First, in various speeches early in 1991, EC Commissioner for Agriculture Ray McSharrie openly criticized the EC's Common Agriculture Policy, on the grounds that it had advantaged only rich farmers and had utterly failed small-scale European agriculture. This undercut the legitimacy of the CAP, and accelerated the reform that was already underway in the EC.

Second, further movement came from the German government, which indicated, in October 1991, it would ease its support for the EC position in agriculture.[5] This was a substantial change from the German position during the Brussels Meeting, and it left the French — as the major supporters of the CAP — in a more isolated position in the EC. The German action increased the probability that a changed position by the United States would actually lead to a meaningful negotiation on agriculture.

Finally, in a meeting between EC President Jacques Delors and U.S. President George Bush, the United States did communicate a changed position with the announcement that it would accept a cut in export subsidies of about 30 percent over five years or 35 percent over six years.[6] By everyone's account, these figures brought the negotiating differences between the two sides into a reasonable range and made agreement possible.[7]

It is unclear at this writing, in January, 1992, what the outcome will be on agriculture. However, it is clear that many GATT Contracting Parties have reached the limit of their capacity to tolerate non-conforming behaviour from the EC on agriculture. The position of a number of influential nations is that liberalization of agriculture is more important than avoiding an enormous setback in the Uruguay Round. The economic history and the contemporary coalition politics of this issue dictate that the onus for resolution of the impasse must fall on the Europeans.

On services, it is the other power — i.e., the United States — that is under widespread pressure to change its position. The services negotiation, which appeared to be one of the success stories of the Uruguay Round in 1990, encountered serious difficulties prior to the Brussels Meeting when the United States announced it could not accept the concept of non-discrimination in a services agreement. This tactic shook the United States' trading partners, and suddenly elevated the services negotiation into a deal-breaking polemic, particularly between the developed countries.

The principle of non-discrimination means that if a service sector is to be liberalized, it must be liberalized for *all* nations. This would mean that if the United States liberalized a particular sector such as telecommunications, all GATT contracting parties could take advantage of this action. In the United States, telecommunications is largely privatized, and therefore foreign private firms would be able to locate in that country and provide services. However, in many nations (such as France), telecommunications are, by law, controlled by a state monopoly, and access to foreign firms is prohibited. It is perfectly legal under GATT to retain state monopolies, but the effect of state monopolies on a services agreement is that it denies to parties in that agreement equal access to each other's market.[8] The position of the United States is that it cannot offer non-discriminatory (i.e., MFN) concessions if the result is an imbalance of market access opportunities. However, to discriminate between nations in a services agreement would violate the most fundamental principle of the GATT; moreover, it would simply authorize the United States to withhold benefits from some selected countries and to seek special arrangements on a bilateral basis.

Given that the United States has often engaged in bilateralism in dealing with smaller and weaker countries, the concern for non-discrimination in services is both a symbolic and a practical political issue.

The issue of services seems to be at the stage of diplomatic negotiation, in contrast to agriculture, where fundamental political decisions still remain to be taken. In services the approach has been to negotiate a general code of conduct, and then to conclude specific (or "access") agreements in various sectors intended to spell out the actual access granted by various parties to one another's markets. Such access agreements are a practical way around the non-discrimination problem faced by the United States, but negotiating these agreements is both tedious and time-consuming. In addition, there are other problems such as "cross compensation," which means the capacity of parties to receive compensation — or to retaliate — in non-service sectors for benefits received or denied in services. This issue boils down to whether services can be traded off for goods, and it is a serious stumbling block in negotiations between developed countries and developing countries. Despite the difficulty of this and the non-discrimination issue, it is expected that these problems are surmountable if negotiators have enough time to craft the web of access agreements that had already reached an advanced phase by mid-1991.

Future of the GATT

New Issues

The issues in the Uruguay Round will continue to occupy the GATT, whether they are part of a negotiated Uruguay Round settlement or not. However, a number of new issues are now crowding on to the agenda. These will have to be dealt with, either in multilateral negotiations or in more piecemeal politicking either inside or outside the GATT. These issues include the relationship of trade to environmental regulations, competition rules, immigration and security.[9]

The interface of trade with other seemingly unrelated issues (such as environment) is an indicator that the world is becoming more of a single society instead of just a group of separate and anarchic societies. The cross impact of one issue area on another is commonplace in domestic politics, and national leaders routinely face questions of whether to support budget allocations for defence versus education, or to promote a reduction of environmental pollution at the expense of employment. However, national leaders who make international economic policy usually do not face as many issue conflicts in international relations as they have to handle internally, owing largely to the fact that the international system is less complicated than domestic systems. Until fairly recently, the international system has been the stage for relatively frequent relations between the citizens of one country and those of others; now it is the main locus of economic activity for many people, and business and political affairs routinely spill over national boundaries to affect citizens in other countries. As a result, national leaders are increasingly confronting policy choices in the conduct of international policy (including trade policy), and they need to resolve priorities in international politics much as they do in domestic politics.

Nowhere is this better seen than in the new issues facing the GATT, especially the environment. It is widely claimed that the environment will be a major issue in GATT in the 1990s, and it has already become one in regional trade negotiations like those preceding the FTA and especially the current NAFTA meetings. Environment and trade tend to interact at two levels: political and legal. At the political level, the environment has been forced on to negotiating agendas by constituents who fear trade agreements will increase environmental abuse by expanding trade and economic activity. This phenomenon first appeared in the Canada–U.S. FTA negotiations, where the environment was a highly charged issue that produced more heat than light in the Canadian "free trade election" of 1988. In the North American Free Trade Agreement (NAFTA) negotiation, the concern is more focused and deals especially with the alleged lower environmental standards in Mexico and the attraction such standards create for U.S. businesses seeking to avoid the cost of environmental regulation. The environment has not been discussed in the Uruguay Round negotiation; it has however, been dealt with recently in the GATT Council, and this body reactivated a long standing but moribund committee charged with handling this issue. It seems clear that the environment will appear prominently on the agenda of future GATT multilateral trade negotiations.

A concrete example of the conflict between trade and environment is the trade dispute between Mexico and the United States over tuna fish.[10] The dispute was occasioned by the U.S. Marine Mammals Protection Act (MMPA) which regulates the harvesting of tuna in U.S. waters. The MMPA requires that fishermen catch tuna in a manner that avoids killing dolphins, which often swim in the vicinity of tuna. The MMPA also imposes a ban on imports of tuna from other countries which use fishing methods that result in a higher incidence of dolphin-kill than American methods do. Further to the restriction on imports, the MMPA provides that the United States may ban imports of tuna products from other countries that have originally bought their tuna from an offending country; and the Act also states that the ban on tuna imports can be extended to all fish products if, presumably, the offending country does not change its practices.

In sum, the United States established an environmental regulation for U.S. fishermen, which was extended more or less equally to foreign fishermen who sought to sell in the U.S. market. The United States assumed the regulation was consistent with the GATT, on the grounds that — under Article III — it accorded "treatment no less favourable" to foreign products than it laid down for U.S. products.

Not surprisingly, the Mexicans saw the situation differently. Instead of focusing on Article III, the Mexicans rested their case on the prohibition against trade restrictions (other than tariffs) found in Article XI.[11] This constituted a strong case, because the language of Article XI is strong and unequivocal. The conflict between Articles III (national treatment) and XI (quantitative restrictions) over tuna was a striking replay of an earlier case between the United States and Canada over lobsters.[12] The lobster case involved a U.S. prohibition against the sale of "short" lobsters, which was then extended to the importation of short lobsters from Canada. Canada took the position that the import ban on short lobsters was an illegal restraint under Article XI, while the United States saw the ban as an Article III requirement fairly applied to nations and foreigners alike. The United States won the case, but the panel was badly split, allegedly along national lines, and hence it is a poor precedent for future law. What is clear from these cases is that the inherent conflict between Articles III and XI will be the terrain for future battles over trade versus environment within the GATT framework.

The tuna panelists decided in Mexico's favour. They took the position that the ban on imports was a trade restriction that violated Article XI, and could not be justified under the concept of national treatment. The panel was particularly alarmed at the extra-territorial application of U.S. law called for by the MMPA, and it argued that if other Contracting Parties were to follow the same course as the United States, then the GATT would be workable only among those countries that had identical internal regulations. The panel was sympathetic to the environmental objectives of the U.S. legislation, but they recommended those objectives be achieved through international co-operative arrangements. Since the United States and Mexico are currently negotiating the NAFTA, it is probable the tuna issue will be settled bilaterally in order not to jeopardize a broader agreement.

The GATT ruling on tuna shocked the environmental movement in the United States, and it even surprised more experienced GATT hands who felt it unlikely GATT rules would ever impair a contracting party's capacity to enact domestic environmental regulations. In the fallout from the tuna affair, several issues became clear. One is that GATT is likely to be seriously troubled in the 1990s by inconsistent national regulations, which will be a stimulus for negotiation but will also offer the greatest obstacle to negotiated agreements.

Second, there will be a need to separate serious environmental concerns on the one hand from a mixture of emotionalism and opportunistic protectionism on the other. For example, in the tuna case a cynic could argue that support for the MMPA was more an emotional response to the incidental killing of dolphins (inspired perhaps by the popular T.V. character "Flipper") than by a concern for the environmental impact of tuna fishing on dolphin populations, since those populations have risen rather than fallen over the last decade. In these circumstances, protectionist interests are usually quick to take advantage of opportunities presented by the political process.

Third, the conflict between environment and trade is likely to get worse as environmental regulations affect products with high trade flows. An example can be seen in the recycling regulations now being applied to paper and newsprint sales in the United States, which will deeply affect Canada's exports of a major trade item.[13] Canadians might object if the U.S. were to apply its recycling regulations to Canadian exports, but it seems unlikely that Canada would be able to get a "tuna-like" policy from the GATT to avoid U.S. regulations. As a result, Canada will likely have to comply with U.S. legislation, or at least attempt to negotiate an alternative arrangement.

The environmental issue points out the growing importance of the judicial process in contemporary international trade policy. GATT is a form of international regulation, but what often occurs today is a form of re-regulation: that is, the adaptation of existing regulatory rules of a regime to take account of new circumstances. The likely course that re-regulation takes is that problems get raised in the judicial process, and then they are moved into the negotiation process as nations seek general solutions to specific problems. All this tests the flexibility of the GATT, which up to this point has been a remarkably flexible structure.

Regionalism

One of the major uncertainties in the future international trade system is the relationship between the GATT and regional trade groups.[14] From the expansion of the European Community to the negotiation of NAFTA, the past decade has seen a series of initiatives to establish regional groups in the trading world. The regionalism that now confronts the GATT is not a new phenomenon. Following the establishment of the European Common Market and the European Free Trade Association, the 1960s saw a series of free trade areas set up in the developing world to promote economic development through trade liberalization. By the end of the 1960s these experiments had collapsed, and with few exceptions developing countries generally headed into a period of high protection and import substitution policies.

Regionalism received considerable impetus from the conclusion of the Canada–U.S. FTA, which is ironic, since neither government was particularly supportive of regionalism in principle. Canada by tradition was committed to multilateralism, while the United States — which historically had promoted the concept of non-discrimination — was a strong defender of the universalistic GATT system. The reason the FTA was concluded is that the agreement was in Canada's economic interests and in the political interest of the United States. Canada's international trade was already substantially bilateralized before the FTA was signed, and the agreement was needed to ensure that trade rules safeguarded Canadian access to the U.S. market. For the United States, which was under pressure, in the context of a stalled Uruguay Round, to demonstrate that trade liberalization could work, the FTA offered an opportunity to carry out a policy of achieving trade liberalization through bilateral agreements if it could not be achieved through multilateral agreements. When it was signed in 1988, the FTA appeared to be a unique and untroubling case of bilateralism. However, that uniqueness is now called into question by the NAFTA negotiation with Mexico, and the possibility that the addition of Latin American nations might eventually turn NAFTA into a hemispheric free trade area (see Chapters 9 and 10). The fact that the United States is involved with all these initiatives means that they inevitably will have an important impact on the GATT.

Prima facie, regional groups are a threat to the GATT because they compromise universality and the non-discriminatory treatment of traded products. While there is some debate about the seriousness of this threat, it is clear some analysts are unconcerned about it and are prepared to shift U.S. trade policy in the direction of a bilateral strategy. For example, U.S. Senator Max Baucus (Democrat, Montana) has called for increased bilateralism on the grounds that progress in GATT negotiations is too slow owing to the large number of interests that must be accommodated.[15] On the other hand, bilateralism creates more flexible fora and a faster negotiating process, with the result that success becomes possible and not an apparently unreachable target, as in the Uruguay Round.

Baucus argues the United States needs new bilateral rules for its relations with its closest trading partners, especially Japan and Mexico, and that it cannot afford to wait for the GATT to address these uniquely American relationships. His argument is realistic and even compelling, because he recognizes the importance of the international economy to America's economic future and he seeks to improve the capacity of the United States to trade openly and effectively in that world economy. It is the tools of trade policy Baucus is concerned with, and he feels the GATT is no longer the most effective tool for the United States.

Senator Baucus' views amount to a call for a fundamental shift in U.S. trade policy, and any such shift would constitute a serious threat to the GATT. The shift would be induced, not so much by Baucus' goals, which are reasonably consistent with liberal trading relations, but rather by the consequences of the policies he espouses. A bilateral strategy risks breaking up what has been an undifferentiated system of contractual obligations into several parts. It has been argued by proponents of bilateralism that there is a difference between liberal trading relations and non-discriminatory relations, and that an insistence on non-discrimination (i.e., the most-favoured-nation procedures of the GATT) in international trade can slow progress toward further liberalization that might be made on a piecemeal basis. This is undoubtedly true, but what is not taken into account is that preferential or discriminatory arrangements create a political structure wherein it is more difficult to pursue liberalism.

Preferential arrangements bring alliance considerations into trading relationships. Preferences and discrimination ultimately introduce into trade policy a search for pragmatic side deals and trade-offs, which often have detrimental consequences for trading partners not party to the deal. Preferential arrangements tend to break the association between free trade and internationalism, and it has been internationalist sentiments in the post-war periods that have been one of the attitudinal bulwarks behind free trade. Preferential or discriminatory relationships present a structural threat to the system of liberal international trade, and the probability is that one cannot threaten the structure of a system without threatening as well the values that help maintain it.

There are risks for the world trade system in a strategy of bilateralism, or even regionalism. However, despite those risks, the world seems to be going in that direction. Are there any positive aspects to this development? An advantage of the development of regionalism — apart from the greater ease of negotiations, noted by Baucus — is that it creates some intermediate organization and structure within the international economic system. The international economy is overwhelmingly vast, and the number of nations is correspondingly large. This system has become too large to be dealt with on an undifferentiated basis. It could be argued that there is a need to "decompose" the system in order to manage it effectively, and regionalism presents a kind of "parts-within-parts" decomposition that is recommended by analysts who have studied complex systems.[16] The key point is perhaps not so much whether regional trading blocks are formed but whether they are internationalist in philosophy and are consistent with GATT obligations. In this respect the Canada-U.S. FTA may serve as a model, for it was consciously negotiated within the GATT framework, and in some places such as the energy chapter it has simply incorporated GATT rules in order to promote Canada-U.S. trade liberalism. If future trade groupings — starting with NAFTA — have as benign an effect on the GATT as did the FTA, then it is possible that regional blocks might improve the conduct and management of multilateral negotiations, while at the same time providing a mechanism that could effectively address uniquely regional problems.

Conclusion

In the next twelve months, the main concern of the Canadian government and the business community will be the outcome of ongoing trade negotiations, namely, the Uruguay Round and the NAFTA negotiations with Mexico and the United States. The completion or non-completion of these negotiations will establish the framework for Canada's trade relations in the 1990s.

The Uruguay Round is particularly critical. If it is successful it will contribute generally to a more liberal trade and investment climate in the world economy. This will wholly benefit Canadian business, and indeed this fact has been recognized by that community in its support for the Round since the Brussels Ministerial Meeting in December, 1990. A successful Round will also bring pressure on Canada, especially in the agriculture sector. Canada's agricultural marketing boards, dealing with products such as dairy, poultry and eggs, are not consistent with the compromise proposals tabled by the GATT Director General in December, 1991, and if these proposals are eventually accepted Canada will probably have to bow to an international consensus.[17]

Arguably, the issue of marketing boards, or supply management, is more one of symbol than reality, at least in the short run. Supply management is partly maintained by a system of import quotas, and is defended by Canada as being permitted under GATT by the wording of Article XI, referring to the use of quantitative measures to protect domestic agricultural management programs. However, one point on which the United States and the European Community have been able to agree, is on the conversion of quantitative agricultural barriers to tariffs, and it is probable that other GATT nations will follow their lead. Tariffication has been strongly resisted by supply-managed agricultural groups in Canada, which see it, correctly, as the first step in the reduction of agricultural protectionism.[18] However, it is widely recognized that initial tariff rates will be set so as to afford the same protection as is now given, with the result that actual liberalization will be postponed well into the future, if indeed it occurs at all.

Another area where an Uruguay Round agreement would put pressure on Canada is intellectual property, but the government has taken the initiative in making changes that are probably inevitable, before any embarrassing showdown can occur with Canada's trading partners. The specific issue is the length of patent protection in the pharmaceutical industry. The norm for patent protection that has evolved in the Uruguay

Round is twenty years; this is currently applied in most industrialized countries and is rapidly being accepted by major developing countries as well. Canada, which has a strong generic drug industry, provided about three years less protection on average but, in January, 1992, moved to adopt a twenty-year period in order to ensure future international investment in the drug industry.[19] The intellectual property issue demonstrates the pressure an international consensus can bring on recalcitrant nations even in the absence of a formal agreement. A similar pattern occurred with respect to the UN treaty on the Law of the Sea.

Failure of the Uruguay Round would undoubtedly worsen the trade policy climate internationally, and this would not work to Canada's benefit as a trading nation. However, it is unlikely the Round will fail outright in 1992. Normally, deadlines in GATT negotiations have been set by the law extending negotiating authority to the U.S. Administration from Congress, and the deadline for that authority in current legislation is June 30, 1993. It seems improbable now that the Round could be concluded in 1992 because of the U.S. Presidential election, but it is equally improbable that parties will terminate the negotiation (and thereby risk blame) before the plausible deadline established by U.S. legislation. It is therefore likely that another "final" effort will be made to settle the Round in early 1993, if it has not been concluded before then.

Finally, with regard to NAFTA, it seems likely the politics of this negotiation will be more difficult than the economics. Trade links between Canada and Mexico are not strong, and therefore the economic benefits Canada has to gain from a NAFTA lie more in the future than the present. Consequently, it may be difficult to mobilize a winning coalition for a trilateral deal, and all the more so because the emotional issue of low-cost Mexican labour will energize opposition from Canadian labour and other parties that earlier opposed the Canada–U.S. Free Trade Agreement (FTA). A further complicating factor is timing. Signals from the U.S. government suggest the Administration will seek to avoid a Congressional fight over NAFTA implementation during the Presidential election, and this would effectively delay the conclusion of the negotiations until 1993. This timetable would in turn increase the pressure on the Mulroney government, which is obliged to hold an election by the fall of 1993. The NAFTA is not as central to Canadian interests as was the FTA, and if it becomes apparent that a fight over NAFTA would seriously damage electoral prospects, it is possible the government might abandon, or more probably defer, Canadian participation in any eventual agreement.

Notes

1 For a resume of the areas of the Uruguay Round negotiation, see Gilbert R. Winham, "GATT and the International Trade Regime," *International Journal*, Vol. XLV, No. 4 (Autumn 1990): 796–822.

2 *United States — Section 337 of the Tariff Act of 1930: Report of the Panel*, GATT doc. L/6439 of January 16, 1989.

3 Personal interview.

4 For general background, see Theodore H. Cohn, *The International Politics of Agricultural Trade* (Vancouver: University of British Columbia Press, 1990); and Grace Skogstad and Andrew Fenton Cooper, *Agricultural Trade: Domestic Pressures and International Tensions* (Halifax: Institute for Research on Public Policy, 1990).

5 "U.S.–EC Leaders Head into Full Week of 'Make-or- Break' Meetings on GATT Talks," *International Trade Reporter*, November 2, 1991, p. 1610.

6 William Dulforce and David Gardner, "Bush makes concession to unblock trade talks," *Financial Times*, November 11, 1991, p. 1.

7 A similar U.S. negotiating tactic was followed in the Tokyo Round, when newly appointed U.S. chief negotiator Robert Strauss substantially reduced U.S. agriculture demands on the EC and thereby unblocked the negotiation which had been stalled for about two years; see Gilbert R. Winham, *International Trade and Tokyo Round Negotiation*, (Princeton: Princeton University Press, 1986) pp. 164–67. As in the Tokyo Round, the characterization of the U.S. action differed between Europe and the United States, and U.S. organs such as *Inside U.S. Trade* and *International Trade Reporter* avoided the term "concession" which was used by William Dulforce of the *Financial Times* (see note 1).

8 Peter Montagnon, "A Review of the State of Play in the Uruguay Round Negotiations and Future Development in the GATT," Ditchley Conference Report No. D91/6 based on a conference held April 12–14, 1991, The Ditchley Foundation, 1991, p. 5.

9 See "Commission Analyzes Problems Posed in Post-Uruguay Round Period," *International Trade Reporter*, September 25, 1991, p. 1405.

10 See "GATT Tuna Ruling Spawns Environmentalist, Congressional Backlash," *Inside U.S. Trade*, Special Report, September 6, 1991.

11 GATT Article XI states: "No prohibitions or restrictions other than duties, taxes or other charges, whether made effective through quotas, import or export licenses or other measures, shall be instituted or maintained by any contracting party on the importation of any product. . . ."

12 *Lobsters from Canada*, Final Report of the Panel (USA 89-1807-01), May 25, 1990.

13 "Pulp and Paper Woes Mount," *The Globe and Mail*, September 4, 1991.

14 See generally Jeffrey J. Schott, *More Free Trade Areas?* (Washington: Institute for International Economics, 1989).

15 Senator Max Baucus, "A New Trade Strategy: The Case for Bilateral Agreements," *Cornell International Law Journal*, 22 (1989): 1–24. See

also in the same issue C. Michael Aho, "More Bilateral Trade Agreements Would Be a Blunder: What the New President Should Do," pp. 25–38.

16 Herbert A. Simon, "The Architecture of Complexity," in Simon, *The Sciences of the Artificial* (Cambridge, Mass.: MIT Press, 1969).

17 "Bush Praises Dunkel Draft Agreement in Effort to Restart GATT Negotiations," *International Trade Reporter*, January 8, 1992, p. 59.

18 Drew Fagan, "GATT proposal poses dilemma," *The Globe and Mail*, January 18, 1992.

19 Rod Mickleburgh, "Ottawa attacked over drug patent decision," *The Globe and Mail*, January 16, 1992.

8

Canada, the Environment and UNCED

Iain Wallace

The United Nations Conference on Environment and Development (UNCED), which convenes in Rio de Janeiro in June 1992, will disappoint most participants. (So don't expect to see the headline, "Earth Summit leaves delegates 'on top of the world'!") But that such sentiments are predictable is a measure of how ambitious is the scope of the conference agenda. Undoubtedly, there will be *some* tangible achievements and the promise of more concerted efforts to respond substantively to the most fundamental global crises of our generation — the threats arising from environmental degradation and the ongoing polarization of prosperity between North and South. In bringing the need to address the *integration* of these two issues squarely on to the mainstream agenda of international affairs, with a salience that is unlikely to be eroded in coming years, the conference will prove to have been, in its own right, a major contribution to human well-being.

The creation of UNCED, from the 1972 United Nations Conference on the Human Environment (UNCHE) in Stockholm, through the ("Brundtland") World Commission on the Environment and Development, is one which has been resolutely fostered, in typically understated fashion, by Canadians, particularly in the persons of Maurice Strong, Secretary-General of both UNCHE and UNCED, and Jim MacNeill, Secretary-General of the Brundtland Commission. But as governments begin to launch in earnest into the value conflicts and complex trade-offs that the UNCED agenda introduces, Canada is unlikely to emerge as a paragon. This has as much to do with our economic history and the politics of environmentalism as with the policies of the Mulroney government.

To say that the scope of UNCED is ambitious is an understatement! The conference agenda has twenty-one major headings (Table 8.1). Delegates will attempt to formulate action that:

- begins to counter the obvious signs of degradation of the global environmental commons (climate change, deforestation and loss of biodiversity, oceanic pollution), which are clearly the prime concerns of the western industrialized nations;

Table 8.1

United Nations Conference on Environment and Development

Agenda Items

Working Group I	**Working Group III**
Protection of the atmosphere	Legal issues
Land resources: forests	Institutions
Land resources: desertification	Earth Charter
Biodiversity	
Biotechnology	
Working Group II	**Plenary Issues**
Hazardous wastes	Financial resources
Solid wastes and sewage	Economic instruments
Toxic chemicals	Transfer of technology
Radioactive wastes	Poverty and population
Oceans	Environment and health
Freshwater	Human settlements

Source: Government of Canada, *United Nations Conference on Environment and Development (UNCED), Third Session of the Preparatory Committee, Geneva 14 August to 4 September 1991, Final Reports* (Ottawa, Environment Canada, 1991), p. 1.

- responds decisively to the barriers to economic development facing most developing nations (now including the members of the former Soviet bloc), which is clearly the priority of that constituency;
- creates institutions and allocates financial resources that will ensure that the two primary thrusts are integrated and implemented.

Not only does this agenda encapsulate clashes of core values such as economic growth versus environmental preservation, and reliance on markets versus reliance on government regulation, but it also involves major clashes of interest (a more liberal trade regime for Third World exports versus the primacy being given to internal market development within emergent northern hemisphere trading blocs, and the relative significance of implications of CO_2 emission reductions for such vastly different nations as Canada and China). Moreover, it calls for policies in fields where the intellectual basis for agreed action is far from settled (how serious *is* the threat of global warming? how *should* one implement national environmental accounting?). For these reasons alone, "success" in Rio will be measured more in *commitments* to policy changes by governments and multilateral agencies than in actions which will transform the world overnight.

In this chapter, we are concerned to define what Canada brings to UNCED and how our national interests may fare in the outcome. To do this involves tracing the rise of environmental issues within the domestic political scene; assessing the strengths and liabilities that a major producer of natural resource staples, such as Canada, carries into the international arena; reviewing the effectiveness of the Canadian response to the novel challenges of integrating economic and environmental goals; and setting these against the experience and priorities of other nations around the world. Of particular interest is the way in which non-governmental organizations (NGOs) and the media have worked both domestically and internationally to shape opinion and define agendas.

The Environment in Canada's Domestic Politics

As in other western nations, environmental issues began to generate increasing interest in Canada in the late 1960s, primarily on the basis of concerns about the health and ecological effects of chemicals, used agriculturally or visibly polluting the Great Lakes. In the early 1970s popularization of *The Limits to Growth* modelling, the first OPEC-induced oil price rise, rapid increases in grain and mineral prices, and international responses to a major Sahelian drought essentially coincided. Visions of impending resource scarcity and recognition of the global interdependencies involved in satisfying human demands on natural resources added new dimensions to the public's environmental awareness. Despite a preoccupation with bread and butter economic issues throughout the recession (in industrialized societies) and the debt crisis of the early 1980s (in most developing countries), the environment retained its high ranking in public concern, supported in Canada by growing evidence of the damage caused by acid rain and by increased questioning of the safety of nuclear power in the wake of the Three Mile Island emergency in Pennsylvania.

One accompaniment of the sustained economic growth of the latter 1980s was a massive increase in the membership and funding of Canadian environmental organizations, broadening their constituency and expanding the capability of their research to highlight the adverse consequences of the human use of the Earth. By now, evidence of global warming and of atmospheric ozone depletion, linked to images of tropical deforestation and warnings about excess sun exposure, had solidified popular awareness that environmental degradation was a global threat and not just a local one. The gazetteer of pollution horrors — Chernobyl, Bhopal, *Exxon Valdez*, Hagersville, St. Basile le Grand — became familiar to the vast majority of Canadians.[1]

The United Nations Stockholm Conference had provided a stimulus to most governments to at least create a department ostensibly responsive to environmental issues. The creation of Environment Canada, in 1971, was a response to these growing domestic and international concerns, but its initial function was to co-ordinate existing environmental monitoring and regulatory activities of the federal government: it was certainly not launched with a visionary mandate. Indeed, the hearings and subsequent best-selling report of the Berger Inquiry into the proposed Mackenzie Valley gas pipeline played a much greater role in getting many of the acute policy dilemmas raised by society's consumptive use of the Earth into the public arena and popular consciousness.[2] Attention through the 1970s and early 1980s to pollution problems such as Great Lakes water quality and acid rain tended to highlight the role of the Ontario government, as the regulatory authority of the Canadian sources of environmental damage, more than the federal role, despite the fact that both issues were clearly in the cross-border category. However, the resurgence of environmental quality as a principal concern of Canadians during the economic recovery of the mid-1980s, and its acceptance into the policy-making process of the main political parties, required that Environment Canada be given a higher and more active profile. This, of course, would represent a significant threat to 'business as usual', not only in the Canadian economy but also in the federal bureaucracy. Taking the integration of economic activity and environmental sustainability seriously was, and remains, a revolutionary change.

The delayed and problematic birth of Canada's *Green Plan* in December 1990 was a reflection of these novel challenges to the status quo. But it also reflected the difficulty that any government has in satisfying the single-minded commitment to improved environmental practice which has been adopted as an agenda by articulate and media-wise environmental interest groups, with considerable public support. Hence, despite real but quiet progress during the latter 1980s in bridging the gap in ideological outlook, and the mutual distrust between environmentalists and their business-sector antagonists, accomplished in fora such as the National Task Force on Environment and Economy and the national and provincial/territorial Round Tables which grew out of it,[3] the *Green Plan* was generally received coolly by both environmental NGOs (for whom it promised too little) and business interests (for whom it threatened too much). This domestic experience of the dynamics of trying to achieve consensus on a broadly-defined program of transition to a more sustainable path of development should caution against an unduly optimistic expectation that international progress towards achieving the same goal will be smoother or judged more favourably by the concerned public.

A Resource Staple Economy in a "Green" Era

If the spotlight in Rio is on the world's environment, Canada cannot help but be visible. Our country is the second largest on Earth, has the greatest reserves of fresh water, contains a major global forest resource, exports more non-fuel minerals than any other, is a major grain exporter, has commercial interests in three oceans, and consumes energy (on a per capita basis) more intensively than any other. Canadian ecosystems may not have the biotic richness of their tropical counterparts, but the sensitive balance of arctic ecozones calls for equally careful stewardship. Even if the Canadian contribution to aggregate global environmental degradation is relatively small, because there are only 26 million of us, the continuing resource-*in*tensity of the Canadian economy (compared to other industrialized western nations) and the *ex*tensive distribution of environmental modifications brought about by mining, forestry, agriculture, etc. make the shortcomings of the environmental stewardship of Canadians difficult to hide. Claims to "greenness" by governments or the nation's corporate and private citizens are vulnerable to the video camera. In an era when environmentalist organizations have learned the power of the visual image, the world's largest traditional staples producer offers plenty of inviting subjects for media exposés both at home and abroad where evasion is more difficult.

Domestic Performance

How well does Canada stand up to a probing of the consistency of its economic and environmental policies? Not marvellously. Let us first look at the federal government's current domestic priority, its constitutional proposals: *Shaping Canada's Future Together* includes a reference to "sustainable development" in the Canada clause. However, the proposed entrenchment of property rights has been widely regarded as hindering the enforcement of environmental protection regulations; and the proposed delegation of exclusive jurisdiction to the provinces in resource sectors such as forestry, has been identified as a potential impediment to the effective implementation, by Canada, of international agreements such as those that might emerge from UNCED, notably undertakings to curtail greenhouse gas emissions.[4] Ottawa's persistent adoption of a permissive approach to the conduct of environmental impact assessments of projects affecting its areas of jurisdiction, in preference to statutory requirements, has been found wanting by the Supreme Court. Challenges by environmental groups to the provincially promoted Rafferty-Alameda and Oldman dam projects (in Saskatchewan and Alberta respectively), which went ahead without a federal impact study, have resulted in clarifying the federal obligation to conduct what, in the words of Mr. Justice

Gerald La Forest, "is now generally regarded as an integral component of sound decision-making."[5]

The depressed state of the economy has already eclipsed the constitution and the environment as the number one priority of Canadians and their provincial premiers. Fiscal constraint and low international energy prices have done more than strong conviction about the environmental implications to prevent Ottawa from responding with job-creating commitments to new resource developments, although the Hibernia project continues. In the face of reduced demand and dramatic cost overruns at the Darlington plant, the provincial NDP government has called a halt, for the time being, to Ontario Hydro's expansion of nuclear generating capacity, despite the significant implications for employment in the provincial equipment supply industries.[6] But elsewhere, old-style resource-intensive growth has maintained its attractiveness. Quebec still sees its economic health as dependent on the further flooding of James Bay catchments; the local coal-burning generating station at Point Aconi, Nova Scotia was approved without benefit of environmental assessment; and Alcan and the federal government are embroiled in a court challenge by the Carrier-Sekani Tribal Council to the legality of a private 1987 agreement between Alcan, Ottawa and the B.C. government exempting expansion of the Kemano power plant from further impact studies.[7]

The real test of a government's belief in sustainable development is its willingness to review comprehensively the environmental implications of all its policies and not just selected programs or projects. The *Green Plan* made such a commitment, but no progress on this score was documented in the first annual report card.[8] Pressed to comment on the likelihood of the 1992 federal budget being so assessed, Environment Minister Jean Charest pleaded the absence of "models that I know of that Canada can borrow from."[9] Meanwhile, the Auditor General found no evidence that either the social or environmental impacts of recent substantial farm subsidies were being investigated. In other words, Canada still has a long way to go before the heady rhetoric of sustainability is given commensurate practical expression. There are genuine intellectual and practical obstacles that all nations face in coming to grips with the revolutionary implications of redirecting the familiar priorities and patterns of economic policy. Undoubtedly, many Canadian institutions have made considerable progress towards adopting more environmentally appropriate practices, but the hardest choices have yet to be made. And although this may be generally true of the rest of the world gathered at Rio, Canada does not stand out as forcing the pace of change; its stance has significant trade implications.

International Trade and Competitiveness

The commitment of the Mulroney government's trade and foreign policies to implementation of its proclaimed environmental agenda is currently quite ambiguous. Recent indications by External Affairs Minister Barbara McDougall, of the shape of Canadian trade policy in the 1990s suggest that neither the economic nor the philosophical thrusts of the *Green Plan* have really registered. By arguing for the need to "pay attention to adjustment costs and . . . avoid the risk of being undercut by environmentally irresponsible competitors,"[10] Ottawa unhelpfully sanctions a 'business as usual' mentality among Canadian firms, despite clear signals that buyers in major export markets, notably the United States and the European Community, are demanding much more rapid adjustment to the supply of what are perceived as "greener" products. The federal government still has to make up its mind whether competitiveness in the resource-based industries lies in using conventional technology on the cheap while limiting and delaying action on environmental damage, or in innovation of the kind recognized in the *Green Plan*, that captures new markets with more ecologically sensitive technologies. Fortunately, some of Canada's leading firms are already clear on which strategy offers the best prospects:[11] but those which are not are increasingly being forced into reactive, damage-limitation strategies that are liable to be overtaken by events.

Canadian resource processors are learning to come to terms with the turbulent business environment of the forest-based industries. The rising groundswell of attempts by government and industry to respond to changing public attitudes towards the environmental consequences of affluent consumption patterns, which has been intensified by the targeted campaigns of international environmentalist alliances, is rapidly reshaping markets for traditional products such as timber and pulp and paper in a manner which is unpredictable and, many (not just those with vested interests) would say, capricious. Shipments of B.C. lumber face well-publicized opposition in Europe, orchestrated to protest clearcutting practices.[12] Now that the chlorine-free production of bleached woodpulp has been demonstrated to be commercially feasible in Scandinavia (and by Howe Sound Pulp and Paper Ltd., B.C.), there are fears that Germany may ban chlorine-bleached paper products within a year or so, threatening $500 million in annual Canadian sales.[13] As a result of moves, first by U.S. metropolitan and state authorities, and more recently by Metropolitan Toronto, to cope with increasing solid-waste disposal problems by mandating a recycled newsprint content for papers sold in their jurisdictions, many Canadian newsprint producers have been scrambling belatedly to adjust their resource procurement practices and incorporate de-inking plants into their production systems.[14]

Such developments raise a number of important questions for Canada as a major resource exporter. There is the obvious issue of the degree to which restraints on trade that purport to be environmentally justified, constitute a new and intractable form of non-tariff barrier, and this is addressed below. For Canadian industries, does questioning the degree to which shifts in market preference are 'scientifically grounded' as opposed to 'emotional', represent a failure to grasp the contemporary cultural climate and its commercial implications? Many resource-based firms have an understandable reluctance to be forced into heavy expenditures on environmental upgrading which lack compelling scientific justification. But for a pulp and paper executive to complain, for instance, that "[t]he case against chlorine is not fair. It is a perfectly sound means of bleaching pulp[.]" is a refusal to acknowledge the decidedly ambiguous and contestable status of much environmental science.[15] It is a form of response, moreover, which presupposes that appeals to the court of public opinion (or buyer sentiment) reach a scientifically literate audience or one disposed to evaluate 'acceptable' pollution limits rather than to demand instinctively 'zero tolerance'. Finally, whatever its technical merits, it is a response which tends to stress the cost penalty of technological change rather than the potential for immediate cost savings which many 'green' technologies have already delivered.

The argument is heard that comparative advantage, based on natural resources, provides a rational "green" justification for maintaining Canada as one of the world's most energy-intensive economies, in per capita terms. It is pointed out that if such commodities as aluminum and nickel have a global commercial future, currently available technologies make it more environmentally benign to process them in Canada than in Europe or even in Australia. But to argue this way is to engage in a form of discourse for which there is little popular sympathy.[16] Environmentalists have the power to capture the high moral ground, and frequently they are entitled to do so, given the past practice of so many firms and governments, not least in Canada. But they are abetted by the media in ways that combine to eliminate reasoned discussion of the precise nature of environmental degradation and the possible remedies. This situation presents Canadian resource exporters and their governments with fundamentally novel challenges in defending their traditional trade interests.[17] At the same time, new market opportunities lie open for firms with the vision and the technologies to take advantage of them.

Canada–U.S. trade is already an arena in which environmental agendas are increasingly intertwined with commercial ones, although neither the Canada-United States Trade Agreement nor the current NAFTA negotiations significantly address this issue. Quebec Hydro's attempts to tie up long-term power suppply contracts with utilities in New York and New England are a clear example, and one which demonstrates the growing commercial impact of the public relations advantage enjoyed by opponents of various forms of environmental resource exploitation. The James Bay Cree campaign to defeat Quebec Hydro's Great Whale project has strategically focused on a receptive audience composed of U.S. environmental groups and the politicians whose interests are aligned with them, rather than on the cool, if not openly hostile, constituencies within Quebec itself.[18] The cross-border softwood conflict has been given an interesting twist by U.S. federal protection of spotted owl habitat in the forests of the Pacific Northwest. It is becoming increasingly clear that far from inflicting material damage on Northwest lumber interests, Canadian imports are satisfying market demand that a declining regional forest resource can no longer fulfil. Indeed, the latest flare-up of subsidy accusations against Canadian producers is essentially a stratagem arising from domestic battles between different northwestern and southeastern interests in the U.S. forest industry, and northwestern producers have openly proclaimed Canada's innocence.[19] Environmental damage caused by Mexican industry, particularly maquiladora manufacturing plants along the U.S. border, has been used (somewhat opportunistically no doubt) by its Congressional foes as a reason for opposing the North American Free Trade Agreement.[20] Given Ottawa's constrained choice regarding involvement in the deal, its evaluation of the environmental implications can hardly prove decisive.

At the multilateral level too, the environment and trade are converging rapidly as forces with a potential to create friction. The working group on this set of issues, which GATT established in 1971 but which had never met until very recently, will need to involve itself rapidly in the increasingly contested questions surrounding the role of environmental regulations as non-tariff barriers. These arise in the wake of the 1991 GATT ruling that a U.S. ban on Mexican tuna (because of the dolphin kill caused by the fishing nets) is in violation of international trade agreements.[21] There are particular fears by developing countries that their resource exports will be constrained by the imposition of northern standards of environmental management. But even among industrialized nations, trade frictions arising from differing environmental policy requirements are multiplying. The European Court backed Denmark against the European Commission over the Danish stipulation that all beer and soft drinks must be sold in returnable bottles, despite the advantage this gives to domestic producers.[22] Germany, where the political weight of the "green" movement is greatest, has introduced legislation calling for levels of packaging recycling by shippers (not end-users) that is described as being of "extraordinary ferocity."[23] But despite the headaches which compliance will create for all exporters to Germany, European Community regulations are likely to follow in the same direction: meanwhile, German attention is turning towards obligatory 'take back and recycle' requirements for auto and electrical goods manufacturers. Once again, firms that innovate to comply are likely to enhance their long-term competitiveness at the expense of those that put their energy into stalling such proposals.

When all is said and done, the European Community's agricultural subsidies reflect *in part* an explicit policy towards the rural environment — that it should be consistently tended by a population that is economically secure. That the mechanisms of the Common Agricultural Policy are frequently counterproductive, both socially and ecologically, and unnecessarily costly and trade-distorting, does not alter the fact that no such coherent vision of the future of rural resources, landscapes and communities exists in North America. Nor is it likely to emerge, for deeply rooted cultural reasons, despite the greening of public opinion. But if something close to the Dunkel proposals finally succeeds in wrapping up the GATT Uruguay Round, and Canadian supply management, particularly in the dairy sector, is consigned to a lingering death, we may expect to see significant changes in the rural environment, especially in Quebec and Eastern Ontario (and in adjacent parts of the United States), which will sharpen popular awareness of the policy vacuum.

Canada's Priorities at UNCED

In Rio the world community is going to be challenged to embark on changes that no individual state has yet come close to seeing through. It will be asked to move on from the phoney war that takes the form of tinkering with the relationship between the economy and the environment, and to come to grips with the real battles of making "development" truly "sustainable." The structure of UNCED provides for this commitment to take shape in the form of three outcomes. The first will be an "Earth Charter," a brief document (if Canada's preferences prevail) outlining a code of environmental ethics which will guide national and international affairs. The second will be "Agenda 21," a wide-ranging action plan whereby each state commits itself to domestic and multilateral measures to reshape economic life, so as to make it compatible with environmental sustainability. Finally, governments will sign specific international agreements to act on major environmental threats, notably global warming, deforestation and the loss of biodiversity. At least, that is the vision! In practice, achievement will fall far short of this: but there are grounds for hope that progress towards the insertion of substance into the rhetoric of "sustainable development" will nevertheless be measurable.

In keeping with Canada's role in getting the environment on to the G-7 agenda and its widespread reputation as being in the vanguard of global responses to environmental threats, one would expect to see Canadians playing an active and constructive role in Rio. So far, work at, and in advance of, the UNCED Preparatory Conferences has seen productive co-operation between the federal participants and the Canadian Participatory Committee (co-ordinating a wide range of NGOs involved with issues appearing on the UNCED agenda). Indeed, the substantial involvement of NGOs, representing both "business" and "environment" perspectives, in the global preparations for the Earth Summit (where they will make their presence felt in a parallel conference) is a distinctive feature of this UN gathering, and one that suggests that governments will not be allowed to place its agenda issues on the back burner once the conference is over. Already, CIDA funding has contributed to underwriting the costs of Third World NGOs participating in the Preparatory Conferences, and to facilitating the preparation of national environmental reports in various developing countries. IDRC, jointly with its Swedish counterpart, funded the work of the Commission on Developing Countries and Global Change, whose report, to be released in March 1992, highlights what is fundamentally at stake for Third World nations faced with the implications of global environmental change.

Without a doubt, UNCED's biggest challenge will be to bridge the North/South gap of interests and expectations, because, unless that can be achieved, substantive agreement on the agenda items will be hard to come by. The acid test of the commitment of Canada and the other industrialized countries to assist adjustment of the developing nations to the implications of current and prospective environmental degradation will be the amount and type of resources they are willing to put on the table in Rio. So far, other nations have been able to hide the actual extent of their support behind Washington's high-profile reluctance to promise cash or concessional access to technology for the purpose of promoting "green" development in the Third World; but when the crunch comes, the North's good faith is likely to be measured in precisely such terms.

How financial and technological assistance from the North should be delivered also needs careful attention. David Runnalls, Director of the Sustainable Development Program at the Institute for Research on Public Policy (IRPP), has outlined a number of multilateral strategies that would be consistent with Canada's interests.[24] Some, such as the redirection of a United Nations Trusteeship Council no longer concerned with a post-apartheid South Africa, giving it the role of guardianship of the Earth, would have to be part of the broader reconsideration of UN structures which is necessary in any case to cope with the new world order of the 1990s. Such a move would therefore take time to implement. A more immediate option would be to build on the very effective role that UNEP has played over the past twenty years by increasing its budget and mandate. But the genuine integration of global economic and environmental priorities will require action to give *sustainable* development strategies greater weight in the decision-making of the World Bank and IMF, and UNEP is an unlikely vehicle for that. Despite the 'greening' of the Bank, which has taken on substance through the U.S. $1.4 billion Global Environmental Facility fund (established in 1990) and is certain to become more apparent when the environmentally focused *World Development Report 1992* is published, the structural adjustment policies which it co-ordinates with the IMF have yet to reflect a real grasp of the environmental implications of the prescriptions issued by either agency.[25] CIDA's enthusiastic alignment of bilateral assistance in support of structural adjustment measures indicates how far the rhetoric surrounding its sustainable development policy pillar has been outrunning the reality,[26] although a more serious commitment to environmentally sensitive aid was promised by Monique Landry earlier this year.[27]

The part of the Rio agenda for which the basis of decision-making has been most fully prepared is the proposed Convention on Climate Change, although this too illustrates the difficulties and ambiguities which surround UNCED's purpose. The 1988 Toronto Conference on the Changing Atmosphere served as a catalyst to international responses to climate change and called for a 20 percent reduction in global CO_2 emissions by 2005. Subsequent work by the Intergovernmental Panel on Climate Change (IPCC) has produced a wide consensus among the scientific community on the need for action, and the drafting of a convention for discussion at Rio is under way. Canada, as part of the *Green Plan*, has made a commitment to stabilizing emissions at the 1990 level by 2000, but a number of European nations have gone further; and the IPCC has made it clear that 20 percent must be seen as a stepping stone to a much more drastic reduction if global warming is to be curtailed.[28]

Many parties have been encouraged by the precedent of the Vienna Convention on Protecting the Ozone Layer (1985), as a result of which a generalized framework of international agreement led quickly to the detailed provisions on phasing out CFCs in the Montreal protocol (1987) and to tightening of those provisions (combined with funding to support Third World compliance) in London two years later.[29] But the climate convention tackles a problem whose order of magnitude is more complex and divisive. To reach any substantive agreement it will be necessary for the North to allow for *increased* emissions by the South, as nations such as China and India continue their economic growth, *and* that it create mechanisms whereby energy-efficient technologies are made available to Southern countries. Moreover, not only are energy sector issues intimately bound up with progress on CO_2 reductions; so too are forestry issues. The reductionistic perspective, which treats forests essentially as carbon sinks in the context of implementing a climate change convention, is being countered by voices stressing the variety of values and uses that forests represent, both to their inhabitants and to the global community at large. Indeed, the coalescence of issues around tropical deforestation, preservation of biodiversity, and ownership of and access to biotechnologies has essentially killed the prospect of international agreement on either a forestry or a biodiversity convention being reached at UNCED.

The critical question about the expected climate change convention is, therefore, whether it will emerge as a loosely worded commitment to action or whether it will enshrine specific emission reduction targets in related protocols. The danger of the former is that governments will take the credit for progress, publics will assume that the problem is under control, and the momentum of support for material changes in global energy consumption patterns will be lost. The threat presented by the latter is that agreement on the necessary policy and resource commitments by governments in the North will prove elusive. It is not at all clear how Canada intends to meet *its* emission reduction goal, and the same is true of most other nations. The federal Management Plan for Nitrogen Oxide (NOx) and Volatile Organic Chemicals (VOCs), introduced after wide-ranging consultation with affected parties, is primarily aimed at improving air quality in Canada's metropolitan areas. No similar action on meeting the CO_2 reduction targets is yet evident.

Conclusion

Over the past twenty years, governments around the world have come to accept that economic well-being and the "health" of environmental systems are not unconnected areas of policy interest. They have arrived at this recognition, however, on the basis of very different perceptions of which of the interests treated hitherto as vital are most threatened by the implications of this fact, with a still embryonic appreciation of the complexity of policy linkages it entails, and with vast disparities in the resources at their disposal for responding to it. For all these reasons, the immediate achievements of the upcoming Earth Summit will be modest at best. Yet there is no doubt of the shift in global sensibilities, among both rich and poor peoples, towards appreciation of the need to ensure that human livelihoods are pursued in an environmentally sustainable manner. Insofar as it is the global commons that is threatened by present forms of development, its future can only be secured by consensual international action. That will require a much greater willingness on the part of materially affluent nations than has so far been apparent to reduce the stresses that their economies impose on the ecosphere.

Seen in that light, the seriousness with which Canadians reassess their patterns of resource use has as much international as domestic significance. The popularity of subsidized blue box waste reduction initiatives is a poor indicator of the support that would be forthcoming for a CO_2 emission reduction program, especially if it took the form of a carbon tax. At a time when federal-provincial relationships are difficult enough to manage, the regional implications of such a tax for Alberta (as an energy source) and Ontario (home of the auto industry) would be highly contentious. Similarly, jurisdictional tensions could arise from federal moves to influence forest management (as a carbon sink) or to promote higher urban planning densities (to encourage less auto-intensive commuting). These are just the sort of uncomfortable adjustments, however, that will need to be faced if Canada's support for the UNCED agenda is to be given substance.

Notes

1 Doug Macdonald, *The Politics of Pollution: Why Canadians are Failing their Environment* (Toronto: McClelland and Stewart, 1991), Part II.

2 Government of Canada, *Northern Frontier: Northern Homeland. The Report of the Mackenzie Valley Pipeline Inquiry: Volume One*, Mr. Justice Thomas R. Berger, Commissioner, (Ottawa: Supply and Services Canada, 1977).

3 Glen Toner, *Whence and Whither: ENGOs, Business and the Environment.* Unpublished manuscript, Carleton University, School of Public Administration, 1990.

4 Nigel Banks, Shaping the Future or Meeting the Challenge? The Federal Constitutional Proposals and Global Warming. *Resources: The Newsletter of the Canadian Institute of Resources Law* No. 36 (Fall 1991): 1–6.

5 "Sharing responsibility for the environment," *The Globe and Mail*, January 27, 1992.

6 "Hydro defers nuclear plants," *The Globe and Mail*, January 16, 1992.

7 "Alcan launches appeal on Kemano," *The Globe and Mail*, December 17, 1991.

8 Canada's Green Plan: The First Year, *News Release*, (Ottawa: Environment Canada, December 10, 1991).

9 "Environmental reviews of budgets put off," *The Globe and Mail*, December 11, 1991.

10 "Ecology takes back seat to trade, paper says," *The Ottawa Citizen*, December 9, 1991.

11 Northern Telecom Ltd. has developed a production process for assembling printed circuit boards which eliminates the need to use CFCs. The technology, which cost $1 million to develop, will save the company an estimated $50 million by 2000. Northern Telecom intends to share its innovation free of charge with other manufacturers. One may hope that this level of

corporate environmental responsibility will prove to be a precedent. See "Process sidesteps use of CFCs," *The Globe and Mail*, January 10, 1992.

12 "Europeans join B.C. logging fight," *The Globe and Mail*, June 10, 1991.

13 "Pulp firms fear chlorine ban spread," *The Globe and Mail*, January 29, 1992.

14 "Paper firms facing recycling problems," *The Globe and Mail*, January 30, 1990.

15 "Pulp firms fear chlorine ban spread," *The Globe and Mail*, January 29, 1992. On the place of science within contemporary environmentalism see Robert C. Paehlke, *Environmentalism and the Future of Progressive Politics* (New Haven: Yale University Press, 1989), chapter 5.

16 There is undoubtedly value in the attempts by groups such as Friends of the Earth to monitor and publicize the environmental performance of nations, but the use of rankings to identify "best" and "worst" performers largely avoids the issue raised here. See "Canada worst in use of energy," *The Globe and Mail*, July 15, 1991.

17 For the use of Hollywood stars to generate heat, if not always light, on environmental issues see "Activists like that star treatment," *The Globe and Mail*, December 10, 1991.

18 "Crees winning U.S. power play," *The Globe and Mail*, November 7, 1991.

19 "Split showing up in U.S. lumber lobby," *The Globe and Mail*, December 30, 1991. For background see earlier articles by Kimberley Noble, "An industry at war," *The Globe and Mail*, November 16, 1991; and "Lumber dispute has absurd roots," *The Globe and Mail*, December 13, 1991.

20 "Just south of the border, down pollution way," *Financial Times*, May 17, 1991.

21 "GATT revives working group on environment," *Financial Times*, October 9, 1991.

22 "World business community fears 'green' dumping," *Financial Times*, April 12, 1991.

23 "A wall of waste: recycling in Germany," *The Economist*, November 30, 1991, p. 73.

24 David Runnalls, "What should be said at UNCED? Institutional choices for the Rio conference." Unpublished manuscript prepared for the National Round Table on the Environment and the Economy, The Institute for Research on Public Policy, Ottawa, September 1991.

25 Jim MacNeill, Pieter Winsemius and Taizo Yakushiji, *Beyond Interdependence: The Meshing of the World's Economy and the Earth's Ecology* (New York: Oxford University Press, 1991). Robin Mearns, Environmental Implications of Structural Adjustment: Reflections on Scientific Method. *Discussion Paper* 284, Sussex University, Institute of Development Studies, 1991.

26 Diminishing Our Future — CIDA: Four Years after Winegard, A Report on Recent Developments in Canadian Development Assistance Policies and Practice. Canadian Council of Churches, Interchurch Fund for International Development, Toronto, 1991.

27 "Foreign aid goes green as CIDA vows to scrutinize effect of all projects," *The Ottawa Citizen*, January 31, 1992.

28 J.T. Houghton, G.J. Jenkins and J.J. Ephraums, eds., *Climate Change: The IPCC Scientific Assessment* (Cambridge: Cambridge University Press, 1990).

29 Fen Osler Hampson, "Climate change: building international coalitions of the like-minded," *International Journal* 45: 36–74.

The New Regionalism
and Global Competitiveness

Canada's Economic Performance:
A Current Overview
Christopher J. Maule

The recession in Canada, which began in 1990, continued through 1991 with declines in industrial production of 1.3 percent, Gross Domestic Product (GDP) of 0.8 percent, and retail sales of 11.3 percent, while unemployment rose from 8.9 percent in 1990 to 10.3 percent by year end 1991. *The Economist* forecasts a real GDP growth of 3.0 percent in 1992 and ranked Canada's likely overall performance for 1992 third among the G-7 countries. In 1991 Canada's overall ranking was equal to last (*The Economist*, Dec. 7th, 1991, p. 123).

Canada's economic performance can be compared to that of other industrialized countries and especially its peer G-7 countries, of which it is the smallest both in terms of population and Gross Domestic Product. The following data are from the OECD, *Economic Outlook*, No. 50, (December 1991).

Growth of Real GDP

Canada ranked sixth out of seven in growth of real GDP, with 0.6 percent for 1989–91, −1.1 percent in 1991, and expected growth of 3.1 percent in 1992. The U.S. economy has had similar growth from 1989–91 but is expected to expand somewhat less than Canada in 1992, with a growth of 2.2 percent (see Chart 1).

Unemployment

Canada had the third highest unemployment rate from 1989 to 1991, and the second highest projected rate for 1992. The rate has been almost 50 percent higher than in the U.S. Canada is now predominantly a service economy with over 60 percent of the labour force employed in services, a category which embraces not only highly paid skilled occupations but workers in wholesale and retail trade and other low-paying service jobs (see Chart 2).

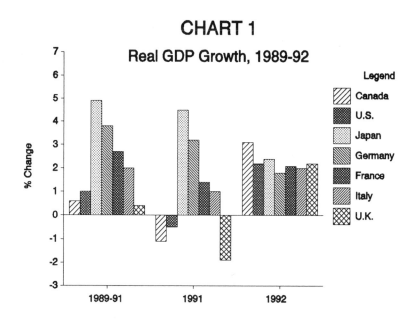

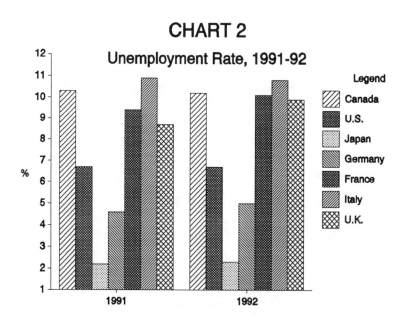

Inflation

Price stability as measured by changes in the GDP deflator shows Canada as the G-7 country with the fourth highest rate of inflation from 1989 to 1991 at 3.8 percent, third lowest in 1991 at 3.6 percent, and forecast second lowest at 2.8 percent in 1992 (see Chart 3).

Public Debt as Percent GNP/GDP

Canada had the second highest debt burden from 1989 to 1991, in 1991 and, according to the forecast, in 1992, with the burden increasing in percentage terms to 77 percent in 1992. Only Italy had a higher figure at 104 percent in 1991. The U.S. debt burden at 59 percent is substantially lower than Canada's (see Chart 4).

Return on Capital in the Business Sector

Canada ranked second highest from 1989 to 1991, third in 1991 and is forecast to rank second in 1992 with 16.2 percent. Notable here is that return on investment is running 3 to 5 percentage points lower in Canada than in the U.S. If investors are planning to invest in North America, then by this measure the U.S. appears to be the more attractive destination (see Chart 5).

Overall, Canada's performance relative to the G-7 countries has been mixed, but in comparison to its neighbour, the U.S., with which it must compete most directly for investment, Canada in 1991 had higher unemployment, higher inflation, a larger public debt burden and a lower rate of return on capital.

Much of what ails the Canadian economy has been attributed to poor productivity performance. Both the Economic Council of Canada and Michael Porter's recent study of Canadian competitiveness have pointed to low productivity growth and rising unit labour costs, the latter measuring the cost of labour adjusted for differences in productivity.

Canada ranked last out of the G-7 countries in terms of growth of total factor (capital plus labour) productivity from 1979 to 1990 with 0.2 percent, as against 0.3 percent in the U.S. and 2.0 percent for first-ranking Japan (see Chart 6).

In terms of changes in unit labour costs in manufacturing (measured in local currencies) the Canadian index rose from 100 in 1987 to 120 in 1991 and a forecast 122 in 1992, an increase larger than in any other G-7 country except the U.K. and Italy, and substantially higher than in the U.S. where the index was 100 in 1987 and is forecast at 106 in 1992. When a similar measure is made using a common currency (see Chart 7), as

CHART 3

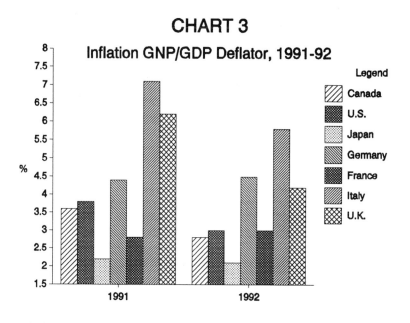

CHART 4

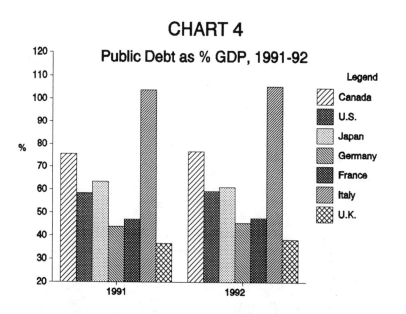

CHART 5

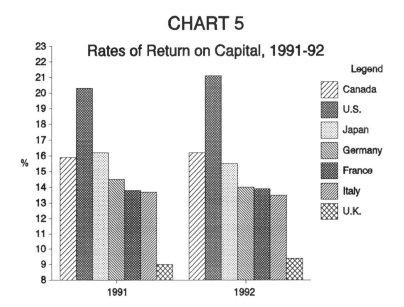

Rates of Return on Capital, 1991-92

Legend
- Canada
- U.S.
- Japan
- Germany
- France
- Italy
- U.K.

CHART 6

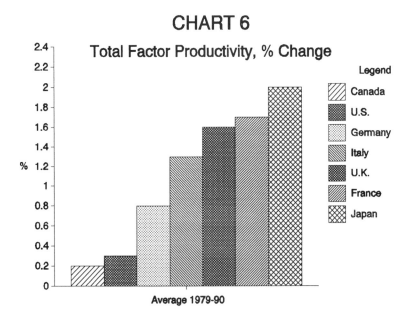

Total Factor Productivity, % Change

Legend
- Canada
- U.S.
- Germany
- Italy
- U.K.
- France
- Japan

opposed to local currencies, the Canadian situation is considerably worse: Canada had the highest increase, from 100 in 1987 to 127 in 1991, while the U.S. had the best performance with the index declining from 100 in 1989 to 81 in 1991.

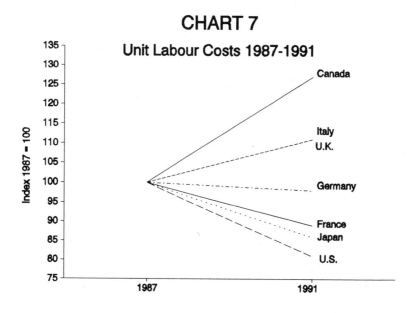

CHART 7

Unit Labour Costs 1987-1991

9

Canadian Continentalism and Industrial Competitiveness

Giles Gherson

Free trade, one of the greatest blessings which a government can confer on a people, is in almost every country unpopular.

–Thomas Macaulay

The 1990s will create a new breed — the continental American.

–Advertisement for a February 1992 seminar sponsored by the New York-based Americas Society

What a difference a recession makes. Only half a decade ago business and government leaders were exhorting Canadians to take a leap of faith. They were urged to shake off the cobwebbed vestiges of Sir John A. Macdonald's 110-year old National Policy of tariff protection, and embrace continental free trade. At the time, Canada's economy was flourishing. Call it luck, but the free trade debate began precisely at the midway point of what was to become North America's longest peacetime economic expansion since the Second World War.

Although the expansion endured slightly longer in the United States, it was, if anything, more robust in Canada. For example, during the decade proportionately more manufacturing jobs were created north of the border. A sharp undervaluation of the Canadian dollar during the mid-eighties, followed by a commodity price boom from 1987–90, together fuelled strong export earnings that propelled fast-growing domestic demand. The country created more jobs per capita than any other member of the OECD (Organization for Economic Co-operation and Development). Everything seemed to be going our way.

The powerful tide of economic growth carried with it a surge of confidence in Canada's economic prospects. Driven largely by an undervalued Canadian dollar, the country's economic momentum, particularly in central Canada, provided a stark contrast to the rust-belt devastation that lingered on south of the border. It was a heady period of industrial buoyancy that seemed to vindicate the free market policies of the Mulroney government. Canada was a confident, rich, resourceful country, Mulroney and his ministers constantly reminded Canadians. It had no need to be afraid of competing openly within North America.

By the late fall of 1991, however, Canadians found themselves aclimatizing to an economy whose prospects had changed almost beyond recognition. The expansion had overheated and crashed. Two full years into a severe manufacturing slump — eighteen months after the officially announced onset of an economy-wide recession — business confidence had plunged. Business executives had exchanged free trade bravado for the vocabulary of self-doubt and defeatism.

Almost overnight, no one was talking about Canada's economic strengths, but rather its numerous shortcomings, from inflated wages and high taxes to soaring land costs, sinking resource prices and an uncompetitive currency. Speaking at a Liberal Party policy conference in Aylmer, Quebec in mid-November 1991, Peter Nicholson, a senior vice-president of the Bank of Nova Scotia conceded: "Many of us who supported the FTA thought Canadian companies would pull up their socks and compete. What was overlooked was that Canadian companies would cut and run. And why not?" Nicholson went on to enumerate the considerable advantages of re-locating in the United States, now that the tariffs sheltering the Canadian economy were being phased out. "You're closer to your major market, you can benefit from a more positive business climate, taxes are lower, inducements are often higher, there is a more modern transportation infrastructure, and you can benefit from broader clusters of suppliers."

Indeed, by 1991, even the Conservative federal government was offering a more sober assessment about Canada's economic prospects. In October, after a year-long study, the Department of Finance and the Department of Industry, Science and Technology jointly released a competitiveness report[1] that concluded Canadian companies suffer from a host of handicaps which, unless rectified, threaten to impede success in international markets.

A further report,[2] commissioned jointly by the federal government and the Business Council on National Issues, and authored by Harvard University business professor Michael Porter, concluded that the Canadian economy suffers from chronic structural weaknesses which are poised to pitch Canada into long-term decline. Appallingly weak growth of labour productivity, a shortage of specialized technical, vocational and engineering skills, a high cost of capital, a poor innovation record, a too heavy reliance on exporting minimally upgraded raw resources, no world-class indigenous machinery and equipment industry, and a high concentration of branch plant manufacturers with no independent product mandate — these all loom as serious barriers to future high growth, he concluded. Under the pressure of relentless competition from aggressive, technologically capable international rivals, Canada's "old industrial

order" is disintegrating. "Canada is already in the throes of a significant economic discontinuity, and profound structural adjustments are
underway."[3]

The growing alarm over Canada's competitiveness gap is prompting searching, fundamental questions about national economic policy. At
stake is more than just the ability of Canadian enterprises — including
foreign-owned subsidiaries — to compete successfully in the U.S. market.
A larger issue, just now coming to the fore with the blizzard of layoff
notices from major U.S. companies as diverse as IBM, General Motors
and Sears Roebuck, is the ability of North America's industrial colossus
to compete in today's relatively open global economy. American firms'
struggle to hold their own against technology-rich, often state-assisted,
supra-national rivals from Europe and Asia will be the epic story of this
decade. For Canadians, it raises the unnerving spectre of being economically tied to a waning economic superpower. As Kenneth Courtis, the
Tokyo-based senior economist for Deutsche Bank, recently told a Canadian audience:

> Japan's huge investments in Asia during the past decade are aimed
> at sourcing new low-value production that will help it take control of
> the mega-markets of the next decade. Take autos. Today, Japan has
> a 38 percent share of world production. In North America, Japanese
> companies are moving from a 32 percent market share to 40 percent.
> North American producers are being thrown on to the defensive.

All this raises large questions about Canadian trade policy, traditionally one of the most vital tools of national industrial policy. Is free trade
with the United States still the right stance? Will it help or hinder Canadian economic restructuring? What about current negotiations to expand
continental free trade to incorporate low-wage Mexico, and beyond that
to include the rest of the hemisphere — President George Bush's so-called
Enterprise for the Americas Initiative (EAI)? Clearly the development of
a hemispheric trade bloc, depending on whether it becomes a truly multilateral trade grouping or a United States-dominated fortress, will have big
implications for Canadian economic development, let alone sovereignty.

With a Canadian election likely in a year or less, the question for the
next federal government will be how to reconcile continental free trade
with what may be mounting pressures to pursue a more activist and
planned industrial policy at home. Put another way, there may soon be
a clash between the demands of a free market trade policy and a growth-
inducing industrial policy not just in Canada, but in the United States
too.[4]

The Origins of Free Trade

When outgoing U.S. President Ronald Reagan saluted the Canada-United States Free Trade Agreement (CUSFTA) in late November 1989 as a "testament to the commitment of our two governments to the principles of the open market,"[5] senior economic ministers in the Mulroney government wholeheartedly agreed. Mulroney himself said: "The choice couldn't be more clear-cut — the voices of the past against a vision of the future." Indeed, at home, the FTA was nothing less than a cornerstone of the Mulroney administration's ambitious free market agenda to reform the Canadian economy. The agenda was first outlined by Michael Wilson, then Finance Minister, in his November 1984 economic statement.[6] Liberalized trade, deregulation, tax reform and government downsizing were the ingredients of a tonic that would encourage domestic business investment and force the sclerotic Trudeau-era economy to start moving once more along the track of rapid post-war expansion. The mix of non-interventionist framework policies was entirely consistent with the international conservative orthodoxy espoused by Prime Minister Margaret Thatcher in the United Kingdom and President Reagan in the United States.

A CUSFTA was not explicitly part of the original Wilson "Agenda for Economic Renewal." Indeed Mulroney had renounced the concept a year earlier during the Conservative leadership contest. Still, by 1985 the term "free trade" was displacing "freer trade" in government thinking. The idea of pursuing a bilateral free trade deal really gained momentum when it was embraced in the Report of the MacDonald Royal Commission on Canada's Economic Prospects, which appeared in the fall of 1985.[7]

What was the reason for recommending such an historic U-turn in Canadian commercial policy? The MacDonald Commission believed that the country's traditional tariff regime had become more of a hindrance than a help. High tariffs had nurtured a domestic manufacturing base, yes. But it was a high cost, inefficient, stunted manufacturing base dominated by U.S.-owned branch plants. Unable to export over the tariff wall, they had simply replicated in Canada miniaturized versions of American parent company operations to serve the small, protected market. These companies manufactured the same broad range of products but in much smaller batches. Short production runs, and constant production line changes, contrasted with the economies of scale found south of the border. Faced with these structural weaknesses, Canada's future as a manufacturing exporter looked bleak.

The striking exception to this unalluring industrial model was Canada's biggest manufacturing industry, automobiles. Under the terms of the 1965 Canada-United States Auto Pact, free trade of sorts had replaced high tariffs for this one sector, dominated on both sides of the border by three Detroit-based companies: General Motors, Ford and Chrysler. Able to import finished cars and components across the border duty free, the Big Three in short order had rationalized their Canadian production. Taking advantage of lower manufacturing labour costs north of the border, they elected to assemble certain models there for the entire North American market.

Trade in cars and parts exploded during the 1970s and 1980s. True, Canada insisted on certain "temporary" production and content safeguards to ensure that the Big Three lived up to undertakings to transform their small Canadian plants into continental scale facilities. Indeed, the safeguards remain to this day as an insurance policy to guarantee Canada a permanent share of North American production. Still, free trade advocates routinely point out that the auto safeguards generally have been exceeded by the Big Three, strong evidence that they have not influenced production decisions. Certainly, Canada has enjoyed a substantial bilateral trade surplus in autos for most of the last two decades. The auto industry's robust good health seemed a promising harbinger of what free trade in other sectors might produce.

Canada, the super-economy that ranked seventh in the world with a population base of only 25 million people, could gear up to take on all comers. And why not? Just sweep away the constraints of government regulatory intervention, give Canadian companies unfettered access to the giant United States market and Canada would compete as never before.

The CUSFTA was not just a product of the free market economics wave that swept Ottawa policy circles following the Tory election victory; and in foreign policy terms it was more than just an expression of the Mulroney rapprochement with Republican Washington. It had an important strategic dimension as well, and it was this that recommended it to Ottawa's senior mandarinate.

The first convert was Allan Gotlieb, former Under-Secretary of State for External Affairs and Canada's ambassador in Washington from 1982 to 1988. He saw free trade as a means to institutionalize Canada's historic special relationship with the United States before that country was swept away in a rising mood of trade protectionism.[8] Gotlieb's arrival in Washington had coincided with the start of the economic recovery of the 1980s. But this expansion, while ultimately long-lasting, was for much of its duration both bumpy and unevenly distributed. Even by 1987, U.S. analysts talked about the "bi-coastal economy," a phrase that captured the sharp contrast between fast-paced, services-dominated growth on the Eastern seabord and Pacific coast, and the continuing troubles of the midwestern industrial heartland, the so-called "rust belt."

The manufacturing shakeout in industries such as steel, autos, farm implements, industrial machinery was strikingly visible in American trade figures. By the mid-1980s, the United States was nursing a staggering

$180 billion trade deficit. The prime culprit was the Reagan administration's ruinous high dollar policy of the early 1980s. But by mid-decade the situation was so serious, and concerns about U.S. de-industrialization so rife, that a Congress dominated by special interests continually debated the imposition of tough new trade restrictions. True, Canada had escaped U.S. import curbs against foreign steel and Japanese autos, even while enjoying persistent trade surpluses in both sectors. But Gotlieb was convinced that it was only a matter of time before the free trade-oriented Reagan Administration would be forced to buckle under Congressional pressure and sign a major piece of protectionist trade legislation. Some means had to be found to ensure Canada escaped the net and safeguarded access to the vital U.S. market. With 75 percent of Canadian exports destined for the U.S. market, 20 percent of the country's gross domestic product was at stake.

In the event, winning secure access to the U.S. market became the Mulroney government's chief argument in favor of free trade. The government's primary negotiating objective was to achieve a special bilateral dispute settlement arrangement that would supersede the operation of the trade remedy laws of both countries on cross-border trade. Since U.S. industry seemed more disposed to bring anti-dumping and countervail cases against Canadian imports than vice-versa, the creation of a more predictable, less costly and less time-consuming trade remedy system would be of particular advantage to Canada.

In the end, Canada won only half a loaf. Washington refused to exempt its biggest trade partner from the scope of its trade remedy law. This was largely due to the lobbying success of a loose coalition of U.S. domestic industries. They managed to convince Congress that Canadian industry was rife with unfair government subsidies — from regional development grants to cheap sources of energy subsidized by provincially owned utilities — and that to remove the threat of U.S. countervail penalties would be only to encourage unfairly traded imports from north of the border. Moreover it would constitute an unwarranted surrender of U.S. sovereignty, setting a dangerous precedent.

One idea canvassed by American negotiators was for Canada to unilaterally agree to terminate a long list of federal and provincial subsidies, including regional development grants. This was unacceptable to the Canadian negotiating team. It was only during the final hours of bargaining that a compromise arrangement was cobbled together: domestic industries in both countries would continue to have recourse to existing national trade remedy laws. However, in the event that one country's industry believed it had been disadvantaged by the improper application of the other country's trade law, a binational dispute settlement panel could be struck to review the matter and issue a binding ruling. Moreover, both sides agreed that this dispute settlement system would be a temporary expedient only, pending a 5–7 year effort to find agreement on a common set of disciplines for North American subsidies.

The other principal Canadian goal, preferential duty-free access to the U.S. market, was achieved with a 10 year phase-out of all bilateral tariffs. Hopes for a staggered phase-out with U.S. tariffs falling faster were rejected by Washington.

And what of the U.S. approach to free trade? Ironically, it was President Reagan who first advanced the idea of setting up a continental free trade zone. During his 1980 election campaign he repeatedly advocated a "North American Accord." So it was all the more surprising that five years later, when Ottawa indicated an interest in exploring a freer trade pact, Washington was caught entirely unprepared. It was consistently viewed as a Canadian-led initiative. Ottawa was cast in the role of supplicant. Let the Canadians set out their objectives, and the United States would respond. The administration's unwillingness to formulate a coherent agenda ensured that Congress would step in to fill the void.

Congress was upset by the Reagan White House's failure to deal with the yawning trade deficit, and was looking for an occasion to vent its anger. Unwittingly, Canada provided it. In April 1986 the Senate Finance Committee scotched what was predicted to be a pro forma vote approving fast track authority to negotiate a CUSFTA. In a bid to highlight their grievance that the Reagan administration was soft on trade and neglecting domestic interests, committee members turned a simmering softwood lumber dispute with Canada into a litmus test of the White House's resolve to act. At the same time, the committee made it clear the FTA negotiations would only proceed if they marked a turning point in the conduct of trade policy. United States Trade Representative Clayton Yeutter was warned that U.S. trade interests were not to be subordinated to the broader foreign policy goals of maintaining a warm and friendly relationship with Canada.

Just to make sure, the Finance Committee's senior Republican, Senate minority leader Robert Dole (Kansas) issued an extensive checklist of demands to the Reagan White House in the form of a Senate resolution. The nine tough demands enumerated the concerns of the Finance Committee and included the following: that Canada be made to open its market for U.S. goods and services; that it curb its use of industrial energy and agricultural subsidies; that it scrap its foreign investment controls; that it shed its compulsory licensing rules for pharamaceutical patents; that provinces end discriminatory sales treatment of U.S. beer and liquor; and that federal and provincial governments open up their purchases to U.S. suppliers. Finally, the Dole resolution demanded that any trade deal must ensure "United States persons retain full access to United States trade remedies affecting imports from Canada."

These demands had the desired impact. They ensured that Congressional special interest concerns formed the centrepiece of the American bargaining agenda. Negotiator Peter Murphy adopted what some observers derisively called an "accounting-ledger" approach to the negotiations, constantly looking over his shoulder at Congress. In the end, instead of a collegial bilateral exercise aimed at forging innovative continental trade institutions, the negotiations became highly adversarial. The Americans used the negotiations mainly as an opportunity to settle a host of bilateral trade irritants. And the emphasis on fair trade and reciprocity, with no concessions to Canada's smaller size and more vulnerable economy, foreshadowed a new U.S. assertiveness in its global trade relations.

Three years have passed since the FTA came into effect, and Canadian public opinion remains sharply divided over its merits. The unanticipated 20 percent appreciation in the value of the Canadian dollar since 1976 clearly has made the adjustment to free trade far more difficult for Canadian companies than either Ottawa or the business community predicted. At the same time, the overheating Canadian economy moved into a wage inflation spiral at the end of the 1980s. Canadian unit labor costs rose over 30 percent between 1986–90, while they stayed static in the United States. By 1991, Canada's industrial wage advantage over the United States had evaporated.

Then came a business cycle recession and, simultaneously, a wave of industrial restructuring. Newspapers overflowed with articles about Canadian manufacturing firms shutting their doors and moving to lower tax, lower wage locations in the United States. At the same time, a series of high profile bilateral trade disputes bolstered the impression that, even under free trade, Americans are still harassing Canadian products at the border. Indeed, in late 1991, no less an authority than the former Canadian deputy negotiator, Gordon Ritchie, publicly declared that the U.S. had demonstrated a worrisome pattern of breaking both the letter and the spirit of the FTA.[9]

On the other hand, FTA-backers can still marshall impressive evidence for the view that the accord has benefited Canada. Despite a U.S. recession and a soaring Canadian dollar, Canada retains a trade surplus with the United States. In fact, in April 1991, Canadian exports to the U.S. posted a record monthly high of $9.7 billion. Moreover, despite stories of Canadian de-industrialization and a manufacturing exodus, net investment inflows reached a record $5.1 billion in 1990. Much of this investment was directed into plant modernization and purchases of upgraded machinery and equipment. Finally, few would disagree that the bilateral dispute settlement procedure has worked reasonably well in protecting Canadian interests when put to the test.

The Drift to NAFTA

In June 1990, President George Bush's sudden interest in launching a new set of FTA negotiations with Mexico caused upheaval in Ottawa's neatly ordered trade world. At that point, Canada's external commercial relations were anchored by two complementary trade treaties. On the one hand, there was a multilateral arrangement, the General Agreement on Tariffs and Trade (GATT), now four decades old. On the other, regulating the terms of trade with its biggest and most valued trade partner, is the CUSFTA.

Updated every decade in successive international bargaining rounds, the GATT sets international trading rules that govern Canada's access to the markets of almost all of its trade partners. The GATT's centrepiece is its most favored nation (MFN) rule, which ordains that trade concessions granted by one nation to another cannot be discriminatory and must be offered to all GATT signatories. That meant that when trade giants such as the United States and the European Community negotiated to reduce trade barriers to each others' markets, smaller countries like Canada could share in the benefits, and for a limited cost. Successive GATT rounds achieved a progressive lowering of tariff protection and spurred world trade. Multilateralism was an entrenched cornerstone of Canadian post war trade policy.

It was only with the resurgence of protectionist sentiment in the 1980s, combined with fears of a proliferation of non-tariff barriers, that Canada acted independently to safeguard its access to the U.S. market. Ottawa was caught completely off guard when President Bush agreed to Mexican President Carlos Salinas de Gortari's request to explore a free trade arrangement. There had been murmurings in Washington in 1989 that the incoming, urbane, Harvard-educated Mexican president might seek a trade deal with the United States to provide a basis for his ambitious growth agenda. But most trade experts believed the likelihood of Washington actually agreeing to talks on that scale was virtually nil.

Undoubtedly free trade with Canada made a lot more economic sense than free trade with an underdeveloped country like Mexico. Yet ironically, where the Canadian deal failed completely to capture Washington's political imagination, Mexico was able to tap an enormous wellspring of sympathy within the U.S. political establishment. A major reason, of course, was the so-called Texas mafia in Washington. President Bush had adopted Texas as his home state. Secretary of State James Baker, and Commerce Secretary Robert Mosbacher — both longtime Bush political allies — are Texans. So is Democratic Senator Lloyd Bentsen, the powerful Finance Committee chairman, who had been a decided skeptic about the merits of a CUSFTA, largely because he knew next to nothing about Canada.

By contrast, for these Texans, Mexico is an important neighbour — and trade partner. Moreover, with its teeming population of 85 million, widespread poverty and volatile political climate, it is a neighbour whose diverse problems increasingly spill over into the United States — largely in the form of massive illegal immigration flows. These flows of often near-destitute, poorly educated peasants are causing significant problems of population absorption in the U.S. southwest.

For the Bush administration, President Salinas' offer of free trade presented an historic opportunity to set the traditionally fragile United States-Mexico relations on a vastly more solid footing. "Politically, we'd like to do something for Mexico to normalize our relationship — remember, we're a country that seized half of Mexico's territory," explained a Bush administration official in an interview last year. Salinas' aggressively reformist, free-market, pro-foreign investment administration provided an opening too favorable to pass up. Not only would free trade — by stimulating investment-led growth — protect the large-scale U.S. financial assistance furnished to Mexico as part of the Brady Plan for third world debt reduction. A bilateral agreement would also lock in Salinas' free market policies, helping to put Mexico's economy on a stable growth path. Stable growth is the key to expanding job opportunities at home, which will soak up Mexico's burgeoning labour force and reduce the northward flight of emigrants. For the Washington Texans, finding a long-term solution to the immigration problem was probably free trade's biggest appeal.

Free trade with Mexico carried with it an additional temptation: in an era of mounting trade friction with Japan and the European Community, Washington was increasingly interested in the idea of a United States-centred hemispheric trade bloc.

For increasingly protectionist-minded Democrats, there was the comforting thought that with the United States in the driver's seat defining the rules, there could be fair trade for American firms, in this hemisphere at least. Meanwhile for liberal-internationalist Republicans like Secretary of State James Baker, brandishing the threat of a 380 million-strong North American free trade zone provided an excellent stick with which to beat trade concessions out of the recalcitrant Europeans and Japanese. For both groups, the product of free trade with Canada was a new enthusiasm for bilateral trade pacts. One on one, Washington could resolve U.S. trade complaints and win commitments for concrete market-opening measures as part of an integrated package. By contrast, multilateral trade rules were based on broad principles that many Americans were coming to see as too loose. The complaint was that GATT rules were often manipulated by aggressive exporting nations that targeted the relatively open American market while raising trade barriers at home. As the U.S. trade deficit climbed during the 1980s, the idea of managing trade by negotiating comprehensive bilateral trade treaties had an intrinsic appeal.

Of course, Canada shared none of these motives for a trade deal with Mexico. Mexico had never been a large trade partner of Canada's and there was no historically close afinity between the two nations. For Canada, the CUSFTA was a unique, preferential and, it was hoped, closed arrangement to protect access to its largest trade partner, not an open-ended model for managing its trade relations with other countries. For that, the multilateral GATT system was the preferred approach.

Moreover, a strictly bilateral U.S.-Mexico free trade arrangement held dangers for Canada. By definition it would erode Canada's preferential position in the U.S. market. It therefore threatened to unbalance the structure of concessions and obligations agreed to between Canada and the United States only a few years earlier. It raised politically sensitive questions about whether Canada had paid too dearly for benefits it would now have to share with the United States' southern neighbour.

After heated debate within the federal government, the Mulroney cabinet concluded in the spring of 1991 that if the United States and Mexico were embarked on a free trade agreement, Canada could not afford to be absent from the table. The posture was purely defensive. The primary objective was simply to protect the terms of trade for Canadian firms in North America. A high proportion of U.S.-Canadian trade, as well as U.S.-Mexican trade, is intra-corporate, and involves identical U.S.-based multinational enterprises. Reduced trade and investment barriers across the Rio Grande could shift North American trade and investment patterns southwards. Canadian exclusion from a U.S.-Mexico pact would accentuate this. It would give American firms preferential open access to both Canada and Mexico, while Canadian firms would have free access only to the United States.

Canada had negotiated the FTA in large measure to make itself an investment magnet for companies interested in serving the entire North American market. But now, if a location in the United States were to provide access to Mexico while a Canadian location did not, the future logic of investment patterns would be clear. For large multinationals, a United States location would offer maximum advantage. Instead of being part of an integrated North American economic hub, as envisioned under the CUSFTA, Canada — and Mexico, for that matter — would end up as separate spokes attached to a U.S. hub. "Our objective had to be to make sure Canadian business competes in Mexico on the same footing as U.S. business," is the way Canada's negotiator, John Weekes, summed up the position.[10]

This concern was particularly acute in the case of automobiles. The North American industry, completely rationalized across the U.S.-Canadian border, greeted the 1990s with a large and growing overcapacity problem. Over the preceding decade, for example, General Motors had lost 35 percent of its market share, mostly to Asian imports and transplant operations. Yet it had undertaken a massive and costly plant modernization program during the same decade — in Ontario, Oshawa's Autoplex I and II plants are examples — expecting to recapture its traditional 55 percent share of continent-wide sales. Its market share currently hovers just under 35 percent. With flat growth projected in the 1990s for North American car purchases, G.M. — as well as Ford and Chrysler — now face the bleak prospect of numerous plant shutdowns to raise operating capacity and reduce costs. But there is one ray of hope: Mexico. Rapid population growth plus rising affluence are combining to make that country a major new market for autos. Indeed, Mexico's car market, now one quarter the size of Canada's, could overtake Canada's by the year 2000. An end to Mexico's highly protectionist Auto Decree, opening up a sizeable export market to cars made in the U.S. and Canada would absorb some of the excess capacity. But, again, if Canada wished to remain an attractive venue for auto investment Canadian plants must have access to Mexico on the same terms as rival American plants.

This imperative of winning preferential access to the emerging Mexican market on the same terms as U.S. companies holds true for indigenous Canadian firms in sectors such as construction, engineering, telecommunications and mining. These are all areas that Ottawa has identified as major export opportunities and that would wither if U.S. competitors were to get there first.

Washington was reluctant to include Canada in its Mexican trade initiative, worried that a third voice at the table would simply impede negotiations and make it harder to meet a short timetable. But the logic of Canada's position — that it had a vital interest in protecting its CUSFTA benefits — was unassailable. The Bush administration and Congress swallowed their misgivings and the notion of a three-way North American Free Trade Area (NAFTA) was born.

Even as negotiations began, in Toronto in June 1991, a core question was left hanging: precisely what kind of a trade deal were the participants aiming for? Canada's hope was that for the most part, the CUSFTA would be the model. After all, as a more or less unwanted player at the table, and with no real bargaining leverage, Canadian officials would be in a poor position if U.S. and Mexican negotiators opted to re-write the rules of North American trade. Under Ottawa's scenario, Mexico would agree to bring its commercial and investment policies in line with North American standards as set forth in the CUSFTA. In return, Canada and the U.S. would extend CUSFTA market access to Mexico.

Mexico agreed to trilateral negotiations — partly to dilute the overwhelming presence of the United States. But Salinas was not interested in signing up to a pre-packaged FTA already designed to suit the trade agenda of the U.S. and Canada. For its part, the United States appeared ambivalent about the possible form of NAFTA. Its goals were located exclusively in the south: it sought to stabilize the Mexican economy while at the same time ensuring that a potentially enormous consumer market would be opened to U.S. firms. Invariably, the U.S. approach was focused less on principle than results — with a micro-agenda defined largely by domestic industrial interests and the trade and investment problems with Mexico that they wanted fixed.

By December 1991, the United States, Canada and Mexico had exchanged initial draft texts, with plans to complete a draft unified text by the end of January 1992. On the surface, progress has been remarkably swift, although at least two key problems remain unaddressed. As of January 1992, the chapter on autos is still blank while negotiators wrestle with the complexities of designing a three-sided auto pact. The United States is also still adamant that Mexico should not obtain the right to use a binding CUSFTA-style quasi-judicial bilateral (or rather trilateral) dispute settlement mechanism, as Mexico has demanded.

While the contents of the NAFTA are still being hammered out, the structure of the arrangement is clearer. And it reflects the degree to which Canada has been swept into a continentalist current — one in which its ability to shape outcomes is quite limited. Originally, Canada's preference was for an overarching NAFTA umbrella agreement that would set out the broad trade principles agreed to by the three parties. But under the umbrella, the CUSFTA would continue to be the primary document addressing bilateral trade, and reflecting Canada's special relationship with the United States. Mexico-U.S. and Canada-Mexico bilateral arrangements would then contain special provisions guiding those separate relationships. But this preferred model quickly lost its appeal for a key reason: the possibility that the continental free trade zone might continue to enlarge to include other countries.

The Enterprise for the Americas Challenge

In June 1990, when President Bush announced his readiness to consider a free trade agrement with Mexico, he also opened the door to an eventual western hemisphere trade bloc. This "Enterprise for the Americas Initiative" was kept deliberately vague. But it appeared to offer free trade with the United States as a carrot to Latin American countries prepared to adopt pro-market economic reforms, including trade liberalization. For the United States, EAI has important resonance in trade policy terms, since it conjures up the idea of recapturing an important regional export market that was lost when the Latin American debt crisis exploded at the end of the 1970s. Many U.S. trade analysts attribute a sizeable portion of the American trade imbalance during the 1980s to the evaporation of Latin American markets.

Canadian trade officials assert that EAI has not surfaced as a concrete factor during the NAFTA talks. But for Canada and Mexico, it has definitely lurked in the background. What if, having signed a NAFTA agreement, the United States proceeds to widen its net of bilateral trade pacts? A deal between the United States and Chile, to choose the most obvious example, would once again prejudice Canada's and Mexico's preferential access to the U.S. market. On the other hand, the United States might offer Canada and Mexico a seat at the new table, but set new conditions. Canada and Mexico might be asked to make further concessions to the U.S. that were not obtained during the CUSFTA or NAFTA rounds. This was precisely the tactic employed when Canada was permitted to join the NAFTA negotiations: U.S. Trade Representative Carla Hills promised Congress she would reopen Canada's cultural industries exemptions in the CUSFTA, and seek improved foreign investment rules and patent rights protection, as well as a higher North American content rule for automobiles.

Canadian negotiators are keen to prevent Washington from using successive bilateral negotiations as a means to erode CUSFTA benefits or to create an occasion to press for unilateral concessions as the price of participation. If the United States wants to open up free trade to new partners, let there be fixed trilateral rules for doing so. The result is that Ottawa is now pushing for a "generic" NAFTA arrangement that would set the terms for hemispheric free trade. Countries that want to join would be free to do so, provided they met the standards established in the NAFTA. This formula would, in effect, "multilateralize" the NAFTA and insulate it from U.S. unilateralism. This has clear benefits for Canada, and presumably Mexico.

On the other hand, creating NAFTA as the "master agreement," for use if Washington decides to make good on EAI, carries a cost. The CUSFTA would be subsumed into the new three-sided pact. Instead of being a stand-alone agreement, the CUSFTA would serve as a Canada-U.S. protocol to the NAFTA, setting out any special bilateral terms. There would also be U.S.-Mexico and Mexico-Canada protocols. Symbolically, the CUSFTA would surely lose importance as a permanent symbol in Washington of Canada's special relationship with the United States. Canada would be sharing with Mexico, and perhaps Chile and Peru, not just the terms of its preferred access to the U.S. market, but the hitherto exclusive institutions of free trade. During the bitterly contested free trade election of 1988, these were precisely the advantages the Mulroney government cited in urging the Canadian public to embrace the bilateral deal.

For Canada both the NAFTA and, more especially, the EAI pose the question: what's in it for us? Certainly, as long as there are prospects for a successful completion of the GATT Uruguay Round, there are few compelling reasons for special trade pacts with Mexico, Latin America, or to cite three countries reportedly interested in joining an EAI, Australia, New Zealand and Korea. Since Canada already participates in a multilateral trade body, what is the merit in setting up another, particularly one in which the United States would be by far the dominant player, with no counterbalance provided as is the case in the GATT, by the presence of other trade superpowers, such as the EC and Japan?

Bilateral and regional trade pacts are normally justified only in special cases. The EC (European Community) with the development of its internal market, is one. Canada, with its regional ties and enormous trade dependence on the United States, is another. Is Mexico another? It may be, given its colossal need for development capital, combined with an acute U.S. desire to curb Mexican immigration flows. But the enormous gap between wage levels in Mexico compared to those in the rest of North America, the gulf between the respective living standards, and the widely different legal and business environments, make it an unlikely experiment that may be fraught with difficulties.

The Odd Couple: Free Trade and Competitiveness

The dilemma over how to handle automobiles within a three-sided NAFTA illustrates the gulf between the rhetoric of free trade and the mounting demands of competitiveness and industrial policy. Mexico is willing to phase out its heavily *dirigiste* Auto Decree but in return wants open access to the United States and Canada for Mexican-built vehicles. Taking into account both its status as North America's only growing car market and its low manufacturing labour costs, Mexico is keen to attract not just additional Big Three investment, but also Asian and European automobile producers (currently, the Big Three, Nissan and Volkswagen constitute its "big five," although production is primarily for the domestic market). The U.S. carmakers, however, vigorously supported by parts producers, the United Auto Workers' union and midwestern Congressmen and Senators, view Mexico primarily as a major export market. They are keen to rationalize their existing production facilities to concentrate on low-end models. But they are fiercely opposed to counting Mexican-made cars in their domestic fleets (as Canadian-built cars are) under U.S. Corporate Average Fuel Economy (CAFE) regulations.[11] (Under CAFE, car companies are penalized if their domestic fleets — defined by 75 percent U.S.-Canadian content — fail to meet specified fuel economy targets.)

Ineligibility for inclusion in the Big Three's domestic fleet would reduce the appeal of Big Three investment in Mexico. At the same time, the American auto industry insists that Mexico should be deterred from exploiting the combination of low cost labour and a North American free trade pact to attract new Asian and European production plants to the continent. This implies that the United States will insist on tough rules of origin standards for cars — including a high North American content rule — to insure against offshore firms using Mexico as an assembly platform from which to invade the already overcrowded U.S. market.

Meanwhile, the expansion of the 27-year-old auto pact to include low-wage Mexico presents a challenge for Canadian policymakers. Rising unit labour costs — and other business costs — have narrowed the cost advantage of assembling vehicles in Canada. In addition, if the GATT Uruguay Round is successfully concluded this spring, Canada's external automobile tariff is likely to decline from its current 9.5 percent level to 6 percent. This will reduce the value of duty remission benefits accorded the Big Three. Under existing rules, auto pact members are permitted to import cars and parts duty-free into Canada from third countries if they exceed their Canadian production and content requirements under the auto pact. The Big Three's need to trim plant capacity and jobs — and to share the pain on both sides of the border — likely mean the glory days for Canada's auto industry are over. Under the CUSFTA Canada was required to give assurances that its Asian transplant operations, owned respectively by Toyota Canada, Honda Canada and Hyundai, would be frozen out of the auto pact for all time. They would not therefore qualify for duty remission on imported parts and cars even if they eventually meet auto pact Canadian content standards. Already this discrimination has slowed expected incremental investment in Canada by Asian car producers and component makers. With no duty remission and high tariffs against imported parts and components in Canada, it makes more sense to set up assembly operations in the United States. Once a 50 percent North American content is achieved under the CUSFTA, they will be able to export to Canada duty free.

Investment in Canada by Asian automakers has been further chilled by a series of tough United States border audits of Canadian made Hondas, Toyotas and GM-Suzuki vehicles. In what Canada claims is a unilateral re-interpretation of CUSFTA North American content rules, Washington is hinting strongly that these companies will be assessed back duties.

As if all this were not enough, President Bush's state visit to Japan in early 1992 — in which he was accompanied by the heads of Detroit's Big Three automakers — was a thinly veiled effort to force a reduction in Japan's soaring $40 billion trade surplus with the United States. In particular, Bush prodded his hosts for more Japanese purchases of U.S. cars and parts, and expansion of major components production in the United

States. This sort of browbeating is likely to nullify Canada's efforts to win similar concessions from Japanese automakers.

Washington's tough stand on autos, and its increasing propensity to manage trade and investment to protect American jobs, pose significant and complex issues for the United States' North American partners. Will Canada and Mexico be protected as the United States increasingly resorts to unilateralism to achieve fair trade with the rest of the world? Or will they be neutralized within a Fortress North America, while the U.S. uses its political and economic muscle to attract investment and open up markets for itself? Furthermore, will Canada and Mexico find themselves side-swiped by retaliatory actions by overseas nations in response to U.S. unilateralism?

The Mulroney government now acknowledges that Canada's status as an internationally competitive economy is waning, raising questions about Canada's ability to maintain its present high standard of living. Free trade, in part, was designed to improve Canada's competitiveness. But in a world where the United States is facing enormous structural problems of its own, the context of free trade has altered enormously.

Dealing with Canada's lack of competitiveness may well require future federal and provincial governments to adopt not just macroeconomic policies geared to low inflation, low public sector deficits and, by implication, a highly competitive cost of capital. It may also mean more than restructured education and training systems geared to technical innovation. All these are quite consistent with free trade. But they may not prove adequate. Competitiveness may require a more activist, European- or Asian-style industrial policy. And that is where it may run afoul of CUSFTA national treatment, open investment and unfair trade practice obligations.

Certainly the free market nostrums of the 1980s, by which Canada's "open door" trade policy was justified, now seem at best inadequate, at worst outdated. How will Canadian governments fashion a microeconomic policy agenda without running afoul of the CUSFTA? Necessary measures may include highly targeted tax incentives or regulatory changes aimed at shifting Canada's industrial structure away from its present over-reliance on a weakening resources base. The U.S. has its own lavish state aid programs for high technology development — Defence Advanced Research Projects Agency (DARPA), National Aeronautics and Space Administration (NASA), Sematech — to cite the best known. But the outrageous premise of U.S. unilateralism is that what other nations are forbidden from doing, American firms may do. As Martin Wolf of the London Financial Times observed recently," Such a stance must reduce international trade law to the law of the bully."[12]

Ultimately, it may transpire that competitiveness and free trade represent quite incompatible policy sets. After all, at its core, competitiveness policy tends towards mercantilism. American authorities on competitiveness, such as Michael Porter and economist Lester Thurow, grade competitive standing by assessing a nation's export balance and a firm's global market share. Increasingly, competitive advantage has little to do with traditional concepts of comparative advantage — endowments of land, people and natural resources. Rather it reflects what Porter terms "competitive advantage," which any nation can build by nurturing and marshalling technological capability, a commitment to product innovation, and marketing prowess. These attributes are made by the country in question and often policy driven. The winners in today's toughly competitive world are those countries and companies that have assiduously built up aggressive export industries, usually targeted at the open North American market.

A final note: the main players in the new competitive world are giant, supra-national corporations. Nations that aspire to be winners in this environment are those with an array of multinational firms they can call their own. Japan, the United States and now Europe, have such corporations. Europe is also moving quickly to adapt to this new order through the creation of pan-European consortia in aerospace, pharmaceuticals and informatics. In the case of Italy and France, these 'national champions' frequently are wholly or partly state-owned and receive major infusions of government capital. By contrast, Canada can claim few of these giant supra-nationals at a time when in many sectors, from airlines and advertising to autos and commuter aircraft — the world is coming to be dominated by a handful of leviathan enterprises. Today, Canada's role as a principal stakeholder in this evolving global order is at risk. Will free trade — and NAFTA — conspire to keep it that way? It seems likely that they will.

Notes

1 *Prosperity Through Competitiveness* (Ottawa: Minister of Supply and Services Canada, 1991).

2 Michael E. Porter and The Monitor Co., *Canada at the Crossroads; The Reality of a New Competitive Environment* (Ottawa: Business Council on National Issues, Minister of Supply and Services Canada, 1991).

3 Porter, p. 151.

4 Peter Morici, *A New Special Relationship: Free Trade and U.S.-Canada Economic Relations in the 1990s* (Ottawa: Institute for Research on Public Policy, 1991). Morici argues a swing towards more activist industrial policymaking in the U.S. during the coming decade will test the special

relationship with Canada. Will Canadian firms and research institutions gain open access to U.S. industrial development programs as part of a drive to make North American industry world competitive? Or will Canadian industry be enviously on the outside looking in?

5 President Ronald Reagan, Signing Ceremony for the U.S.–Canada Free Trade Agreement, The White House, Washington, D.C., July 25, 1988.

6 Minister of Finance, "Economic Statement," House of Commons, Ottawa, November 8, 1984.

7 *The Report of the Royal Commission on the Economic Union and the Development Prospects for Canada* (Ottawa: Minister of Supply and Services Canada, 1985).

8 Interviews with the author, 1987, 1988.

9 Drew Fagan, "Ritchie accuses U.S. of abusing free trade," and *The Globe and Mail Report on Business*, December 17, 1991.

10 John Weekes, interview with the author, December, 1991.

11 *Position of Chrysler Corporation, Ford Motor Company and General Motors Corporation on the Key Objectives of the North American Free Trade Agreement*, Washington, D.C., September 1991.

12 Martin Wolf, "Fair trade or foul?" *The Financial Times* (London), January 10, 1992.

10

North American Free Trade: Co-operation and Conflict in Canada-Mexico Relations

Maxwell A. Cameron, Lorraine Eden and
Maureen Appel Molot[1]

Mexican President Carlos Salinas de Gortari and United States President George Bush announced on June 11, 1990, that talks would begin on a comprehensive bilateral trade agreement. Canadian policy makers were then forced to choose Canada's best response to this initiative. The Canada-U.S. Free Trade Agreement (FTA) had just come into effect (in January 1989) and the Canadian government was reluctant to contemplate another round of trade talks — especially with a country with which there were few trade and investment ties, that had a much lower standard of living and level of wages, and that was a clear competitor for the U.S. market.

In the late summer and fall of 1990 the Canadian government conducted public hearings under the auspices of the Standing Committee on External Affairs and International Trade, to seek the views of business, labour, and other sectors of Canadian society likely to be affected as to whether Canada should participate in negotiations aimed at a prospective North American Free Trade Agreement (NAFTA). On September 24, 1990, before the committee had finished its work, John Crosbie, the Minister of International Trade, announced that Canada would seek a seat at the bargaining table with Mexico and the United States. After a period of uncertainty about the unwillingness of Mexico and the United States to include Canada in the talks, the three countries announced on February 5, 1991 that they would begin negotiations to create a trilateral trading area.

The purpose of this paper is to outline the stakes and bargaining postures of the two smaller players in this drama — Canada and Mexico. First, we document the asymmetries of interdependence between the two "spoke" countries and the U.S. economic "hub,"[2] focusing on trade and foreign direct investment (FDI) patterns in the late 1980s. Second, we discuss how these patterns of asymmetrical interdependence prompted each "spoke" country's interest in a NAFTA, and its bargaining posture, as well as some of the economic, political and cultural problems involved in a

Table 10.1

The Distribution of Intra-North American Trade, 1988

	Canadian Exports to U.S.	to Mexico	U.S. Exports to Canada	Mexico	Mexican Exports to Canada	to U.S.
Value (U.S. $ billions)	79.3	0.4	69.9	20.6	1.1	23.3
XO = Export Orientation (percent)	71.2	0.4	22.2	6.5	5.6	67.0
MP = Import Penetration (percent)	17.3	2.0	62.3	67.0	1.0	5.0

Notes:

XO = export orientation e.g., 22.2% of U.S. exports go to Canada.

MP = import penetration e.g., 17.3% of U.S. imports come from Canada.

trilateral arrangement. Finally, we examine the process of negotiation and point to areas of conflict and co-operation between Canada and Mexico in the trade bargaining.

The Structure of Interdependence and Dependence

Trade Patterns

The structure of trade between Mexico and Canada provides the underlying basis for co-operation and conflict between the two countries in the NAFTA negotiations. In 1987, total intra-North American trade was $US 163.57 billion, distributed as 46 percent Canadian, 41 percent American and 13 percent Mexican exports. Intra-regional North American trade presently accounts for about 36 percent of the combined total of U.S., Canadian and Mexican merchandise (or goods) trade. In the European Community (EC) intra-EC trade accounts for 60 percent of member country exports.[3] Thus trade links within North America are not as well developed as those within the EC, reflecting the longer history of tariffs and non-tariff barriers within North America.

We can illustrate these merchandise trade linkages as a triangle where the intensity of linkages among the three parties varies in strength depending on the dollar value of bilateral trade flows. Table 10.1 shows these linkages for 1988.[4]

The effective trade pattern is that of a hub and spoke with the U.S. as the hub or economic centre and two trading spokes, a large northern one with Canada and a small southern one with Mexico. Trade flows between the two spokes are so small as to be almost non-existent. As Table 10.1 shows, 1988 American exports to Canada totalled $US 69.9 billion. In terms of Canadian *import penetration* MP (where MP is the share of one country's exports in the total imports of the other country), this flow represents 62.3 percent of total Canadian imports. In terms of American *export orientation* EO (where EO is the share of one country's total exports going to another country), this represents 22.2 percent of U.S. exports. While the value of Canadian exports to the U.S. is similar but larger ($US 79.3 billion), these exports represent only 17.3 percent of all U.S. imports but 71.2 percent of all Canadian exports. Therefore Canada is more *trade-dependent* on the U.S. because American trade with Canada bulks larger as a share of Canadian trade than it does of U.S. trade flows.

A similar but smaller relationship holds true in terms of U.S.-Mexican merchandise trade. As Table 10.1 shows, in 1988 the U.S. exported $US 20.6 billion, representing 6.5 percent of U.S. exports and 67 percent of Mexican imports. U.S. imports from Mexico of $US 23.3 billion represented 5 percent of U.S. imports and 67 percent of Mexican exports. What is particularly noteworthy is the rapid growth in Mexican manufactured exports to the U.S. Until the early 1980s petroleum was the major Mexican export to the U.S.; since 1985, manufactured goods have constituted the largest export category. Now 80 to 85 percent of Mexico's manufactured output, the most rapidly expanding category of Mexican exports, go to the U.S. market.[5]

Canada-Mexico two-way trade in 1989 amounted to some $2.3 billion. Trans-shipment of goods from one spoke to the other spoke through the U.S. probably understates these statistics, although estimates are not available.[6] Canada currently ranks sixth amongst Mexico's trading partners and Mexico seventeenth among Canada's partners. Mexico has consistently had a trade surplus with Canada in recent years and its exports to Canada are growing rapidly. Despite efforts to stimulate Mexico-Canada economic linkages, the increase in trade since 1989 has been one way, i.e., a rise in Mexican exports to Canada: Mexico's exports to Canada grew by 23 percent in 1989.[7] In 1990 the trade balance in Mexico's favour increased as Canadian exports to Mexico fell by 4.2 percent. Canadian exports to Mexico fell again during 1991.[8]

It is perhaps surprising, since we think of Mexico as a developing country and Canada as a developed one, to find that Mexico exports a higher percentage of fully manufactured goods to Canada than vice versa; i.e., 69 percent versus 24 percent.[9] Almost 80 percent of Canadian exports to Mexico are in two groups: agricultural products (half of all exports) and machinery and transport equipment (a third). Given the importance of Canadian exports to Mexico of agricultural products and raw materials (e.g., sulphur), which are subject to dramatic price fluctuations, the

Canadian government hopes that Canada's exports to Mexico will change in the coming years from commodity-based goods to manufactured ones. Mexican exports to Canada are even more concentrated, two-thirds being machinery and transport equipment. Canada-U.S. trade is also heavily weighted towards machinery and transport equipment, with almost half of all Canadian merchandise exports to the U.S. and two-thirds of U.S. exports to Canada in this category. Over 40 percent of Mexican exports to the U.S. and 50 percent of its imports from the U.S. are in this sector. Clearly, the three-way trade in machinery and transport equipment dominates intra-North American trade patterns. It reflects the combination of the Big Three auto producers in all three economies, the 1965 Canada-U.S. Auto Pact, and the combination of the Mexican maquiladoras and U.S. 806/807 tariff provisions.[10]

Investment Patterns

Table 10.2 provides a picture of the triangular FDI patterns among the three economies; the statistics are 1989 stocks of FDI in billions of U.S. dollars, based on Investment Canada data.[11] What is striking about Table 10.2 is its similarity to Table 10.1: while the dollar amounts are smaller, their relative size is the same. The importance of U.S. investment in the Canadian and Mexican economies is obvious. Thus the two spokes are as investment dependent on the U.S. hub as they are trade dependent.

Foreign ownership of Canadian industry has declined in recent years but more than two-fifths of Canadian manufacturing and mining industries remain in foreign, primarily U.S., hands. Canada still has a higher percentage of its economy controlled by foreign investors than any other OECD country. As Table 10.2 shows, in terms of import penetration, the American share of the total FDI stock in Canada of $100.7 billion was 67.7 percent in 1989. This compared to Canadian ownership of 25.1 percent of the $400.8 billion stock of inward U.S. FDI, which represented about 70 percent of the Canadian outward FDI stock.[12]

The stock of U.S. direct investment in Mexico in 1989 was far less than in Canada. It stood at $US 16.7 billion, representing an import penetration of 62.8 percent.[13] The stock of inward FDI in Mexico grew at an average annual rate of 11.6 percent between 1980-85, which increased to 16.1 percent for 1985–89. U.S. investment as a percent of the total has actually fallen from 69 percent in 1980 to the 1989 figure of 62.8 percent. American FDI grew rapidly in Mexico over the period, but not as rapidly as FDI from other countries (e.g., Germany, Japan) and thus the U.S. share fell. Given increasing competition from European and Japanese multinational enterprises (MNEs), U.S. multinationals have made heavy use of maquiladora factories as a cost-driven method of responding to foreign competition. Over one-third of all U.S. FDI in Mexico is in the maquiladoras.[14] At present the majority of the more than 1900 maquila

Table 10.2

The Distribution of Intra-North American

Foreign Direct Investment, 1989

	Canadian FDI Stock in U.S.	in Mexico	U.S. FDI Stock in Canada	Mexico	Mexican FDI Stock in Canada	in U.S.
Value (U.S. $ billions)	31.5	0.4	100.7	16.7	0.005	1.0
XO = Export Orientation (percent)	31.3	0.4	17.0	4.2	0.02	3.8
MP = Import Penetration (percent)	25.1	1.5	67.7	62.8	0.005	0.2

Notes:

XO = export orientation e.g., 31.3% of Canada's stock of FDI is located in the U.S.

MP = import penetration e.g., Canada's FDI in the U.S. accounts for 25.1% of the stock of FDI in the U.S.

firms are owned by American MNEs and medium-sized U.S. companies. At least 57 of the Fortune 500 largest U.S. corporations have maquila plants, including the "Big Three" U.S. auto producers and the major players in the consumer electronics industry. Offshore sourcing in low labour cost sites, which has become critical to the competitiveness of U.S. manufacturing firms, is clearly also a factor more closely connecting the two economies.

The amount of Mexican investment in Canada is negligible at $5 million, or .005 percent of all FDI in Canada. Canadian FDI in Mexico historically has been quite limited and currently stands at about $US 400 million, or an import penetration rate of 1.5 percent of total FDI in Mexico. This places Canada seventeenth among countries with investments in Mexico. In 1989 there were 214 companies in Mexico in which Canadians had investments.[15]

Canadian investment has been primarily in the extractive industries, but in the last few years there has been some FDI in manufacturing as Canadian firms have either established joint ventures with Mexican firms (necessary in the past, and still required in some sectors, under Mexican foreign investment regulations) or moved production to Mexico. In contrast to the huge numbers of U.S. owned maquila firms is the small number of such Canadian owned companies, less than a dozen and primarily in the auto parts industry. Mexico has traditionally had far more stringent restrictions on FDI than Canada and many of these continue.

However, during the 1980s both countries relaxed their limitations on foreign investment.

Trade in automotive products between Canada and Mexico illustrates the way in which the activities of MNEs have linked the two economies, despite their overall limited economic connections. Because of the way in which the Auto Pact and the maquiladoras program have facilitated rationalization of production there is already something akin to a free trade arrangement amongst the U.S., Canada and Mexico in automotive products. Over 98 percent of automotive imports from Mexico into Canada enter duty free under the terms of the U.S.-Canada Auto Pact.[16]

Although only passing attention can be given to Japan in this chapter it is important to note the growing level of Japanese investment in Mexico and the reasons why Japanese firms have found Mexico a more attractive investment location than Canada. Japanese firms, particularly automotive and electronics multinationals, have been heavy investors in Mexico in recent years. Japanese FDI in Mexico, both in maquiladoras and outside them, totalled $1.5 billion in 1990[17] and has risen during 1991. Japan ranks as Mexico's largest trading partner after the U.S. and third as a source of foreign investment.

Japanese investment in Mexico illustrates the ongoing nature of corporate restructuring of production by MNEs to facilitate market access. Intense global competition in autos and consumer electronics has prompted the location of Japanese plants in Mexico to take advantage of lower labour costs as well as proximity to the U.S. Szekely and Wyman argue that "the United States has replaced the Mexican market as the chief target for Japanese producers expanding their operations in Mexico."[18] These plants supply components to Japanese industries located in the U.S. as well as finished goods. Moreover, maquila exports can circumvent the voluntary restraints which the U.S. requires on exports from Japan.

While our federal and provincial governments have attempted to attract Japanese multinationals to Canada, we have been less successful than the Mexicans in this regard. Rugman argues that Japanese FDI in Canada is concentrated in extraction of resources for Japanese use and wholesale distribution of Japanese products; that the Free Trade Agreement has not attracted an increasing amount of this FDI; and that Japanese firms prefer to invest in the United States.[19]

The impact of a NAFTA on the maquiladoras and the consequences of Japanese investment in these in-bond factories are likely to be contentious issues in the free trade negotiations. We now turn to an analysis of the stakes and postures of Canada and Mexico in the NAFTA negotiations, and their relationship to the patterns of trade and investment dependency we have outlined here.

Stakes and Postures

The Canadian Perspective on NAFTA

Economic theory tells us there are mutual gains from reducing barriers to trade, particularly for small open economies, such as Canada. The statistics presented above demonstrate the trade and investment dependence of two small open economies, Canada and Mexico, on the United States and the low level of economic ties between them. Given this combination of theory and economic reality, why were many Canadians reluctant to seek free trade with the United States and even more uncertain about a North American Free Trade Agreement? The answers lie in the complexities of Canadian political life, the continuing uncertainty about the benefits of bilateral free trade and the limited direct economic linkages between Canada and Mexico. If there were expectations of economic gain for Canada from the FTA, there are not so many immediate expectations from a NAFTA. Indeed, as this section of the paper will argue, Canada's decision to participate in the trilateral talks was made for defensive reasons — to ensure no diminution in the terms of its access to the U.S. market — rather than for the more positive reason of new market opportunities.

The Mulroney Government's decision to seek free trade with the United States was a dramatic policy reversal that resulted from a harsh reassessment of Canadian economic alternatives. Pushed by senior officials in the Department of External Affairs, leading segments of the Canadian business community (most notably the Business Council for National Issues and the Canadian Manufacturers' Association) together with some provincial premiers, the Government agreed that, given Canada's trade dependence on the United States and growing U.S. protection, the only route for Canada was to seek an FTA. Such an agreement would broaden access for Canadian exports in the U.S. market and prevent Canadian goods from being caught in the widening web of U.S. neo-protectionist policies.[20]

Some three years into the agreement debate continues over the wisdom of that decision. Canadian adjustment to the new North American economic regime has been hindered by a serious recession in both Canada and the United States. Pushed by difficult economic times, the challenge of goods produced more cheaply elsewhere, and a high Canadian dollar, multinational enterprises, which had begun to plan for the rationalization of their North American operations prior to the signing of the FTA, implemented new organizational structures. These have resulted in plant closures in Canada and the movement of jobs to cheaper labour sites in the southern United States, Mexico[21] or Asia. Labour, strongly opposed to an FTA from the outset, points to the loss of more than 20 percent of Canada's manufacturing jobs since the implementation of the FTA.[22]

Canadian public opinion, never strongly supportive of free trade, registered clear opposition to it in polls conducted in late summer and then again in late fall 1991.[23] That the FTA is of uncertain benefit to Canada is a view that would also seem to be supported by statistics presented by a U.S. Customs officer to the Senate Finance Committee which suggest that free trade has increased U.S. exports to Canada more than Canadian exports to the U.S.[24] For its part, the Mulroney Government maintains that "the recession would have been worse without" the FTA.[25]

Although it is too early, three years into the life of an agreement as broad as the FTA, to definitively assess its economic impact, the FTA experience shaped the parameters within which Canadians examined the new trilateral free trade option. NAFTA was pushed by Mexico, for reasons spelled out below. Although Canada may have appreciated the reasons that led President Salinas de Gortari to seek free trade with the U.S. (reasons which were not unlike those which prompted a similar Canadian decision in 1985), NAFTA presented the Mulroney government with a serious dilemma. Canada, which had focused all its energies on the successful negotiation of the FTA, was surprised when the United States responded positively to Mexican overtures for free trade. For Canada, the exigencies of adjusting to one free trade agreement and the challenges of ongoing constitutional debate meant that the need to consider another free trade opportunity was rather untimely. After a brief series of House of Commons Committee hearings[26] and a debate within the bureaucracy, the Tories decided that they had to seek a place at the NAFTA table. Recognition of the potential costs to Canada of a series of U.S. hub and spoke arrangements explained the Canadian decision to join the NAFTA talks, rather than any deep interest in a wider free trade agreement. Given its trade dependence on the U.S., Canada cannot risk diluting any of the advantages it has gained through the FTA.

That Canadian business is less enthusiastic about a NAFTA than it was about Canada-U.S. free trade is not surprising, given the relatively low levels of Canada-Mexico economic linkages and the present difficulties of adjustment to free trade with the United States. There is considerable concern about competition with Mexican goods for the U.S. market and uneasiness about the anticipated future adjustment to a lower cost partner. Nonetheless, those major Canadian business interests which supported bilateral free trade — the Business Council on National Issues (BCNI), the Canadian Manufacturers Association and the Automotive Parts Manufacturers Association — all argued strongly that Canada had to be a party to discussions which would structure the rules of trade and investment in North America. Canadian auto parts producers, for example, are anxious to ensure that content and rules of origin requirements strengthen, not weaken, their position as players in the North American auto industry. Firms and industries already finding adjustment to the

FTA difficult, such as the furniture, shoe and garment industries, are disturbed at the prospect of yet another free trade agreement. Small business is much more worried about a NAFTA than it was about Canada-U.S. free trade, according to a Canadian Federation of Independent Business survey of members, conducted in April 1991.[27] Canadian labour cites job losses from the FTA and argues that a NAFTA, which would promote competition with lower paid Mexican workers, would simply increase the incentive for many plants to relocate out of Canada.

The Mexican Perspective on NAFTA

The Mexican decision to negotiate a free trade agreement with the United States and Canada was the culmination of efforts to open the Mexican economy that started in earnest during the Presidency of Miguel de la Madrid (1982–1988). The widely perceived exhaustion of import-substituting industrialization, the unwillingness of international banks to continue lending in Latin America after Mexico nearly defaulted on its loans in August 1982, and the decline of oil revenues after 1982 and 1986, were among the factors that forced the Mexican government to liberalize the economy, promote manufacturing exports, and redefine the role of the state in the economy. Mexico joined the General Agreement on Tariffs and Trade (GATT) in 1986. Over the next four years it reduced the maximum tariff to 20 percent and the average tariff to 9.8 percent. Mexico participated actively in the Uruguay Round of Multilateral Trade Negotiations; the foreign investment law was modified to broaden the areas in which foreign investors were allowed full ownership; intellectual property rights legislation was reformed; and over 800 state-owned enterprises were privatized.

The nomination of Salinas de Gortari to be the candidate of the Partido Revolucionario Institucional (Revolutionary Institutional Party, or PRI) in the 1988 presidential election consolidated the power of the more outward-oriented and technocratic wing of the ruling party. The major opposition party led by Cuauhtémoc Cárdenas won slightly over 30 percent of the vote — to the PRI's 50.7 percent — the best showing of the opposition in the post-revolutionary period. A decade of stagnation in which real wages declined by 50 percent contributed to the decline in support for the PRI. Salinas needed to take bold measures to show Mexicans that the government could reactivate the economy. Opinion polls suggest substantial support for economic reforms leading to recovery. In one poll, 59 percent of Mexicans said they would be "willing to form a single nation with the U.S. if it meant a higher standard of living."[28]

In early 1990 Salinas visited Europe in an effort to stimulate trade and investment with Mexico. His disappointment with Europe's response convinced him that Mexico's future lay in economic integration with North America. Salinas said integration is "a fact of the modern world. Look at the blocs that are being created: Europe in 1992, the Pacific Basin countries, the United States and Canada. I don't want to be left out."[29]

What could Mexico do to avoid being "left out"? As previously noted, standard economic theory suggests that when a small country liberalizes trade with a larger country the benefits flow disproportionately to the small country.[30] Mexico stands to gain far more access to new markets through NAFTA than either the United States or Canada. How could the Mexican administration convince Canada and the United States that they should be interested in freer trade with a small economy like Mexico?

A large country may pursue trade liberalization in order to increase its political influence. Trade liberalization gives large countries asymmetrical power. Thus, U.S. policy makers justly expect to have greater influence in Mexico as a result of NAFTA. John D. Negroponte, the Ambassador of the United States to Mexico, said that "an FTA would institutionalize acceptance of a North American orientation to Mexico's foreign relations."[31] Mexico can "sell" NAFTA to the United States by pointing out that the United States has an interest in a politically stable and prosperous southern neighbour: "the United States would rather have Spain than Peru on its border."[32] Moreover, powerful states pursue free trade to strengthen their allies.[33] Concern for Mexico, which intensified in Washington after the dramatic results of the 1988 presidential election, made the United States more receptive to the Salinas initiative. The narrow margin of victory — and widespread accusations of fraud — suggested that the post-revolutionary authoritarian system was crumbling. The prospect of political chaos in Mexico created anxiety among U.S. policy makers. Instability south of the border could lead to massive immigration and border security problems, with implications for U.S. commitments around the world.[34]

President Salinas may be counting on the fact that the U.S. administration wants a stable Mexico. In the past, U.S. concern about Mexican domestic politics would have been unwelcome. Mexico remains wary of U.S. geopolitical interests in the region and suspicious of interference in domestic Mexican affairs; however, in recent years Mexico has become less concerned about its political vulnerability to the United States and more attentive to specific economic vulnerabilities. Since the mid-1980s Mexico has viewed itself as having a more modest regional role, has focused increasingly on domestic economic issues, and has sought to consolidate closer bilateral relations with the United States. This change in the Mexican attitude is largely due to the perceived need to avoid exclusion from the formation of regional blocs, as well as Mexico's desire to distinguish itself from a stagnant and debt-ridden Latin America. Mexico is now more concerned to sustain the current recovery, increase capital inflows (especially FDI), and avoid commercial frictions with its major trading partners.

Trade agreements, in principle, can insulate smaller economies from the future loss of export markets. Both Canada and Mexico have sought trade agreements to shield their economies from the political use of United States trade remedy law. NAFTA is perceived by policymakers in Mexico City as one way in which Mexico can diminish its commercial vulnerability to U.S. protectionism.[35] Thus, Mexican officials have made a dispute settlement mechanism a major objective in the negotiations. The Canadian experience suggests, however, that free trade agreements do not eliminate the political use of U.S. trade remedy laws, particularly when the "hub" economy is under intense competitive pressures and the adminstration faces a protectionist Congress.[36]

The Mexican initiative was also a response to the Canada-U.S. FTA. According to Gustavo Vega, "Mexico and Canada compete in exporting various automotive, textile and apparel, furniture, petrochemical and other products. To prevent Canada from gaining a margin of preference through its free trade agreement with the United States, Mexico feels that it too must pursue the free trade option."[37]

In addition to open and secure access to the United States market, Mexico needs an infusion of external capital. Since the debt crisis began in 1982, Mexico has become a major capital-exporting nation (debt repayments exceeding new investment). The decline of petroleum prices in 1982 and 1986 further reduced the overall level of investment. Until recently, economic growth was sluggish. A NAFTA would help sustain the economic recovery that began in 1989 by "locking-in" Mexico's economic reforms and providing guarantees to capital. A NAFTA "would not only bolster investor confidence by offering an important signal of future intentions but it would also encourage it more directly by the improved market access for export-oriented activities and the 'concessions' to U.S. capital that would undoubtedly be a part of an overall deal."[38]

One of the most sensitive issues in NAFTA negotiations is energy. The Persian Gulf War heightened the perception in the United States that sources of petroleum outside the Middle East should be pursued. Mexico has seen petroleum as a major source of bargaining power in bilateral U.S.-Mexican relations and is reluctant to give it up in the negotiations. However, making concessions to the U.S. in energy pricing, distribution, and ownership of PEMEX, may be necessary to get a favourable deal. Oil is one commodity that can be used to swing support for NAFTA in the U.S. Congress. Canadian officials have recognized Mexican "sensitivities" in the energy sector. However, Canada's motivation in keeping energy off the table is to avoid direct competition with Mexican petroleum producers in the U.S. market.

The Negotiations: Some Tentative Speculations

Mexico initially sought Canadian involvement in NAFTA negotiations to pacify domestic critics who argued that Salinas placed excessive emphasis on the U.S.-Mexican bilateral relationship. The Canadian reaction to a NAFTA, however, was mixed. It soon became apparent that, for domestic reasons outlined above, Canada could be a disruptive partner in the negotiations. When the Canadian government finally decided to join the talks, the Minister of International Trade had to lobby hard to overcome Mexican objections that trilateral negotiations would be too complex and Canada would cause unacceptable delays.

The Canadian government became convinced that, although the idea was not a popular one, it was necessary for Canada to take a seat at the table. Canada was successful in its effort to be included in the discussions. However, negotiators from the three countries agreed that no one country would be able to hold up the talks. If, during the negotiations, Canada was unable to agree with Mexico and the United States in any given area of bargaining, separate bilateral U.S.-Mexican clauses could be written into the final accord. This restricts Canada's ability to hold up the talks to extract concessions.

Canada and Mexico have few economic interests in common. This paper has demonstrated that the current level of trade and investment between the two countries is limited. Where Canada and Mexico have the sharpest difference of interests concerns the status of the existing FTA. Mexico's negotiators have insisted that their country is mainly interested in its bilateral relationship with the United States and wants to negotiate from a "clean slate." Canada, on the other hand, wants the final agreement to be an extension or "trilateralization" of the FTA. Canadian negotiators will oppose any concessions to Mexico that Canada did not achieve in the Canada-U.S. Free Trade Agreement and that would give Mexico preferences in the U.S. market. For Canada, the negotiations are basically about how to include Mexico in the North American economy, not an opportunity to re-open the FTA or deal with the "unfinished American agenda." Canada's basic position is defensive — to protect the FTA.

Mexico is more interested in its bilateral relationship with the U.S. and sees Canadian participation as a potential hindrance to a final agreement. Thus, Mexico aligned itself with efforts by U.S. negotiators to have cultural industries included in a NAFTA. Initially, United States Trade Representative Carla Hills stated that the FTA would not be re-opened. After Canada was included in the talks, however, Hills promised Congress to use the NAFTA negotiations to beat down Canadian barriers in cultural industries. Mexican support for this position illustrates an area of antagonism with the Canadian negotiators.

The evolution of the NAFTA talks illustrates the political complexities of economic dependence: not only are Canada and Mexico both economically dependent on the U.S., but they are also dependent on the U.S. political agenda and the sensitivities of Congress to domestic electoral realities. Formal trilateral discussions on a NAFTA began in June 1991 and the expectation was that a NAFTA agreement could be put before the U.S. Congress for approval prior to the summer commencement of the 1992 election campaign.

As 1991 drew to a close this timetable was being revised. The positive atmosphere surrounding the talks was replaced by the realities of difficult negotiations and a less hospitable economic environment in the United States. A consolidated draft of a NAFTA agreement was expected to be completed by the end of January, 1992. However, many differences remain amongst the three parties; amongst the most difficult areas are textiles, oil, automobiles and a dispute settlement mechanism.[39] At a December 1991 Camp David meeting with President Salinas President Bush reiterated his commitment to the early conclusion of the NAFTA negotiations.[40] Although Washington remained committed to a NAFTA the combination of a U.S. recession and the realities of election politics have made the Americans less enthusiastic about pushing for an early completion of the trilateral talks. If a NAFTA accord is not presented to the U.S. Congress until after the November U.S. election, that is, in early 1993, the timing might pose serious difficulties for the Mulroney government (which must face the electorate no later than October 1993) and for President Salinas (whose term expires in 1994).[41]

Conclusions

This chapter has explored the asymmetrical nature of economic linkages across the three North American economies and analyzed the way in which the patterns of dependence on the United States prompted Canada and Mexico to seek a free trade arrangement with the United States. Although both Canada and Mexico are heavily dependent on the United States, the economic linkages between them are limited. Multinational enterprises, particularly in the auto industry, have played an important role in linking all three North American economies. We argued, further, that Canada, already in the throes of adjusting to the FTA, had little alternative but to seek a seat at the NAFTA talks. The stakes in the NAFTA negotiations are high for both Canada and Mexico. There are points of co-operation and conflict between them over the contents of a NAFTA agreement. In the end, however, the successful conclusion of a trilateral accord will be heavily influenced by U.S. interests and the U.S. political timetable.

Notes

1 The authors would like to acknowledge the Social Sciences and Humanities Research Council of Canada for its support through a research grant for Maxwell A. Cameron and a strategic grant for Lorraine Eden and Maureen Appel Molot. The authors alone are responsible for the ideas expressed in this chapter.

2 The term "hub and spoke" is used by Richard Lipsey and Ronald Wonnacott to depict a series of agreements between the United States (the hub) and a variety of partners (the spokes). Such an arrangement would give the U.S. preferential access to each spoke market but the spokes would have preferential access only to the U.S. market. With the addition of each new spoke, the value of preferential access for previous signatories of free trade agreements with the U.S. would be diminished. See Richard Lipsey, "Canada at the US-Mexico Trade Dance: Wallflower or Partner?" *C.D. Howe Institute Commentary* No. 20 (Toronto: C.D. Howe Institute, 1990) and Ronald J. Wonnacott, "US Hub and Spoke Bilaterals and the Multilateral Trading System," *C.D. Howe Institute Commentary* No. 23 (Toronto: C.D. Howe Institute, 1990). We argue that a de facto hub and spoke relationship already exists in North America whereby trade and investment linkages produce bilateral flows between the U.S. and its northern and southern neighbours. See Lorraine Eden and Maureen Appel Molot, "The View from the Spokes: Canada and Mexico Face the US," in Stephen Randall, ed., *Canada, Mexico and the United States: The Debate Over North American Relations* (Calgary: University of Calgary Press, forthcoming).

3 The EC comparison refers to the Community's twelve current members. House of Commons, Standing Committee on External Affairs and International Trade (SCEAIT). Hearings on Canada-U.S.-Mexico Trade Negotiations, Vol. 68: 35–36 (Ottawa: House of Commons, 1990).

4 The trade data for 1988 is based on Michael Hart, *A North American Free Trade Agreement: The Strategic Implications for Canada* (Halifax: Institute for Research on Public Policy, 1990). The data have been adjusted to include the value added produced in the Mexican maquiladora plants, which the Mexican balance of payments statistics normally counted as transformation service transactions rather than as merchandise exports.

5 Sidney Weintraub, "The Impact of the Agreement on Mexico," in Peter Morici, ed., *Making Free Trade Work* (New York: Council on Foreign Relations, 1990), p. 106.

6 Hart, p. 7.

7 Department of External Affairs and International Trade, *North American Free Trade: Securing Canada's Growth Through Trade* (Ottawa: Supply and Services Canada, 1991).

8 Drew Fagan, "Canada's trade deficit with Mexico soars," *The Globe and Mail*, January 24, 1992.

9 Hart.

10 The maquiladoras are Mexican in-bond assembly and processing factories located in export processing zones set up to attract FDI and encourage local assembly by taking advantage of low Mexican wage rates and reduced taxes and tariffs. The establishment of the maquilas in 1965 marked the initial opening of the Mexican economy to FDI. With the U.S. 806 and 807 tariff regulations levying duties only on the difference between the value of goods imported from Mexico net of U.S. inputs, U.S. multinational enterprises (MNEs) were directly encouraged to set up offshore factories in Mexico and shift subassembly functions to these Mexican locations. Nearly half of all Mexican manufactured goods are produced in the maquiladoras. While the older maquila plants continue to produce labour-intensive products such as textiles and simple components, the newer maquilas are capital-intensive, sophisticated plants producing auto engines and advanced electronics. See Gary Gereffi, "Mexico's Maquiladoras Industries: What Is Their Contribution to National Development and Transnational Integration in North America?" in Randall, ed. (see note 2).

11 Investment Canada, *The Opportunities and Challenges of North American Free Trade: A Canadian Perspective*, Working Paper No. 7 (Ottawa: Investment Canada, 1991), Chart 3, p. 33.

12 Alan Rugman and Alain Verbeke, "Canadian Business in a Global Trading Environment," *Research in Global Business Management*, Vol. 1 (1990): 12.

13 Investment Canada, p. 36.

14 Peter Morici, *Trade Talks with Mexico: A Time for Realism* (Washington: National Planning Association: forthcoming), p. 36.

15 Investment Canada, p. 42.

16 The remaining 2 percent are imported by non-Auto Pact companies and are imported at the generalized preferential rate of six percent. SCEAIT, Issue 61, p. 12.

17 *The New York Times*, April 29, 1990, p. E2; Investment Canada, Table 9, p. 37.

18 Gabriel Szekely and Donald Wyman, "Japan's Ascendance in U.S. Economic Relations with Mexico," *SAIS Review*, Vol. 8, No. 1 (Winter-Spring 1988): 181.

19 Alan Rugman, *Japanese Direct Investment in Canada* (Ottawa: The Canada-Japan Trade Council, 1990), p. 36.

20 For a detailed discussion of the politics of the free trade decision as well as the negotiations, see G. Bruce Doern and Brian W. Tomlin, *Faith and Fear: The Free Trade Story* (Toronto: Stoddart Publishing Co., 1991).

21 Reports of plant closures and job losses have been frequent. See for example the report of the closure of an appliance manufacturer in Waterloo, Ontario and the relocation of jobs to the United States and Mexico. Officials with Electro Porcelain Co. Ltd. attributed the plant closure to reduced demand, foreign competition and the high Canadian dollar. "200 jobs going to U.S. and Mexico," *The Globe and Mail*, November 14, 1991, p. B6.

22 Alan Freeman, "Job loss alarm sounded," *The Globe and Mail*, August 29, 1991, p. B3.

23 Bruce Little, "Recession erodes support for Canada-U.S. pact," *The Globe and Mail*, November 25, 1991, p. B1. The level of public support for the FTA was an issue immediately after the 1988 election when opponents of the agreement noted that, despite the Conservatives' election victory, more than 50 per cent of Canadian voters voted for either the Liberals or the NDP, both of whom opposed the FTA. Various opinion polls suggest that in early 1990 public opinion was about evenly divided on the issue; by the middle of 1991 and after 55 per cent of Canadians opposed the agreement while 38 per cent supported it.

24 Rod McQueen, "Statistics show Canada as loser under free trade pact," *The Financial Post*, February 21, 1991, p. 6.

25 Drew Fagan, "Wilson defends free trade deal," *The Globe and Mail*, August 19, 1991, p. A5.

26 The House of Commons Standing Committee on External Affairs and International Trade held hearings on a NAFTA through much of 1990.

27 "Trade deal raises fears: Small business wary of Mexico," *The Globe and Mail*, October 11, 1991, p. B3.

28 See Matt Moffett, "Mexicans, weary of 10-year debt crisis register little opposition to trade pact," *The Wall Street Journal*, May 13, 1991. Further results from the same survey are reported in "Integración económica y nacionalismo: Canadá, Estados Unidos y México," *Este país* (April 1991): 3–9.

29 From *Newsweek*, October 16, 1989, cited in Adolfo Gilly, "The Mexican Regime in its Dilemma," *Journal of International Affairs*, Vol. 43, No. 1 (1989): 285.

30 Gerald K. Helleiner, "Considering a U.S.-Mexican Free Trade Area," paper prepared for a conference on "Mexico's International Trade Options in the Changing International Economy." Universidad Tecnológica de México, Mexico City, June 11–15, 1990, p. 12.

31 From a statement in a cable to Assistant Secretary of State for Interamerican Affairs, reprinted in *Proceso*, No. 758, May 13, 1991: 7.

32 M. Delal Baer, "North American Free Trade," *Foreign Affairs*, Vol. 70, No. 4 (1991): 138.

33 Joanne Gowa, "Bipolarity, Multipolarity, and Free Trade," *American Political Science Review*, Vol. 86, No. 4 (1989): 1252.

34 Baer, p. 138.

35 We are grateful to Fen Osler Hampson for this observation.

36 Doern and Tomlin argue that Canada failed to win agreement to have U.S. trade remedy laws subject to the FTA.

37 Gustavo Vega, "Consolidating a North American Free Trade Agreement: A Mexican Perspective," Paper prepared for the workshop "The Politics of North American Free Trade," at the Center for Latin American Studies, University of California, Berkeley, November 21–22, 1991, p. 3.

38 Helleiner, "Considering a U.S.-Mexico Free Trade Area," p. 8.

39 Rod McQueen, "Top-level talks expected in bid to speed free trade," *The Financial Post*, January 20, 1992, p. 4.

40 On the preparation of draft texts and the continuing U.S. commitment to a NAFTA see "Free-trade deal near: Salinas," *The Globe and Mail*,

December 16, 1991, p. B4 and "Bush says no delay on free trade deal," *The Financial Post*, December 20, 1991, p.8.

41 See discussions by John Saunders, "Mexico deal unlikely till '93," *The Globe and Mail*, November 22, 1991, p. A1 and Drew Fagan, "Tories fear free trade will haunt them again in '93," *The Globe and Mail*, November 23, 1991, p. A1.

11

Europe 1992:
Implications for North America
Fanny S. Demers and Michel Demers

"The 'ship' of opportunity . . . is not 'leaving the dock' and 'Fortress
Europe' is no greater a threat than ' America'."
–Douglas E. Rosenthal

The Post-Maastricht Europe

For the past few years one single date, 1992, has seemed to capture the
hopes, dreams and aspirations of all Europeans, as a turning point for Europe. The completion of the internal European market is well under way.
At the December 1991 Maastricht Summit meeting, the twelve European
nations reached a historic agreement concerning the establishment of a
single currency by 1999, as well as some limited, though important, form
of political union including co-operation in matters of security, an extension of citizenship rights and a strengthening of the European Parliament.
In the past forty years, by deciding to impose constraints on their own
sovereignty, the member states of the European Community (EC) have
made significant headway towards realizing Jean Monnet's dream of a
federal Europe, a Europe of citizens, a Europe capable of rivalling the
United States and Japan.

European integration, culminating in the Maastricht Summit, did not
follow a smooth progression. Whereas the Treaty of Rome of 1957 had
created a common market, the 1960s and 1970s witnessed the growth of
non-tariff barriers as well as countless obstacles to the functioning of a
single European market. By the end of the 1970s many questioned the viability of the European Community, but the "Eurosclerosis" of the 1980s
gave new impetus to the search for a "European solution." The high
unemployment rates accompanied by low rates of GNP growth[1] experienced by most members of the EC, coupled with the fear of American and
Japanese competition, led to the EC White Paper, "Completing the Internal Market," and to passage of the Single European Act whose objective
was to create a genuine customs union and common market within the
EC by the end of 1992. Whereas political leaders provided the impetus

for the Treaty of Rome, business leaders were at the forefront of support for the White Paper's recommendations. The core of Europe 1992 consists of eliminating the physical, technical and fiscal barriers to the free movement of goods, services, capital and labour. Although complete agreement on some issues, such as tax harmonization and company law, has not yet been reached and there still remain 56 directives that have not yet been ratified, substantial progress has been made on all counts.[2]

The architects of the Single European Act had not anticipated the end of Communism in East Europe, the reunification of Germany, the end of the Warsaw Pact, the disintegration of the Soviet Union, and the explosion of nationalistic tensions unleashed after the demise of communism. However, the EC has responded robustly to this unfolding of events. In November 1989, the former French Defense Minister Jean-Pierre Chevènement, a "Euro-skeptic," declared: "The fall of the Berlin wall has made only one victim: Jacques Delors." History proved him wrong. European leaders moved swiftly to anchor the reunified Germany within the EC, an important accomplishment of the Maastricht Summit.

In October 1991 the twelve EC nations and the seven European Free Trade Area (EFTA) members (Austria, Finland, Iceland, Liechtenstein, Norway, Sweden and Switzerland) agreed to form a European Economic Area (EEA) as of 1993. In December 1991, however, the European Court of Justice invalidated the EEA treaty by ruling that the proposed EEA court (composed of five judges from the EC and three from the EFTA) which was designed to settle disputes, violated the EC treaties.[3] If the EEA is successfully renegotiated, it will become the world's largest free trade area with a population of 380 million and with 46 percent of world trade.

What developments will take place in this decade in which Europe will be striving to regain its status at the centre of world affairs? History testifies to the vital importance of European stability for North America and the world. In view of the rising ethnic tensions in the Eastern part of Europe, which the Western World would be misguided to ignore, what strategy will the EC adopt to avoid the repetition of the Yugoslav conflict? While the Czech and Slovak Republic (formerly Czechoslovakia), Poland and Hungary have been granted associate membership in the EC, it has been argued that East European countries do not presently have suitably developed market economies to qualify for an economic association with the EC in the near future. Will the EC then allow some form of political union with its East European neighbours to precede an economic association such as was proposed by Alain Minc, among others, with the objective of guaranteeing the respect for democracy and the recognition of minority rights, together with the acceptance of EC arbitration to settle territorial disputes and of EC intervention if necessary?[4] In this thinking, a form of political union would pave the way for a future economic union.

In the next millennium, are we to anticipate a European Community with concentric circles of progressively looser free trade zones, encompassing Western *and* Eastern Europe, or perhaps even an EC of 40 from the Atlantic to the Pacific as predicted by Jacques Attali? What are the possible implications for countries such as Canada which find themselves outside this European microcosm?

The Canadian view of Europe 1992 appears to be indifference tinged with some apprehension. Are we to anticipate Fortress Europe or Partner Europe? As the world enters the hyper-industrial age, is the centre of gravity in economic matters going to shift away from North America to Europe or Japan? What are the implications for Canada's competitiveness? While the European club becomes more influential in the determination of international outcomes, will Canada, internally torn by divisions and indecision, helplessly and irrevocably drift towards a lower standard of living and reduced influence on the international scene?

In this chapter we examine developments in Europe from a Canadian and North American viewpoint. First we look at current Canadian-EC relations and the prospects for Canada resulting from the integration process in Europe. Next, we analyze whether the fears of "Fortress Europe" are well founded. Finally, we discuss possible Canadian strategies in response to the present developments in Europe.

Opportunity Europe

How will European integration affect Canada? This is a question of considerable importance since the EC is Canada's second largest trading partner (after the U.S. and before Japan: see Figure 11.1), and is the second most important destination for Canadian foreign direct investment after the U.S. (see Table 11.1).

Europe 1992 will undoubtedly facilitate access to the EC market for Canadian exporters and direct investors. In fact, due to the principle of mutual recognition, one of the most important mechanisms facilitating the harmonization and integration process in Europe, it will be less costly for Canadians to penetrate the EC market. Under the principle of mutual recognition, the regulations and standards adopted by one member state will have to be recognized by all other member states of the Community. Therefore, non-EC firms will have to meet the requirements of only one country as opposed to twelve in pre-1992 situations. Firms involved in either export activities or direct investment will be able to choose as their point of entry the country with the most advantageous regulations. Furthermore, member states, regions and localities, eager to attract foreign investment and employment opportunities, will compete fiercely with one another in offering the most favourable conditions for entry into the

Canadian Trade, 1990

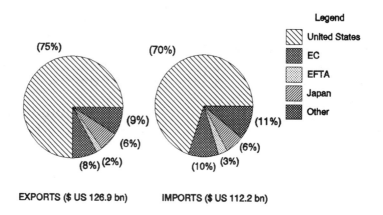

EXPORTS ($ US 126.9 bn)   IMPORTS ($ US 112.2 bn)

Source: Eurostat External Trade Statistical Yearbook 1991, Table C, p. 134.

EC market, to the benefit of potential entrants. The principle of mutual recognition will also make it harder for any EC-country to discriminate against an EC-based subsidiary of a non-EC firm.

Table 11.1

Direct Foreign Investment Flows (1989)

Billions of U.S. dollars

From ↓ To →	Canada	U.S.	EC	Japan
Canada	—	43.3	12.0	0.3
U.S.	65.5	—	150.0	19.4
EC	22.8	234.8	—	2.6
Japan	4.0	104.4	42.0	—

Source: Prosperity Secretariat, "Prosperity Through Competitiveness," Ottawa, 1991, p. 35.

Europe 1992 will also open up government procurement to non-EC firms. As shown in more detail below, there may be a preference margin for bids from EC firms when foreign bids do not have 50 percent local content. However, given the strength of Canadian and American firms in telecommunications and the projected growth rate of 67 percent between 1986 and 1995 of the telecommunications equipment market in the EC, there appear to be important opportunities, especially as the EC has indicated that, once a country outside it eliminates its "buy national preference" in bids at all levels of government, the Community will eliminate its preference margin altogether.

Canadian firms will also benefit from the European Monetary Union (EMU), which will lead to the adoption of a single currency by 1999, thereby eliminating all exchange rate uncertainty among EC countries and the transaction costs involved in operating in more than one currency. The single EC financial market offers Canadian banks and their investment dealer affiliates interesting opportunities. Canadian banks have expertise in mergers and acquisitions, one of the most important areas of activity in the completion of the single market. Moreover, being unaffiliated with industrial groups in Europe, they would be considered impartial and their services would be in demand.

Direct investment by Canadian firms may be complementary to Canadian exports, as previous empirical work has demonstrated for U.S. multinationals.[5] For example, investment in distribution channels and service facilities which provides customer services in local markets promotes exports by the home company. Alternatively, when a Canadian parent can sell components to its affiliate in Europe, exports will follow Canadian foreign investment in the EC, whereas without the Canadian presence in Europe the EC market could be lost to competitors. With a view to creating such advantages, Canadians have the opportunity to seek acquisitions, mergers or alliances with EC firms during the ongoing restructuring process taking place in many European industries. In some cases, seeking such opportunities may be vitally necessary. One example is the pulp and paper industry, which currently accounts for 30 percent of Canadian exports to the EC. As European manufacturers attempt to secure their pulp supply, a failure to form joint ventures or mergers may endanger future export prospects in this area.

In other cases, the choice between exporting to the EC or investing in the EC may also be affected by protectionist measures adopted by the Community. For example, a Canadian firm in telecommunications may face the choice between expanding plant, equipment and research & development (R & D) in the EC or in Canada, and may decide to locate in the EC simply because of origin and local content rules, even if cost considerations would have otherwise favoured a Canadian location.

Thus, protectionist tendencies in the EC could lead to distortions in direct investment patterns as well as a reduction in the benefits of the integration process for Canadian and non-EC firms (as well as to EC firms themselves in the longer run). In the next section we first document current EC practices which may be deemed protectionist, and then investigate whether protectionism is likely to dominate EC trade policy in the near future.

Fortress Europe?

While Europe 1992 is a continuing process of increasing trade liberalization among the EC members, it has also raised some fears with respect to the EC's trade practices with respect to non-member countries. What is the evidence for protectionist moves on the part of the EC? While this is a complex issue, one indication of protectionism may be the extent of trade diversion taking place, for which one rough measure is the increase in the "regional bias ratio," that is, the ratio of intra-regional trade to the share of total world trade.[6] The regional bias in the EC rose from 1.28 in 1980 to 1.77 in 1989, a more important increase in regional bias than in other regions such as North America or East Asia. While these figures are by no means a decisive indication of protectionism, firms of non-EC countries, especially Japan, are intensifying their direct investment activities in order to pre-empt any attempts on the part of the Europeans to erect barriers. Thus, while most Japanese direct investment is undertaken in North America, Japanese direct investment in the EC, as a percentage of total Japanese direct investment world-wide, increased markedly between 1987 and 1990: the increase was 5.4 percent, as compared to only a 1.8 percent increase in North America.

Trade diversion is due to the common tariff barriers that protect all EC members with respect to imports from the rest of the world, as well as to the multitude of non-tariff barriers, regulations and other practices which also lead to trade diversion. Our discussion will emphasize non-tariff barriers to trade with third countries, such as anti-dumping duties, rules of local content and origin, technical standards, environmental regulations and state aid, corporatism, state *dirigisme* and managed trade.

Anti-dumping

In the past, dumping was a term used to identify the practice of selling the same product at a lower price in the foreign market than at home, thus conferring an unfair trade advantage on the perpetrator. However, as Flamm humorously points out, today the term "has come to mean 'less than my calculation of what your full average cost ought to be'."[7] In fact, accusations of dumping have prompted more regulations that restrict trade than any other unfair trade practice, and have become, in many instances, a favoured tool of protectionists. As Messerlin argues, since anti-dumping action is often brought against a firm at the instigation of import-competing EC firms, these regulations have, in effect, led to "the privatization of administered protection."[8] Anti-dumping regulations are accompanied by "anti-screwdriver" regulations which are measures to prevent the circumvention of anti-dumping duties by firms which undertake the major stages of the production process outside the region and only very minor aspects (assembling parts with a "screwdriver") within the region. Thus, according to EC ruling, foreign firms which have been found guilty of dumping are required to have 40 percent of the value of their product originating in countries other than their home country (but not necessarily in EC member-countries) so as to avoid dumping penalties. However, in practice, EC officials indicate to the firms involved that their chances of settling the case would be better if they have a higher EC content, leading again to trade diversion.[9]

Anti-dumping and anti-circumvention regulations often distort not only trade patterns but international investment patterns as well by forcing foreign firms to undertake costly investments in the EC. These additional production costs lead to higher prices and a loss of consumer welfare.

Rules of Origin and Local Content

Among the numerous protectionist measures in place, rules of origin and local content constitute an important non-tariff barrier. They are also often used as "anti-screwdriver" measures. Local content rules classify goods according to the percentage of value added in a given geographical region — say, the EC — while rules of origin, as the name implies, determine the national origin of goods or of components of goods. Yet, given today's vertically integrated multinationals, with operations that span nearly the entire globe, it is becoming increasingly difficult to determine the national origin of a product. In the words of Hufbauer, "[R]ules of origin and local content are two mind-numbing concepts that, when linked together in certain ways, can create almost impenetrable trade barriers....The coupling of stringent local content requirements with tight rules of origin can essentially exclude products made outside of the Community."[10]

In the sensitive case of semiconductors, ". . . rules of origin have become the litmus test for the attitude Europe will be adopting toward the trade regime . . . ."[11] Semiconductors are today as strategic an input to the computer and high-tech industries as petroleum is to the more traditional manufacturing industries. In February 1989, the European Commission altered the interpretation of the rule of origin for chips: whereas the old interpretation considered "assembly and test" to be an important part of the production process for semiconductors and a determinant of the origin of the chip, the new interpretation required that the process of laying the circuit on the chip (the "diffusion" process) be done in the EC in order for the product to be considered EC-made. This ruling had an especially negative impact on Japanese producers since the percentage of the sales of Japanese semiconductor firms operating in Europe that qualified as being of EC origin fell from 39 percent to only 12 percent. This redefinition on the part of the EC has led to substantial trade diversion, as all firms in the EC using semiconductors as inputs had to change their sourcing and purchase chips deemed to be EC-made, in order to satisfy local content rule requirements imposed on them and to evade anti-dumping duties.

Furthermore, when national government procurement in energy, water supply, transportation and telecommunications becomes finally accessible to non-nationals, governments will be able either to reject outright any bid with more than 50 percent non-EC content, or to adopt a three percent preference margin for European bids relative to those with more than 50 percent non-EC content.[12] Until Canada is able to negotiate reciprocal treatment with respect to government procurement, these protectionist rules will lead to trade diversion, and may be harmful to Canadian firms. As a result, EC-based firms currently using Canadian parts would now replace them by European parts that might be less efficiently produced, with an ensuing loss of Canadian exports. Moreover, in industries such as telecommunications, where Canadian firms such as Mitel and Northern Telecom are internationally competitive, a large share of the value added of a specific piece of equipment is contained in the more general R & D effort of the companies. The 50 percent EC-content rule applied on a project by project basis would discriminate against non-EC based firms. This is prompting a greater transfer of R & D and software activities, as well as other production facilities, to the EC. In fact, since 1987, Northern Telecom has made moves to penetrate the EC market by purchasing a 28.5 percent share in the British firms STC and by building a PABX (private automatic branch exchange) plant in France.[13]

While contributing to a reduction in EC trade with the rest of the world, rules of origin and local content have increased the incentive for foreign direct investment in the EC. However, as illustrated by the recent agreement on automobiles between the EC and Japan, direct investment is not always successful as a means of circumventing the local content rule. The European Commission has indicated that it wants to increase the import quotas on Japanese cars from the present 11 percent to 16–17 percent, but that it will count as Japanese those cars that are produced by Japanese-owned plants in Europe.[14] Thus, the local content rule has become an elastic concept that is reinterpreted at will. For example, the local content rule is 60 percent for automobile imports from the EFTA to be duty free, but 35–45 percent for other goods to escape national quotas.[15]

As the EC gains increasing importance and weight in international trade relations, agreements between the EC and its non-EC trade partners came to affect indirectly third countries such as the U.S. and Canada. The EC-Japan automobile agreement may again be taken as an example: Honda wants to export Accords made in the U.S. to France, but France may decide to consider these as Japanese, just as it had attempted to do with the Nissan Bluebirds produced in Britain, in spite of their 70 percent British content.[16] Even though the U.S. would like to contest this interpretation as a protectionist measure that restricts its exports to the EC, it may refrain from doing so, and instead follow the same procedure itself by imposing duties on Japanese cars made in Canada under the pretext that they are Japanese and not North American. The alternative chosen will depend on how successful the U.S. thinks it can be in contesting the French interpretation and on the relative importance of the EC and Canadian markets.

The reinterpretation by the EC of the rule of origin regarding semiconductors also has a significance beyond its direct impact on firms currently operating in Europe, and may affect trade negotiations in the rest of the world by redefining the meaning of "origin." Since the location of assembly and test has been the traditional determinant of origin in international negotiations, the EC ruling may set a dangerous precedent with respect to this definition.

Indirect Effects of Government Policies

Some policies that are directed ostensibly towards environmental or other national concerns may, sometimes unwittingly, have a protectionist implication, at least in the short run. Alternatively, governments may attempt to disguise protectionist moves by emphasizing some other motive for their policies. One example of such an attempt is a recent German regulation regarding environment-friendly packaging. The Germans seem to be more sensitive to the issue of environmental protection, perhaps due to the political importance of the Green movement in that country. However, some recent policies, apparently aimed at environmental protection, may have a protectionist impact by favouring packaging produced only by German companies.[17]

The EC ban on hormone-injected North American beef is another example of a protectionist move disguised as a health protection measure, initiated in response to the vociferous European agricultural lobby whose activism has at times reached unimaginable proportions.

The next target (directly involving Canadian exports) may very well be the pulp and paper industry, as the public starts questioning the pollution standards or the reforestation practices of particular firms. As the environment gains importance, and the demand for recycled fibres increases, some types of pulp produced by processes that do not conform to specific emission standards could be banned.[18]

Other developments such as concern with the pinewood nematode (PWN), a micro-organism found in softwood, could hinder access to the EC market. Although the probability of undetected PWN in Canadian softwood that has been examined under the Canadian mill certificate program is very low and the risk of transmission to European forests almost non-existent, Ireland has banned the import of green Canadian softwood unless it is kiln-dried. The European Commission is currently debating whether or not kiln-drying should be made mandatory.

This type of protectionism is particularly insidious because the outward motive is a commendable one. As public opinion becomes more vocal about environmental issues opportunities multiply for invoking environmental protection in order to ban certain imports. Since this is, of course, true for *all* countries and not only for Europe, it is the fear of retaliation that may keep such activity in check.

Technical Standards

An essential aspect of the completion of the single market is the harmonization of the often disparate rules, standards, testing and certification procedures that various EC-members use to regulate almost all industries, including pharmaceuticals, construction, and telecommunications, especially in areas related to health, safety and the environment. Such a harmonization of standards is essential for both EC firms and EC-based foreign firms if they are to realize the benefits of a unified market.

However, if the adopted set of harmonized standards differs too markedly from those in the EC's trade partners, it would increase the adjustment costs of foreign firms which wish to penetrate the EC market. For example, the construction products directive and Eurocode 5 could have important implications for Canadian industry. The objective of the construction products directive is to harmonize aspects of the design and construction of buildings and civil engineering structures by the end of 1992. Eurocode 5 deals with product and testing standards for wood. If some of the EC standards, such as those that apply to fire-testing, prove to be inconsistent with Canadian standards, there could be adjustment problems for Canadian firms.

Corporatism, State dirigisme *and Managed Trade*

The completion of the internal market in the EC is inevitably accompanied by a major restructuring of many of its industries as they attempt to take advantage of the opportunities for greater efficiency and greater economies of scale provided by a "single market." This process has led to numerous mergers, acquisitions and joint ventures.[19] However, this restructuring of firms, especially when involving state-aid, has led to fears that the EC countries might start to promote "national champions," especially in high-technology industries, and call for a redefinition of antitrust and competition policy to mean "competition in world markets" so as to allow for the formation of giant conglomerates.

High-technology industries are perceived to be the key to competitiveness and military security. The former Defence Minister of France,

Jean-Pierre Chevènement, rejected the advice of the French Navy to purchase U.S.-made F-18s, claiming that protecting the French aeronautics industry was a national security issue in itself.[20]

Except in the area of aerospace, Europe has lagged behind the U.S. and Japan in high-technology industries. Many Europeans seem to prefer state aid and collusion to competition as the means of successfully competing with giant Japanese and U.S. firms, especially in the high-tech industries.[21] As Charles Shultze notes, a "major area of concern . . . is the extent to which the European Community, through unification, hastens a trend — already in evidence around the world — to subsidize, protect, and otherwise pursue policies to expand its *high-technology industries* at the expense of those based in other countries."[22] (emphasis in original). The EC could intensify the use of anti-dumping laws, prevent the admission of foreign firms into European consortia, favour European firms in government procurement of high-tech products, subsidize high-tech production, and allow anti-competitive behaviour in the EC in order to foster the development of giant firms. Caught in a vicious circle, the EC may then find itself obliged to support these giant firms if in the end they turn out to be unsuccessful in world markets.

The 1985 White Paper and the implementation of the Single European Act of 1987 were seen as the remedies that would help Europe emerge from the crippling unemployment and stagnation that characterized what Hoffman has called the "dark age" of the EC, during which economic difficulties had given national governments the traditional excuse for state intervention.[23] After about five years of recovery, growth and optimism, Europe is now starting to feel the brunt of the North American recession. Together with rumours of a double-dipped recession (or, at best, stagnation) in the U.S., a certain malaise is apparent in many EC countries, as some business and opinion leaders are calling for greater state aid. Now that national governments are constrained by EC regulations in the amount of aid that they can provide, firms are turning for aid to Brussels. Some governments (especially, but not only, France and Italy) openly support an EC-wide "industrial policy" to help their industries.[24]

In Germany, banks are allowed to be important shareholders in German corporations, and they can use their position to ward off hostile take-over bids from non-German firms. In France, the government is still an important shareholder in many firms and, according to some, may have tried to prevent some takeovers by foreign firms.[25] The British, Dutch and the Italian also have in place some legal provisions which can be used to block unwanted take-overs.[26]

Many intellectuals and business leaders in Europe are also in favour of increased state intervention and are criticising the tendency of the EC to adopt the "American model" of capitalism. Michel Albert, head of the Assurances Générales de France, rejects the American model of capitalism characterized by "unbridled competition, individualism and hedonism," and advocates the Japanese-Swiss-German model characterized by "a concern for collective success and consensus building."[27] Neil Kinnock, the leader of the Labour Party in the U.K., while being an ardent supporter of Europe, also favours the German model with its consensus-oriented social-market philosophy.[28] Bernard Cassen writes:[29]

> The French government, which has sacrificed a great deal for the sake of a European entity until now of a strictly neoliberal persuasion, . . . would like to see the implementation of common policies other than those — incarnated by Mr. Leon Brittan — of competition, which amounts to the same thing as having no policy to counter competitors who do have one. Health, culture, education, training and *especially industry* are the candidates being put forward by Paris. [emphasis added]

The corporatist tendency may be accentuated because of the adoption at the Maastricht Summit of an à la carte social charter allowing eleven member states — Britain chose not to opt in — to formulate EC social policy in matters such as working conditions, information and consultation for workers, and equal rights for men and women in the work place. Laws pertaining to layoffs and social security will require unanimity. Federations of employers and unions will be granted the right to reach agreements on their own with the option of turning them into law. Britain chose not to adhere to the social charter because of the implication that labour markets would be less flexible in responding to local conditions and the EC would become less attractive as a source of foreign investment. However, the situation could change if a Labour government is elected in Britain.

Partner Europe?

It is clear that the protectionist forces at work in Europe have led to the adoption of numerous measures that hinder free trade and competition. However, some of these measures have been taken in retaliation against protectionist moves by trading partners. Furthermore, since protectionism would negate some of the benefits of the completion of the internal market, it runs counter to the underlying philosophy that motivated the Single Market Act. Besides, there do exist some built-in safeguards against protectionism.

Existing Safeguards against Protectionism

It is of some significance that, the EC has espoused the principle of free trade and competition as its main guiding philosophy, and has on many occasions declared its commitment to the essential tenets of free trade. In fact, the Commission of the EC has urged the involvement of the European Round Table (a business association representing European multinationals) in the Uruguay Round of the General Agreement on Tariffs and Trade (GATT) negotiations.[30] Furthermore, the current EC Competition Commissioner, Sir Leon Brittan, who has acquired a reputation for being very strict about enforcing the EC antitrust regulations, has indicated his belief that nurturing national champions does not constitute a successful strategy. In a speech delivered in 1989 he explicitly stated that

> ... companies that are allowed to operate in a monopolistic way in their own home markets, whether those are national or European, are in fact unlikely to become world beaters. Without the spur of competition in their own market they will inevitably be tempted to rely on and reinforce their dominance of that market and will not have the cutting edge needed to secure success on the world stage.[31]

He has also demonstrated his commitment to enforcing Article 92 of the Treaty of Rome forbidding state aid, by reviewing 15 cases involving Italy, Belgium, Britain, Germany and France. These actions signal the EC Commission's resolve to adhere to the principles of competition and free trade.

Since about 30 percent of EC exports are with non-EC and non-EFTA members, the threat of retaliation may itself be an important deterrent to the adoption of protectionist measures. The EC remains the most trade-oriented bloc in the world. In 1990, its external exports amount to 9.3 percent of EC gross national product, compared to 7.8 for North America and 6.2 for Japan.[32]

An additional safeguard is provided by the evolution in trade patterns. Today, the bulk of direct foreign investment (DFI) is undertaken by footloose multinational corporations which invest in a given market in the pursuit of lower costs. This has led to an international interpenetration of DFI. As Bhagwati notes "we are past the days of one-way DFI portrayed by Jean-Jacques Servan-Schreiber."[33] In fact, not only do we observe inter-industry DFI but also, frequently, intra-industry DFI, as multinationals in the same industry penetrate each other's home market and even export back to the home country.[34]

Firms and states are developing increasingly looser ties. The cross-national joint ventures and strategic alliances increase trade between blocs, and thus create important pro-trade interests offering a safeguard against protectionism, which, by closing markets and increasing costs, jeopardizes the returns to global investments. In this way a constituency that is strongly in favour of free trade is thus created: for example, in Canada, the Business Council on National Issues and the Canadian Manufacturers' Association; in the U.S., the Business Round Table, the

U.S. Council for International Business, the National Association of Manufacturers, and the U.S. Chamber of Commerce; and in the EC, the European Round Table. All these have been supporters of free trade.

Furthermore, pro-trade interests may even spark opposition to specific protectionist measures. In the U.S., a coalition of exporters, importers and manufacturers, called the Pro-Trade Group, voiced its opposition to the U.S. anti-dumping laws because "greater international interconnections today cause antidumping decisions to have wide repercussions for American business."[35] In another example, China's threat to decrease grain imports from the U.S., in retaliation against restrictive American quotas proposed during the multifibre negotiations led to vigorous lobbying against the quotas by the American agricultural lobby.

While the emergence of coalitions at the level of Europe is clearly a relatively new phenomenon, the creation of strong pro-trade interests in Europe is sparking action of the kind described above. For example, the President of the European Chemical Industry has strongly argued in favour of multilateral free trade, indicating that it is in the best interest of the industry, and has undertaken lobbying activities in support of this position.

Protectionism Negates the Benefits of Integration

Perhaps the most compelling reason why Europe should not, and probably will not, hide behind a protectionist wall, is that such a move would negate some of the anticipated benefits from the integration process. Protectionism often works to reduce competitiveness in unexpected places. The protection of the agricultural sector in Europe is one of the causes of the lack of competitiveness of its chemical and pharmaceutical industries. The income support programs for agricultural producers has made starch and sugar (fermentation feedstock) so prohibitively expensive that a liquid sweetener was commercialized in the U.S. rather than in Europe, where it had originally been developed. These handicapped industries may provide some pressure to help bring about the all-round reduction of agricultural subsidies, an issue which is hindering the progress of multilateral trade negotiations.

Another example is offered by the privatized British electricity firms, which are put at a competitive disadvantage due to a contract which forces them to purchase coal from the economically inefficient state-owned British coal firms. It is unlikely that the European Commission will allow the renewal of this contract, due to expire in 1993–94.[36]

The absence of competition leads to inefficiency, as is documented by Cowhey in the context of the central office switch (COS) market, the largest and most important component of the telecommunications market (and a sector in which Canada has a comparative advantage). The average cost per switched line provided by "national champion" European firms in the EC is from two to five times that provided by North American firms. This large cost differential is gradually inducing European telecommunications agencies to abandon their almost exclusive supply contracts with European firms in favour of North American producers. Thus, even though the COS market is characterized by high R & D costs and substantial economies of scale, and therefore may be a typical example of an industry which would qualify for protection according to the proponents of strategic trade policy, we observe the essential failure of this approach which, due to intermarket linkages, achieves the protection of one industry (the COS) only to the detriment of another, the telecommunications industry.[37]

Protectionism also hinders the structural adjustments in traditional sectors such as textiles and clothing required by considerations of worldwide comparative advantage. Although labour in southern Europe enjoys a substantial cost advantage relative to northern Europe, it is at a disadvantage in relation to some developing countries (and to Eastern European countries, as trade relations with these countries intensify). In fact, even South Korea, Hong Kong and Singapore have reduced the proportion of textiles and clothing in their total manufacturing activities, as they face a similar disadvantage in labour-intensive activities when compared to other countries such as India.[38] Therefore, exposure to foreign competition would permit some much-needed adjustments in Southern Europe, whereas protectionist measures would lead to inefficiencies.

Those who favour the formation, and subsequently the protection, of large national high-technology firms, often argue that this industrial sector is characterized by economies of scale due to high research and development costs, (hence the need for large firms and high market concentration), and that R & D activities have important spill-over effects to the rest of the economy (hence the strategic nature of these industries and the need to protect them). However, as is argued by Jacquemin and Sapir,[39] policy intervention should not divorce the firm from the beneficial market signals and should not shield it from international competition. Cohen notes that by nursing its high-tech firms on government contracts, the French government has reduced the incentive for French firms to compete in international markets, thus contributing to the difficulties of the computer firm Groupe Bull, to name one.[40] There are no simple criteria for "picking winners."

The technology policy in the completed EC market encourages the formation of research joint ventures. According to the Cecchini Report, "co-operative behaviour for R & D coupled with tough competition in the end market, might further the general welfare more than totally non-co-operative behaviour."[41] Economic theory indicates that such co-operative behaviour may be warranted when the private benefits of R & D fall short of the social benefits. Furthermore, even in areas where such market failure occurs, it does not necessarily imply that only EC research joint ventures will be favoured. The EC could very well promote joint ventures between EC and North American or Japanese firms.

In high technology, there exist several consortia and R & D programs in the EC. Some of these are EUREKA, RACE, ESPRIT and JESSI.[42] Foreign firms can participate in EUREKA projects as long as they are in partnership with at least two European firms. In fact several Canadian firms participate in various EUREKA projects — DMR, a leading Canadian firm in information technology, co-operates in the development of advanced software technology; Zenon Environmental Inc. in a water filtration and waste water treatment project; and National Optic Laboratory works on the development of an advanced laser system within the consortium "Eurolaser."[43]

The EC has not, thus far, allowed the participation of foreign firms in research consortia such as RACE, ESPRIT and JESSI, claiming that EC firms based in North America do not have reciprocal access to U.S. R & D programs, and cannot obtain research contracts from the U.S. Department of Defence. However, this policy stance merely aims at obtaining reciprocal treatment.

Contrary to what may be perceived, there is growing public recognition that increasing protectionism and state intervention would tend to offset the gains from liberalizing the internal market. Even while government officials take a protectionist and interventionist stance, domestic public opinion may favour competition. While Prime Minister Cresson seeks greater state control over the economy, a recent opinion poll in the French periodical *L'Express* indicates that the vast majority of French citizens favour the privatization of public firms so that they may compete with private firms, the promotion of the competitiveness of firms even if it were to require cutbacks of social programs, tax cuts on savings, and income tax cuts even for high income earners.

EC Protectionism as a Reaction to North American Protectionism

Ironically, present tendencies indicate that in the near future "Fortress America" is as likely to take shape as "Fortress Europe." Note, for example, the increasing tendency in the U.S., (and to a lesser extent in Canada) to blame Japan for its trade deficits and even for the current recession. In what seems like an echo of Cassen's words, Clyde Prestowitz, president of the Economic Strategy Institute in Washington, D.C. and former adviser to President Reagan on Japanese affairs, states ". . . if Japan's industrial policy and giant *keiretsu* firms push for leadership in a particular industry while the American government sticks to laissez-faire, the dominance of Japan in that industry is a foregone conclusion."[44] On the eve of U.S. presidential elections, the purpose of President Bush's visit to Japan in January 1992, asking for Japan to increase American car imports, was evidently motivated by the growing protectionist mood in the U.S. Congress and among some business leaders.

We have argued that the EC has relied heavily on non-tariff barriers to trade. Yet the U.S. itself has adopted a variety of protectionist measures. In particular, it has made a dramatic use of both countervailing duties (CD) and anti-dumping duties, often against minute subsidies or dumping margins. From 1980 to 1985, Finger and Nogues[45] report the initiation of 252 cases of CD by the U.S., twelve by Canada and seven by the EC. During the same period, the U.S. initiated 280 anti-dumping actions, Canada 219 and the EC 254. In the U.S., the filing of an unfair trade practice complaint has often been followed by negotiated voluntary export restraints.[46]

In view of the 1988 Omnibus Trade and Competitiveness Act and one of its clauses, Super 301, the U.S. cannot claim that its policies are entirely aimed at free trade. Some "protectionist" actions taken by the EC were adopted as retaliation to perceived U.S. threats to European interests. In fact, the EC redefinition in the case of semiconductors of the rule of origin as the location of the "most" substantial process rather than the "last" substantial process, was, in part, a response to the Semi-conductor Trade Agreement (STA) signed between the U.S. and Japan in 1989, which effectively assured twenty percent of the Japanese market to U.S. producers.[47] The Europeans were not only economically hurt by the STA, but more importantly, they realized that they could be powerless to secure a very strategic input such as the semiconductor due to bilateral negotiations among third parties.

"Fortress Europe" or "Partner Europe"?

Doubtless there exist protectionist forces in Europe. However, they are currently being counterbalanced by groups who truly believe in the virtues of the free market. The future orientation of the EC and the relative importance of these two opposing persuasions will, to some extent, depend on developments in the rest of the world, in particular in North America and Japan. In this context, it is important to emphasize multilateral negotiations through the GATT in order to lower trade barriers all around, and prevent retaliatory behaviour from leading to an escalation of protectionism in the world.

One factor that may have an important impact on the future direction of trade relations between the EC and its partners is the extent to which EC member countries are affected by the current prolonged recession, since hard economic conditions tend to strengthen the position of protectionists in the eye of the public, while diminishing tolerance for (and encouraging retaliation against) what is perceived to be protectionist by trade partners. The weakening of the German economy after reunification is also a negative influence. And, of course, the Uruguay Round of

GATT negotiations may also be affected by a surge of protectionism in the industrialized world due to the impact of the recession.

The change in political leaders due to upcoming elections may also influence the future orientation of the EC. Thus, the election of a Labour prime minister in the U.K., the outcome of presidential elections in France in 1993, and, not the least, the election of a new president of the EC, will all influence the future dynamics of world trade relations. Jacques Delors has exerted a positive influence against protectionist tendencies. As his second mandate comes to an end an important question is: will Delors seek another mandate as President of the EC or will he return to France to become Prime Minister and eventually President of France? And, if so, will his successor be as committed to free trade? One current contender, Ruud Lubbers, the Prime Minister of The Netherlands, who held the rotating presidency of the Council of Ministers for the last six months of 1991, would in all likelihood pursue similar policies. Taking into account all positive and negative influences on the protectionist stance in the EC, we remain cautiously optimistic that the pro-free-trade forces will prevail.

Canadian Strategies

In view of these developments in the EC what strategy should Canada adopt in order to take advantage of the benefits offered by the unified European market, and at the same time, counter some of the protectionist moves of the EC?

Multilateral Trade Negotiations

It is important for Canada to pursue multilateral trade negotiations in the context of GATT.[48] Canada is currently bargaining for zero tariffs on forest products and minerals. This would enable Canada partly to counter the preferential access to the EC that the EFTA members presently enjoy. In contrast to the EFTA members, Canada has to pay export duties on lumber, wood products and softwood plywood exports, and has a duty-free quota of only 600,000 tons for newsprint.[49] While Canada's lower fibre costs have, thus far, permitted it to compete, negotiating a zero tariff would also allow Canada to position itself in advance of any future decision by the EC to move towards free trade (in these natural resources) with Eastern Europe, and especially with the Ukraine and Russia. Such a move by the EC would subject Canadian firms to unfair competition in the EC market, leading to a loss in its market share. Similarly, Canada should pursue the reduction in protection in the agricultural sector, a move which will benefit the export of its high quality grain products.

Through multilateral negotiations, Canada should also try to promote the establishment of standards that are as close as possible to Canadian ones in order to minimize the extent of adjustment that Canadian firms will have to undergo to penetrate the EC market.

Bilateral Trade Negotiations and the Principle of Reciprocity

In such areas as single bank licensing, open government procurement, mutual recognition of technical standards or pan-European television, the EC is not obliged to confer the benefits of the single market to non-EC members, but may do so provided reciprocal treatment is granted. In these areas, Canada must offer reciprocal access to EC firms in order to benefit from the single European market.

The Canadian Bank Act stipulates that no single non-resident can control more than 10 percent of an institution's shares and non-residents in the aggregate cannot control more than 25 percent. Under the Free Trade Agreement (FTA), American nationals have been exempted from this Canadian regulation. In order for Canadian financial institutions to obtain unrestricted access to, and fully benefit from, the unified European financial markets, the Canadian government will have to offer the same treatment to EC firms as that obtained by U.S. firms under the FTA. EC financial institutions must receive national treatment in Canada since, according to the Second Banking Directive, the EC will only extend the benefits of the single market to non-EC countries if it receives reciprocal treatment.

The same is also true in the area of open procurement, where the EC has agreed to permit non-EC firms to compete under the same terms as EC firms provided that EC firms based, say in Canada, receive reciprocal treatment.

Co-ordinating Competition Policy

There appears to be a need to co-ordinate EC-North American anti-trust policies in evaluating corporations involved in transatlantic mergers or strategic alliances. The recent case involving the Canadian firm De Havilland highlights the importance for a more global oriented competition policy. On October 2, 1991, the European Commission prevented two publicly owned aerospace firms, France's Aérospatiale and Italy's Alenia, from acquiring Canada's De Havilland, claiming that the takeover would have given the purchasing firms 50 percent of the world market and 65 percent of the EC market for 20- to 70-seat commuter airplanes and would have adversely affected British Aerospace and the Dutch company Fokker. Yet, if the takeover had been permitted, potential competition would have still existed, from Bombardier, Airbus, and Daimler-Benz.

While, on the one hand, the decision to prevent the acquisition indicates the resolve of the Competition Commission of the EC to promote competition, it would seem that anti-trust action is not always taken in an even-handed manner. For example, in February 1991, the Commission decided to allow the merger of Aérospatiale's Helicopter division with Germany's Messerschmitt-Bolker-Blohm.

North American competition policy is concerned with efficiency and lies outside political influence, whereas the European approach has more room for political influence since it is determined at the level of the Commission. In this regard, it has been suggested that EC competition policy be given to an independent agency (such as Germany's Federal Cartel Office), to ensure that it is coherent and free from political influence. More importantly, the formation of a supranational agency, a World Trade Organization such as has recently been suggested by Canada, may provide the best forum for the resolution of transnational issues.

Trade Diplomacy and the Future of Canada

With the formation of trade blocks and the tendency for national governments to favour industrial policy, trade diplomacy becomes an important tool for smoothing out conflicts and resolving them in line with a country's best interest. An important economic benefit of a united Canada lies in the conduct of trade diplomacy. The size and strength of the Canadian economy enable it to exert an important influence in international trade negotiations as well as in the management of international economic relations.

Canada's current constitutional difficulties raise the possibility of a break-up of Canada into two or more independent countries. The disintegration of Canada would mean a considerable loss of weight in the international arena. According to Murray Smith,

> Canada would no longer be a member of the G-7 or the Quadrilateral Trade Ministers (representing the European Community, Japan and the United States as well as Canada). The rest of Canada would be a diminished middle power like Australia, and Quebec would be comparable in population to Austria. Clearly the constituent parts of Canada would have less access to the international economic system particularly the informal corridors of power.[50]

As Smith argues, Quebec and the rest of Canada would be less likely to reduce their trade barriers bilaterally because countries are less interested in reciprocal negotiations with smaller partners.[51]

Ironically, at a time when Europe strives to complete its internal market and to achieve a monetary union by 1999, and at a time when belonging to an economic union is deemed to be a necessary condition to achieve prosperity in the next millennium, Canada stands to lose the high degree of integration it presently enjoys. If, as seems likely, a customs union cannot be preserved between Quebec and the rest of Canada and a free-trade area is the only possible economic association, Canada would in fact be moving in a direction opposite to that of the Europe of 1992![52]

As Europe becomes stronger, Quebec and the rest of Canada will risk losing an important asset which they possess in attracting foreign investment from the EC and Japan: a free-trade zone with the United States. It is certain that the FTA would need to be renegotiated and additional concessions would have to be made at a time when the FTA has little public support, partly due to the costly adjustment process, and when the protectionist forces in the U.S. Congress are gaining strength.

In reopening the FTA, the U.S. would scrutinize various protectionist policies of the Quebec government: the subsidizing of electricity by Hydro-Québec and Quebec's industrial policy in general, including the activities of various public corporations such as the Société de Développement Industriel and the Caisse de Dépôt, as well as those of the rest of Canada, such as the bail-out of De Havilland by the Ontario and federal governments. The U.S. would also require of both Quebec and the rest of Canada substantial modifications to the Auto-Pact (which in 1989 contributed 9.3 percent and 26.5 percent respectively of manufacturing output in Quebec and Ontario), the abolition of the exemption of cultural industries and of the mandatory screening of the takeover of Canadian firms with assets in excess of $150 million, allowed under the FTA. Such demands for concessions, especially on the part of the U.S. Congress, may even lead a future New Democratic or Liberal government in the rest of Canada to reject an amended FTA. This would induce foreign firms seeking to service the entire North American market to establish themselves in the U.S. or in Mexico. If the disintegration of Canada were to be acrimonious, trade wars could erupt, thus further weakening each economy.

What other trade options could Quebec or the rest of Canada pursue as sovereign states? Could they, as is sometimes argued, seek preferential access to the EC? The report of the Bélanger-Campeau Commission makes an implicit assumption that the U.S. would not renegotiate the FTA with Quebec under unfavourable conditions, since Quebec could look elsewhere, implying association with the EC. However, this outcome has little plausibility. Although trade relations with the EC are complementary to those with the U.S. and should be actively courted by Canadian firms and officials, they are not a substitute for access to an integrated Canadian market nor to the U.S. market. Furthermore, it appears unlikely that the EC would wish to give special status to either the rest of Canada or Quebec, for it has a heavy task of deepening and widening itself to include new members from Eastern Europe.

The resolution of Canada's constitutional problems will require considerable vision and leadership on the part of elected officials and opinion leaders. Contemplation of the fragmentation of Canada in the coming hyperindustrial age and in the context of a changing world of regional blocs should suffice to discourage the seemingly irreversible trend towards tribalism. Whether the EC constitutes a fortress or not, Canadian trade diplomacy and national unity will remain of overwhelming importance in dealing with both the EC and the U.S.

Notes

1 From 1979 to 1986 GNP growth averaged 1.6 percent while unemployment rose above 11 percent in 1988. The unemployment rate rose above 10 percent in France, Belgium and Italy, while it reached 19.1 percent and 16.7 percent in Spain and Ireland respectively. See Richard Jackman, Christopher Pissarides and Savvas Savouri, "Labour Market Policies and Unemployment in the OECD," *Economic Policy* (Oct. 1990): 454, Table 1.

2 *The Economist*, January 4–10, 1992, p. 43.

3 *The Economist*, December 21, 1991–January 3, 1992, p. 58.

4 Alain Minc, "Europe: pour l'élargissement politique," *L'Express*, 17 janvier 1992, p. 5; Jean-François Poncet, "Maastricht: un début prometteur," *Les Cahiers de l'Express*, janvier 1992, pp. 104–105; Daniel Vernet, "Les trois Europes," *Le Monde*, 14 décembre 1991, p. 1; Pascal Bruckner, "Punir l'armée serbe," *L'Express*, 27 décembre 1991, p. 7; Jean-Pierre Casanova, "Après Maastricht, avant l'Europe," *L'Express*, 27 décembre 1991, p. 8; Bernard Cassen, "Impuissance face à la crise yougoslave: l'Europe à hue et à dia," *Le Monde Diplomatique*, Octobre 1991, p. 1; Thierry Desjardins, "Regretter Tito . . . ," *Le Figaro*, 1er juillet 1991, p. 1.

5 Robert E. Lipsey and Irving B. Kravis, "The Competitiveness and Comparative Advantage of U.S. Multinationals, 1957–1983," NBER Working Paper no. 2051, (1986).

6 It is misleading to look solely at growth in intra-regional trade, since this expansion may be due to an increase in the region's share of world trade and not necessarily to trade diversion. See Jeffrey Frankel, "Is a Yen Bloc Forming in Pacific Asia," *Finance and the International Economy*, Vol. 5 (1991): 8.

7 Kenneth Flamm, "Semiconductors," in Gary Clyde Hufbauer, ed., *Europe 1992: An American Perspective* (Washington D.C.: The Brookings Institution, 1990), p. 273.

8 Patrick A. Messerlin, "The Anti-Dumping Regulations of the European Community: The Privatization of Administered Protection," in Michael J. Trebilcock and Robert C. York, eds., *Fair Exchange: Reforming Trade Remedy Laws* (Toronto: C.D. Howe Institute, 1990), pp. 107–139.

9 Flamm, p. 275.

10 G.C. Hufbauer, "An Overview," in Hufbauer, pp. 39–40.

11 Flamm, p. 225.

12 Hufbauer, p. 42.

13 Peter F. Cowhey, "Telecommunications," in Hufbauer, p. 184.

14 *The Economist*, July 6–12, 1991, p. 63.

15 Horst Siebert, "The Single European Market — A Schumpeterian Event?" Kiel Institute Discussion Paper 157 (FRG: Kiel Institute of World Economics, November 1989), p. 18.

16 Joseph Greenwald, "Negotiating Strategy," in Hufbauer, p. 373.

17 "Germany enforces recycling," *The Globe and Mail*, December 2, 1991, p. B12.

18 Gordon Pitts, *Storming the Fortress: How Canadian Business Can Conquer Europe 1992* (Toronto: Harper Collins, 1990), p. 134.

19 According to a study that analyzes takeovers in the U.K., France and Germany, the number of takeovers and joint ventures per year has increased dramatically since 1985 in all three countries. See Julian Franks and Colin Mayer, "Capital Markets and Corporate Control: A Study of France, Germany and the U.K.," *Economic Policy*, Vol. 10 (April 1990): 191–231.

20 Douglas E. Rosenthal, "Competition Policy," in Hufbauer, p. 337.

21 In the 1986–88 period, subsidies in general were on average 82 billion ecus (1 ecu = $US 1.30) per year for ten members of the Community (i.e., excluding Spain and Portugal which joined in 1986). Sectorally, agriculture was the recipient of 11 billion, coal 13 billion, railways 26 billion and industry 32 billion ecus. See "Of State and Industry," *The Economist*, June 8–14, 1991.

22 Charles L. Schultze, "Introduction," in Hufbauer, p. xxi.

23 Stanley Hoffman, "The European Community and 1992," *Foreign Affairs*, Vol. 68 (Fall 1989): 29.

24 See "Europe's Industrial Tug-of-War," *The Economist*, January 25–31, 1992, pp. 65–68 and "Of State and Industry," *The Economist*, June 8–14, 1991.

25 Franks and Mayer, p. 209.

26 Rosenthal, p. 335.

27 From Bernard Cassen's review article, "Capitalisme en panne," *Le Monde Diplomatique*, Novembre 1991, p. 12. See Michel Albert, *Capitalisme contre capitalisme* (Paris: Le Seuil, 1991). In our opinion, the Japanese system differs in important ways from the German and Swiss approaches.

28 *The Economist*, November 16–22, p. 74.

29 See Bernard Cassen, "Les logiques contradictoires du sommet de Maastricht: Parler d'une seule voix, mais pour quelle Europe?" *Le Monde Diplomatique*, décembre 1991, pp. 4–5. It is hardly surprising to see such opinions expressed in Europe when, even more disturbingly, they are being voiced across the Atlantic in the U.S., the very homeland of the laissez-faire market-oriented approach to business and economics. Admittedly, however, these voices are far fewer than in Europe.

30 Sylvia Ostry, *Governments and Corporations in a Shrinking World* (New York: Council on Foreign Relations, 1990), pp. 34–35.

31 Sir Leon Brittan, "1992: Priorities on Competition Policy," *European Access*, April 2, 1989, p. 20.

32 Siebert, Table A4.

33 Jagdish Bhagwati, *Protectionism* (Cambridge, Massachusetts: MIT Press, 1988), p. 74.

34 This phenomenon has been observed for U.S. multinationals by Lipsey and Kravis. Whereas in 1966 offshore exports by foreign affiliates were equal

to 25 percent of mainland U.S. exports, in 1983 this percentage had risen to 75 percent.

35 Quoted in Ostry, p. 43.

36 See Norman Macrae, "A Future History of Privatisation 1992–2022," *The Economist*, December 21, 1991–January 4, 1992, pp. 15–18. Macrae hypothesizes that even Neil Kinnock, the leader of the Labour Party would, if elected, privatize coal and the railways.

37 See Peter F. Cowhey "Telecommunications," in Hufbauer, pp. 182–83. Even proponents of "managed trade" acknowledge the inefficiency of some protectionist measures, such as anti-dumping regulations, as a means of protecting national firms producing high-tech goods. The higher prices of the protected products, say semiconductors, penalize other national industries that use semiconductors in their production, causing them to become uncompetitive as a result. See Laura D'Andrea Tyson, "Managed Trade: Making the Best of the Second Best," in R. Z. Lawrence and Charles L. Schultze eds., *An American Trade Strategy: Options for the 1990s* (Washington D.C.: Brookings Institution, 1990), pp. 142–191.

38 André Sapir, "Europe in the 1990s: Coping with Internal and External Economic Change," in Douglas M. Brown and Murray G. Smith, eds., *Canadian Federalism: Meeting Global Economic Challenges?* (Kingston: Institute of Intergovernmental Relations, Queen's University, 1991), p. 39.

39 Alexis Jacquemin and André Sapir, "Competition and Imports in the European Market," in Alan Winters and Anthony Venables, eds., *European Integration: Trade and Industry* (Cambridge: Centre for Economic Policy Research, Cambridge University Press, 1991), pp. 82–91.

40 Elie Cohen, "Le Colbertisme high tech" (Paris: Conseil national de la recherche scientifique, 1991). See also *The Economist*, January 4–12, 1992, p. 64.

41 Paolo Cecchini, *The European Challenge 1992: The Benefits of A Single Market* (Aldershot, U.K.: Wildwood House for the Commission of the European Communities, 1988), p. 86.

42 ESPRIT, the European Strategic Program for Research and Development in Information Technology, consists of 450 co-operative projects which aim at improving microelectronics technology, for instance in integrated circuit design. EUREKA comprises over 300 research projects in areas as diverse as high definition television and external automobile guidance systems. JESSI, the Joint European Submicron Silicon Initiative, has as its objective the development and manufacture of a new generation of semiconductors. RACE consists of dozens of projects and companies and is aimed at developing European telecommunications technologies for a Europe-wide high speed data telecommunications network. For an examination of some strategic alliances arising out of these programs see Lynn Mytelka, *Strategic Partnerships and the World Economy* (London: Pinter, 1991).

43 Canada, Department of External Affairs and International Trade, *Moving into Europe* (Ottawa, 1991), p. 25.

44 *The Economist*, November 30–December 6, 1991, pp. 22–23. Both Cassen's and Prestowitz's comments are directed against Japan.

45 J.M. Finger and J. Nogues, "International Control of Subsidies and Countervailing Duties," *World Bank Economic Review*, Vol. 1 (1987): 707–26.

46 Bhagwati, pp. 52–53.

47 In addition to being protectionist, this could lead to the establishment of a world cartel of semiconductor firms and thus should be of concern to antitrust agencies as well. See Rosenthal, p. 340.

48 For a similar view see Lawrence Schembri, "Canada and International Trade: Policies for the 1990s," in Fen Hampson and Christopher Maule, eds., *Canada Among Nations 1990–91* (Ottawa: Carleton University Press, 1991), pp. 41–64.

49 Canada, Department of External Affairs and Trade, *1992: Implications of a Single European Market: Forest Products* (Ottawa: February 1990), p. 30.

50 Murray Smith, "The Quebec Sovereignty Scenario: Implication for Canadian Trade Policies," in Robin Boadway, Thomas Courchene and Douglas Purvis, eds., *Economic Dimensions of Constitutional Change* (Kingston: John Deutsch Institute for the Study of Economic Policy, Queen's University), Vol. 2, p. 484.

51 For a discussion of other implications of Canada's national unity crisis see Gilles Paquet, "The Canadian Malaise and its External Impact," in Fen Hampson and Chris Maule, eds., *Canada Among Nations 1990–91* (Ottawa: Carleton University Press, 1991), p. 25; and Gerald Schmitz, "The Pathbreaking Politics of European Integration," Library of Parliament Research Branch, Background Paper, no. BP-240E, (November 1990), p. 63.

52 Since sovereignty-association is a contradiction in terms (as the experience of Europe demonstrates) what economic association is likely to emerge between an independent Quebec and the rest of Canada? It seems improbable that a monetary union or even a customs union between Quebec and the rest of Canada could survive, for each type of union would require a political union. On the customs union issue see Smith, "The Quebec Sovereignty Scenario," and Ronald J. Wonnacott, "Reconstructing North American Free Trade following Quebec's Separation: What Can Be Assumed?" in G. Ritchie, R.J. Wonnacott, W.H. Furtan, R.S. Gray, R.G. Lipsey and R. Tremblay, eds., *Broken Links* (Toronto: C.D. Howe Institute, 1991), pp. 20–44; and Richard Lipsey, "Comments on the Bélanger-Campeau Commission's Papers on Trade Relations," in *Broken Links*, pp. 58–69.

New Agendas

12

Canada and International Development: New Agendas

Maureen O'Neil and Andrew Clark

The overwhelming global changes and developments of the last two years have overshadowed Third World issues on the foreign policy agendas of Canada and the West. These changes include a litany that has become all too familiar: the end of communist rule in Eastern Europe, the re-unification of Germany, the release of Nelson Mandela and steps toward majority rule in South Africa, the Gulf War, the Soviet coup, the independence of the Baltic states and the breakup of the Soviet Union. For very good reasons our world has been altered significantly. Each of these events has set in motion a chain of consequences that lead to more rather than less uncertainty. Each set of events has its own particular impact on poor countries.

The Third World certainly does have its own dramatic problems. Many countries remain mired in economic crisis — their "lost decade" (the 1980s) continuing into the 1990s. During the 1980s, per capita incomes actually fell for much of Latin America and most of Africa. In Canada, the perception is also one of economic decline, although Statistics Canada data show that household incomes have remained relatively unchanged over the decade.[1] But compare this with the situation in sub-Saharan Africa where per capita income fell by fully 25 percent from levels that were already abysmal.

Over the last year there were shattering events in the region which aggravated continuing economic distress. Their significance was ignored (with the exception of political developments in South Africa) because of events elsewhere. The 1991 famine in the Horn of Africa, on a par with that which shocked the world in 1984, received very little media attention. The thirty-year Ethiopian civil war came to a merciful end, one of the first benefits of the end of the Cold War. All over Africa the push for multi-party rule gained strength, old one-party regimes began to fall. Last year many African countries had "national conferences" which were, effectively, a means of bludgeoning old leaders into seeing that their time was past. Benin, Congo, Côte d'Ivoire, Mali, Niger, Togo have all made substantial changes in the past year. In anglophone Africa, an October election saw Frederick Chiluba oust Kenneth Kaunda, President of Zambia for 27 years, with an overwhelming majority, while Ghana and Nigeria are moving toward elections in 1992.

It is within this context of international flux that Canadian foreign policy has been attempting to operate or at least stay abreast of events. More specifically, this is the context within which Canada has been applying its principal policy instrument for dealing with the Third World: foreign aid policy. In 1991–92 the net Official Development Assistance (ODA) program was $3.12 billion. Over the last three years, the dominant influence on Canada's ODA program has been the federal government's primary economic policy objective of deficit reduction through tight monetary and fiscal controls (primary because even a recession did not cause them to loosen the purse strings!)

ODA Cuts

For those who hoped that Canada's ODA would be spared after two successive years of restraint, Michael Wilson's last budget, in February 1991, was a disappointment. A three percent per annum cap in the growth of ODA was announced, to come into effect in 1992–93 as part of the government's continuing Expenditure Control Plan (with 5 percent growth permitted in 1991–92 in accordance with the February 1990 budget). It was expected that this measure would save the government $1.6 billion through 1994–95, bringing the total savings from ODA budget cuts since 1988–89 to approximately $4 billion over the seven year period ending in 1995–96 (see Table 12.1).

These cuts have made a mockery of Canada's commitment to achieve an ODA level of 0.7 percent of GNP; this figure has been a benchmark for donors advocated by the Organization for Economic Co-operation and Development (OECD) and the United Nations (UN), and it can be traced back to the 1969 World Bank Commission headed by Lester B. Pearson.

The percentage is a receding target which now appears to have disappeared entirely. Canada first accepted it in 1970. In 1980, the objective was to reach 0.7 percent by 1990–91; by 1984 the target was moved back again to 1995–96; in 1987, the year the government published *Sharing Our Future* (a strategy document for Canada's ODA) it retreated to the year 2000. That is the last mention of a date, although the North-South Institute calculated in 1989 that at the rate budgets were being cut, the figure could only be reached in 2040.[2]

The last three budgets have clung lamely to an ODA/GNP ratio of 0.47 percent, offered as a target (or hope) for 1994–95. This is actually less than the high ratio of 0.52 percent achieved in 1975! As the November 1990 Review by the Development Assistance Committee (DAC) of the OECD pointed out, Canada's real commitment to its announced

Table 12.1

ODA Restraint Measures 1989-91

April 1989	Cut $360 million for '88–'89 and '89–'90	$1.8 billion
February 1990	5 percent cash growth for two years	$0.5 billion
February 1991	3 percent cash growth from 1992–93	$1.6 billion
Total Savings		**$3.9 billion**

ODA/GNP target must be in question.[3] Whether or not a clear statement is eventually made that the 0.7 percent is being *abandoned*, budget decisions indicate that it is already gone. This is a significant change in Canadian aid policy.

Meanwhile the government's efforts to reach even 0.47 percent by 1994–95 are open to question. With an ODA/GNP ratio of 0.44 percent in 1990, Canada ranked eighth among OECD countries, outpaced by Norway, the Netherlands, Denmark, Sweden, Finland, France and Belgium, in that order.[4] The ratio may go up as a result of an actual decline in GNP owing to the recession rather than a real increase in ODA. Unless inflation is lower than 3 percent in 1992–93, it is hard to see how 3 percent capping will cause the ratio to increase. One way this might be achieved would be to make non-cash increases in ODA by forgiving loans held by the Export Development Corporation (EDC) and the Canada Wheat Board.

Indications in the February 1991 budget are that the government expects "the pace and magnitude of debt relief agreed upon multilaterally" will be a non-cash element of ODA which will increase sizably.[5]

The budget paper also foresees that the non-cash elements in the ODA budget may increase owing to 1. "the speed with which international environmental agreements affecting ODA-eligible countries are concluded," and 2. the profile of Canada's commitments to the multilateral agencies such as the World Bank or the regional development banks.[6] Thus, the promised growth in the ODA/GNP ratio may be more likely to come from growth in the non-cash elements of ODA rather than ODA cash levels.

The Expenditure Control Plan did hit other government spending programs, some of them harder than ODA. For example, in the last two budgets Established Programme Financing (federal health and education expenditures) has been capped at population growth levels of around one percent per annum through 1994–95. However, in terms of its relative budget size, the ODA program has probably borne the largest burden of any of the major government programs over the last three years of fiscal restraint. (Prior to the Gulf War, Defence cuts over the period 1988–1995 were only $3.3 billion out of a $12 billion annual program, compared to $3.9 billion of cuts out of the $3 billion annual ODA program.)

These cuts occurred in spite of active protest by Canada's NGO and church communities and the presence of Joe Clark, a powerful Secretary of State known to be pro-aid. The fears that this program was especially vulnerable to cuts in times of fiscal restraint have been proven correct. In fact, contrary to the spirit of the Winegard Report's recommendation to legislate the program's spending levels at minimum ODA/GNP ratios,[7] the February 1991 budget indicated that the government plans to introduce legislation in Parliament to *limit* program spending.

Part of the reason the aid budget is perceived as vulnerable is that its constituency within Canada is not as numerous or as geographically concentrated as other constituencies. Surveys indicate that Canadians' support for increased aid is slipping. While the clear majority of Canadians (60 percent) still believe we spend the right amount or not enough on aid, a steadily rising percentage — 16 percent in 1988, 25 percent in 1991 — think we are spending too much.[8]

Having imposed its important fiscal restraint measures, the Canadian government, because of world events, now has new international demands on its budget:

1. Requests for "aid" from Eastern Europe and more recently from the former Soviet republics cannot, in practical terms, be ignored by the West. Jeffrey Sachs at Harvard University has estimated that the Commonwealth of Independent States will require $32 billion of Western assistance in 1992.[9]
2. The environment issue has moved from the periphery to the mainstream of the public policy agenda as preparations for the United Nations Conference on the Environment and Development (UNCED), in 1992 continue.
3. Renewed demands for official debt reduction.

The government's main budgetary response has been the creation of the International Assistance Envelope.

International Assistance Envelope

This envelope was created in the February 1991 budget. Resources in this envelope will be used to fund not only ODA but also assistance to Eastern Europe and now, probably, the republics of the former Soviet Union. According to the government, "this approach is designed to improve fiscal planning and control by balancing the available resources against the total demands for international assistance."[10]

The grouping of ODA funds destined for Third World nations together with funds for the Eastern bloc underlines the reality that these two areas will be forced to compete with each other for resources. This fact has been pointed out by the developing countries as a reason for genuine concern. Already the 1991-92 main estimates for ODA include some money in the program reserve for "partial funding for aid projects in Eastern Europe."[11] It remains to be seen whether the Development Assistance Committee of the OECD will consider these amounts as ODA that can be accepted for purposes of calculating the ODA/GNP ratio.

Although one can see the sense of establishing the "envelope," concern will be justified if funds for the Eastern Bloc are to be provided at the expense of an already shrinking ODA budget, given the continuing high demand from the Third World. If Eastern Europe is to be accommodated *without* an injection of new funds, then this is, effectively, an additional loss for Canada's "traditional" aid recipients.

Aid restraint has not been without its impact, although lack of data prevents analysis of specific program impact in the Third World. Many organizations have felt the pinch: the International Development Research Centre has laid off 60 people, or 10 percent of its staff; Petro-Canada International Assistance Corporation has been wound up; Canadian International Development Agency (CIDA) decentralization has halted and staff cuts are expected at the Agency. There has also been revision of cost-sharing ratios applying to NGOs. For example, CUSO's small projects ratio was reduced from 3:1 to 2:1. This translated into a dollar cutback of $175,000 in 1991.[12]

Cuts to the aid budget within CIDA have thus far been borne largely by forms of assistance that are quickly disbursed: program aid, food aid, and voluntary contributions to UN agencies. Expenditures for capital project assistance have been relatively less affected and allocations for CIDA's industrial co-operation program (CIDA INC) have actually been increased. Cuts were almost equally distributed between bilateral and multilateral programs. With regard to regional distribution: Asia suffered the largest proportion of the cuts, followed by North Africa and the Middle East, Latin America and the Caribbean and finally, sub-Saharan Africa. These cuts were, therefore, generally in proportion to regional per capita income levels, but they hide some particularly severe cuts in aid to certain individual countries, like Bangladesh.[13]

Sustainable Development

There has also been an impact on the content of Canadian aid policy itself, although some of these changes would have occurred even without the cutbacks. The best and most recent indication (if somewhat unofficial) of CIDA's new policy direction is contained in a memo to all staff from CIDA president Marcel Massé, dated March 28, 1991.

This memo contains an expanded definition of what CIDA considers to be "Sustainable Development," It provides useful headings under which to briefly evaluate recent Canadian aid policy performance. According to the memo, there are five pillars of sustainable development: economic, social, political, environmental and cultural.

Economic Sustainability (Structural Adjustment)

Economic policies must be sustainable in the long run: that is, policies which allocate resources "inefficiently," or which lead to unsustainable trade or fiscal deficits, are not developmental.

Much has been made in recent literature of CIDA's new policy focus on structural adjustment.[14] Since *Sharing Our Future*, where it was one of the six thematic objectives of Canadian aid policy, structural adjustment has been a primary concern.[15]

While this issue was given greater visibility in 1989 when Canada, as chair of the Guyana Support Group, undertook to mobilize funds for Guyana's structural adjustment program (SAP), it was not a new policy for Canada. Structural adjustment has been around as an international development objective since the early 1980s. Canada, through its votes in favour of structural adjustment lending at the Bretton Woods institutions, has given de facto support to these policies since the beginning.

The federal Department of Finance is the lead agency with the IMF and World Bank, and has been a supporter of SAP policy, if one may judge from Canadian support of the Bank's third General Capital increase and International Development Assistance (IDA) fund replenishments over the decade.[16] As these policies grew in importance, and especially in the case of Africa where they came to dominate the development co-operation agenda, CIDA took a more active role.

CIDA's first direct involvement in mitigating the effects of structural adjustment policies came in 1987 in Ghana, where it took the lead with UNICEF in setting up PAMSCAD: a Plan of Action to Mitigate the Social Costs of Adjustment (CIDA's contribution was $8.4 million). Thus CIDA's initial policy approach took its lead from the UNICEF "Human Face" critique of SAPs. Canada's support of programs to mitigate the social impact of structural adjustment has often been referred to by External Relations Minister Monique Landry.

However, over the last two years, CIDA, working with the Department of Finance, has become more directly involved in the initial formulation of adjustment programs themselves. This has been done primarily by influencing the Policy Framework Papers (the SAP blueprints designed essentially by the IMF), and by input into the Bretton Woods institutions both at the field level and in Washington through the Canadian Executive Director's offices.

There has also been increased linking of CIDA's bilateral aid to adjustment programs. Thus, CIDA lines of credit, balance-of-payment support and food aid have been linked to the conditionalities of structural adjustment programs.

This policy shift toward bilateral aid support for SAPs has come under considerable attack from Canada's NGO, church and academic communities. In February 1991, the Canadian Council for International Co-operation (CCIC) put out a "Report Card" critical of CIDA's current policy approaches.[17] This was followed in October 1991 by the Interchurch Fund for International Development's evaluation, "Diminishing Our Future: CIDA, Four Years After Winegard." It called for a re-appraisal of CIDA's present course, characterizing it as "a betrayal of its best contributions in the past."[18]

Social Sustainability

One important way of targeting the poorest is through support for the social sector, specifically primary health care and basic education (especially if this support is even more specifically targeted at women, who make up the majority of the world's poor).

This development "truth" is not new, going back to the basic needs agenda of the 1970s. For a while, it got lost in the focus on structural adjustment and the need for economic stabilization and growth. UNICEF's *Human Face* report put it back on the map in moral terms. The realization that adjustment would not ensure sustainable economic growth if human resources i.e., a country's populace, are illiterate or in poor health is shared by developing countries themselves, academics and recently the World Bank.[19]

"Social sustainability" received substantial attention in the lead-up to the World Children's Summit in September 1991, co-chaired by Prime Minister Mulroney. The point has best been made, however, in the UNDP's *Human Development Report 1991*.[20] In addition to calling into question developing country spending priorities with regard to the social sectors as a whole and within those sectors, it critically examines the aid policies of donor countries.

Using an OECD data base, the report argues convincingly that most donor countries have neglected the social sectors, and what aid there is to these sectors is often channelled to curative health care (hospitals) or post-secondary education. Canada's performance is worse than most.

In 1989 only 20 percent of Canada's ODA budget went to the health and education sectors. An even more critical aspect was that only 25 percent of this aid went to primary health care, basic education and water and sanitation. Thus only five percent of Canada's ODA reaches these sectors which specifically concern the poorest (see Table 12.2). Clearly there is room for restructuring and redirecting Canada's aid budget.

Environmental Sustainability

Another of CIDA's thematic objectives in *Sharing Our Future* was "environmentally sound development." This is an area in which CIDA has

Table 12.2

Analysis of ODA Social Spending, 1989

	Aid human expenditure ratio (%)	Aid expenditure ratio (%)	Aid social allocation ratio (%)	Aid social priority ratio (%)
Average	0.026	0.32	22.6	36.6
Netherlands	0.128	0.94	25.2	53.8
Denmark	0.110	0.94	22.4	52.2
Sweden	0.070	0.97	13.8	51.9
France	0.053	0.54	39.1	25.1
Finland	0.051	0.63	29.3	27.4
Switzerland	0.047	0.30	20.1	78.7
Germany[a]	0.047	0.41	25.6	44.4
Australia	0.029	0.38	30.7	25.2
United Kingdom	0.028	0.31	24.8	36.6
Canada	0.023	9.44	19.9	25.9
Italy	0.017	0.42	18.0	22.4
United States	0.012	0.15	17.1	46.1

[a] Excluding the former German Democratic Republic.
Note: Column 1 is the percentage of a donor's GNP allocated to priority sectors (primary health care and basic education) in recipient countries through ODA. It is calculated in columns $2 \times 3 \times 4$.
Source: Reprinted from UNDP, *Human Development Report 1991*.

known some success. Both the CCIC "Report Card" and the DAC evaluation report commented favourably.

CIDA has implemented *environmental assessment procedures* for projects likely to involve environmental risks; its ability to do this has been strengthened by staff training and the creation of an environment division. Its Environmental Management Development project in Indonesia (EMDI) has been quite successful and has attracted interest from other donor countries.

While CIDA's approach has received relatively good marks at the project level, at the policy level it is wanting. CIDA needs a more *proactive* general policy stance on the environment rather than the largely *reactive* project policy it now has. Further, it needs to consider the environmental as well as the social impacts of its structural adjustment policies. Policies

such as export promotion, food self-sufficiency, taxes and subsidies all
have environmental as well as economic implications. The debt crisis also
has direct effects on developing country environments. Efforts to service
unmanageable amounts of debt can lead to environmentally unsustainable
export growth.[21]

Measuring development simply in terms of per capita incomes or GNP
growth, without taking into account environmental quality indicators and
natural resource depletion is misleading, and is similar to the failure
to take measures of human development into account (an omission the
United Nations Development Programme's (UNDP) human development
index (HDI) has attempted to correct). There are environmental issues
that go beyond CIDA's mandate and must involve the Canadian government as a whole, in particular Environment Canada and the Department
of Finance.

Indeed, as the 1992 UN Conference on Environment and Development
(UNCED) in Brazil approaches, it is clear that the view of environmentally
"sustainable development" that is current in the North is quite different from the perception held in the South. In the North, the so-called
"global change" issues of ozone depletion, global warming and tropical
deforestation are at the top of the environment agenda. Environmentally
sustainable development in the South concentrates on more localized issues, such as soil degradation and availability of fresh water. In the South,
"global change" issues are viewed as problems induced by developed countries and of concern to them. If the North wants these problems addressed,
then it is going to have to consider additional transfers of resources to the
South. The World Resource Institute estimated $20–50 billion per an-
num in the 1990s. Saving "spaceship Earth" is not going to be cheap.
This is one of the few areas where the South has leverage on the North;
indications are that the South intends to use it in Brazil.[22]

Political Sustainability

Economic and social development cannot take place in an insecure political environment, such as war or civil insurrection. Nor can it occur when
a government's development policies do not have the support of the people. However, political sustainability also means respect for fundamental
human rights and the possibility for people to have a say in who governs
them.

There has been considerably more interest and agreement that the
form of government matters, since the events of the fall of 1989 which
brought changes in Eastern Europe. The lesson that seemingly eternal
autocratic rule could in fact be ended almost overnight through popular
protest was not lost on the Third World, and in particular sub-Saharan
Africa. This lesson may have originated in the Third World itself with
the ouster of Marcos in the Philippines by Corazon Aquino in 1986.

In 1991, the people rose up in protest all over Africa to call for the end of dictatorial regimes and the establishment of multi-party democracy. In Benin, Congo, Gabon, Kenya, Mali, Togo, Zambia and Zaire, movements for multi-party democracy made their voices heard. In light of these developments, the creation in Canada of the International Centre for Human Rights and Democratic Development by act of Parliament in 1988 seems timely.

For Canadian aid and human rights, the policy has been to reduce or deny bilateral government to government aid where "human rights violations are systematic, gross and continuous."[23] Annual decisions as to a country's record on human rights and its aid eligibility by Cabinet have been marked by secrecy and a certain degree of controversy. This has been most true with respect to continued Canadian bilateral aid to such countries as Zaire, Kenya and Guatemala.

Prime Minister Mulroney may have put some teeth into existing policy by his remarks in advance of and at the Harare Commonwealth Heads of Government meeting in October 1991, and his subsequent statements at the Francophone Summit in Paris in November, in which he stated that Canadian aid would be conditional on human rights performance. In the last quarter of 1991, Canada moved to suspend its bilateral aid program to Zaire, Haiti and Indonesia owing to human rights concerns. However, it took particularly dramatic incidents in all these countries to bring these actions about.

The very public initiative by the Prime Minister will certainly require CIDA to focus its attention on the human rights issue and the related issue of aid conditionality. However, this will require particularly close co-operation between CIDA, External Affairs and the Prime Minister's Office (PMO).

Cultural Sustainability

This is still a rather vague notion: it means taking into account the values and cultures of a people. It could be in conflict with furthering women's status, where cultural values and practices are usually an impediment.

Women are not explicitly referred to in the list of aspects of sustainability. Although the response from CIDA to criticism along these lines would be that CIDA *integrates* women in all policy areas, that is really not sufficient. In fact, the evaluations of CIDA's Women in Development (WID) policy, to be done in 1992, should be an occasion to reflect on whether the rhetorical success Canada has had with its WID policy in international fora has a solid counterpart in demonstrable improvements in real women's lives. It is expected that in the future there will be objectives in addition to sectoral integration, with the more explicit aim of changing women's political, economic, health, education and legal status.

Operational Principles for Implementing CIDA's Policy of Sustainable Development

Massé's memo also includes a section on operational principles for implementing sustainable development. The following statement augurs significant change in the Agency's policies: "CIDA will move gradually to give more emphasis to influencing policies and institutions which promote sustainable development in the developing countries."[24]

Reading between the lines, one may infer that less emphasis will be given to CIDA projects and that aid will be increasingly policy-based and consequently more conditional, requiring e.g., structural adjustment for economic sustainability, protection of human rights for political sustainability, and perhaps more general conditions regarding the environment. (Such requirements would apply mostly at the project level.) This policy implies a further retraining of CIDA staff as well as the hiring of more policy analysts, instead of project management personnel, to reflect these new priorities.[25]

The Agency also apparently intends to become more "partnership-oriented in the sense of using partners more in conceiving and delivering programs."[26] CIDA's partners are an extremely diverse group and include organizations which receive funds from CIDA's ODA budget and, in effect, implement CIDA policies, including the World Bank, UN agencies, non-governmental organizations (NGOs), churches, consultants and private companies. By being more partnership-oriented, CIDA will probably be contracting out even more of its project work, most notably to NGOs and the private sector, so as to devote its attention to broader policy objectives. The extent to which these contracts will go to non-profit organizations, rather than the private sector, remains unclear.

CIDA may also embark on considerable organizational changes. Indeed much of Massé's memo seems to foreshadow conclusions reached by Groupe SECOR, a Montreal management consulting group, which produced a "strategic management review" of the Agency at Minister Monique Landry's request. Released in November 1991, it will be the object of extensive consultation with CIDA staff, NGOs, business, universities (the key "stakeholders") during the first quarter of 1992.

SECOR focused on many long-standing CIDA concerns: broad dispersion of aid to more than 150 countries and regions, and the increased cost of doing business. The report identified five major reasons for rising costs: dispersion of countries, sectors and channels; a large number of institutions and organizations funded; cumbersome and complex contracting processes (probably to meet excessive demands for accountability and protect the Agency from criticism); increased use of consultants to cope with staff freezes imposed (as elsewhere in the government) by Treasury Board; and the support required for the Minister after the creation of the Cabinet post in 1984.

SECOR's main conclusions were that "CIDA should either reduce the scope of its mandate in proportion to the availability of resources, both monetary and human, or maintain its mandate but increase the level of its resources."[27] Given current tight fiscal conditions it is not hard to imagine which option the government might favour. The report also implies that CIDA should move away from micro to macro management of its contracts. CIDA's energy should be spent on the development of strategic skills and abilities. This will have major implications for the Agency's culture, systems, philosophy, management practices and employee profile. CIDA needs relief from the pernicious effects of accountability as understood and interpreted by the Auditor General.

Three organizational models for bilateral aid delivery are proposed:

- the "dual entity model," which would split up CIDA and assign operations to a non-profit public sector entity;
- the "brokerage model," which would let CIDA develop country policy frameworks and then respond to proposals from the Canadian voluntary and private sector development community; and
- the "comprehensive management model," which would have CIDA develop sustained relationships with a pool of pre-qualified entities, drawn from the private and voluntary sector development community to act as executing agents. It is this third option which Groupe SECOR seems to favour.

Given this new focus on policy and the reality of aid cutbacks, it is not surprising that CIDA intends to play an increasing role in non-aid issues of development, attempting to influence both the Canadian government and international fora on trade, debt and environmental policies.

Debt

While the debt crisis may be over in the North and gradually reaching resolution in some developing countries in Latin America, in Africa it is still very much an ongoing concern. Many countries are using up to a third of their export receipts to service their debt, or are accumulating unpayable arrears.

Canada has taken some important, though ad hoc, initiatives on debt, including the forgiveness of $1.15 billion of ODA debt over the last 12 years and a lead role in developing the so-called Toronto terms at the G-7 summit in 1988. However, there remains much to be done.[28] This was made clear in a June 1990 report issued by the Standing Committee on

External Affairs and International Trade (SCEAIT) entitled *Securing Our Global Future: Canada's Stake in the Unfinished Business of Third World Debt.*

The $1.15 billion that has been forgiven was originally lent on very soft terms, so, in actual fact, the cost to the Canadian Treasury and the benefit to Third World countries was at most only 10 percent of the amount forgiven. The Canadian government, primarily through two Crown corporations, the EDC and the Canadian Wheat Board, is still owed at least $3 billion by Third World debtors, most of it on hard commercial terms.[29] Forgiving all or part of this debt will cause significantly more financial pain to Canada but will bring correspondingly greater benefit to the countries concerned.

In March 1991, Canada, along with the Paris Club of creditor nations, agreed to reduce the net present value of Polish debt stock by as much as 50 percent (for Canada this represents as much as $1.5 billion in EDC and Canadian Wheat Board debt with 30 percent of it to be written off immediately). Strict equity would suggest an even more generous treatment for the much poorer African nations — arguments that Poland is a "special case" notwithstanding!

At the Paris Club meeting of December 1991, however, the agreement reached to deal with the poorest indebted countries of the world ended up by being *less* generous than that accorded to Poland. The agreement contains concessional options which allow for a 50 percent reduction in the net present value of debt *maturing* over the agreement period rather than the country's entire stock of debt. The agreement also contains a non-concessional option for creditors (notably the United States) which would not agree even to the 50 percent reduction in maturities. While Canada may have wanted to be more generous, 50 percent was the highest figure which all non-U.S. Paris Club members could agree on and thus maintain burden-sharing.

Canadian Trade Policy toward Developing Countries[30]

Canada had a total two-way trade with developing countries of $24 billion in 1989. This may be compared with 1991–92 aid of $3.12 billion, or with foreign direct investment in developing countries of $5 billion in 1986. So while one dollar's worth of trade is not the same as one dollar's worth of aid, trade was our largest direct economic link with the developing world.

Compared to the activity of other industrial countries, Canada's trade with developing countries is small (12 percent of our imports originate in the Third World as compared with 17 percent for the EC, 40 percent for the United States and 48 percent for Japan). It is, in the words of G.K. Helleiner, "under-utilized potential."

Despite the small size of Canada's trade with developing countries, Canadian trade policy continues to be overly protective. We impose an average tariff of over 10 percent on our industrial imports from lesser developed countries (LDCs) (while the average tariff faced by developed countries is less than 5 percent). Even our top 30 aid beneficiaries face an average duty of 9 percent.[31]

More important are quotas on clothing imports, in place for over a decade and affecting the largest single export category from developing countries to Canada, in an industry which is a major stepping-stone to industrialization.

The World Bank estimates that developed country protection costs developing countries twice as much as they receive in aid. There is room for Canadian policy improvement, improvements which could have a significant beneficial impact on developing countries.

Of course, if policy changes do occur, Canada's domestic adjustment policies for the workers and industries affected will have to be strengthened. This issue will likely be brought home to us if the NAFTA materializes (see Chapter 10) and the Canadian economy is forced to adjust to Mexican competition.

Canada has made important policy contributions to the GATT Uruguay Round negotiations, which will be of benefit to developing countries. It has supported the Cairns Group — the thirteen-country coalition on agricultural issues — in which Canada is the largest trading country. It has acted as a bridgebuilder on issues such as investment measures and intellectual property rights, where it shares some concerns with developing countries.[32] Canada also made offers on tariffs and on textiles and clothing and worked for the strengthening of GATT's institutional base. CIDA now recognizes that it has the task of persuading our trade negotiators to keep the door open to Third World products.

Conclusion

The steady erosion of aid flows, the increasing tendency of developed countries to trade with each other, and the increased mobility of capital (together with that of well-trained people in the developing countries) leave most people in the Third World very badly off. However, even in the presence of these bleak economic trends, there is hope that the political transformation which is now gathering speed in many developing countries will result in governments that are, in fact, accountable to their people.

Canada's policies toward the Third World have been encouraging stronger support for human rights and democratic government in developing countries, and continuing support at the Uruguay Round for issues on their agendas as well as our own. However, severe cuts to the aid budget and limited movement on debt forgiveness remind us of how much more could and should be done. Destitution in the Third World is still not seen as a threat to our security whether it be environmental, moral or otherwise. But it should be.

Notes

1 Roger Love and Susan Poulin, "Family income inequality in the 1980s," *Canadian Economic Observer* (Ottawa: Statistics Canada, September 1991), p. 4.2.

2 The North-South Institute, "The 1989–90 Federal Budget and the ODA cuts," Ottawa, April 28, 1989 (press release).

3 OECD, Development Assistance Committee, "Aid Review 1990–1991." Report by the Secretariat and Questions on the Development Assistance Efforts and Policies of Canada (Paris: OECD, November 1990), p. 7.

4 OECD, *Development Cooperation: Efforts and Policies of the Members of the Development Assistance Committee* (Paris: OECD 1991 Report), p. 126.

5 Department of Finance Canada, *The Budget* (Hull: Supply and Services, February 26, 1991), p. 70.

6 *Ibid*, p. 70.

7 *For Whose Benefit: Report of the Standing Committee on External Affairs and International Trade on Canada's Official Development Assistance Policies and Programs*, House of Commons, Ottawa, 1987 — known as the Winegard Report.

8 CIDA, *Public Attitudes toward International Development Assistance, 1991*, (Hull: Supply and Services, 1991), p. 11.

9 "L'aide occidentale sera cruciale pour éviter la catastrophe en Russie," *Le Devoir*, January 4, 1992, p. A10.

10 Finance Canada, p. 70.

11 Government of Canada, CIDA, *1991–92 Estimates. Part III Expenditure Plan* (Hull: Supply and Services, 1991), p. 6.

12 The North-South Institute, "Shake-up in CIDA," *North-South News*, no. 13 (Spring 1991).

13 OECD, Development Assistance Committee, pp. 8, 12.

14 *Canada Among Nations 1989*; *Diminishing our Future: CIDA Four Years After Winegard* (Canadian Council of Churches, Interchurch Fund for International Development Churches' Committee on International Affairs, October 1991).

15 *Sharing our Future: Canadian International Development Assistance*, (Ottawa: CIDA, 1987).

16 Protheroe, David, "Canada and Multilateral Aid," (Ottawa: The North-South Institute, 1990), pp. 57, 64.

17 Canadian Council for International Co-operation, "Report Card on the Government of Canada's Foreign Aid Program." Background Materials, Ottawa, February 1991.

18 Interchurch Fund for International Development, *Diminishing Our Future: CIDA, Four Years After Winegard.* A Report on Recent Developments in Canadian Development Assistance Policies and Practice (Toronto: Canadian Council of Churches, October 1991), p. 9.

19 The World Bank, *Sub-Saharan Africa: From Crisis to Sustainable Growth 1989. A long-term perspective study* (Washington, D.C.: World Bank, 1989), p. 6.

20 United Nations Development Programme, *Human Development Report 1991* (New York: Oxford University Press, 1991).

21 This section draws on Roy Culpeper and David Runnalls, "The International and Canadian Policy Context for CIDA Institutions in Environment and Development: A Working Paper," (Ottawa: The North-South Institute, November 1990).

22 Culpeper and Runnalls, p. 7.

23 CIDA, *Sharing our Future: Canadian International Development Assistance* (Hull: Supply and Services, 1987), p. 31.

24 Marcel Massé, "Memo to Staff," CIDA, March 28, 1991.

25 Many CIDA personnel have been given a short course in macroeconomic policy over the last two years.

26 Massé, "Memo to Staff."

27 Groupe SECOR, "Strategic Management Review." Working Document. A study completed for the Canadian International Development Agency (mimeo: October 30, 1991), p. 40.

28 Department of External Affairs and International Trade, *Government Response to the Report of the Standing Committee on External Affairs and International Trade on Third World Debt* (Ottawa: Supply and Services, 1990), p. 32.

29 Estimated using: Government of Canada, *Public Accounts 1990–91*, Vols. I and III.

30 This section draws heavily from a speech by Ann Weston entitled: "The Canadian Economy and Third World Development: Some Introductory Comments," delivered at the IDRC Media Seminar, Ottawa, September 19, 1991.

31 Weston, Ann, "Canadian Aid and Trade Relations with Developing Countries: Consistent or Conflicting?" (Ottawa: The North-South Institute, July 1991).

32 The North-South Institute, "A Whole New World: Regionalism as a building block, not a barrier," *Review '90 / Outlook '91* (Ottawa, 1991), p. 4.

13

Human Rights, Democratization, and International Conflict

Gerald J. Schmitz[1]

"It was the best of times; it was the worst of times . . ."
—Charles Dickens, *A Tale of Two Cities*

"A pessimist is an informed optimist."
—Soviet definition

"Once again, history has accelerated its pace."
—Mikhail Gorbachev, last President of the Soviet Union

The dilemma for anyone surveying the dizzying march of globally significant events during 1991 is to discern whether they are the bearers of coherent and durable trends, or whether the attempt at systematic synthesis is not an artificial projection of one's own wishful thinking upon a very disorderly canvas. We are living through one of those extraordinary historical moments which seems to justify both intemperate optimism and unlimited pessimism.

Certainly the demise of Cold War bipolarity has unblocked the global system. The previously unthinkable is not only possible, it is happening in many parts of the world. There is much talk of an apparently irresistible progressive movement supporting human rights, liberalization (both political and economic), democratization, and the building of pacific (or at least relatively demilitarized) international security regimes.

At the same time, contradictions abound. While human rights violations, political repression and violence remained endemic in the international system in 1991, the relationships among these variables became more complex, and sometimes perverse and unnerving — as when newly-won democratic freedoms released ancient ethnic hostilities. While the United Nations was seen to reassert its decayed authority and to extend the principles of humanitarian intervention, this happened in the context of a calamitous war — the largest since 1945 — the aftermath of which continues to claim innocent victims. The global ethic of interventionism that began to take shape and was actively promoted by Canada, was still more fragile hope than established consensus.[2] The rhetoric of a "new order" faced, perhaps, its severest test in the Middle East, notably in the very uncertain prospects of the historic U.S.-brokered peace conference which convened in October.

With the concept of national sovereignty increasingly in question, the UN nonetheless added seven new members at the start of its 46th session in September (bringing the total to 166), with more surely to follow as Communist unions fell apart from Yugoslavia to the Kazakhstan. The European Community, the advance party of supranational integration, tried in vain to douse the nationalist flames on its doorstep. Only months after the Paris conference supposedly laid to rest the ghosts of the Second World War, European powers were once again in a wartime alliance and a war was being fought on European soil. The abortive Soviet coup of August (and others which toppled civilian governments in Thailand and Haiti) were further sobering reminders of the threat still posed by military force to constitutional due process in the era of the elusive "peace dividend."

In all directions, governments appeared beset by a rising tide of domestic and external pressures. It is hardly surprising that the attention to issues of human rights, democratic accountability and "good governance" coincided with the impatience and assertiveness of many of the governed. In the world economy as a whole observers noted the concomitant trends represented by globalizing economic forces and the apparent acceptance of market-oriented solutions to problems of depression, stagnation and poverty. Growth and recovery were, however, spread very unevenly. There was for many little evidence of the promised improvements in their material welfare. Indeed, the UN reported the first yearly decline in total world product and income since 1945.[3]

Against this backdrop of conflict interwoven with high expectations, whither the human prospect for the world's poor majority? Will the pain of unprecedented political transitions and economic "adjustments" lead to structural transformations that will bring long-term gains? There are reasons for being in the camp of the informed optimists. But one need not be carried along by new world order rhetoric to recognize that 1991 opened up still further exceptional and challenging opportunities for collective action to affirm human rights and democratic freedoms, and to work towards real peace and security. Canadian initiatives, pursued in a credible and consistent manner, can contribute in selective and modest ways to a forward internationalist impulse. Beyond that there are no guarantees.

A Year of "People Power"?

Even with the shadow of the United Nations deadline for Iraq to withdraw from Kuwait looming large, the year 1991 began auspiciously for friends of democratic change. While it had been perhaps premature to speak of a "global revolution" signalled by the whirlwind of change in Eastern Europe, liberal democrats could be forgiven some enthusiasm for a view that saw history as, if not ending, at least "unfolding as it should." As one put it: "Democracy still has shallow roots in many parts of the world, but autocracy is in retreat everywhere."[4]

This was an arguable assertion in the light of the failure of political liberalization in China, which remained Communist, and in other countries. But it was supported by a number of positive developments during 1990. The high point of these in the North was undoubtedly the signing of the Paris Charter in November, in which thirty-four countries represented in the Conference on Security and Co-operation in Europe (CSCE), which grew to thirty-eight members with the addition of Albania and the three Baltic republics, committed themselves to the pursuit of human rights, political democracy and liberal economies. In the South, too, there was impressive movement forward, in part stirred by the popular revolutions in Europe.[5] Under international supervision, Haiti held its first free election in December with liberation theologian Fr. Jean-Bertrand Aristide winning the presidency, with an overwhelming mandate for reform. In Africa, one-party regimes were put on the defensive, a charter on "popular participation" was proclaimed, there were national conferences on political reform and less polite democracy campaigns were waged from the street. Even in Asia, where concerns about stability and productivity were seen to hold pride of place, the demand for political rights seemed to achieve "take-off" in authoritarian societies with dynamic economies (South Korea, Singapore, Hong Kong, Taiwan).[6]

A year later, the momentum of political liberalization and democratization faced a more uncertain outlook. In the Americas, the military overthrow of President Aristide in Haiti provoked unprecedented action by the Organization of American States (OAS) to try to restore constitutional government, including the dispatch of a high-level mission in early October and the imposition of comprehensive sanctions. But for the moment the hopes of the Haitian people have been dashed yet again. In Guyana there have been doubts about a clean electoral process going ahead. The results of elections in Mexico in August, although seen by most outside observers to be reasonably fair, have strengthened the hold of President Carlos Salinas de Gortari's Institutional Revolutionary Party (PRI), which has not lost power in over 60 years. Mexico is not out of the woods yet. Overall, Latin American elites faced the immense challenge of simultaneously opening up their political and economic systems. In many countries the depth of commitment to human rights and democratic reform had only begun to face real tests.[7]

In Africa, the record was mixed. There had been courageous movement forward:

> From Mauritania to Zaire, opposition political groups are challenging the one-party rulers and military dictators who have dominated African politics since decolonization. In *samizdat* articles and at political demonstrations, activists push for democracy and greater freedom of expression. Countries where pressure for change is intensifying include Cameroon, Benin, Congo, Ivory Coast, Nigeria, Togo, Zambia and Madagascar.[8]

Yet the costs were also high in often deadly civil strife, and the results of some national constitutional dialogues and concessions towards multi-partyism were of uncertain benefit. One-party autocrats survived elections in Côte d'Ivoire and Gabon (October and December 1990); in other cases the ruling party lost, but voter turnout was very low (only 25 percent in Cape Verde in early 1991). The peaceful transfer of power to the opposition Movement for Multi-Party Democracy in Zambia, following its first free elections on October 31, was hailed as a model for the rest of Africa. But again the turnout was under 50 percent and the new government faced a very difficult situation. Late in 1991, there was an attempted military takeover in Togo, and the Mobutu dictatorship survived amid chaos in Zaire. Some important countries like Kenya, which had stubbornly resisted political pluralism, did finally cave in to the pressures of aid donors. Still, it was obvious the road to African democracy would be long and rocky.[9]

In Asia, Malaysia and Bangladesh managed to hold reasonably successful elections (October 1990 and February 1991 respectively). But elsewhere democratic prospects remained frozen — China, Myanmar (Burma), North Korea — or dimmed, as in the following examples: the aftermath of the downfall of Benazir Bhutto in Pakistan and the assassination of Rajiv Gandhi in India; the ironically peaceful and popular military coup in Thailand in February which would entrench a military-dominated "civilian" regime of the Indonesian type. In Singapore elections produced only a tiny opposition, and in Hong Kong, although pro-democracy candidates won, there was only a one-third turnout for the less than one-third of legislative seats opened to electoral contests. In the Philippines, where the seminal "people power" revolution had overthrown the Marcos dictatorship in 1986, the human rights situation has deteriorated and the democratization process remains precarious as the country prepares for elections, scheduled for May 1992.

In the Middle East, liberal democrats probably have the least going for them. Notwithstanding the war to liberate Kuwait, there have been greater democratic gains in Jordan, which suffered for not supporting the coalition forces. Saddam Hussein survived in Iraq while an equally oppressive tyrant in Syria became an "ally." Amid the evidence of deep discontent, feudal monarchies, theocracies, and autocratic Arab regimes from Morocco to Iran were swept more by Islamic fundamentalism and the venting of collective frustrations (an observation confirmed by Algeria's ill-fated elections and army takeover) than by any movement towards Western-style democracy. And of course the rights of stateless peoples (Kurds, Palestinians) were still being denied.[10]

The most celebrated manifestation of people power occurred not in the Third World but around the Russian parliament in Moscow, hastening the collapse of the Soviet internal empire, and soon the extinction of the Soviet state itself. The resurrection of civil society in the East momentarily became prime-time television drama, as the heroic populist forces defeated the evil Kremlin plotters. On August 30, Yeltsin and Gorbachev paused in their burial of the Communist party, and appeared together to answer questions from American viewers on a live ABC television news program![11] Yet in the presence of widespread alienation and economic despair, no one can be sure what these manoeuvres portend. In the ex-Communist world there are varying degrees of confusion, as well as fear and a profound weariness after so much traumatic change amid present and prospective hardship. In Poland a majority did not vote in the first fully free elections in October, and recycled former Communists did as well as anyone in the hopelessly splintered competition for parliamentary seats.[12]

The undeniable expansion of global communications and media power contained mixed messages. The response to the plight of the Kurds indicated that the development of a global audience can be a significant factor in the advocacy of interventions based on humanitarian concerns and human rights. As *The Economist* observed: "Increasingly, world opinion, when confronted by television pictures of genocide or starvation, is unimpressed by those who say, 'We cannot get involved, national sovereignty must be respected.'" At the same time, it could be argued that much media coverage of the Gulf conflict ignored the human consequences of high-tech warfare and failed to provide a forum for education.[13]

There is a danger of fickle attentions, which seldom outlast the headlines, leading perhaps to an Andy Warhol world in which each region of conflict and struggling "distinct society" competes for its moment of notoriety. The resurgence of ethnic nationalism has complicated an already fragmented picture of a hopeful yet troubled global village.[14] The millions once again at risk from famine in Africa should not therefore recede from our consciousness as a major human rights story. If history is indeed speeding up, it will be important to resist the temptation to avoid long-running or recurring problems by "flipping the channel" to what seems new and different.

In 1991, the good news was that great numbers of people did demand their rights and put political leaders and regimes on notice. But we ought not to forget that many also perished as silent victims or voted with their feet. At the height of the Gulf crisis, over 1.5 million people fled across borders to neighbouring countries. The United Nations High Commission for Refugees (UNHCR) estimated there were 17 million refugees worldwide; in addition, estimates of internally displaced persons ran as high as 30 million — most of them being in the South.[15] Meanwhile the UNHCR's budget was declining in real terms and Northern countries were strengthening their border defences against this vast human flow. A more democratic world was trying to be born. But it was not as yet a noticeably kinder, gentler or more stable one.

Human Rights and International Policy: Promise and Performance

The emergence of human rights as one of the great issues of international politics was confirmed by a number of events during 1991. Although the war against Iraq was fought on the classical grounds of interstate aggression, the coalition made much of human rights atrocities by Iraqi forces. Subsequently, the intense pressure to come to the aid of the beleaguered Kurdish minority overrode some of the White House's strategic reservations. UN Security Council resolutions explicitly defended the rights of people against their government within a member state, which was given no choice but to comply. Later, in Haiti, where traditional collective security considerations could not be invoked, international action dramatically breached still further the taboo of "non-intervention" in another state's internal affairs. The United States again acted multilaterally, and perhaps more surprisingly, gave its full backing to a left-wing democratic leader.

However, the use of human rights issues as a potent international instrument, whether under UN auspices or supported by U.S. muscle, raised grave doubts in the minds of human rights activists. The dire post-war situation inside Iraq has already been noted. Overall, it was not obvious that global human rights violations were decreasing in proportion to the intent of the sermons and exhortations (and this statement takes no account of the social and economic rights which may be put at risk by celebrated transitions to democratic capitalism). Human rights criteria continued to be applied selectively, inconstantly and often incoherently, if at all. In the United States, a renewed linkage of human rights concerns to foreign policy interests found new converts. But it also disturbed critics who are sceptical as to how much the pattern of American interventions has really changed.[16]

Canada's policy on the "linkage" of human rights to foreign policy, which had been non-aggressive and often carefully understated, suddenly took on a higher profile as a result of strong statements by Prime Minister Mulroney in September and October at the time of the Haitian coup and the Commonwealth heads of government meeting in Harare, Zimbabwe. The principle of linking aid to progress on human rights and democratic "good governance" was reiterated at the Francophone summit in November. Subsequently, Canada suspended new aid to Indonesia following reports of a massacre in East Timor. The Guyanese government, with which Canada has leverage as the principal donor, was pointedly warned not to rig forthcoming elections. This tougher line should not have come as an unexpected development. Joe Clark, as Secretary of State for External Affairs, had been a forceful advocate of international human rights promotion. However, Canadian government responses to ambitious parliamentary committee recommendations (the most recent were formulated in November 1990), while appearing positive, had remained quite equivocal and restrained.[17] In practice, Canada was supporting a number of human rights activities in developing countries, often under trying circumstances, but without the benefit of a clear operational framework.

According to the existing policy, ministers were provided with human rights assessments from the Department of External Affairs as an "integral part" of annual aid allocations. However, this information and the decision process itself remained confidential. There were only a few human rights officers (one person in CIDA), the criteria were very few (or very vague and general), and the weight given to human rights considerations was often ambiguous, or appeared to be slight, especially in regard to non-aid relations (export credits, military exports, trade and finance).

By the fall of 1991, the Canadian stance, at least at the formal political level, became demonstrably bolder. The new external affairs minister, Barbara McDougall, who had seemed shaky in initially reacting to the attempted Soviet coup, put herself on the line in supporting the vigorous response of the OAS to the military takeover in Haiti. A position was being staked out, giving the moral and legal authority to act to uphold basic rights priority over the principle of non-intervention. On September 25, McDougall told the UN General Assembly: "the concept of sovereignty must respect higher principles, including the need to preserve human life from wanton destruction." A few days later, addressing an audience at Stanford University, Mulroney declared: "We must recognize that there are certain fundamental rights that all people possess — and that, sometimes, the international community must act to defend them."

In October, the Prime Minister went further. Stopping in Gabon on the way to Harare, Mulroney used the occasion of a toast to its plutocratic ruler Omar Bongo to talk about a "new international solidarity" arising in large part from "the acceptance of the primacy of human rights." Addressing the Commonwealth leaders, Mulroney was pointedly blunt:

> In Canada's judgement, it is indispensable to the credibility of the Commonwealth that its Harare declaration make clear that nothing in international relations is more important than the respect for individual freedoms and human rights. For Canada, the future course is clear: we shall be increasingly channelling our development assistance to those countries that show respect for the fundamental rights and individual freedoms of their people. Canada will not subsidize repression and the stifling of democracy.[18]

The Canadian position provoked resistance from leaders of developing countries, sensitive about their sovereignty and defensive about their domestic human rights records. Only nine of fifty member states had ratified the full International Bill of Rights and thirty-one countries, including host Zimbabwe, had yet to ratify any of its instruments. A number of Commonwealth governments have been cited for gross human rights abuses.[19] In the end, the pious and vague language in the final declaration was disappointing. There was no agreement to establish the kind of human rights monitoring capacity recommended by an NGO advisory group chaired by former Canadian external affairs minister Flora MacDonald.[20] Canadians had recently also expressed disappointment about the lack of an agreed effective mechanism for human rights surveillance at the conclusion of a month-long CSCE human rights conference in Moscow.[21]

The domestic Canadian reaction to the Prime Minister's rhetoric was, on the whole, to support linkage in principle, but to turn a critical spotlight on the gaps in Canadian policy and practice. Questions were raised about the continuing flows of economic assistance (both ODA and export lines of credit) to rights-abusing regimes — citing, for example, China, Indonesia, Pakistan, Iran — and about the shadowy assessment/decision-making process.[22] Equally troublesome were questions about the weight given to human rights in other areas of foreign policy. Had this been just a solo prime ministerial sortie with more drama than governmental substance or follow-up? At one point the Prime Minister seemed to indicate that human rights would be closely linked to aid but separated from trade — notably from the trilateral talks involving Mexico (although that country had been anxious to show its commitment to human rights reforms since the release in September of an Amnesty International report on torture by its security forces). Yet Agriculture Minister Bill McKnight did put undiplomatic stress on human rights concerns during commercial discussions with Chinese officials in Beijing in late October.[23] (Canada subsequently protested the expulsion of three MPs on a human rights mission to China early in 1992.) The government had also been sensitive to charges that its export controls policy and advocacy of a global arms-control regime were undermined by a proposed major sale of armoured vehicles to Saudi Arabia and small but continuing sales of military goods to developing countries with dubious human rights records.[24]

In short, by the end of 1991, human rights were clearly established as a central item on the foreign policy agenda. Important principles had been enunciated in international fora. Following through was another matter. To a degree, practice could follow, as examples multiplied of ways to provide concrete external support for human rights objectives. But, in Canada as in other nations, ambivalent and inadequate policy frameworks still served to create uncertainty about the political commitment to a really new global order.

Next Steps towards Democratic Development Assistance

Concurrent with the increased attention to human rights by major Western donor governments and international organizations was an increased linkage of progress on human rights to a process of "democratization" — usually understood very liberally to include "market-friendly" economic development and reform. The vexed linkage of political to economic liberalization will be taken up later. What has been less contested is the principle that human rights include democratic rights and freedoms, and that part of human development is the capacity to provide equitable opportunity for participation by all members of society in decisions affecting their lives. Similarly, the case has been made that, without honest and effective "good government" that is accountable to civil society, many development efforts are doomed to fail. "Support for participatory and democratic development is becoming an essential part of the aid mission," concluded the 1991 *Report* of the OECD's Development Assistance Committee.[25]

The democracy agendas of powerful international actors are nonetheless complicated by their less fashionable interests and by the understandable suspicion they arouse with respect to their motives. Virtually all aid donors (including the largest, Japan, and the most technocratic, the International Monetary Fund — IMF) now apply some degree of broadly political "conditionality," which includes commitments by recipient governments to domestic reforms and possibly decreased military spending. Germany and Japan have most clearly adopted a position of linking aid to lower arms expenditures. But the most aggressive promoters of conditionality are the "hegemonic" states of the past two centuries, the United States and the United Kingdom. The U.S. Agency for International Development (USAID) released a comprehensive "Democracy Initiative" in

December 1990. In June 1991, the British minister for overseas development announced substantially increased spending on direct help for good
government, which covered "the processes and institutions needed for
democratic and pluralistic structures, a free press and human rights."[26]

Both countries disclaimed any intentions of engaging in ideological
imperialism, or of attempting to redirect aid resources from an offending
Third World to more promising partners in newly liberated eastern Europe. The initial record of the nineties, however, reveals some disturbing
patterns. The U.S. and the U.K. were the major military partners in a war
which failed to bring democracy, but did carry very high costs for millions
in developing countries. At the same time, the U.S. remained the stingiest
of the large aid donors (at 0.21 percent of GNP) even after including in its
totals the forgiveness of military debt extended to Egypt. British ODA
dropped to 0.27 percent of GNP in 1990, its lowest level ever. This came
at a time when developing countries could no longer expect help from a
disintegrating Soviet bloc that had itself turned into a competitor and
supplicant.[27] Yet within the G-7, the U.S. and Britain also remained the
least enthusiastic about direct aid to their former foes despite dire pre-
dictions about the sustainability of reforms at a time of collapsing living
standards. They were long on advice about free politics and markets, but
short on cash transfusions, and while preaching support for pluralism to
the South, presented the world with a telling contradiction: as per capita
aid to Africa declined, Malawi's pro-Western "president for life" received
increased *military* assistance from the U.S. and Britain in 1990.[28]

Following the swift defeat of the Soviet military *putsch* in August
1991, the Wall Street Journal proclaimed: "All recent evidence suggests
that the world is about to embark on an era in which membership in the
club of nations will turn on the Jeffersonian principle that governments
derive their legitimacy from the consent of the governed." However, a
later editorial in *The Economist* was more accurate: "The democratic
world is in a muddle about its dealings with the non-democracies."[29]

Canada's foray into the perilous adventure of assisting democratic
transitions remained rather more circumspect and modest, perhaps wisely
so. The International Centre for Human Rights and Democratic Development (ICHRDD) had its first full year of operations in 1991. Its $15
million budget from Parliament (voted in 1988) is to last to the end of the
1992–93 fiscal year. The Centre has been able to fund only a fraction of
the project requests it receives (and even that was too much for some Conservative party members who resolved at their national convention that
it should be abolished). As an arms-length agency, ICHRDD has been
somewhat hesitant about its role in policy development. For its part, the
government supported various initiatives with a democratic development
component: through its Task Force on Assistance to Central and Eastern

Europe, the CSCE's Office of Democratic Institutions established in Warsaw; election monitoring and technical assistance from Elections Canada; the OAS Unit for the Promotion of Democracy; assistance to planning a democratic transition in post-apartheid South Africa; the Commonwealth's human rights work; a proposed human rights information unit and secretariat to support democratization within La Francophonie; and a development and democracy thrust in preparation for the 1993 UN world conference on human rights in Berlin.

Addressing the Department of External Affairs' annual consultations on human rights with Canadian NGOs on January 20, 1992, Barbara McDougall indicated that the government was considering applying to its international assistance a number of "good governance" criteria including: "commitment to democratic processes, sound economic management, non-excessive levels of military expenditure, probity and transparency of public accounts, and priority to basic social programmes, as well as respect for human rights." Yet notwithstanding the ministerial advocacy, the bureaucratic momentum and the articulation of "securing democracy and respect for human values" as priority objectives of foreign policy, the Department of External Affairs and International Trade (DEAIT) was finding it difficult to obtain new resources to respond to increasing requests for "political" assistance.[30]

CIDA was also concerned about fiscal constraints, even as it engaged during 1991 to get up to speed on "participatory development" issues, given the prominence being attached to them within the OECD's Development Assistance Committee (DAC).[31] This was not entirely new territory for CIDA, but the agency could derive little confidence from its limited experience of using aid directly to encourage democratic reforms. There was recognition that integrating human rights and democratization objectives, from policy development through to the level of field operations, often under unfavourable conditions, was a task which had just begun.[32]

Conflicting "Governance" Agendas: Structural Adjustment and Political Participation

A growing area of policy tension during 1991 was the clash between the "neoliberal" (i.e., pro-market) economic conditionalities of Northern donors and lenders and the deeper democratic visions of popular movements in the South and their international partners in NGO networks. This tension was especially pronounced in Africa, sometimes resulting in sharp public disputes about who and what were to blame for that continent's evident failures in economic management and governance. At the final review in September of the UN African recovery program (UNPAAERD, begun in 1986 with strong Canadian backing), the World

Bank's Edward Jaycox declared: "Africa needs to get competitive again
. . . . The real cause of many of today's problems lies in the mistaken [i.e.,
statist] economic policies of the past." But a UN director-general, Antoine
Blanca, lamented that as a result of current market-driven "adjustment"
policies, "Entire health systems and education systems are in jeopardy
. . . . There can be no democracy with hunger and starvation."[33]

Noted Nigerian scholar Claude Aké has been sharply critical of the
late Western conversion to the cause of democracy and human rights in
Africa, arguing that the implementation of the free-market structural adjustment programs to which "good governance" has been attached have
in fact required coercive state imposition in the face of popular democratic resistance. Similarly Canadian Africanist Richard Sandbrook, while
welcoming the move away from a strictly economistic approach to adjustment, saw major problems ahead.[34] Provocative parallels were drawn to
the difficulties of simultaneous economic and political transformations in
Eastern Europe.[35] But at least the East Europeans did not, as yet, have
to fear political conditionalities as an ironic concomitant of dependence
and marginalization. (Some estimates predict that per capita assistance
to ease their transition will soon be 20 times the amount granted to developing countries.)

A major source of unease with the governance agendas of the big
players, especially the Bank, has been the sense that they are far more
committed to an essentially Western design of liberalization — economic
and political ("free markets and free votes") — and to continued policy leverage, than to accepting democratization as empowering the poor
and including socio-economic welfare and equality rights.[36] Alternative
governance agendas have included, as an essential element, the right to
policy choice and to the self-determining development of civil society. As
a North-South parliamentary declaration in July 1991 put it:

> . . . the promotion of democracy in Africa is the supreme goal. . . .
> Economic reform, including structural adjustment programmes must
> be fully transparent, answering to the interest and will of the African
> peoples. Conditionality, whether economic or political, must not be
> imposed, but rather agreed upon with the free consent of African lead-
> ers and citizenry. It should be applied only as a last resort to encourage
> and ensure the survival of democracy and protection of human rights.[37]

Another contentious aspect of the dominant governance approaches
was that they seemed to put the primary onus to change on poor countries
while accepting a very inequitable and undemocratic international system.
Would getting politics as well as prices right mean accepting an order
of economic "globalization" in which political choice was reduced? How
"transparent" and democratic were international trade negotiations or the
operations of international financial institutions and donor governments?

How "accountable" were powerful international bodies and regimes to the world's peoples? to the poor?

Critics argued in 1991 that Canada had embraced too closely the dominant perspective of political structural adjustment. The prime minister's Commonwealth address in Harare advised that:

> ... the global community must not marginalize the poorer countries .... But, equally, developing countries must not marginalize themselves outside of the emerging global mainstream of human rights, political pluralism and market based economies. ...
>
> Political and economic freedom are two sides of the same coin. Free economies are not an adjunct to development but integral to it .... Those countries that embrace sound economic policies and stable democratic institutions — and thereby make themselves attractive to private investment — will prosper most ....

CIDA, under its president Marcel Massé, was seen as basing its five-dimensional approach to "sustainable development" — including political sustainability — to an excessive degree on this combined orthodoxy of liberal politics and neoconservative economics.[38] Some churches and NGOs sharply challenged that direction in a report released in October, arguing that the effect of structural adjustment, even with a "human face," was to hurt, not help, the poor.[39] Canadian policy was confronted with the dilemma that too great an insistence on market-driven economic medicine might be denying the very human rights (civil-political and social-economic) which the same policy claimed governments of developing countries should respect as a condition of receiving assistance, — in effect, and ironically, a potential recipe for conflictive and unsustainable governance.[40]

Born Again Multilateralism?
Human Rights, Democracy and Peace-Building

The "new world order" rhetoric which flowed from the Gulf war worried many, especially in the Third World, who saw in it not a renewed multilateralism but a virtually unipolar direction, with the United States bearing the official ideology of democratic capitalism, and using United Nations authority as a mere flag of convenience to impose its version of global justice. Of course, it may be, as some suggest, that the action against Iraq resulted from a unique combination of circumstances and that the manner in which it was executed makes it unlikely ever to be repeated. It could, in this view, catalyze real UN reform.[41] As well, the ability of the remaining superpower to control a complex, fluid and still highly conflictive post-Cold War landscape may be vastly overstated.[42] Nevertheless, leaving aside the most cynical Chomskian interpretation of U.S. motives and power, many analysts were more concerned that opportunities created for multilateral co-operation of real benefit to the world's peoples could be squandered.[43]

The camp of the multilateral optimists, which included the Canadian government, saw in the post-war situation the basis for a new ethic of lawful interventionism. The situation was not unlike the immediate post-1945 years of liberal internationalism, and now the time was never better to complete the global "architecture" of peace and security, human rights protection and democratization.[44] The declaration of the G-7 London Summit in July noted:

> . . . the urgent and overwhelming nature of the humanitarian problem in Iraq caused by violent oppression by the Government required exceptional action by the international community, following . . . Security Council Resolution 688. We urge the UN and its affiliated agencies to be ready to consider similar action in the future if the circumstances require it. The international community cannot stand idly by in cases where widespread suffering from famine, war, oppression, refugee flows, disease, or flood reaches urgent and overwhelming proportions.[45]

Prime Minister Mulroney, in his Stanford speech in September, called for "re-thinking the limits of national sovereignty in a world where problems respect no borders," and for the creation of "a commonwealth of universal democratic values," echoing Barbara McDougall's address to the UN General Assembly a few days earlier:

> . . . we must look beyond a system which only inhibits armed confrontations. I believe that we need a new definition of the concept of multilateral security, a definition that takes into account the new and varied threats to global peace and security. These include the depletion of the ozone layer, the degradation of our seas, the debilitating scourge of illicit drugs, and worldwide epidemics such as AIDS, mass exoduses of people from one country to another, and the desperate poverty which persists in many parts of the world.
>
> We recognize as well that our collective security depends upon democracy and respect for human rights.

The Liberal Party was also active in presenting its own "new internationalist" agenda, centred around a reformed United Nations system.[46]

Events in 1991 certainly challenged and tested the linkages of democratization, human rights, and the building of a working peace or common security system. The thesis that democracies never fight each other was resurrected, but analysts cautioned about expectations of an era of peaceful co-existence. One major study concluded that, by itself, " 'democracy' does not appear to be a force for peace in any straightforward, uniform, or consistent fashion."[47] Democratization, in the sense of a loosening of centrally or externally imposed constraints, could even exacerbate a host of local and ethnic conflicts — major sources of human rights violations in many regions.

The UN seemed to reach a high point in human rights and peace-brokering activism (in Central America, Cambodia, Western Sahara, possibly Afghanistan), though it was, paradoxically, on the sidelines in the post-war Middle East process. The civil war raging in Yugoslavia defied efforts at outside mediation, although new UN efforts early in 1992 held out a glimmer of hope. In Africa, the positive examples of Namibia and Angola could be contrasted with the tragedies of Liberia, the Horn of Africa (Sudan, Ethiopia, Somalia) and Mozambique.

Regionally, however, there were hopeful signs and models for the future. In May, in Kampala, Uganda, the UN helped to organize a conference with the "African Leadership Forum" which hammered out a statement on "Security, Stability, Development and Co-operation in Africa," containing proposals on non-aggression, conflict resolution, democratization and human rights. One recommendation was for an "African Peace Council" under the auspices of the Organization of African Unity (OAU); another for an "African Court of Justice" to monitor human rights commitments. In June, in Santiago, Chile, the OAS concluded several historic accords linking security to democracy, human rights and social justice. One resolution set out parameters for OAS intervention when "democratic institutions" are threatened or when "the legitimate exercise of power by a democratically elected government" is interrupted. This was invoked within months in the case of Haiti.[48]

In Paris, in October, agreement was reached on a complex political settlement for Cambodia to be supervised by a United Nations Transitional Authority (UNTAC). However, the operation, the largest ever undertaken by the UN, was criticized for giving legitimacy to the genocidal Khmer Rouge and as lacking credible human rights safeguards.[49] More promising, perhaps, was the UN Observer Mission in El Salvador (ONUSAL), which was entrusted with an explicit human rights verification role and which was also unprecedented in that it intervened with domestic combatants in a member state, well in advance of the dramatic New Year's Eve ceasefire. ONUSAL began field operations in July 1991, and in September an additional New York Accord was signed establishing a National Commission for the Consolidation of Peace (COPAZ).

These early moves were very positive, certainly when compared to the bleak situation in neighbouring Guatemala. But, as has been extensively documented by Canadian NGOs, many obstacles remained to the securing of real democracy and a just peace: the issues of land reform, impunity of the armed forces, non-compliance, restrictions on humanitarian work, etc. In the Salvadorean case, continued international pressure and Canadian assistance were deemed important. At the same time, NGOs were concerned that multilateral measures applied to rights-abusing regimes (e.g.,

OAS sanctions against Haiti), or to regions of conflict, should not have the paradoxical effect of cutting assistance to democratic and peace-building forces within the civil society. Channels for leverage and assistance should be designed accordingly.[50] What was being called for was a truly new multilateralism — one based on relations of solidarity and support within an international vision of civil society, yet often frustrated by the old rules of statist 'realpolitik.'

New Norms of International Order — Canada's Role

What does a Canadian "informed optimist" conclude from the confused messages of the past year: that superior force still "works" in the crunch, but that henceforth global law and order should serve a new orthodoxy of human rights, democracy and benign Western-style capitalism? The long-term Canadian view is likely to be less pushy and ideological. In part that is because we are: aware of the Achilles' heel represented by the treatment of our native peoples; struggling to define rights (property rights or a "social charter"?) in the midst of economic recession; deeply worried for the democratic health of our own political system; concerned that cultural and territorial divisions could destroy our exemplary "peaceable kingdom".

Looking abroad in 1991, Canadians saw much that was wrong. But they also saw a rising tide of popular democratic and humanitarian demands that would eventually have to be met, as authoritarian, rights-violating regimes ran out of friends and excuses. Canadian policy, for its part, balanced on the horns of several dilemmas: supporting "just" war yet calling for humanitarian and peacemaking interventions; tying foreign aid to human rights yet doing business with some nasty governments. In Myanmar (Burma), where 1991 Nobel Peace Prize winner Suu Kyi continued to be kept under house arrest by the military junta and her National League for Democracy was denied its overwhelming victory in 1990 elections, Petro-Canada was allowed to continue exploring for a strategically important resource. The donors' preaching about democratic pluralism and human rights often seemed to fall on deaf ears in the places where it most needed to be heard.[51]

At the end of 1991 new norms of international order, capable of transcending not only East-West but eventually North-South divides, remained more dream than reality. Yet important breakthroughs were made and ambitious reform options seriously debated. The rights of peoples and citizens made a significant if unsteady advance against the prerogatives of states and governments. In that context, Canadian international policy faced a time of critical examination and testing that could, hopefully, spur it to grow in clarity, consistency, maturity, and hence, credibility.

If nothing else, 1991 proved the need for more independent, moderating voices to put the building of a *better* world order on the agenda of future years.

Notes

1 The author gratefully acknowledges the assistance of Daniela Zane, graduate student at The Norman Paterson School of International Affairs, in the early stages of preparing this chapter.

2 Infant mortality in Iraq was reported to have increased four-fold since the end of the Gulf war. A. John Watson, "Something Has Gone Terribly Wrong in Post-War Iraq," *The Ottawa Citizen*, October 24, 1991. John Hay, "UN interventionism idea needs a little work before it will sell," *The Ottawa Citizen*, December 2, 1991.

3 Global GDP was expected to drop by 0.5 percent in 1991. "World economy at its worst since 1945," *The Ottawa Citizen*, October 2, 1991.

4 William Maynes, "The New Decade," *Foreign Policy*, No. 80, (Fall 1990): 4; Dankwart Rustow, "Democracy: A Global Revolution?" *Foreign Affairs*, Vol. 69, No. 4, (Fall 1990): 75–91; and for more critical perspectives the special issue on "The Global Context of Democratization," *Alternatives: Social Transformation and Humane Governance*, Vol. 16, No. 2, (Spring 1991).

5 See, for example, Kofi Kumado and Nana K.A. Busia Jr., "The Impact of Developments in Eastern Europe on the Democratization Process in Africa: An Exploratory Analysis," in Bard-Anders Andreassen and Theresa Swinehart, eds., *Human Rights in Developing Countries 1990* (Kehl: N.P. Engel Publisher, 1991), pp. 3–18. More generally, see the emphasis on human rights and democratic reforms in *The Challenge to the South*, Report of the South Commission (Oxford: Oxford University Press, 1990).

6 For several rather contrary views of this political-economic relationship see "Freedom and Prosperity," *The Economist*, June 29, 1991, pp. 15–18; Richard Gwyn, "Western-style democracy is no cure-all," *The Toronto Star*, November 13, 1991; Martin Wolf, "Paths to Progress," *The Financial Times of London*, November 15, 1991.

7 See Tina Rosenberg, "Beyond Elections," *Foreign Policy*, No. 84, (Fall 1991): 72–91.

8 Craig Forman, "Africa's Tide of Reform Lapping at Zaire," *The Wall Street Journal*, September 26, 1991. See also Gwynne Dyer, "Change sweeps Africa," *The Toronto Star*, November 13, 1991.

9 For mixed reviews see Jonathan Manthorpe, "Pushing Democracy," *The Ottawa Citizen*, December 4, 1991. Linda Hossie, "New Voices of Africa," *The Globe and Mail*, December 14, 1991. On the phenomenon of national conferences which began in Benin in early 1990 see *Africa News*, Vol. 35, No. 1, (August 26, 1991): 3–5; also *Netherlands Quarterly of Human Rights*, Vol. 9, No. 3, (1991): 326–31.

10 For a pre-Madrid assessment see "Out of Joint: A Survey of the Middle East," *The Economist*, September 28, 1991, 22 pages; Mustapha K. Al-Sayyid, "Slow Thaw in the Arab World," *World Policy Journal*, Vol. 8, No. 4, (Fall 1991): 711–38.

11 "Why the Soviet Union Died," *Maclean's*, September 16, 1991, p. 27.

12 No party won more than 14 percent of Sejm seats. Patricia Clough, "Vote confusion may prompt the rise of a strongman," *The Ottawa Citizen*, November 2, 1991.

13 "New ways to run the world," *The Economist*, November 9, 1991, p. 11. According to *Middle East Report*, heavy viewers of American television were twice as likely as light viewers to believe Kuwait was a democracy, and three times as likely to believe that Saudi Arabia was a democracy. (Noted in *Compass*, November/December 1991, p. 5.)

14 See Linda Hossie, "An angry world of distinct societies," *The Globe and Mail*, September 28, 1991.

15 "The Dispossessed," *The New Internationalist*, No. 223, (September 1991).

16 For views supporting U.S. foreign policy as convergent with democratic human rights promotion see Brad Roberts, "Human Rights and International Security," *The Washington Quarterly*, Vol. 13, (Spring 1990): 65–75; Morris Abram, "Human Rights and the United Nations: Past as Prologue," *Harvard Human Rights Journal*, Vol. 4, (Spring 1991): 69–83. For critical human rights perspectives see Richard Falk, "Refocusing the Struggle for Human Rights: The Foreign Policy Illusion," *Harvard Human Rights Journal*, (Spring 1991): 47–67; and in the same journal, Edward Herman, "The United States Versus Human Rights in the Third World," pp. 85–104.

17 See "Government Response to the Third Report of the Standing Committee on Human Rights and the Status of Disabled Persons Entitled *Human Rights Considerations and Coherence in Canada's Foreign Policy*" (Ottawa: Secretary of State for External Affairs, November 15, 1990); Gerald Schmitz, "Between Political Principle and State Practice: Human Rights 'Conditionality' in Canada's Development Assistance," in Irving Brecher, ed., *Human Rights, Development and Foreign Policy: Canadian Perspectives* (Halifax: The Institute for Research on Public Policy, 1989), pp. 467–85; and for a current assessment, T.A. Keenleyside, "Human Rights," in Cranford Pratt, ed. *Canadian Development Assistance Policies* (forthcoming).

18 "Notes for a Speech by Prime Minister Brian Mulroney — Global Report: World Political Overview," Commonwealth Heads of Government Meeting, October 16, 1991, p. 2.

19 The International Bill consists of the International Covenant on Civil and Political Rights, its Optional Protocol, and the International Covenant on Economic, Social and Cultural Rights. See the ratification chart in *Human Rights Update*, Newsletter of the Human Rights Unit of the Commonwealth Secretariat, No. 9, October 1991, insert after p. 6. On documented abuses see Linda Hossie, "Top abusers found in Commonwealth," *The Globe and Mail*, October 22, 1991.

20 Its report was entitled *Put Our World to Rights: Towards a Commonwealth Human Rights Policy* (London: Commonwealth Human Rights Initiative,

August 1991). The Commonwealth's tiny human rights unit was also, despite its constraints, doing impressive work. See, in particular, Dilys Hill, *Development Assistance and Human Rights: Principles, Criteria and Procedures* (London: Commonwealth Secretariat, June 1991).

21 Jim Sheppard, "Human rights meeting disappointing, Canadian says," *The Ottawa Citizen*, October 5, 1991.

22 Cf. G.J. Schmitz, "Nice talk, but will there be action?" *The Globe and Mail*, October 24, 1991; Julian Beltrame, "Aid and rights: Tough talk is not new, but action would be," *The Ottawa Citizen*, October 17, 1991; Ed Broadbent, "Tying aid to human rights," *The Toronto Star*, October 25, 1991; Michael Hanlon, "Can Cash Buy Human Rights?" *The Toronto Star*, October 26, 1991.

23 Officially sanctioned delegations from both China and Mexico were in Ottawa during that month, specifically to discuss human rights.

24 See Geoffrey York, "Canadian rockets make big impact," *The Globe and Mail*, August 19, 1991. The government agreed to a parliamentary investigation of these issues. But note also the critique by Douglas Roche, "Canada's hypocrisy on human rights," *The Toronto Star*, November 28, 1991.

25 Organization for Economic Co-operation and Development (OECD), *Development Co-operation 1991 Report* (Paris: OECD, December 1991), p. 66.

26 Lynda Chalker, "Good Government and the Aid Programme," Speech to the Overseas Development Institute, Chatham House, London, June 25, 1991.

27 OECD, pp. 150–51; John Hay, "Dissolution of Soviet Union will worsen Third World's distress," *The Ottawa Citizen*, September 30, 1991.

28 Neil Henry, "Banda a model African dictator," *The Ottawa Citizen*, September 10, 1991.

29 "The New Democratic Order," *The Wall Street Journal*, August 22, 1991. "Spreading democracy," *The Economist*, October 5, 1991, p. 18.

30 See the statement by Joe Clark, "Human Rights and Democratic Development," presented to the International Conference on Human Rights, Banff, November 11, 1990. (A two-day seminar sponsored by the DEAIT on the theme "Democratic Development: By Whom — For Whom?" was held at Meech Lake, March 21–22.) Policy Planning Staff, "Foreign Policy Themes and Priorities, 1991–92 Update" (Ottawa: External Affairs and International Trade Canada, December 1991), pp. 11–12. Lack of funds was confirmed in conversations with DEAIT officials.

31 OECD, esp. pp. 33–66. For exploratory analysis originally commissioned by CIDA, see David Gillies and Gerald Schmitz, *The Challenge of Democratic Development* (Ottawa: The North-South Institute, 1992). The author has also done work on "governance" issues for CIDA's policy branch.

32 See the cautionary observations by David Gillies, "The Philippines: Foreign Aid and Human Rights in an Uncertain Democracy," in *Human Rights in Developing Countries 1990*, pp. 27–45.

33 Cited in John Stackhouse, "Africa Inc., where the bottom line is starvation," *The Globe and Mail*, September 14, 1991.

34 Claude Aké, "Rethinking African Democracy," *Journal of Democracy*, 2:1, (Winter 1991): 32–44; Richard Sandbrook, "Taming the African Leviathan," *World Policy Journal*, Vol. 7, No. 4 (Fall 1990): 673–99.

35 See Irina Galunina, "Interaction Between Economic Reforms in Eastern Europe and the Structural Adjustment Process in Africa: Political and Social Impacts," Paper presented to the Seminar on Reintegration of Eastern Europe and the Soviet Union: Implications for Developing Countries (Ottawa: The North-South Institute, September 25–26, 1991).

36 This holds for even the most persuasive presentations of the official thesis. See Pierre Landell-Mills and Ismail Serageldin, "Governance and the Development Process," *Finance & Development*, (September 1991): 14–17; John Johnson, "Aid and Good Governance in Africa," *The Round Table*, Issue 320, (October 1991): 395–400. The UNDP's much-debated "human freedom" index in its *Human Development Report 1991* also revealed liberal conception which is open to question. (Cf. Douglas Williams, "UNDP World Freedom Index: A Comment," *Human Rights Intermet Reporter*, 14:1, (Summer/Autumn 1991): 83–85.)

37 "The Abidjan Declaration on Debt Relief, Recovery and Democracy," July 8–9, 1991. (Available in Canada through co-sponsor Parliamentarians for Global Action.)

38 For an earlier critique of the latter see Robert Clarke, "Overseas Development Assistance: The Neo-Conservative Challenge," in Maureen Appel Molot and Fen Osler Hampson, eds., *Canada Among Nations 1989* (Ottawa: Carleton University Press, 1990), pp. 193–206.

39 *Diminishing our Future, CIDA: Four Years After Winegard*, Interchurch Fund for International Development and Churches' Commission on International Affairs, Canadian Council of Churches, October 1991.

40 On the primary importance of both sets of rights to the sustainability of democratic transitions, see Zehra Arat, *Democracy and Human Rights in Developing Countries* (Boulder, Colo.: Lynne Rennier Publishers, 1991).

41 See Bruce Russett and James Sutterlin, "The U.N. in a New World Order," *Foreign Affairs*, Vol. 70, No. 2, (Spring 1991): 69–83.

42 Cf. Stanley Hoffman, "A New World and Its Troubles," *Foreign Affairs*, Vol. 69, No. 4, (Fall 1991): 115–22; Robert Rothstein, "Democracy, Conflict, and Development in the Third World," *The Washington Quarterly* Vol. 14, No. 2, (Spring 1991): 43–63.

43 See Jerry Sanders, "Retreat from World Order: The Perils of Triumphalism," *World Policy Journal*, Vol. 7, No. 2, (Spring 1991): 227–50; Delia Boylan and Richard Feinberg, "The 'new world order' and the Third World," *The Boston Globe*, October 3, 1991.

44 See, for example, B.G. Ramcharan, "Strategies for the International Protection of Human Rights in the 1990s," *Human Rights Quarterly*, Vol. 13, No. 2, (May 1991): 155–69.

45 Cited in David Gillies, "Human Rights and State Sovereignty," Background Paper prepared for a meeting at ICHRDD (Montreal, October 8–9, 1991), p. 13.

46 The party organized several colloquia and conferences on these themes. See Jean Chrétien, "Pursuing a Vision: Canadian Foreign Policy and the New

Internationalism." Speech given at Trinity College, Toronto, June 14, 1991; Lloyd Axworthy, "Perfect Chance to Repair the UN Charter," *The Globe and Mail*, August 14, 1991.

47 T. Clifton Morgan and Sally Howard Campbell, "Domestic Structure, Decisional Constraints, and War: So Why Can't Democracies Fight?" *Journal of Conflict Resolution*, Vol. 35, No. 2, (June 1991): 210; Rothstein, pp. 46–52; Bernard Wood, "The Curious Link Between Democracy and Peace," *Peace and Security*, Vol. 6, No. 3, (Autumn 1991): 16.

48 For more details see *Netherlands Quarterly of Human Rights*, 9:3, (1991): 322–31; John McClintock, "OAS's 'Kuwait': Haiti ultimatum could lead to use of force," *The Ottawa Citizen*, October 5, 1991, p. B8.

49 Ian Filewood and Bill Janzen, "Hold Khmer Rouge accountable for their crimes," *The Ottawa Citizen*, October 29, 1991.

50 See The Central American Monitoring Group, "El Salvador: In for the Long Haul," (Ottawa, November 1991).

51 For an astute American perspective, see David Steinberg, "Democracy, Power, and the Economy in Myanmar: Donor Dilemmas," *Asian Survey*, Vol. 31, No. 8, (August 1991): 729–42.

14

Post-Communist Transitions: The Background, Challenges, and Canadian Response

Lenard J. Cohen

> The so-called reforms and changes to communism, right through perestroika were really symptoms of its disintegration. . . . It is a system which cannot be restored.
>
> —Milovan Djilas (1991)

> The communist heritage survives not only in the economy and in political institutions, but in minds as well. . . . The coming years will not bring any radical solutions to the recently decommunized countries.
>
> —Leszek Kolakowski (1991)

The decline and fall of the "Soviet Empire" in the Eurasian and Eastern European regions constitutes a major watershed in contemporary history. This chapter will explore a number of fundamental questions relating to the atrophy and residual impact of communism in Eastern Europe and the Soviet Union. What are the principal factors which contributed to the deterioration and dramatic collapse of the "Marxist-Leninist" states in Eastern Europe, and eventually the disintegration of the U.S.S.R. itself? What obstacles stand in the way of current efforts by the post-communist regimes to achieve political democracy and the establishment of free market economic systems? How did Canada respond to the twilight of *perestroika*, and what challenges does the advent of post-communism present to Canadian foreign policymakers?

The Demise of Communism

As with any major revolutionary upheaval, the collapse of communist rule in Eastern Europe and the Soviet Union is a complex phenomenon characterized by the convergence of both long-term and short-term factors. A combination of internal and external stimuli must also be considered in explaining this demise. Keeping in mind that it is hazardous to generalize about the reasons for communism's failure in so many highly diverse societies — each case naturally having a particular context of revolutionary causes and a specific pattern of transformation — the following survey will identify the key factors responsible for the profound changes recently experienced in the Soviet Union and Eastern Europe.

The Economic Factor

Probably the most important long-term factor responsible for the demise of the Soviet and East European communist regimes was the very weak performance of their economic systems, and their related inability to satisfy popular expectations of an improved standard of living. Experimentation with different schemes of economic reform varied considerably from one communist state to another, but at each stage in their respective country's development the ruling communist elite hesitated to take the necessary steps to jettison the dysfunctional features bequeathed to them by the Marxist-Leninist and Stalinist models of economic organization.

In most communist regimes, the failures of economic reform can be traced to various political and ideological obstacles which perpetuated negative aspects of state intervention in the economy. Such intervention included state regulation of prices and of the production of goods and services; subsidization of unprofitable areas of economic activity; and restrictions limiting both the development of private entrepreneurial activities and material incentives to stimulate economic productivity and innovation. State socialism's aversion to market economic principles not only prevented accurate measurement of profitability and efficiency, but also resulted in unbalanced patterns of production and constant shortages of consumer goods. Efforts to tinker with the old economic system either by the partial and inconsistent incorporation of various capitalist features intended to create a new "market socialism" or, alternatively, by campaigns for the enhanced efficiency and technological upgrading of the centrally planned economic system (e.g., a kind of cybernetic or computerized scientific socialism), proved to be futile and unable to compensate for the innate defects of communist economic organization.[1]

Popular cynicism and disappointment arising from the gap between the exaggerated claims of the communist regimes and the dismal reality of their economic performance also became an important factor contributing to their delegitimation. This delegitimation, caused by the state of the economy, can additionally be traced to the various privileges and perks of power enjoyed by the rulers of the communist states, together with the rampant corruption and nepotism manifest in their ruling circles. Presiding over clearly deficient economic systems, the failures of which they frequently exacerbated by blatant mismanagement, communist decision-makers added insult to injury by pressuring the working population to achieve unrealistic standards and levels of economic performance. This pattern of "asymmetrical verification," whereby the leaders of the one-party state remained unaccountable to the citizens, but the citizenry was bullied into performing and monitored by the rulers, contributed to a gradual erosion of popular support for the communist system.[2]

Efforts by the communist elites to save their economies through the infusion of borrowed funds from the West and the partial importation of capitalist ideas also proved ineffective and counter-productive. Thus, money alone could not overcome the inefficient grafting of capitalist methods on to the residual features of the communist system. Moreover, popular resentment often increased when borrowed funds were siphoned off by the communist elites for their personal benefit. Each communist country, of course, had a unique trajectory of economic failure. Cases ranged, for example, from the highly market-oriented model of Yugoslavia, where the pioneer socialist reform of the 1950s and 1960s was later undermined by elite corruption, mismanagement, and rampant ethno-regional autarky, to Romania, where the regime's already tenuous legitimacy completely evaporated, due to the imposition of strict neo-Stalinist rule and the ruling family's primitive effort to pay off the country's entire foreign debt by denying the population the most elementary necessities.

Another important source of economic dissatisfaction in the Soviet Union, and in Eastern Europe up to the end of 1989, derived from the contrast between the standard of living in Western countries and in the communist states. Thus, while the ruling communist elites took a certain justifiable pride in how far their societies had advanced economically beyond the levels of the pre-communist period (albeit at very great cost and with unnecessary hardship to the population), the citizens of those societies generally focused upon their low standard of living as compared to the inhabitants of neighbouring capitalist states. During the 1970s and 1980s, the "demonstration effect" of non-communist economic success had a heightened impact on citizens of the Soviet Union and Eastern Europe. Partially due to the worldwide communications revolution (e.g., increased access to copying machines, satellite T.V. from the capitalist states, circulation of dissident views on tape cassettes, etc.), and also as a result of greater opportunities for travel and the direct exchange of information during the period of détente, citizens of the communist states became more aware of the sharp contrast between their own living conditions and developments in the outside world. Most Soviet and East European citizens came to believe that foreign models of socio-economic organization were preferable to their own, an attitude which together with the previously mentioned sources of discontent, cynicism, and alienation, contributed to the delegitimation and eventual collapse of the communist states.

Political and Moral Factors

In addition to weak economic performance, the political and moral failings of the communist regimes must also be considered as a major factor in their eventual demise. Through their outright monopolization of power, and the use of various techniques to repress or harass those who practiced forms of political dissidence and non-conformism (first quite violently, and after Stalin's death through a variety of less violent but still coercive sanctions), the communist regimes gradually undermined their already tenuous legitimacy, and also engendered a sense of moral indignation among growing numbers of their citizens.[3] Although communist elites temporarily preserved their hegemony by obstructing any genuine pluralism of opinion, they gradually destabilized their regimes by failing to co-opt or incorporate potential centres of political opposition, as well as forces that could have played a positive role in reforming the socialist system. Burdened by their brutal Stalinist history and poor economic record, and moreover, imprisoned in their own anti-pluralist ideology, communist leaders found it almost impossible to generate support for their increasingly isolated and marginalized regimes.

Devotion to political monism by the elites also stimulated the growth of clandestine political networks and organizations which gradually crystallized as "alternative" or "parallel" political systems, functioning outside the official political order. This phenomenon, which is often identified as the growth of "civil society" in the Soviet Union and Eastern Europe," typically began as an expression of citizen and group protest regarding some special social or political issue, such as environmental causes, peace and disarmament, nationality and religious rights, and workers' grievances.[4]

While these activities of socio-political groups were usually the target of official harassment during their initial stages, and only attracted support from a small portion of the population during the 1970s and 1980s, their number and size gradually increased, as did their reciprocal contacts and links with similar organizations in other communist and non-communist countries. Typically led by poets, philosophers, and other members of the non-technical intelligentsia, the alternative movements served as magnets for the classical "desertion of the intellectuals" from the established order which is characteristic of a pre-revolutionary period. As the structure of civil society became more complex, communist regimes were challenged by a kind of shadow political sub-system, complete with counter elites, as well as alternative political ideas regarding the reorganization of society. The fact that this system of "parallel politics" generally did not receive the attention it deserved from political analysts until after the collapse of the communist regimes, is mainly due to its unconventional characteristics — a collection of politically fragmented and inexperienced dissidents — and also to exaggerated evaluations of the ability of the communist apparatus to retain power.

One of the most significant facets of the burgeoning group pluralism in the U.S.S.R. and Eastern Europe during the 1980s was the emergence of ethnic and religious nationalism as a political force.[5] To a large extent the renewed salience of nationalism in communist states represented the failure of the ruling ideology to transcend or eliminate traditional ethnic and communal loyalties through the creation of a new and wider frame of reference for the definition of identity. Efforts to drum up enthusiasm for ideological notions such as "proletarian internationalism," or the creation of the new pan-ethnic "communist man," had little effect or promise within a society where political power was often very obviously stratified along ethnic lines. Thus, long-standing societal resentments and divisions were aggravated by the political hegemony of dominant nationalities, such as the Russians in the U.S.S.R., the Serbs in parts of Yugoslavia, Romanians in Romania, non-Moslem Slavs in Bulgaria, and Czechs in Czechoslovakia. Often the political nationalism of subordinated ethnic groups was reinforced by feelings of economic exploitation, a situation that was partially due to the regionally unbalanced pattern of economic development in the multinational communist states.

Structurally, a number of the communist countries were formally organized as federations, and all of the regimes accorded some constitutional recognition to minority rights. In practice, however, such governmental arrangements and legal protection were largely spurious, and did little to forestall a deterioration in ethnic relations. Communist ideology's failure to supplant traditional loyalties and beliefs also extended to the area of religion. The reawakening of religious feeling throughout the communist world in the post-Stalin period often reinforced regional ethno-nationalism (e.g. among the Catholics in Ukraine, Lithuania, Croatia, Slovenia and Slovakia, or the Moslems in Yugoslavia and Soviet Central Asia), while in more ethnically homogeneous countries it was expressed primarily in the expanded influence and popular support for the religious authorities (e.g. Poland, Hungary and the German Democratic Republic). As the growing weakness of the communist authorities became more apparent in the second part of the 1980s, claims by ethnic and religious groups for a share in power and even political autonomy became noticeably evident as part of the emerging system of "parallel politics."

The Gorbachev Factor

While the serious intrinsic defects and flawed policies of the communist regimes played a key role in their gradual deterioration and delegitimation, well-intentioned, but delinquent and piecemeal efforts to revamp communism also tended to hasten its eventual demise in the Soviet Union and Eastern Europe. Most significant in this regard was the ambitious program of *perestroika*, or restructuring, launched by Mikhail Gorbachev not long after his assumption of power in March 1985. Designed to end the stagnation and political malaise which had become starkly apparent within the Soviet Union by the mid-1980s, *perestroika*'s political and economic reform measures, and especially the new political thinking displayed in Soviet foreign relations, opened a Pandora's box of festering problems and unintended consequences. Indeed, rather than revitalizing communist rule, *perestroika* would significantly undermine both the Soviet "internal empire," i.e., the Soviet Communist Party's control over the many regions and nationalities comprising the U.S.S.R., and also the Kremlin's "external empire" of allied communist regimes in Eastern Europe.

Within the U.S.S.R. itself, the liberalizing policies of *perestroika* created a profound break with earlier Soviet development and generated enormous momentum supportive of economic change and political democratization. Unfortunately, despite Gorbachev's seminal role as an agent of progress, the Soviet leader's constant vacillation between more radical and more conservative proponents of *perestroika* hindered the successful realization of his reform vision, and led to a sharp decline in his popular support by 1990. "The effect of democratization," observes the Soviet historian, Roy Medvedev, "was not to cause people to express their goodwill, their suggestions, their constructive ideas, but rather to show their animosity. Instead of enthusiasm, an enormous negative potential rose to the surface."[6] Hungry for change, increasingly dissatisfied with the politics of the central authorities, and faced with a seriously deteriorating economic situation, Soviet citizens increasingly turned to political spokesmen from their various ethnic groups, republics, and regional governments to provide a new road out of the growing crisis.

While Gorbachev aimed at a controlled expansion of pluralism and decentralization, his criticism of earlier Soviet nationality policy, and also his vision of a less centralized Soviet state, actually fostered ethnic and regional assertiveness, and unintentionally detonated an explosion of political nationalism throughout the U.S.S.R. As one Soviet journalist supporting *perestroika* proudly asserted in 1988: "abscesses and sores which were lying somewhere beneath the surface concealed and unseen, have now burst open in the conditions of *glasnost* and have made it possible to resolve the problems."[7] Regrettably for Gorbachev, while recognition and open expression of ethnic conflict grew in intensity, the regime had little success at managing such conflicts, or satisfactorily reconciling the proliferation of ethnic and regional demands throughout the country. Paradoxically, Gorbachev's own liberal program generated a combustible mixture of economic and ethnic expectations which he proved unable to fulfil. Consequently, by the onset of the 1990s, as the Soviet Union's economic crisis worsened, and as ethnic conflicts became more extreme and violent (e.g., in the Baltic republics, the Caucasus, and Central Asia), both conservative and liberal support for *perestroika* and Gorbachev rapidly evaporated, as did popular confidence in the capacity of the communist system to reform itself.

In Eastern Europe, *perestroika*'s break with the past and the heightened expectations it created, proved equally detrimental to the prospects of continuing communist rule. For example, Gorbachev's decision to concentrate on shoring up the economic security of the U.S.S.R., rather than wasting scarce resources on the military sector and the escalating arms race with the Western Alliance, completely altered the Kremlin's perceptions about the value and costs of maintaining a Soviet military and political hegemony over Eastern Europe. Thus, while Gorbachev initially attempted to maintain the institutional cohesion of the Soviet alliance system in Eastern Europe — including renovation of the Warsaw Treaty Organization and Comecon — he also confirmed the need for radical political and economic reforms within the East European states, and pointedly signalled that the U.S.S.R. would no longer intervene in the internal development of other socialist states. This new Soviet view directly contravened the spirit of the well-known Brezhnev Doctrine, which had been used to justify Soviet intervention in Czechoslovakia in 1968, although Gorbachev was careful not to formally renounce such "old thinking" until the fall of 1989.

Nevertheless, by clearly disassociating himself from the previous policy of Soviet intervention in East European affairs, however, Gorbachev gradually removed the security blanket, or safety net, which had protected the region's ruling communist elites. This shift in the policy of the Kremlin, together with constant pressure on its allies to emulate the liberalizing features of the U.S.S.R.'s *perestroika* reform package, caused considerable consternation within the more conservative East European communist regimes in East Germany, Czechoslovakia, Romania and Bulgaria. Leaders in these states felt irritated and threatened by Soviet disavowal of policies which had buttressed the communists' monopoly control, and particularly by *perestroika*'s endorsement of "openness," which promised to fully expose the bankrupt policies and anachronisms of the unreformed communist regimes.

According to the former Soviet Foreign Minister Shevardnadze, the Kremlin's urging of reform in Eastern Europe in the second half of the 1980s created a "conservative backlash," or a "fraternal alliance of Party-state elites" in the region, that worked together with opponents of *perestroika* within the U.S.S.R.: "Now in greater danger than ever, they sought one another out, easily found a common language, and consolidated into a club for those disgruntled with Soviet *perestroika*, and pledged to fight against it."[8] While the ideas of *perestroika* were disconcerting to conservative communist leaders in Eastern Europe, and sometimes provoked them to take more repressive measures, Gorbachev's ideas attracted considerable popular support throughout the region. The reform winds blowing from Moscow also emboldened the growing opposition forces to take more decisive action against the authorities. Indeed, throughout Eastern Europe, just as within the U.S.S.R. itself, the growing perception that the waning communist systems no longer had the determination or the capability to obstruct pluralist development stimulated an upsurge of powerful opposition forces seeking fundamental political change and often a complete end to communist rule.

From Perestroika *to Post-Communism*

The last stage of the communist regimes in Eastern Europe and the Soviet Union, beginning in 1989 and continuing through to the end of 1991, resembled a kind of "rolling revolution" or domino effect that ended the monopoly of the communist party in one state after another. Among the many remarkable features of this dramatic political transformation was the relatively small amount of force that proved necessary to finally remove the communist authorities from power in the so-called triangle countries of East Central Europe (Poland, Czechoslovakia and Hungary), and also in the German Democratic Republic. Weakened for years by the numerous difficulties discussed above, the communist elites in these countries had little capacity to mount a sustained struggle for survival, and little support.

This final period of communist rule in Eastern Europe began in Poland, after non-communists won a large majority in semi-free elections held in June 1989. These elections followed protracted negotiations on the future of Poland between communist officials and activists from the opposition Solidarity movement. In some respects, the Polish transition to post-communism had been in progress since the rise of the Solidarity trade union movement in 1980. That development had been cut short by the communist regime's declaration of martial law in December 1981, and had been followed by several years of political manoeuvring between an essentially illegitimate regime and the repressed but growing Solidarity opposition. By the end of 1988 it was clear to the communist regime of General Jaruzelski, and to Gorbachev as well, that there was no hope of economic improvement or political stability in Poland without the legalization of non-communist parties, which might result in their coming to power.

The Soviet Union's acceptance of the Polish non-communist government that was finally installed in power in September 1989 was perceived throughout Eastern Europe as a major turning point by both hopeful opposition forces and anxious communist elites. The collapse of the anti-reformist Honecker regime in East Germany in October 1989, just weeks after the regime change in Poland, occurred after only a short period of mass demonstrations and clashes between the police and the opposition. Honecker had rebuffed Kremlin urging to reform his regime along the lines of *perestroika*, despite Gorbachev's unequivocal message that the G.D.R. would not be propped up by Soviet military intervention. Shortly before resigning, Honecker told his colleagues that the demonstration against the communist regime might still be stopped: "What if we call in tanks just to scare them?" When the proposal was met in dead silence, Honecker capitulated: "All right, forget it," he said.[9] The previous May, Honecker had claimed that the Berlin Wall would stand for one hundred years "if necessary," but in fact it ceased to stand as a barrier on November 10, 1989, and by October 1990 the G.D.R. itself no longer existed.

The collapse of the G.D.R. was soon followed by similar events in Czechoslovakia, which caused the fall of that country's conservative communist regime in the face of the so-called "velvet revolution." By early 1990, the prominent dissident leader, Vaclav Havel, and a non-communist government were in power. The ascendancy of non-communists also came about relatively smoothly in Hungary, where the slowly evolving exit of communists from power occurred between the removal of Janos Kadar in July 1988, and free elections in March-April 1990. The road to post-communism was to be far more protracted and violent in Romania, Bulgaria, Yugoslavia and Albania for reasons connected with the political traditions and divisions in those countries. But even in Southeastern Europe the tide had turned against monolithic communism, and the position of various "born again" communists who tried to maintain power rapidly crumbled during 1990–91. For example, by the fall of 1991, the Bulgarian communists had lost their control in free elections, and in Yugoslavia former communists retained authority in only two republics of the disintegrating and war-torn country.

In the U.S.S.R., meanwhile, the failed effort by conservative communists to remove Mikhail Gorbachev from power in August 1991 was followed by the end of the Communist Party's "leading role," and indeed the suspension of that party as a legal organization. During their three-day tenure in office, coup leaders brought tanks into Moscow as a measure to "scare" the public and opposition forces into compliance, but just like Honecker's colleagues in October 1989, the Soviet military and police had lost their stomach for a struggle against the population. Faced with stiff resistance by forces that had coalesced around Russian President Boris Yeltsin and radical opposition forces in Moscow, the coup quickly collapsed as its rather clownish leaders scattered in all directions. Immediately after his return to Moscow, following three days of captivity in the Crimea, Gorbachev announced his continued support for socialism and the "unchangeability" of his reform path. Within days, however, the

Soviet leader had been forced to change course, and to disband the Communist Party. The "architect of reform," as one astute Soviet observer put it, "was reforming before our eyes."[10]

The communist regime in the Soviet Union finally collapsed when its leaders' collective self-confidence and cohesion had been sapped. Moreover, after years of elite failure and corruption, very few citizens remained willing to actively follow the communist banner. The seriously weakened Gorbachev managed to retain his post as the formal head of state for only four months after the August coup, and the policy of *perestroika* — or what one Polish writer called "the transition from Communist party dictatorship to President Gorbachev's authoritarian regime" — approached its end.[11] In the wake of the coup, Yeltsin and his political supporters temporarily emerged as heroes, but with the linchpin of communist rule gone and central authority emasculated, the U.S.S.R. tottered on the brink of economic breakdown and political collapse. By December 1991, political life in the Soviet Union, as well as throughout Eastern Europe, was no longer consumed by discussions of how to end or reform communist control, but rather of how to design viable and legitimate post-communist regimes.

Post-Communist Transition in Comparative Perspective: Political and Economic Dimensions

For the long-suffering populations of the Eastern European states and the U.S.S.R., the end of traditional communist rule — whether achieved by peaceful or violent means — was initially greeted with considerable euphoria and high expectations. Once "post-revolutionary hangover" ensued, however, it became clear that each new regime faced daunting problems, many of which they had inherited from the previous rulers.[12] Communist rule had been jettisoned, but post-communism entailed another and longer transitional stage defined by two closely related challenges: (1) a *political transition*, which involves both the dismantling of residual features of the communist political system, and also the establishment of stable democratic institutions, and; (2) an *economic transition* which requires scrapping the centrally planned or only partially liberalized economic system, and the creation of a free market economy. How the newly established post-communist regimes in Eastern Europe and the successor states of the former U.S.S.R. deal with these two complex areas of transition will largely determine whether their citizens enjoy a better life, or simply experience another phase of dashed hopes and lost opportunities.

Political Transition and the Problems of Democratization

Any discussions of political change in former communist party states can benefit from a clear distinction between different aspects of the general process of democratization, including the concepts of *liberalization*, the *establishment* or restoration of democracy, and the *institutionalization* of democracy.[13] Liberalization refers to very limited concessions toward expanded political participation and civil liberties made by authoritarian regimes. The establishment of a democratic political order is related to the elaboration of various genuine democratic institutions, such as an accountable executive, a vital legislative system, a competitive party and electoral system, and an independent judiciary. The creation of such institutions does not, however, ensure the operation of a stable democracy, but is only the first step in the democratization process. Thus, the "founding" competitive elections held in Eastern Europe during 1990 and 1991 are important events in the democratic process, but provide no guarantee of an orderly and persistent democratic political system.

The institutionalization of democracy is a protracted process, whereby democratic political structures and activities acquire value and stability. Whether a democracy has reached a substantial level of institutionalization can only be reasonably assessed if the political system has successfully undergone one or more important challenges; held a number of free elections over a considerable period of time; experienced the alternation of different political parties or coalitions of parties in power; and survived some major threat to the continued operation of the political system (e.g., a wartime situation or serious internal subversion by anti-democratic forces). The use of such conceptual distinctions regarding democratization will clearly show that in different degrees the various republics in the Soviet Union, and the East European states, underwent some democratic liberalization near the end of the communist period, and also had, in almost all cases, established democracies by the end of 1991. The new regimes all remained, however, at the very first stage of their quest to become institutionalized democracies.

How successfully the post-communist states will accomplish the task of institutionalizing democracy remains a very open question at the onset of 1992. Speculation about the likelihood of democratic institutionalization in a particular country must take into account a variety of different factors. One of the most important considerations is a country's degree of earlier experience with democracy. For example, the lack of a well-grounded democratic political culture in most regions of the former Soviet Union, and in the various Balkan states, is a major liability for them as they begin the process of democratic development. Czechoslovakia's experience with democratic institutions and a competitive party system throughout the interwar period gives that country a marked advantage, although by no means an adequate or sufficiently durable experience to ensure democratic continuity in the 1990s.

Democratic liberalization during the latter stages of communist rule can also be considered as a facilitating factor in the smooth establishment and institutionalization of democracy but, like Czechoslovakia's interwar experience, cannot be a guarantee of future democratic development. Thus, regime liberalization by the communists in Hungary and Poland during the late 1980s, and in the Soviet Union during the halcyon days of *perestroika* (1987–89), may only be said to have facilitated the initial democratic transition which occurred before and directly after the collapse of communist rule. Conversely, the lack of communist liberalization, together with an absence of democratic traditions in countries such as Romania, Bulgaria, and Albania, certainly intensified the violence and conflict connected with the transition to post-communism in those countries, and also leaves room for serious doubts about their process of democratic institutionalization.

Of course many additional factors besides the extent and timing of communist liberalization must also be considered with regard to the character of post-communist democratization in a particular country. In Czechoslovakia, for example, the liberalization of the communist regime was hurriedly improvised on the eve of the regime's replacement at the end of 1989, but the country's short history of pre-communist democracy, and the presence of an exceptionally talented post-communist leadership dedicated to democracy, helped to compensate for the absence of sustained liberalization under the communists (some additional credit should also be given to the short-lived communist "thaw" during 1967–68). Meanwhile in Yugoslavia, a long period of highly original communist liberalization (1949–89) has not guaranteed a stable transition to democratic rule. The lack of uniformity among Yugoslavia's regions with respect to pre-communist democratic experience, combined with a pattern of very strong, elite-led, regional and ethnic nationalism, has both seriously undermined the cohesive establishment of democratic structures throughout the federation, and quickly led to the outbreak of bloody civil war.

One of the most serious factors threatening the process of democratization in the post-Soviet successor states and the Eastern European countries during the initial stages of post-communism has been the absence, or fragility, of political consensus regarding democratic institutions and democratic rules of the game. To some extent, such political discord is an outgrowth of the natural fragmentation and polarization which followed the end of communism. After years of artificially induced political unity, pent-up forces and radically different political perspectives finally received an opportunity for direct expression and organization on the political stage. Another source of political fragmentation has been a breakdown in the unity of the opposition forces that led the struggle against communist rule. Once the target of such opposition was removed, the reasons for the anti-communist coalitions evaporated, and internal differences of opinion in the ranks quickly emerged. As a member of the Solidarity caucus in the Polish parliament observed, when explaining the intense splintering of political forces in his country after the fall of the communist regime: "We do not have a common enemy. We are short of communists."[14]

Post-communist democratization is also jeopardized by the fact that not all the anti-communist or pre-1989 anti-authoritarian forces were in favour of democracy, but were often channelled by political activists seeking to replace one non-democratic political order by another.[15] Fervent opposition to communist rule and oppression does not in itself indicate support for the political toleration and political competition so necessary to democratic institutionalization. Emotionally devoted to their sectarian and other quite restrictive notions of "democracy," post-communist leaders often seek to prohibit or politically emasculate political forces which express open disagreement with newly established regimes. In some cases, lack of commitment to democratic norms, or a misunderstanding of the appropriate parameters of democratic competition, can be traced to the authoritarian background of post-communist leaders. For example, in some cases post-communist decision-makers may have spent much of their political careers in the apparatus of communist party organizations before deciding to embrace new ideologies and policies that are currently in vogue.[16] However, efforts by other post-communist leaders with a purer non-communist background to ban all former communist officials from public service in the post-communist regimes reveals a similar misunderstanding of how democracy works. Such low tolerance for democratic competition seriously complicates the problem of establishing autonomous political institutions, such as an independent judiciary, politically neutral civil bureaucracies, and a free press.

The problems of achieving political consensus and commitment regarding democratic norms, as well as political stability, has been especially difficult for those post-communist states which have serious ethnic divisions. In some cases, such as Czechoslovakia, Romania and Bulgaria, the intensification of nationalism, and sometimes ultra-nationalism, has complicated the already difficult early stages of democratization. For example, two years after non-communist parties took power in Czechoslovakia, disagreement between Czechs and Slovaks over the distribution of powers between the regional and federal government in Prague paralyzed legislative decision-making in the country, and forced President Havel to seek stronger executive powers. "Today," Havel remarked, "the point is whether we will become a civilized European democracy or a despised area of incessant conflicts and disorders."[17]

In the most extreme cases, such as the former U.S.S.R. and Yugoslavia, ethnic conflict and political polarization among the country's principal regions has led to regional civil wars and the collapse of central authority. In such disintegrating countries the preoccupation of most political forces with programs advocating either ethno-regional independence on the one side, or the reconstitution of inter-regional unity on the other, detracted from the processes of communist liberalization and post-communist democratization. Thus, plans for a new Union Treaty that would have reorganized the U.S.S.R. along more decentralized lines were not just a key factor precipitating the conservative coup of August 1991; they continued to disrupt political life after the coup, as demands for sovereignty and independence multiplied throughout the Soviet Union. As 1992 began, the war-torn Yugoslav state was doomed as a united federation, or even a loose confederation, while the quarrelling remnants of the former U.S.S.R. strained to reach agreement on the details necessary for the re-establishment of a viable political "centre."

To a certain extent, the surge of politicized nationalism in the post-communist period can be traced to flawed regime strategies adopted during the last years of communist rule. The advent of post-communism, however, has in many cases provided additional reasons for nationalist expression. For example, adherence to nationalist parties and programs may offer citizens psychological solace during a highly disruptive period in which established ideological beliefs break down, and popular *angst* spreads because of the weakness or vacillation of newly established authorities. Searching for a new focus of identity in difficult times, religious nationalism can offer a "quick fix," and also a way to seemingly disentangle one's group or region from the problem of the large multinational society. Because the new regimes and ruling parties have still not been able to generate a sense of commitment to new symbols and programs — mainly due to their own economic and political programs which are still not fulfilled — nationalist expression may be the only alternative and will be seen as a way of channelling political participation, or of protesting the current situation. Paradoxically, the very success of the post-communist regimes in creating a freer atmosphere for groups and political pluralism allows both nationalistic and ultra-nationalistic forces to take part in a political process and state structure which they generally seek to destroy (much the same phenomenon occurred in communist Yugoslavia after the death of Tito, and in the Soviet Union during *perestroika*). In that regard, nationalism can be viewed as part of the "noise" of emergent democracy, which at its highest decibel level and range can endanger the fragile process of democratic institutionalization.

Economic Transition

The economic performance of each post-communist regime will have a major bearing on its capacity to dampen political extremism and successfully institutionalize democracy. Well aware that the collapse of the former regimes was closely tied to popular dissatisfaction with the economy, the post-communist elites of the former Soviet Union and East European states almost all advocate rapid transition to free market principles of economic organization. Thus, while Marxist ideology may be discredited as a basis for economic development in the region, Lenin's dictum that politics is essentially "economics in concentrated form," remains an apt summary of post-communist political debate. Earlier models of economic restructuring designed to create a "mixed economy" combining elements of capitalist and communist economic organization — the well-known goal of "market socialism" or the so-called "third way" — are now viewed as having been a waste of time necessitated by the limits of communist-inspired liberalization.

Developing and implementing plans for the creation of a market economy have proved extremely difficult in practice. Because there is no historical precedent for fully dismantling a communist economic order, or replacing it with a market system, the new regimes lack any "transition theory" to guide their efforts. Consensus about the general prerequisites for market liberalization is limited to some fundamental points: price liberalization to eliminate the artificial and subsidized value of goods under the old economic system; wage stabilization to prevent runaway inflation; radical reduction in the size of the state bureaucracy and the end of support for unprofitable and obsolete state firms; privatization through both the sale of state firms and the encouragement of a new private entrepreneurial sector; reduction of barriers to free trade and investment; and creation of a convertible currency.[18]

While an understanding and basic consensus exists regarding the general features of liberalization, there are many different views within and outside the former communist states about the speed with which such measures should be introduced, and also about methods of adjusting general principles to the needs and problems of particular countries. Worried over the potential disruption and socio-political backlash which may be generated by adopting the free market, some observers and experts have argued for a cautious and incremental shift away from the old economic system, and for the elaboration of a "safety net" to aid those most adversely affected by the process of change. Others have advocated a much faster strategy — variously referred to as "shock therapy," the "big bang," "crash capitalism," or the "bitter pill" — which calls for the rapid introduction of market-based principles. According to this latter view, the temporary disruption and tension caused by the rapid introduction of a market economy is far outweighed by the accelerated access to the benefits of the market, such as an end to shortages, more efficient production, and the ability to attract trading partners and investment.

Proponents of rapid economic transformation can point to the former U.S.S.R. as an example of the negative consequences of excessive vacillation regarding marketization, and the dangers of piecemeal and inconsistent economic reforms. Thus Gorbachev, it is argued, by generating popular expectations at the outset of *perestroika* in 1985, about imminent and fundamental change in the Soviet system but hesitating to implement economic reforms, failed to produce results over the next six years, and gradually lost popular support for his entire program of reform.[19] Such a strategy and the disruption it caused, also dangerously exacerbated socio-political conflicts and instability in the U.S.S.R.

The most ambitious effort to implement a "shock therapy" approach to economic transition has been made by Poland's post-communist leadership, beginning in January 1990. In a short span of time prices were freed, strict limits were put on wage increases, the zloty was made convertible to foreign currencies, and trade barriers were lowered. The results over the next two years have appeared to be quite mixed. On the downside, there was a rapid increase in unemployment, inflation remained quite high, popular dissatisfaction in various sectors mounted, and there was a noticeable increase in corruption and economic crime as individuals sought ways to survive or exploit the radical changes. On the positive side, however, Poland's private sector rapidly expanded and absorbed a portion of the unemployed work force, production rose, shortages of goods diminished, and queuing for goods all but disappeared.[20]

Although the economic benefits of Poland's rapid transition to the market features certainly did not immediately translate into political support and legitimacy for the post-communist regime, the early results of the "big bang" did not produce political revolt and chaos as many had feared. Poland's first completely free post-communist elections, held in October 1991, revealed signs of popular cynicism, apathy (turnout was only 40 percent), as well as sharp political polarization and fragmentation in the party system, but the regime's basic strategy of economic change remained temporarily on course. When a national strike of factory workers against the government's market reforms became a real possibility in early 1992, President Lech Walesa treated the development as quite normal, and indeed a sign of the post-communist regime's success in broadening citizen rights. He also noted ironically: "the full victory of Lenin has been achieved by us. In the moment when the proletariat finally feel they are the proletariat, we propose to them capitalism."[21]

During 1991, Czechoslovakia and Hungary also implemented programs of transition to a market system that were ambitious but somewhat different from the trail-blazing Polish model, and even Bulgaria and

Romania embarked on limited schemes of market liberalization. Circumstances at the time also propelled forces in the U.S.S.R. toward more radical economic reforms, but the collapse of central authority following the failed August coup left in doubt the prospects for any comprehensive program of economic change. Following the coup, Gorbachev was grudgingly forced to scrap Communist Party rule and embrace the idea of radical reform, but the weakened founder of *perestroika* remained very much in the shadow of Russian President Boris Yeltsin, who introduced his own radical program of economic transition along lines closely resembling the Polish strategy. Observers remained sceptical as to whether Yeltsin was actually committed or capable enough to carry out a "shock therapy" type of economic transformation in Russia, although it was clear that he appreciated the need for a change in direction. As Yeltsin put it: "Russia has inherited from the Soviet Union, a shattered economy, a ruined natural environment, a miserable standard of living, and heavy debts. But this is our inheritance, and we have accepted it. And despite all the difficulties, we will cope with it."[22] Only days after Gorbachev's departure from power at the end of December 1991, Yeltsin pushed ahead with his "shock therapy" for the Russian economy, and quickly found himself coping with a strong aftershock of complaints and problems. It was still open to question, however, whether radical economic reforms in Russia would be continued, as in Poland during 1990 and 1991, or would engender serious socio-political instability, and possibly even lead to a coup d'état by conservative political and military forces. Meanwhile, in Yugoslavia, the spreading civil war and the disintegration of federal authority in 1991 completely postponed economic reform, as the breakdown of the internal market, military destruction, and disrupted production drove the economy into a steep decline.

In the first months of 1992, the prognosis for economic transition, and especially its impact on political development, remained very unclear throughout Eastern Europe, and within the post-Soviet states of the Eurasian region.[23] For example, all the post-communist regimes, whatever the design of their market liberalization programs and internal political difficulties, were experiencing serious problems attributable to the complexity of denationalizing state industries. Finding sufficient capital for the development of the private sector also proved more difficult than expected, and it became evident that there was a shortage of native entrepreneurial talent and initiative. The situation was further complicated by the disruption of former trading ties between Eastern Europe and the former Soviet Union, and the prospects of reduced Russian energy exports. Consequently, the economic difficulties of the Soviet Union's successor states not only jeopardized their own tentative transitions toward market economies and democracy, but also endangered the post-communist transition of neighbouring regions and states.

Canada and the Twilight of *Perestroika*

> Our future is in trying to help Gorbachev succeed.
>   –Joe Clark, November 15, 1990

> As a result of the newly formed situation — creation of the Common-
> wealth of Independent States — I cease my activities in the post of
> the U.S.S.R. President. . . . The process of renovating the country and
> radical changes in the world community turned out to be far more
> complicated than was expected.
>   –Mikhail Gorbachev, December 25, 1991

Adjusting to the advent of post-communism, and particularly the political decline of Mikhail Gorbachev, has been a difficult challenge for
all the states in the Western alliance. During the first five years of
the "Gorbachev revolution" the Canadian government approached the
transformation of the U.S.S.R. with considerable reserve and scepticism.
Preoccupied for much of the time with the complex and controversial negotiations over the Canadian-American Free Trade Agreement, Ottawa
had a special interest in demonstrating that Canada was a team player
and junior partner in the process of making a Washington-led Western
policy toward the Soviet Union. Determined to maintain close relations
with the conservative Reagan and Bush administrations, and ideologically
sceptical regarding communism's ability to reform itself, the Mulroney
government avoided taking bold or original initiatives toward the Soviet
Union.[24]
    It was only in the second half of 1989, after Gorbachev's demon-
strated magnanimity towards post-communist transformation in Eastern
Europe, that Canada became more willing to assertively recognize the
liberal features of Soviet *perestroika*. Prime Minister Mulroney's visit
to the U.S.S.R. in the fall of 1989, accompanied by a large entourage
from the Canadian business community, and a short visit by President
Gorbachev to Ottawa at the end of May 1990, generated "forward momentum" in Canada-Soviet relations,[25] and increased hopes for improved
economic links between the two countries. Unfortunately, the serious deterioration of the Soviet economy during 1990 considerably dampened
Canadian enthusiasm for investment arrangements or expanded trade
with the U.S.S.R.[26] By the Fall of 1990 Canadian government support
for *perestroika* was focused mainly on shoring up President Gorbachev's
weakening political position through joint initiatives of the G-7 countries
to provide economic assistance to the Soviet Union. Hopes remained high,
however, that the Canadian-Soviet bilateral relationship would continue
to develop. At the end of November 1990, Secretary of State for External Affairs Joe Clark — who had earlier been a leading sceptic regarding
perestroika's positive potential — observed that: "in region after region,

on problem after problem, the Soviet Union now brings a welcome flexibility, and assessments remarkably similar to Canada's . . . Disagreement with the Soviet Union was once the rule; it is now the exception."[27]

Less than one month after Clark's optimistic remarks, Gorbachev's swing in a decidedly conservative direction seriously disrupted Canadian-Soviet relations. When a Soviet military crackdown in Lithuania and Latvia resulted in numerous civilian deaths during January 1991, Canada responded by suspending credit and technical assistance to the U.S.S.R. "We have drawn a direct linkage between Canadian assistance and the continuation of Soviet reform," Joe Clark now told the House of Commons.[28] The Soviet Foreign Ministry characterized the Canadian decision as intervention in the U.S.S.R.'s internal affairs.[29]

Canada's decision to react decisively to the January 1991 incidents in Lithuania and Latvia contrasted with the more cautious approach to the Baltic question taken in early 1990. For example, in April 1990, Canada had gone along with the other members of the Western alliance in ignoring Lithuanian requests for recognition as an independent state, despite the harsh economic blockade imposed against that republic by Moscow. At the time, Washington suggested that "quiet diplomacy," rather than encouragement of self-determination, was the most appropriate method to achieve a resolution of nationality and inter-regional conflicts in the U.S.S.R. When Canada's Baltic community urged that Ottawa take strong action against the Soviet Union for its economic sanctions against Lithuania, and also send the Lithuanians badly needed supplies, External Affairs Minister Clark responded that Canada did not contemplate taking such measures (although some managerial expertise and training was offered to Lithuania), and preferred to encourage "constructive conversations" between Soviet and Lithuanian leaders.[30] Canada's more vigorous reaction to Baltic developments in January 1991 — following Gorbachev's ambiguous denial of any association with the use of violence in that region — coincided with the general dissatisfaction now expressed in Washington regarding Moscow's drift away from internal reforms and a liberalized nationality policy.

Despite their disagreements over developments in the Baltic region, Ottawa and Moscow remained committed to the broader improvement of Canadian-Soviet commercial relations that had been taking place for the past several years. For example, in the 1990–91 crop year, the Soviet Union moved back to the top of the list of countries purchasing Canadian grain. By the spring of 1991 the Lithuanian crisis had temporarily abated, and when Gorbachev proceeded to elaborate new institutions for restructuring the Soviet federation on a less centralized basis, Canada became more actively involved in debating with the other G-7 countries the best method of providing direct aid to the U.S.S.R.'s troubled economy. At the London Summit of the G-7 countries in mid-July, the Canadian government lifted the suspension of credit and other assistance to the Soviet Union which had been imposed in January. Prime Minister Mulroney still expressed strong scepticism, however, about the state of the Soviet economy and its capacity to utilize Western aid productively:

> Mr. Gorbachev happens to be President of that country, whose system brought about the downfall of the economy. . . . He has been very constructive internationally, but he's got very serious problems that can only be addressed by fundamental reforms in his economy. . . . So the response to him from all of us will be constructive and helpful . . . but on this we are all from Missouri. . . . We're not going to throw good money after bad.[31]

Ottawa's decision to restore assistance to Moscow was supported by the Canada-U.S.S.R. Business Council, the main non-governmental organization working to promote Canadian commercial investment in the Soviet Union. Gorbachev's announcement of a Draft Union Treaty to reorganize relations among the Soviet republics was viewed as a particularly promising development by the Council, but considering the uncertain political and economic climate in the Soviet Union the Council cautioned that future Canadian private and governmental support for the U.S.S.R. should be premised on "enlightened self-interest."[32]

During the last four months of 1991 Canadian-Soviet relations entered a period of some confusion and considerable uncertainty, as a result of the short-lived August coup by hardliners against Gorbachev, the fragmentation of power following his temporary return to the position of Soviet President, and the rapid disintegration of the U.S.S.R. as a governmental and territorial entity. Gorbachev's sudden removal from power by the so-called "State Committee on the State of Emergency in the U.S.S.R.," on August 19, 1991, presented the Canadian government with a particularly difficult challenge. As was the case in other Western capitals, Ottawa was at first caught off balance by the anti-Gorbachev coup. Still not having co-ordinated a joint response with other members of the Western Alliance, Barbara McDougall — Joe Clark's successor at External Affairs — initially suggested that Canada was not focusing on the reinstatement of Gorbachev, and also hinted that Ottawa would have no problem doing business with the self-installed coup leaders in Moscow, so long as they continued to adhere to democratic "principles."[33] That pragmatic response — not unlike the initial position of the Mitterand government in France — was quickly amended by the embarrassed McDougall when more information became available to Western observers regarding the weak political support enjoyed by the leaders of the coup, and the possibility that Gorbachev might be reinstated by co-ordinated external leverage (see Chapter 2).

Gorbachev's quick return to Moscow from Crimean captivity initially called forth a collective sigh of relief among Western political and business leaders. Prime Minister Mulroney sent Gorbachev a "Dear Mikhail" note indicating his delight that the Soviet President had been restored to his "rightful role," and looking forward to a continuation of their joint work in "creating the new world order."[34] Rapidly evolving developments within the U.S.S.R., however, made it difficult for Canada and other countries to re-establish their traditional relationship with that country. The enhancement of the political power of Russian President Boris Yeltsin in the wake of the coup, and particularly the weakening of the political authority of the central government as each republic moved to assert its own sovereignty and independence, seriously jeopardized Gorbachev's political position, and altered the prospects for Western governmental and commercial contacts with his regime. Having struggled for over two years with the problem of how best to provide assistance to the Soviet economy, Western political and economic decision-makers now faced the question of precisely who was governing the U.S.S.R., and indeed if the U.S.S.R. could still be said to exist at all.[35] For Canada, which was undergoing its own internal debate about national unity and the distribution of power in a federal system, adjustment to the political decline of the Soviet "centre" manned by Gorbachev's team, and the territorial disintegration of the U.S.S.R., became especially discomforting.

Problems regarding recognition of a newly emerging political reality became more concrete when various republics initiated — or in some cases re-initiated — their departure from the Soviet federation. When the Baltic states became the first republics to leave the U.S.S.R. framework, less than one week after the coup, Canada jumped ahead of the United States and established full diplomatic relations with Lithuania, Latvia and Estonia. In view of the new circumstances within the U.S.S.R., high profile public pronouncements of recognition had replaced "quiet diplomacy" as Canada's preferred course of action. Still chafing from earlier criticism that Ottawa had traditionally mimicked, or trailed behind, Washington on Soviet policy, and also suffering from residual embarrassment over the hasty nod to the coup leaders immediately after Gorbachev's removal, the Mulroney government welcomed the opportunity to take a front-runner position on Baltic recognition. Prime Minister Mulroney also indicated that Canada would recognize the independence of the Ukraine if that republic voted to secede from the U.S.S.R. in a referendum scheduled for the beginning of December.[36] Canada's avant-garde approach to diplomatic recognition was not, however, without its downside for the government. For example, journalists and pundits speculated that Ottawa's recognition of Ukraine's independence constituted a dangerous precedent for Canadian unity. Specifically, would not Ottawa's position justify international recognition of Quebec's independence, if the citizens of that province were to opt for such a course of action in a proposed referendum? Mulroney rejected any such parallels: "The Soviet Union came about as a result of the totalitarian and illegal integration of states which resulted in the Soviet Union," the Prime Minister observed, while "Canada was the result of the great democratic coming together of people, English and French, who sought freedom."[37]

As various components of the U.S.S.R., and also the disintegrating Yugoslav federation, pressed forward with plans for independence in late 1991, Ottawa's position regarding the diplomatic recognition of emergent post-communist states became the object of mounting criticism. Increasingly the Canadian government found itself caught in the middle of a debate. On the one side, domestic ethnic groups urged the speedy recognition of areas such as Ukraine, Armenia, Croatia and Slovenia, that had declared their independence.[38] Other citizens and groups viewed Ottawa's tilt towards such independence-seeking regions as a hasty effort to achieve originality in foreign policymaking, that might also boomerang on Canada where the cohesion of the Canadian polity was concerned. Canadian officials adamantly rejected both perspectives, claiming that they were simply moving in a careful and deliberate manner to recognize new realities, and that any comparisons with domestic Canadian issues were spurious. For example, visiting Kiev in September 1991, External Affairs Minister McDougall claimed that Canada was still withholding recognition of Ukrainian independence in order to judge the results of the upcoming referendum, and also to determine what kind of relationship the republics "will have with the centre. . . . We have nothing to apologize for as far as Canada goes in terms of relations with Ukraine." She added that "Quebec is very, very different. There is no comparison."[39]

At the beginning of December, Canada became the first Western country to recognize Ukraine's independence directly, after a large majority of voters in that republic registered their support for departure from the U.S.S.R. in a popular referendum. Although such imminent recognition had already been signalled by Prime Minister Mulroney in August, he was nonetheless accused of pandering to the large group of potential voters from Canada's Ukrainian community, an insinuation allegedly supported by the double standard displayed by the government in not immediately extending the same diplomatic treatment to other post-Soviet republics such as Armenia, or, in the context of the Yugoslav break-up, to Croatia and Slovenia.[40]

Ukraine's acquisition of independence hastened the termination of the U.S.S.R. as a legal and territorial entity. As the Soviet Union entered its final stage of existence, Mikhail Gorbachev warned his fellow citizens of dire consequences ahead should they fail to organize a "renewed union" along the lines which he advocated: "Only the union can protect us against the most tragic of the impending dangers from separation and loss of bonds by which history linked peoples over centuries in an area amounting to one-sixth of the Earth's surface. Disintegration of this multi-ethnic country will bring to millions of citizens misfortunes that will prevail over all possible temporary advantages of separation."[41] Gorbachev's pleading did nothing to obstruct the forces of centrifugal momentum. On December 8, the leaders of Russia, Ukraine and Byelorussia (Belarus) met in Minsk to sign an agreement establishing a new Commonwealth. In Ottawa, Barbara McDougall, who had become cautious about reports of newly created political regimes, hailed the Commonwealth's birth as a "very positive development" that promised to facilitate co-ordination on questions of nuclear weapons, debt and finance, and human rights.[42] Although signalling approval of the new Commonwealth, Canada continued to support Mr. Gorbachev's effort to preserve some form of central government. "It's far too soon to suggest that Mr. Gorbachev is irrelevant," McDougall said on December 10, pointing out that Canada had not been asked to recognize the three-state Commonwealth. She also denied that Canada's cautious approach to recognition of newly formed post-communist states had been driven by the domestic national unity question, but conceded that "foreign policy is a reflection of domestic values, domestic interests. Since national unity is a domestic issue, it is also part of our foreign policy consideration."[43] By December 21, a broader 11-member Commonwealth of Independent States (C.I.S.) was created at Alma-Ata, Kazakhstan, including all the former republics of the U.S.S.R., with the exception of the already independent Baltic states and strife-torn Georgia. In the last two weeks of December, Russian President Yeltsin boldly moved to extinguish the remaining authority of the U.S.S.R. and Gorbachev by decreeing Russian control over the Kremlin, the K.G.B., and the Soviet Foreign Ministry, and also advancing Russia's application to supplant Soviet membership in the UN and other international bodies. The cessation of Soviet central governmental authority, with the resignation of Gorbachev on December 25, 1991 and Canada's recognition of Russian independence, brought 67 years of Canadian-Soviet relations to an end. Canadian relations with Russia and the other individual member states of the C.I.S. had begun.

At the beginning of 1992, Canada faced an entirely new agenda with respect to the countries that had emerged from the breakup of the U.S.S.R. For example, in view of Canada's own economic difficulties and broad-ranging commitments in various regional areas, would Ottawa be able to find the resources to assist the large number of new states from the former U.S.S.R., and also the several new post-communist regimes in the Kremlin's former "East Bloc"? What impact would the "demonstration effect" of ascendant regional nationalism in the former U.S.S.R. and other post-communist states of Eastern Europe have on Canada's own inter-regional conflicts and constitutional evolution? Would the newly organized and economically speaking, potentially viable regions of the former U.S.S.R. continue to import Canadian agricultural products, or would they become competitors in Canada's traditional export markets? Having become accustomed to playing the "honest broker" between the two superpowers throughout the protracted Cold War, and during its immediate aftermath, how would Canada adjust to a world with only one superpower, and several new actors seeking Canadian-like "middle power" status?

Outlets for Canada's traditional mediative role in international affairs remained, as exemplified by acceptance in December 1991 of Ottawa's proposal that NATO troops be used as part of a relief program for the Soviet Union, and also by Canadian participation in a UN team of peacekeepers sent to Yugoslavia in 1992.[44] But, as the various emerging states of the former U.S.S.R. joined the countries of the Soviet Union's former East European empire in the difficult transition to post-communism, Canadian elites were challenged to establish new relationships, secure new markets, and reorient Ottawa's role in international relations.

Notes

1 On the major difficulties affecting reform in communist centrally-planned economies see, for example, Stanislaw Gomulka, et al., eds., *Economic Reforms in the Socialist World* (Armonok: M.E. Sharpe Inc., 1989); and Ilpyong J. Kim and Jane Shapiro Zacek, eds., *Reform and Transformation in Communist Systems: Comparative Perspectives* (New York: Paragon House, 1991).

2 Ryszard Kapuscinski, "A Warsaw Diary," *Granta*, Vol. 15 (1985): 214–23.

3 See, for example, Daniel Chirot, ed., *The End of Leninism and the Decline of the Left: The Revolution of 1989* (Seattle: University of Washington Press, 1991); and J.F. Brown, *Surge to Freedom: The End of Communist Rule in Eastern Europe* (Durham: Duke University Press, 1991).

4 See, for example, H. Gordon Skilling, *Samizdat and an Independent Society in Central and Eastern Europe* (Columbus: Ohio State University Press, 1989); Vladimir Tismaneanu, *In Search of Civil Society: Independent Peace Movements in the Soviet Bloc* (New York: Routledge, 1990); and also Judith B. Sedatis and Jim Butterfield, *Perestroika From Below: Social Movements in the Soviet Union* (Boulder, Colo.: Westview Press, 1991).

5 For an excellent overview of this issue see, Ronald Linden, "The Appeal of Nationalism," *Report on Eastern Europe*, Vol. 12, No. 24 (June 14, 1991): 29–37.

6 Roy Medvedev, "Politics After the Coup," *New Left Review*, No. 189 (September/October, 1991): 94.

7 Eduard Rozental, cited in Igor Modnov, ed., *The Turbulent Years in the Caucasus* (Moscow: Novosti, 1988), p. 10.

8 Eduard Shevardnadze, *The Failure Belongs to Freedom* (London: Sinclair-Stevenson, 1991), p. 116.

9 Igor Maximychev, "End of the Berlin Wall," *International Affairs*, No. 3 (March 1991): 104.

10 Alexander Ghelman, "Gorbachev and Freedom," *Moscow News*, Nos. 34–35 (September 1–8, 1991), p. 4.

11 Adam Michnick, "We Are With You Our Soviet Friends," *Moscow News*, Nos. 34–35 (September 1–8, 1991), p. 13.

12 Leszek Kolakowski, "The Post-Revolutionary Hangover," *Journal of Democracy*, Vol. 2, No. 3 (Summer 1991): 70–74.

13 For insights on conceptualizing post-communist change see Scott Mainwaring, *Transitions to Democracy and Democratic Consolidation: Theoretical and Comparative Issues, Working Paper No. 130* (Notre Dame: The Helen Kellog Institute for International Studies, 1989); and Pietro Grilli di Cortona, "From Communism to Democracy: Rethinking Regime Change in Hungary and Czechoslovakia," *International Social Science Journal*, No. 128 (May 1991): 315–31.

14 *The New York Times*, July 23, 1990, p. 6.

15 Adam Przeworski, *Democracy and the Market: Political and Economic Reform in Eastern Europe and Latin America* (Cambridge: Cambridge University Press, 1991), pp. 94–95.

16 On the difficulties of such personal reorientation see, for example, John Morrison, *Boris Yeltsin: From Bolshevik to Democrat* (New York: Dutton, 1991).

17 *The Globe and Mail*, November 18, 1991, p. A8.

18 See, for example, Keith Bush, *From the Command Economy to the Market: A Collection of Interviews* (Aldershot: Dartmouth Publishing, 1991); Peter Havlik, ed., *Dismantling the Command Economy in Eastern Europe* (Boulder: Westview Press, 1991); Nicholas Spulber, *Restructuring the Soviet Economy: In Search of the Market* (Ann Arbor: University of Michigan Press, 1991); Aslund Anders, *Gorbachev's Struggle for Economic Reform* (London: Pinter, 1991); and Marshall Goldman, *What Went Wrong With Perestroika?* (New York: W.W. Norton, 1991).

19 Roy Medvedev, "Politics After the Coup," *New Left Review*, No. 189 (September/October 1991): 91–110.

20 Zbigniew M. Fallenbuchl, "Poland: The Case for Cautious Optimism," *The World Today*, Vol. 47, No. 11 (November 1991): 185–88.

21 *The New York Times*, January 14, 1992, p. A2.

22 Stephen Kinzer, "Yeltsin's Free Market Promise Leaves His German Hosts Sceptical," *The New York Times*, November 23, 1991, p. 4.

23 As steep price rises, unemployment, and general socio-economic dislocation continued in Eastern Europe and in Russia in early 1992, the negative side of post-communist "crash capitalism" came under closer scrutiny and criticism. See, for example, Valtr Komarek, "Shock Therapy and its Victims," *The New York Times*, January 5, 1992, p. 13.

24 Lenard J. Cohen, "The Soviet Union and Eastern Europe in Transition: Trends and Implications for Canada," in Maureen Appel Molot and Fen

Osler Hampson, eds., *Canada Among Nations: The Challenge of Change* (Ottawa: Carleton University Press, 1989), pp. 19–42.

25 Leigh Sarty, *Détente, Cold War, and Perestroika: Canadian-Soviet Relations Since 1980* (Ottawa: Centre for Canadian-Soviet Studies, Carleton University, 1991), Occasional Paper, No. 1.

26 It is interesting to compare the enthusiasm for business contacts with the U.S.S.R. expressed at the conference on the subject held in Toronto in early 1990, with the pessimism and uncertainty expressed at a similar meeting held at the end of the year. See Rein Peterson, ed., *Getting Down to Business in the U.S.S.R.: The Soviet Market in the 1990s, Proceedings of the Conference Held February 19 and 20, 1990* (Toronto: The Canada-U.S.S.R. Business Council, 1990); and, *Canada-U.S.S.R. Business Council, First Annual Meeting, November 28, 29, 30, 1990* (Toronto: The Canada-U.S.S.R. Business Council, 1991).

27 "Notes for a Speech by the Right Honourable Joe Clark, Secretary of State for External Affairs, at a Conference on Canadian-Soviet Relations," *Statements and Speeches*, 90/17, November 28, 1990, p. 3.

28 *Canadian Press Newstex*, January 22, 1991.

29 "Soviet Official on Canadian Reaction to Baltic Events," *News Release, Press Office of the U.S.S.R. Embassy in Canada*, No. 14, January 26, 1991.

30 *Canadian Press Newstex*, April 25, 1990.

31 Estanislao Ozewicz and Ross Howard, "No Miracles for Soviets," *The Globe and Mail*, July 10, 1991, p. A1.

32 *Canada-U.S.S.R. Business Council Bulletin*, Vol. 2, No. 4 (July 1991), p. 1.

33 Ross Howard, "Ottawa Resists Calling for Gorbachev's Return," *The Globe and Mail*, August 21, 1991, p. A6.

34 *Canadian Press Newstex*, August 22, 1991. The executive director of the Canada-U.S.S.R. Business Council was ecstatic regarding the commercial opportunities under post-coup *perestroika*. "The way for foreigners is going to be much, much faster." *Canadian Press Newstex*, August 26, 1991.

35 As the Soviet Union's central political authority and territorial cohesion eroded in the last months of 1991, Canada adopted a "wait and see" approach to the question of economic aid for the U.S.S.R. Although Canada lifted its freeze on $150 million of food credits to the Soviet Union in July, and also produced a $10 million package of other, small-scale measures (including assistance for victims of the 1986 Chernobyl nuclear accident), additional aid was not forthcoming in the months immediately following the August coup. Discussions of assistance did occur, for example, at the Bangkok meeting of finance ministers in October, but the focus was almost entirely on trade credit to facilitate Canadian grain sales to the U.S.S.R. Even in this area, however, there was some concern about the economic viability of the measures discussed. "We would like to sell them more grain," one Canadian official observed. "The question is, what are the terms and conditions on which they are likely to be able to meet the payments" *Canadian Press Newstex*, October 10, 1991. Despite such concern, on November 1, 1991 Canada and the Soviet Union signed a two-year extension to a long running grain sales agreement that called for the U.S.S.R. to buy a minimum of four million tonnes of Canadian grain annually. Wheat Board

Minister Mayer indicated, however, that Ottawa was also willing to open direct negotiations with former Soviet republics which declared their independence. *Canadian Press Newstex*, November 1, 1991.

36 *Canadian Press Newstex*, August 26, 1991.

37 *Canadian Press Newstex*, August 26, 1991. The Prime Minister's speech at Stanford University at the end of September, arguing that the political situation and very serious ethnic problems in a country might sometimes demand UN intervention, and that in such cases traditional notions of "national sovereignty" might have to be set aside, unintentionally invited further comparisons between Eastern Europe and the potential evolution of Quebec. *The Globe and Mail*, October 1, 1991, p. A19.

38 Some foreign critics felt that all the members of the Western alliance were slow at breaking ties with the multinational U.S.S.R. For example, Yelena Bonner, the widow of Andrei Sakharov, argued that: "having staked everything on Mikhail Gorbachev, who had proclaimed *perestroika* but impeded actual changes that would inevitably limit his power, the West tirelessly strove for the preservation of the Soviet Union. . . . On March 12, 1990, Lithuania declared its independence. Why did it take a year and nine months to recognize its legitimacy, as well as that of Latvia and Estonia? For that matter, what could possibly explain why the West refused to recognize the right to independence of Slovenia and Croatia from the very start? Is it easier to normalize international relations after a blood-bath? *New Perspectives Quarterly*, Vol. 8, No. 4 (Fall 1991): 15.

39 *Canadian Press Newstex*, September 9, 1991. Although recognition of Ukraine was temporarily withheld, McDougall also announced a Cdn. $50 million line of credit to help Canadian businesses invest in the breakaway Soviet republic, as well as $5 million in technical assistance. In November, the Canadian Banknote Company of Ottawa won a contract worth U.S. $30 million to print new currency for an independent Ukraine.

40 *Canadian Press Newstex*, August 28, 1991; December 8, 1991.

41 *The Globe and Mail*, December 4, 1991, p. A10.

42 *Canadian Press Newstex*, December 10, 1991.

43 *Canadian Press Newstex*, December 10, 1991.

44 On January 15, 1992, Canada became one of the first countries outside the European Economic Community to recognize the independence of Slovenia and Croatia.

15

Arms Transfers and International Security: The Evolution of Canadian Policy

Keith Krause

The war in the Persian Gulf pushed an old issue — controlling the international trade in arms — near the top of the foreign policy agenda in several states, including Canada. Initiatives were announced, meetings were held, speeches were made, but (at least by early 1992) few concerted steps had been taken to reduce the global flow of weapons. Canada's policy initiatives were forthright and high-level, but had little direct influence on concrete measures to control the arms trade. In addition, the exercise revealed the policy dilemmas and pressures that face arms-exporting states. Although Canada is not a major arms producer or exporter, the deep conflict in its foreign policy between "value-driven impulses" and considerations of trade (in this case, related to the defence industries) manifested itself in Canadian actions. In the end the heightened interest in arms control the difficulties states will face as they attempt to move beyond the rhetoric of a "new world order" to tangible measures to increase international peace and security.

Canada's high-profile initiatives to control the arms trade received sustained attention throughout 1991. They built on the work done in relatively low-level discussions and initiatives that occurred prior to the Gulf War, but assumed a greater significance as the Mulroney government sought to demonstrate a longer-term commitment to conflict resolution in the Middle East; in this way it hoped to counterbalance the effect of the departure it was perceived to have made from Canada's traditional policies by dispatching warships and aircraft to the Persian Gulf. The centrepiece of Canada's initiatives was the announcement, on February 8, 1991, of a proposal for a "world summit on the instruments of war and weapons of mass destruction." This proposal, which included a range of ideas on controlling the arms trade, was simultaneously announced in speeches by Prime Minister Mulroney and Secretary of State for External Affairs Joe Clark.[1] In subsequent months, variations on the proposal were promoted at meetings of the Commonwealth, the Group of Seven (G-7), the Conference for Security and Co-operation in Europe, and elsewhere.

Before we discuss the content of this proposal, it makes sense to examine why the arms trade emerged as a focus of Canadian foreign policy during the Gulf War, given Canada's relatively low international involvement in it. This chapter therefore begins by working backwards from the February initiative to uncover its immediate sources and deeper roots. It then examines the way in which the initiative was promoted in the international arena, assessing the degree of impact Canada has had (or can have) on the arms trade issue. Finally, the chapter examines the relationship between Canada's policies towards the arms trade, and towards defence production and arms exports, especially in light of the June 1991 debate over the multi-million dollar sale of armoured vehicles to Saudi Arabia.

The Roots of the Initiative:
Political Imperatives or Institutional Memory?

Given Canada's relatively low profile in the international arms trade and the small size of its defence industrial base, it is rather hard to see why a Canadian initiative in the area of "international peace and security" would focus on the arms trade. There are essentially two interrelated reasons which explain why the February proposals took the form they did: they were (1) a natural bureaucratic and institutional response — given past activities — to a request for some Canadian policy initiatives, and (2) a politically driven response to a perceived need for a "peacemaking" initiative in light of Canada's more aggressive role in the Gulf War. These motivations are not exclusive, and their interplay helps explain why the arms trade was a logical focal point for the diverse interests contributing to Canadian foreign policy, in spite of its otherwise low salience to Canada.

In bureaucratic and institutional terms control of the arms trade has been prominent, since at least 1985-86, in public discourse on foreign policy and in bureaucratic planning. The 1986 report of the Special Joint Committee of the Senate and the House of Commons on Canadian Foreign Policy (the Hockin-Simard Committee), whose recommendations were based in part on a series of public hearings held across Canada in 1985-86, concluded that:

> we are attracted by proposals for an international system to register exports and imports of weapons and munitions as one means of controlling the expanded trade in conventional weapons, and we believe that Canada should seek international support for this concept.[2]

It is important to note, however, that in response the government argued that "the usefulness of an arms export and import register is questioned by many. . . . Moreover, there is little evidence that transparency inhibits either weapons exporters or importers."[3] The government's opposition to an arms transfer register in 1986 was not strong, but nonetheless was clear. This position had changed by 1991.

On the non-governmental organization (NGO) side, several groups either actively campaigned against the arms trade (and in favour of particular initiatives such as the register), or acted to raise the public profile of the issue. The Ploughshares Project at the University of Waterloo, the Coalition to Oppose the Arms Trade (COAT), and (to a lesser extent) the Centre for Arms Control and Disarmament, all released publications or raised campaigns against Canada's role in the arms trade and the perceived weakening of its export control policy.[4] The efforts of COAT included the organization of demonstrations against the annual ARMEX defence products exhibition. In addition, proposals to increase the transparency of the arms trade continued to receive attention within and outside of government (these will be discussed below). Finally, the Canadian Institute for International Peace and Security (CIIPS), in the fall of 1987, convened a conference on the arms trade that examined in some detail various aspects of the global arms trade, including the prospects for its control.[5] Thus there existed an active NGO community raising the issue of controlling the arms trade, which made it a relatively easy issue for policy planners to latch on to when concrete policy measures were being sought during the Gulf War. Although active NGO communities exist around many peace and security issues, it is difficult without this backdrop to imagine the arms trade being selected as the focus for Canada's post-Gulf War initiatives because Canada's role in it is otherwise marginal. It should be noted as well that, outside this relatively small NGO community, the matter did not receive sustained public attention (either in the media or through public opinion) and was not in other respects high in public consciousness.

Within the bureaucracy, there were, before the Gulf War, two initiatives on the arms trade that help explain the direction of the Canadian initiative. The first, a direct follow-on from the Hockin-Simard report's recommendation, was an informal consultative group commissioned by Fred Bild, Assistant Deputy Minister of External Affairs (Political and International Security Affairs Branch) to examine the security and trade implications of measures designed to inject greater transparency into Canadian arms exports. Up to that time, the Canadian government released only general figures of dollar values of arms transfers to foreign countries, and considered details of specific transactions to be commercially sensitive information that could not be released publicly. The Bild committee (which included government and industry representatives) examined some of the implications of changes to the policy, in order to find the limits of what was acceptable to Canada as a baseline for Canadian foreign policy initiatives. Consultations among government officials from various departments produced consensus that greater transparency would neither pose a security threat nor undermine confidentiality of commercial transactions, if the information was presented in an aggregate fashion.

The second initiative, which was closely connected to the first, was an examination of the possibility of a United Nations arms transfer register. This proposal had been informally discussed for many years in and around the United Nations, but it emerged formally on the United Nations agenda through a 1988 General Assembly Resolution establishing an "expert group" to study "ways and means of promoting transparency in international transfers of conventional arms on a universal and non-discriminatory basis."[6] A Canadian representative (Ernie Regehr of Project Ploughshares) participated in the deliberations of the group of 18 experts and, perhaps significantly, he was one of only two non-governmental participants (the majority being External Affairs or National Defence officials). Although he worked relatively closely with the appropriate officials of the Department of External Affairs, his participation was not fettered by prior Canadian policy commitments, which is a somewhat unusual arrangement. As he noted, "I reported to them in fair detail the line I was taking in various arguments [and] in virtually every case, their position was 'if you can get the rest of the group to go with that, then we have no problem with it'. . . . I also felt under some constraint to push for a report that Canada could support."[7] What is important to recognize is that both these efforts created an institutional memory around this issue that could serve as a focal point for Canadian policy initiatives during the Gulf War.

In the fall of 1990 the question of controlling arms transfers and increasing transparency was raised in several Canadian statements. On September 26, 1990, well after the Iraqi invasion of Kuwait but before the fighting began, the Secretary of State for External Affairs raised the matter in his speech to the UN General Assembly. It was also here that he pledged to release an annual report on Canadian arms exports. On October 26, 1990, Joe Clark spoke publicly against "the grotesque trade in conventional weapons, a trade which keeps societies poor and which makes war more devastating when it occurs."[8] At this point, no specific measures were suggested, but the question was clearly on the public agenda. By early 1991, references to the destructive consequences of the arms trade in the Middle East were being made in most speeches and declarations on the Gulf War, only now they were coupled with a general commitment to "devote as much energy to the construction of peace after this conflict as we must now devote to the conduct of that conflict."[9]

The proposal made on February 8 represented the emergence of a concrete policy from these inchoate thoughts. It specifically suggested a program of action to deal with the proliferation of weapons, including measures to deal with nuclear weapons, missile systems, biological and chemical weapons, and conventional arms. Enveloping the program was a three-part proposal for:

- a "gathering of world leaders under United Nations auspices" to condemn the proliferation of conventional weapons and weapons of mass destruction and endorse a comprehensive program of action, to be followed by:
- individual negotiations in appropriate multilateral forums, and;
- a subsequent conference in 1995 to "celebrate completion of the comprehensive network of specific non-proliferation regimes."[10]

The specific measures contained in the conventional arms "basket" included a meeting of major arms exporters to encourage greater transparency, restraint and consultation; an information exchange system; a commitment from the states that had signed the Conventional Forces in Europe (CFE) treaty not to retransfer treaty-limited items to regions of tension; and the release of statistics on Canadian arms exports (as a gesture to encourage increased transparency). In general, the proposal was a grab-bag of global arms control measures that encompassed several ongoing efforts (those concerning nuclear, biological and chemical weapons will not be dealt with here) and included some particularly vague wording on specific measures (such as "pressing for a global consensus," urging "serious examination" and "encouraging a formal commitment to greater sensitivity"). This type of formulation allowed much credit to be taken for unrelated successes, and little blame to be incurred for specific failures. The "world summit" initiative was also proposed to the UN Secretary General as a meeting to be convened under his auspices.

The proposal appears to have been born at a fairly high level — in the office of the Director-General of the Policy Planning Staff of External Affairs and with the participation of the Assistant Deputy Minister for Political and International Security Affairs.[11] It was the work of a few individuals, and was generated directly from discussions in the fall of 1990 with the External Affairs Minister concerning imaginative long-term proposals for Canadian post-Gulf War policy. Public opinion played no direct role, but as one official said, the initiative was based on "a clear understanding that we had to keep an eye on the post-crisis situation," and that "the support for having Canadian Forces used in this conflict was that [our policy] did not follow single-track thinking."[12] Many of the specific initiatives (concerning the renewal of the Non-Proliferation Treaty (NPT), strengthening of the Missile Technology Control Regime, or emphasis on the need to conclude a Chemical Weapons convention) were restatements of existing policies and built upon continuing efforts. Others, such as the "world summit" proposal, were new. It is difficult to determine where this idea came from, although it perhaps drew from the United Nations "world summit on children," held in the fall of 1990, which 82 world leaders attended. This more expansive aspect of the policy was not particularly attractive to the on-line bureaus of External Affairs (in particular the Arms Control and Disarmament Division), although the exact degree of discontent is unclear. References to the "world summit" soon disappeared from view, as the initiative became focused on increasing transparency and raising the issue in various multilateral fora (although it should be noted here that the world summit garnered no significant international support).

The sustained attention given to the problem of arms transfers by a small number of interest groups and interested foreign policy elites ensured that it remained higher on the foreign policy agenda than would otherwise have been expected in the years before the 1991 Gulf War. Although the proximate source of the February initiative was a ministerial request for concrete policy measures Canada could take to promote peace and security in the aftermath of the Gulf War, it was the activity of the immediately preceding years that facilitated a focus on conventional arms transfers. In a sense, the February initiative appeared to respond more to vague domestic pressures (to do something positive) than to external stimuli. That this domestic pressure was perceived by policy makers was confirmed by the Under-Secretary of State for External Affairs, de Montigny Marchand, when he noted that "we recognized that Canadians' support for the war effort was in part conditional on the government doing everything in its power to make sure we would not find ourselves in a similar situation a few years down the road."[13] This perception is reinforced by an examination of the way in which Canada's proposals played themselves out in the international arena.

Canada's Proposals in the International Arena

After the February announcement Canada launched a broad effort to promote its ideas in diverse bilateral and multilateral forums. It should be emphasized that these efforts were extremely high-profile, as they included statements by the responsible ministers or ambassadors in fora such as the Conference on Security and Co-operation in Europe (CSCE), the Organization of American States (OAS), the UN, the North Atlantic Treaty Organization (NATO), the G-7, the Commonwealth, and in bilateral contacts. In most cases, the goal was not merely to put the issue up for discussion, but to elicit a public pledge to take concrete action. In London on February 20, Joe Clark outlined before the Royal Institute for International Affairs the main elements of the February 8 package, renewed (and expanded upon) the plea for a summit of world leaders, and highlighted the issue of (and difficulties of) controlling arms transfers to the Middle East. The case for the summit was argued in terms of the need to secure the political will to change attitudes and spearhead action, and it was compared with the 1990 UN "world summit on children." Already, however, some equivocation on the subject of the summit appeared, with the admission that the proposal "will be greeted with cynicism by officials in some capitals in the West."[14]

The initiative was also pursued privately in inter-governmental consultations with major allies (Britain, France and the United States), and by Joe Clark with Middle Eastern leaders during his March visit.[15] Perhaps the first discussion to become public was the one held between Prime Minister Mulroney and President George Bush, at a meeting in Ottawa on March 13, 1991. At this meeting the Prime Minister referred clearly to his proposal, but the President was cautious. When asked directly about the summit idea, he noted that "I'm not sure exactly what the proper structure is, but clearly that idea might have some merit . . . it's a little early . . . I would like to talk to [Mulroney] before I commit ourselves further on it."[16] Although the summit idea was reportedly pursued with other governments after the Americans had poured cold water on it, this was to be its last public promotion on the international stage. Clark did advocate the idea in his testimony before the Standing Committee on National Defence and Veterans Affairs, March 20, 1991, although he admitted that "some of the early response is negative."[17] The Europeans in particular were lukewarm to the summit idea.

This policy setback did not stop the initiative, which was pursued fairly persistently over the summer and fall in almost all of the multilateral organizations in which Canada held membership. In May, the Canadian Ambassador for Disarmament argued before a United Nations conference on disarmament in support of two specific measures: the promotion of transparency for the arms trade, and the establishment of consultative mechanisms for situations "where arms build-ups in excess of legitimate defence requirements appear to be developing."[18] No mention of a world summit was made, and she admitted that no consensus existed even on the need to control conventional arms buildups. In June, a minor success was scored when the OAS General Assembly adopted a resolution calling for a halt to proliferation of weapons of mass destruction, and for the exercise of sensitivity in transfers of arms and related technologies, especially to regions of conflict or arms buildups.[19] Given Canada's relatively recent accession to the OAS, it could be said that Canadian action had achieved a notable and clear result.

Similar initiatives were pursued at the NATO Foreign Ministers' meeting, the meeting of the CSCE Council of Ministers in June, the G-7 leaders' summit in July, the United Nations General Assembly in September, and the Commonwealth heads of government meeting in October. The CSCE adopted a declaration along the lines proposed by the Secretary of State for External Affairs, Barbara McDougall, encouraging restraint and transparency in arms transfers.[20] The G-7 issued a long declaration on arms proliferation and agreed to increase consultation, transparency and action against egregious arms buildups.[21] Canada apparently fought hard to have a serious proposal for control on the agenda, although opposition was strong from some states which (among other objections) did not want economic summits to deal with security and arms control issues. Secretary of State McDougall's speech to the General Assembly reiterated the Canadian proposal in some detail, but the "world summit" proposal was dropped, and the concrete steps suggested were all, with the exception of endorsement of a UN arms transfer register, statements of previous Canadian policy (extension of the NPT, conclusion of a chemical weapons convention, strengthening of the biological and toxic weapons convention).[22] Finally, the communiqué of the Harare Commonwealth meeting "underlined the need to . . . curb the build-up of conventional weapons beyond the legitimate requirements of self-defence."[23]

Canada was not, however, alone in promoting discussion of this issue, for in the aftermath of the Gulf War, control of the arms trade received higher priority on the foreign policy agendas of many states, including leading arms exporters. In April, British Prime Minister John Major pledged British support for the idea of a UN arms transfer register (a position supported by the European Community).[24] Japanese Prime Minister Kaifu undertook in May to introduce the register resolution at the UN in the fall.[25] France, as part of a comprehensive initiative that included adherence to the Nuclear Non-Proliferation treaty, also agreed in June to the register idea and suggested monitoring of unusual weapons buildups.[26] Finally, after some months of policy confusion, President Bush announced on May 29 a comprehensive plan to control arms proliferation and destabilizing weapons buildups in the Middle East (although this was not a global plan).[27]

Following on from these diverse initiatives, the Americans managed to convene a meeting of the Permanent Five (P-5) members of the Security Council in June, at which they agreed to begin discussions on formal and informal measures to control the arms trade to the Middle East. At a further meeting October 17–18, the P-5 established common guidelines for arms exports, agreed to exchange information on transfers to the Middle East, supported UN efforts to establish an arms trade register and (perhaps the most important point in the long run) agreed to meet at least once a year to pursue these issues.[28] The guidelines include consideration of whether the transfer meets legitimate self-defence needs or is an appropriate response to potential threats, and a pledge to avoid transfers that might prolong or aggravate existing conflicts, introduce destabilizing military capabilities to a region, undermine recipients' economies, or support terrorism. In other words, the P-5 agreed to establish a tacit, informal arms control regime focused on supplies, and at the end of 1991 it was the P-5 that had become the forum for concrete action on controlling the arms trade, not the CSCE, the UN or the G-7.

Correction and Adaptation:
Responses to International and Domestic Reaction

These moves by different states had a great effect on the shape of action taken by Canada. From the Canadian point of view, the issue of arms transfers had been taken up (and perhaps taken over) by the great powers and principal arms suppliers (in particular Britain and the United States), which of course had a strong interest in controlling the agenda on this issue. This left Canada in the awkward position of claiming credit only for the first statement advocating action, or for "galvanizing the international community on this issue," a position which does not in itself reflect a great deal of either international influence or agenda-setting power.[29] More interestingly, the content of Canadian initiatives had by the end of the summer been significantly altered from what had originally been proposed in February in order to handle international reception of the proposal. Gone was the world summit idea, and in its place was an express desire to mobilize political will and gather "political commitments at the highest level," in the belief that this would "generate and maintain the momentum necessary to free specific negotiations and processes from the complacency or technical minutiae in which they have tended to become mired."[30] The promotion of the idea of controlling the arms trade in various multilateral fora became, in a sense, an alternative way of achieving the same end as that of the world summit. Canada's efforts also included the convening of a meeting of "like-minded" states on the margins of the United Nations in September, whose goal was to explore ways in which they could work together on a range of multilateral arms control issues, as yet unspecified. This group was the most direct spin-off from the world summit idea, and it will likely continue meeting on a regular basis in New York.

The highest profile issue on which Canadian attention concentrated turned out to be the United Nations arms trade register. In one sense this was a policy shift, given the government's mild opposition to the idea in its response to the Hockin-Simard report; on the other hand the government had subsequently supported UN resolutions in favour of a register. In any case, the reasons behind the shift were *not* connected with any change in the logic of the arguments against a register — as was pointed out then and now, a register would add no real information to existing sources would discriminate in favour of arms-producing states (which do not have to reveal their internal acquisitions), would not be clearly linked to specific controls, and would not probably be comprehensive if disclosure were voluntary. The most scathing critics argued that the register "will do exactly what it is designed to do, and that is prevent anything meaningful from happening" by serving as a convenient fallback initiative for governments that do not wish to address the issue with concrete measures.[31] In fact, as late as the February proposal, the Canadian government refused to give unequivocal support to a UN register, arguing instead for "early action on an information exchange system regarding arms transfers, including serious examination by all states of the recommendations of the United Nations Experts Group."[32] Supporters of the register argue that its primary value is that it will focus public attention on the arms trade, and perhaps help to build confidence as states voluntarily disclose their weapons acquisitions and acknowledge the interest of the international community in controlling weapons buildups.

The question was finally dealt with in a UN resolution passed in December, mandating the establishment of a UN register.[33] Here too Canada's role was merely ancillary, as the final resolution was drafted primarily by the European Community (EC) and secondarily by Japan, not Canada. According to officials, Canada considered putting forward a draft, but decided that this would complicate the process, and sought instead to provide informal input into the EC and the Japanese efforts. The main negotiations occurred between the EC, Japan, and six representatives of the non-aligned movement. Canada chaired (and spoke for) an informal group of about fifteen "like-minded states" (including Australia, the Nordics, and the East Europeans) that sought to have some input into the main negotiations. On one particular issue (the expansion of the register to include domestic weapons holdings and procurement), Canada apparently lobbied hard (and successfully) for its inclusion in the resolution, seeing this measure as a way to bridge the gap between the arms-producing sponsors and the non-aligned states, many of which had objected to the discriminatory nature of a measure that would not affect arms-producing states. Of course, the mere passage of a UN resolution establishing a register does not guarantee its success, and the ultimate value of this measure is yet to be determined. The precedent set by the UN mechanism for registering military expenditures is not a strong one, as few states submit information and little public attention is paid to this source of information.

In this situation, there is reason to be sceptical about the degree to which promoters of the modified Canadian initiative believe it will contribute in a concrete way to controlling the arms trade. Another indication of equivocation that is closer to home was provided by the March 1991 report, *Export of Military Goods from Canada 1990*. It offered dollar values (by country) of Canadian arms exports in 1990, but excluded exports to the United States (which account for about three quarters of Canada's arms exports), and gave no specific details on the goods transferred. The goods involved are only described by their Export Control List number, which permits one to identify general categories (such as "large calibre armament," or "vehicles") but not to assess quantities, qualities, and any other characteristics. If this represents the degree of transparency acceptable to the Canadian government (and to be emulated by others), it is hardly likely to be a major force in contributing to control of the arms trade. The form of this report is also evidence that the interests of the defence industry (and its bureaucratic champions), which were strong in 1986–87, had not been totally overruled by the arms controllers within External Affairs before and after the Gulf War.

Finally, even within Canada the February initiative was not without its critics. Perhaps the most visible set of comments was contained in the hearings and recommendations of the Standing Committee on National Defence and Veterans Affairs, which held a series of hearings on arms transfers in February and March 1991. Witnesses divided evenly on the value of a summit, although none advocated it as a goal in itself.[34] The final committee report supported in principle the summit idea, but noted that "this overarching interest might well be served by an initial emphasis on regional agreements. It is here that Canada has comparative advantages that should be put to good use." It recommended that "Canada should concentrate its efforts on helping to establish regional systems of arms transfer transparency, and these efforts should be targeted towards areas of Canadian diplomatic advantage."[35]

Seen against this backdrop of domestic and international reaction, the shift in Canada's overall arms transfer control policy towards promotion of a UN register (and related measures within the UN) can be explained by two considerations: it provided a vehicle for some concrete, though limited, foreign policy successes, and it ensured that Canada had its "fingers in the pie" during multilateral discussions on control of the arms trade. The summit idea was a dead letter, repeated declarations from multilateral organizations would soon wear thin, domestic critics were vocal, and the real measures to control the conventional arms trade were being taken by other states without Canadian participation. Canada would therefore be left "gathering political commitments" while practical work was done by others, unless it could play an active role in promoting at least a minimal measure, such as the UN register, and in related activities centring the UN. What this implies for Canadian policy initiatives in the realm of peace and security is discussed briefly in the conclusion.

The "Problem" of the Canadian Defence Industry

Somewhat ironically, the Canadian initiative on control of the arms trade, and the vigorous denunciations of the trade from the Prime Minister and the Secretary of State for External Affairs, coincided with the process of seeking final approval (secured in June 1991) of a major sale to Saudi Arabia, worth hundreds of millions of dollars, of Light Armoured Vehicles (LAVs) armed with automatic weapons. The debate on Bill C-6 served to highlight the real economic interests — trade, high technology, employment — that are at stake in any attempt to control the arms trade. In a sense, the dilemmas of promoting controls and transparency while attempting to protect an indigenous arms industry, dilemmas that face all major producers, became clear even to Canadians. A coherent value-driven foreign policy was the first victim.

Before describing the specific issue of the Saudi debate, one ought to put Canadian defence production and arms exports in a global perspective. Overall, Canada ranks about seventh or eighth in the list of world arms producers, with annual production of about $3 billion, or just above one percent of the world total.[36] In comparison, the United States produces about $90 billion per year in arms, the Soviet Union slightly more, France, Britain and Germany $19, $14 and $8 billion respectively, and other producers such as Italy and Poland are in the same range as Canada. Canadian arms exports, which fluctuate considerably from year to year, averaged $1.36 billion a year over the 1980s (with boom years for the industry in 1984–87). Fully three quarters of Canadian production is exported to the United States, and most of this is in the form of components or licensed production of sub-systems (conducted under the Defence Production Sharing Agreement), as Canada produces few stand-alone weapons systems. Canadian arms exports to other NATO allies accounted for a further 10–12 percent of the total, leaving roughly $136 million a year for other states (including the developing world). These figures place Canada low in the list of major arms exporters, compared to the United States (about $10 billion a year), Britain ($1.4 billion), France ($4.3 billion), or China ($1–1.5 billion). Canada is a small second-tier producer and exporter, hardly a major player in the world's weapons market.

The Canadian industry as a whole is relatively export-dependent, with about 50 percent of production being exported. This figure is similar to that for producers such as Britain, France and Italy. About 35,000 jobs depend directly upon arms production, and hence about 17,000 on arms exports.[37] This is not a large number, but it is concentrated in a few firms — the top ten arms-producing firms probably account for 50 percent of total production, and perhaps three of them export more than 50 percent of their military production.[38] In addition, the industry is heavily subsidized by the government, and receives about $300 million annually under the Defence Industry Productivity Program (DIPP), representing 10 percent of the total value of production![39] Evidently, changes in overall export policy that reduce arms exports can (especially in a time of declining demand and great competition) have a direct impact within Canada.

The control mechanisms for Canadian exports are quite restrictive and comparable to those of suppliers such as Sweden, Japan and Germany. The 1986 export policy states that Canada would closely control, and in principle not allow, military exports to:

1) countries which pose a threat to Canada and its allies;
2) countries involved in or under imminent threat of hostilities; and
3) countries under United Nations Security Council sanctions; or
4) countries whose governments have a persistent record of serious violations of the human rights of their citizens, unless it can be demonstrated that there is no reasonable risk that the goods might be used against the civilian population.[40]

In practice, since the late 1980s sales had been evaluated not on the basis of a "blacklist" that banned all military exports to specified countries, but on a case-by-case basis that involved high level and often Ministerial review. One reason for adopting this measure was the need to deal with the rapidly changing international conditions that made blacklists difficult to maintain without frequent review.

The specific issue at stake in the debate over Bill C-6 need not concern us here, as the bill was intended to rectify a legal anomaly in the Criminal Code that prevented Canadian firms from selling automatic weapons to buyers other than the Canadian government. This outright prohibition on sales was much more restrictive than the overall military export policy, and conflicted with two potential transactions involving sales of automatic rifles to the Dutch armed forces and of LAVs armed with small automatic cannon. The "problem" with the Criminal Code provisions had become clear in the mid-1980s, and a bill to correct the anomaly, while at the same time ensuring tight export controls over automatic weapons (by means of an Automatic Firearms Country Control List), had been prepared several years earlier.[41]

But the broader issue raised by the potential sale by General Motors of Canada to Saudi Arabia of 393 (and perhaps up to 1,117) Light Armoured Vehicles was important, in light of Canadian arms export policy and its stated goal of controlling the arms trade. The Saudi contract would create (more correctly, maintain) about 700 direct jobs for a period of up to ten years, and have a dollar value between 200 million (for 393 vehicles) and 500 million (for 1,000 vehicles). It is one of the largest single export contracts for the Canadian defence industry that is not with the United States. More importantly, testimony by company and union officials suggested that without this contract the plant manufacturing the LAV might close, with the concomitant loss of defence production expertise that had been built up (with government assistance) over many years.[42]

The Saudi sale could have been seen to contradict point two (threat of hostilities), and certainly point four (human rights), of the export principles noted above. The somewhat acrimonious debate in the House of Commons revolved around the extent of the contradiction. Not surprisingly, the Ministers of External Affairs and International Trade saw no contradiction. With respect to the possible violation of point two of the guidelines, it was argued that the defence by Saudi Arabia of its oilfields was part of that country's legitimate self-defence, and, in light of the Gulf War, that Saudi Arabia was under no imminent threat of hostilities.[43] Ministers were silent on point four, but officials claimed that on human rights matters "we have a dialogue with the Saudis [on this]."[44] With respect to the possible conflict with the government's arms control initiative, the Secretary of State for External Affairs argued that:

> no such inconsistency exists . . . under the proposed amendments, exports of automatic weapons will be subject to the same stringent controls that have long been applied to the export of other military goods from Canada. These controls fully reflect Canada's arms control and disarmament policies.[45]

Perhaps more significant than the reasons offered for not opposing the sale were the overall justifications. In both potential sales (the Dutch and the Saudi), the argument was that production for Canadian forces had come to the end of a procurement cycle, exports to the United States were not foreseeable in the immediate future, and arms exports to other countries were necessary to maintain defence industrial capabilities (and related jobs). As the Minister for International Trade, Michael Wilson, argued, "neither production facility can survive on the basis of Canadian requirements alone. Both will fail if new flexibility with respect to exports of automatic firearms to selected countries is not introduced."[46] Evident here is the central dilemma facing smaller arms producing states: in a situation of rising unit costs, shrinking defence procurement budgets and increased competition in the export market, arms exports (even to unpalatable customers) are crucial for industrial survival. But there can be little doubt that the sale to Saudi Arabia conflicted with the spirit of Canada's stated arms export policy and of its post-Gulf War arms control initiative, even if it did not do violence to the positions formally adopted; in the case of Saudi Arabia even this latter interpretation might have been questioned, because of the human rights issue.

Conclusion:
Sniffing the Wind or Setting the Agenda?

What lessons can be drawn from this flurry of activity, with regard to the light it throws on Canadian foreign policymaking, its impact on the arms trade, and its implications for the future? The active pursuit by Canada of conventional arms trade controls clearly reflected a high-level political commitment to resolving the issue, derived primarily from domestic concerns over Canada's role in the Gulf War, and secondarily from a desire to pursue a policy of "peacemaking" consistent with our overall foreign policy on peace and security issues. The willingness to take a lead in this area, and the ability to overcome some resistance on the part of other states (especially in the G-7 and OAS) to discussing controls on the arms trade, were evidence of a relatively strong middle power policy.

But one cannot infer from the statement of a Canadian initiative and subsequent international action that Canada greatly influenced the outcome. Canada's ability to achieve even limited progress was derived in no small part from the fact that the issue emerged high on the foreign policy agendas of several other states: it follows that resistance to Canada's initiative was based on differences over specifics, rather than a complete rejection of the idea. This fits the traditional pattern of Canadian foreign policy, where moderate success can be achieved in promoting an issue of relatively high salience and attracting low dissent. Canada's role in the evolving debate on controlling the arms trade cannot be characterized as that of a "leader" or a "follower," but rather as that of a "shaper" of the international debate.

On the other hand, when Canada took the diplomatic high road by advancing the world summit idea and proposing the goal of "gathering political commitments" its action did not result in any concrete measures or proposals that would (directly or indirectly) lead to control the arms trade, and its rhetorical victories may prove to be hollow. Canada's own role in the international arms trade is also sufficiently small that it has few real interests at stake and hence is accorded little right by other states to participate in the formulation of multilateral controls in this field. This implies that Canada's 1991 initiatives should be seen as a somewhat ephemeral foray into a field of arms control in which, whatever progress is made, Canada will remain a peripheral actor. If control of the arms trade and other similar security issues become highly salient multilateral issues in a post-Cold War "new world order," it can be forecast that Canada's foreign policy on international peace and security will be increasingly marginalized.

The arms trade is ultimately woven into the fabric of international politics as a self-help system, through which states that cannot guarantee their own security continually seek to "buy" it in the form of advanced weapons. Current measures by suppliers to control the diffusion of advanced technologies (specifically the P-5 initiative, but also such measures as the Missile Technology Control Regime) are driven more by a desire to protect their existing monopoly and reduce the threats they might eventually face than by any belief that controlling the arms trade is a desirable objective in itself. This makes the potential for far-reaching supply-side controls rather limited, and implies that genuine progress must come from, and involve, recipient states in different regions.

Finally, larger producers and exporters (and indeed Canadian citizens) may suspect the Canadian government of some hypocrisy when it promotes an initiative the price of which will have to be paid by others. Canada's own behaviour concerning the Saudi sale, and the issues raised in the ensuing debate, justify such criticism and highlight starkly the inherent difficulties that proposals for genuine control of the arms trade will continue to encounter.

Notes

1 See Canada, Department of External Affairs, "Proposal for a World Summit on the Instruments of War and Weapons of Mass Destruction," *Backgrounder*, February 8, 1991; Secretary of State for External Affairs, "Canada and the Challenges of the Post-war Period in the Gulf," *Statement*, 91/10, February 8, 1991; Prime Minister Brian Mulroney, "Address on the Situation in the Persian Gulf," February 8, 1991.

2 Conclusion/Recommendation 17, as cited in Department of External Affairs and International Trade (DEAITC), *Canada's International Relations: Response of the Government of Canada to the Report of the Special Joint Committee of the Senate and the House of Commons* (Ottawa: Supply and Services Canada, December 1986), p. 48.

3 DEAITC, p. 48.

4 See, for example, Ernie Regehr, *Arms Canada* (Toronto: Lorimer, 1987); John Lamb, "Canada, arms transfers and arms control," paper presented to the Canadian Institute for International Peace and Security conference on international arms transfers, October 1987. The *Ploughshares Monitor* (produced by Project Ploughshares at the University of Waterloo) and "Press for Conversion" (the newsletter of the COAT), also contain frequent articles on the arms trade.

5 This conference was suggested in the government's response to the Hockin-Simard report. See Keith Krause, *The International Trade in Arms: Problems and Prospects*, conference report (Ottawa: Canadian International Institute for Peace and Security, October 1987).

6 United Nations, General Assembly, resolution 43/75, 7 December 1988. A draft resolution on an arms transfer register was proposed as early as 1968 by Denmark, Malta, Iceland and Norway (after a 1965 Maltese initiative failed), and the issue resurfaced in 1976, 1977, 1978, 1981 and 1982. Canada

had more or less consistently expressed support in the UN for the idea of a register since 1968. See "An Arms Trade Register," unpublished paper of the Canadian Institute for International Peace and Security, July 1987, reprinted in Krause, pp. 35–46.

7 Personal interview, *The International Trade in Arms.*

8 Secretary of State for External Affairs, "The Persian Gulf, International Order and Canadian Foreign Policy," *Statement*, 90/63, October 26, 1990, p. 9.

9 Statement by the Secretary of State for External Affairs before the House of Commons Standing Committee on External Affairs and International Trade, January 21, 1991. See also Secretary of State for External Affairs, "Peacekeeping and Peacemaking: The Persian Gulf Crisis and its Consequences," *Statement*, 91/05, January 24, 1991. This latter speech contained an extensive diatribe against the arms trade (describing "a free market in arms [as] a suicidal market"), and a call for "an attitude of co-operative security" in the region. The concept of "co-operative security" has become a *leitmotif* of Canadian foreign policy since the end of the Cold War.

10 Details in this paragraph from *Backgrounder*, February 8, 1991.

11 The officials in those two positions were Howard Balloch and Jeremy Kinsman.

12 Interviews, External Affairs officials.

13 Address to the Canadian Institute for International Peace and Security conference on the Supply-Side Control of Weapons Proliferation, Ottawa, June 21, 1991.

14 Secretary of State for External Affairs, *Statement*, 91/12, February 20, 1991.

15 Clark reported to Parliament that he had raised the issue, although he gave little indication that a positive response was received (and suggested that the reflex in the region might be to acquire more arms). *Hansard*, March 15, 1991, p. 18534. Prime Minister Mulroney also noted the demarches to allies in *Hansard*, March 14, 1991, p. 18468.

16 Text of joint press conference, United States Information Service, March 15, 1991. President Bush did also say that "the idea of coming together in a multilateral way to do something about the proliferation of weapons into the Middle East is something that has some appeal to me." Privately, External Affairs officials have acknowledged that the United States opposed the summit idea.

17 House of Commons, Standing Committee on National Defence and Veterans Affairs, hearings on arms transfers, March 20, 1991, pp. 7, 11. One official noted, "that part of the proposal has almost disappeared"; another that "it wasn't exactly a big hit."

18 Ambassador Peggy Mason, "Proliferation of Weapons Systems and Disarmament Issues — Non-Proliferation Regimes vs. Partial or Comprehensive Prohibitions," address to the United Nations Conference on Disarmament issues, May 27–30, Kyoto, Japan.

19 See Secretary of State for External Affairs, *Statement*, 91/30, June 3, 1991. The text of the resolution (with an accompanying analysis) is reprinted in *Disarmament Bulletin*, 17 (Fall 1991), p. 4.

20 Secretary of State for External Affairs, *Statement*, 91/32, June 19, 1991; *The Globe and Mail*, June 21, 1991.
21 Declaration of the G-7 reprinted in *Disarmament Bulletin*, No. 17 (Fall 1991).
22 Secretary of State for External Affairs, "Notes for a Statement to the Forty-Sixth Session of the United Nations General Assembly," *Statement*, 91/43, September 25, 1991.
23 Commonwealth Heads of Government Meeting, "The Harare Communique," (October 1991), item 15.
24 As noted in Canadian Institute for International Peace and Security, *Guide to Canadian Policies on Arms Control, Disarmament, Defence and Conflict Resolution, 1991* (Ottawa: CIIPS, 1991), p. 2.
25 CIIPS, p. 3.
26 *Le monde*, juin 2–3, 1991; *Libération*, juin 4, 1991.
27 See President Bush's address to the Air Force Academy, May 29, 1991, and the accompanying White House fact sheet detailing the proposals. The policy confusion included contradictory statements by Bush and his advisors on arms control. Although Secretary of State James Baker said in February 1991 that "the time has come to try to . . . reduce arms flows into an area that is already overmilitarized," President Bush argued in March that arms control "doesn't mean we're going to refuse to sell anything to everybody," and Secretary of Defense Dick Cheney announced that arms control in the Middle East would only cover ballistic missiles and chemical and nuclear weapons. All quoted in *Newsweek*, April 8, 1991.
28 See Meeting of the Permanent Five on Arms Transfers and Non-Proliferation, *Joint Declaration*, October 18, 1991: *The New York Times*, October 20, 1991.
29 This claim was made at the G-7 summit (*The Globe and Mail*, July 17, 1991), in a speech by the Under-Secretary of State for External Affairs in June, and in interviews with External Affairs officials. The quote is from an interview with an External Affairs official.
30 Address by Mr. de Montigny Marchand, Under-Secretary of State for External Affairs, to the Canadian Institute for International Peace and Security conference on the supply-side control of weapons proliferation, Ottawa, June 21, 1991, p. 2.
31 Barry Blechman, quoted in *The Globe and Mail*, July 17, 1991. These objections were also raised in the CIIPS report and conference. See Krause, *International Trade in Arms*, pp. 26–30, 40–42.
32 *Backgrounder*, February 8, 1991.
33 See United Nations, General Assembly, "Study on Ways and Means of Promoting Transparency in International Transfers of Conventional Arms," report of the Secretary General, A/46/301, September 9, 1991, and UN General Assembly Resolution 46/36L (December 9, 1991), "General and Complete Disarmament: International Arms Transfers. Transparency in Armaments." The resolution was co-sponsored by about 40 states, with 150 votes in favour, none against, and two abstentions. China was notably absent from the deliberations and was not counted in the vote. (Information in this paragraph from External Affairs officials).

34 House of Commons, Standing Committee on National Defence and Veterans Affairs, Hearings on Arms Transfers, February 26, 28, March 5, 7, 14, 20, 25, 26, 1991.

35 Standing Committee, March 25–26, 1991, p. 6.

36 Data in this paragraph, unless otherwise noted, from Keith Krause, *Arms and the State: Patterns of Military Production and Trade* (Cambridge: Cambridge University Press, 1992), pp. 93–107.

37 Employment figure from Department of External Affairs, "Export Controls Policy," *Communiqué*, No. 155, September 10, 1986. A much higher figure (50,000 jobs in Quebec alone) is given in Yves Bélanger and Pierre Fournier, *Le Québec militaire: les dessous de l'industrie militaire québécoise* (Montreal: Éditions Québec-Amérique, 1989).

38 Derived from "Canada's Largest Military Contractors," *Ploughshares Monitor*, Vol. 12, No. 4 (December 1991), pp. 17–18.

39 See Ken Epps, "The Defence Industry Productivity Program, Contributions, 1969 through 1990," *Ploughshares Working Paper 91-2* (Waterloo: Project Ploughshares, 1991).

40 Department of External Affairs, "Export Controls Policy," *Communiqué*, September 10, 1986.

41 Interviews with External Affairs officials.

42 Information in this paragraph derived from statements by Mr. Doug Rutherford, plant chairperson, Canadian Auto Workers Local 27, and Mr. William Pettipas, Director, Government Relations, General Motors Diesel Division, before the House of Commons Legislative Committee E on Bill C-6, June 12, 1991.

43 Minister for International Trade Michael Wilson, in *Hansard*, May 30, 1991, p. 790.

44 Interview, External Affairs official. Under the legislation, Canada would also have to negotiate a defence research, development and production agreement with potential customers. To that point, Sweden had been the only non-NATO country with such an agreement.

45 Department of External Affairs, *Statement*, 91/27, May 30, 1991, cited in CIIPS, p. 7.

46 *Hansard*, May 30, 1991, p. 789. Wilson's words were echoed by MP John Reimer, who argued that "we have a limited need [for these weapons]. If we want that expertise to exist in Canada . . . and if we want those kinds of people to develop that expertise into the future, then they have to be able to export, at least to our friends and our allies." *Ibid.*, p. 802. Further elaboration of these positions can be found in the hearings of Legislative Committee E on Bill C-6, issues 1–4, June 11, 12, 13, 17, 1991, and of the Senate Standing Committee on Foreign Affairs, June 20, 1991.